Witness To Miracles

Remembering
the
Cokeville Elementary School Bombing

A Compilation Project by
The Cokeville Miracle Foundation

www.pronghornpress.org

...God is not dead,
nor doth he sleep
The wrong shall fail,
the right prevail...

—Henry Wadsworth Longfellow,
I Heard the Bells on Christmas Day

Acknowledgments:

We wish to thank the many people outside of the Cokeville Miracle Foundation for their help in this project. For those who gathered stories and helped us locate survivors, thank you. To Annette Chaudet at Pronghorn Press in Greybull, Wyoming, thank you. To the Town of Cokeville, past, present, and future, thank you. To all the contributors of stories, thank you. For allowing every single one of you heroes, the survivors, to live, we thank an eternal Heavenly Father who has His own reasons for everything.

Witness To Miracles

Witness To Miracles

Preface

On May 16, 1986, the little town of Cokeville, Wyoming, faced a life-changing event that rocked its peace and security as a man and his wife held hostage 154 children, teachers, and visitors in the community's sole elementary school.

This story shocked the nation as a whole school was forced into a crowded classroom with a bomb as well as an armed man and his accomplice who terrorized their captives for three hours. The bomb did detonate and fire, thick black smoke and toxic fumes filled the room. Although many were burned, some severely, only the perpetrators of this horrible incident died. One of the miracles that day was that not a single person was lost. Other miracles were reported and some of those are documented in this compilation.

With the goal of remembering the faith, courage, and blessings experienced that day, the Cokeville Miracle Foundation (CMF) embarked on its memorial project, this book. Feeling a desire and need to give back in some small way to the community they love, a book committee was formed and the members sought out personal accounts and insights from these now grown up survivors along with the stories of civic workers, law enforcement and emergency personnel, relatives, and medical staff. Herein are the stories submitted that recall the event, reflect on insights and lessons learned, and share individual feelings and perspectives twenty years later.

At first the task of collecting the stories was overwhelming. The survivors had scattered and there was no list of the emergency workers who had responded that day. Relying on faith and prayer the committee found themselves guided to what they needed to do and how they needed to do it.

We are asked, "Why now? Why after almost twenty years are you doing this?" The answer is very simple. People weren't ready at five years. People weren't ready at ten years. Even now, after twenty years, some people are still not ready to share their stories. Their emotions or feelings, for many different reasons, do not allow them to share. Some stories are very private, sacred, and reserved for the intimate moment. Some stories are filled with fear or anger.

We respected all of those feelings and the wishes of those who chose not to share their stories. Still others want to remember and acknowledge the hand of God that guided the miracle that spared a generation of children. One mother, Cheryl Buckley, said, "Every May 16th all of my kids can expect a call from their mother reminding them...of that day and how thankful I am to have been a part of a modern day miracle. I will never forget God's mercy to us that day! I will never forget!"

What happened during this labor-intensive collecting process was, of itself, marvelous and impacted the lives of many involved on both sides of this project. Some have, for the first time, recounted their stories of the events of that day. Many found healing and closure by writing about their experiences. In some cases family members openly discussed their experiences together for the first time.

For many the experience became a witness of God's love. "The miracle of the bombing was no random act of luck. It is by the grace of God that Cokeville, Wyoming, did not lose a generation of children that day," says Kara Thornock Titensor, a third grade survivor. Others remember their heroes as exemplified by the reflection of H.J. Esterholdt, another third grade survivor. He said, "The thing I remember most about that day was the unflappable strength that the adults showed in that room. That day there was no one better to handle the events than those adults."

One of those adults even saw special symbolism in the smoke blackened classroom as Sherrie Cornia, a survivor's mother, recalls, "I stepped over to the corner and studied the graceful folds of red, white and blue hanging in quiet dignity, altered only by a thin film of black dust. A symbol of freedom that had been held hostage, the standard had been tested and terror had failed. Our freedom was intact. Our children were alive."

In this book each person was allowed to share a reflection in his or her own words with little or no editing. Recognizing that each person saw, felt, and witnessed those tense hours differently, no effort has been made to correlate these stories. However, the stories are grouped by grade or other classification to help the reader. They are not offered for comparison or critique. If you look for errors and inconsistencies, you will find them. That's not what this compilation is about. We share for the historical significance of this event and the twenty-year retrospection. We share so that others who are in traumatic events might find hope of healing through these stories. We share to declare and acknowledge that Heaven's hand in life is nothing to be afraid of or ashamed of. The title refers to the collective witness of people to the many miracles of that day and beyond, and to the God behind them. Each survivor can be considered a miracle themselves.

As some in the next generation have begun to forget or ignore the important experiences of that day, the witnessed miracles become especially valuable. "I feel a tremendous responsibility as a survivor, not only to value my life, but to live it the best way I can. I also feel a responsibility to share my experiences of that day and my testimony...I think it is important that we never forget. If there is any way that I can possibly show gratitude for all that happened, it is to always remember what the Lord did for us that day," said Lori Nate Conger, 5th Grade survivor.

The Cokeville Miracle Foundation agrees. This book, *Witness to Miracles: Remembering the Cokeville Elementary School Bombing*, seeks to rekindle and renew this legacy.

Cokeville, Wyoming May 25,1986
Courtesy of the Casper Star Tribune Collection, Casper College Library

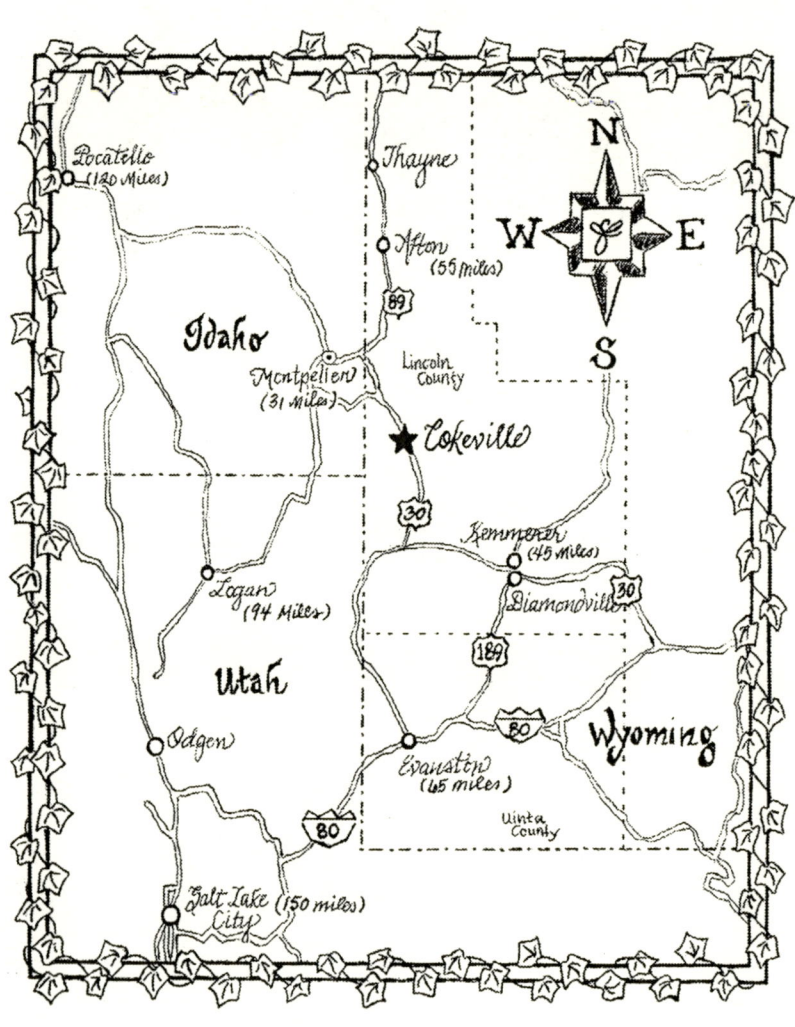

Introduction

The Cokeville Miracle Foundation thought lead investigator Ron Hartley could introduce the story better than anyone else. The first part of his remarks will explain the days leading up to the Cokeville Elementary School bombing with factual data that was gathered during the original investigation. The second part recounts his own very personal story.

Ron Hartley, Lead Investigator.
Photo by Rick Sorensen
Courtesy of the Casper Star Tribune Collection, Casper College Library

Ron Hartley

Lincoln County Sheriff's Office Investigator
Father of four student survivors
(Email Submission)

This is a summary I have of some interviews conducted by various agencies of the Cokeville School hostage incident that occurred on May 16,1986 in Cokeville, Wyoming. This is a condensed story of the incident, as I recall it:

On May 16, 1986 at approximately 1:30 p.m. David and Doris Young backed a rented Toyota van into the south Cokeville Elementary School entrance and unloaded numerous items including a shopping cart with the bomb, components to make additional bombs, rifles, handguns, diaries, and two boxes of photography slides David had taken during his life. He and Doris ordered all of the faculty and children to be brought to the second classroom from the south end of the school on the east side. David threw his keys at his daughter, Princess, and told her to get out. Princess and the two handcuffed men, Gerald Deppe and Doyle Mendenhall, drove to the Cokeville Town Hall and reported the incident. Sheriff Wolfley reported that David demanded $300 million dollars, or $2 million a child as ransom. All communication went through the school's principal. At approximately 3:40 p.m. the bomb detonated.

A more detailed time line of the incident was developed through witness testimonies gathered and compiled over the next few days and was reported as follows:

Gerald Deppe knew David Young since childhood. They were raised together in Grinnell, Iowa. Upon graduation, they drifted apart and had only seen each other briefly since that time. Doyle Mendenhall met David Young in 1979 while they were employed at Beker Industries in Soda Springs, Idaho. Approximately a year before the bombing, both men were contacted by David and were solicited to invest in a business venture. This venture was never specifically described to either of them. David told them that he was working on a "formula that would revolutionize the system." "The system" was never defined and the investors were led to believe David was working on a technological energy-related formula. Both men stated David Young was very intelligent and thought to be capable of making such a breakthrough. For the next seven months, Gerald Deppe contributed $100 per month and Mendenhall made a contribution of $1,000.

Timeline

David and Doris Young were living in Arizona.

Approximately the first of May 1986, Doris telephoned the men and told them there would be a meeting in Wyoming about the formula and that they should plan to attend. Doris told Deppe that David would pick him up on May 12, 1986.

Also, approximately the first of May 1986, David Young purchased a two-wheeled shopping cart at Safeway on Valencia Street in Tucson.

May 11, 1986—Doris telephoned to confirm the meeting dates.

May 12, 1986, 12:05 a.m. —Doris and Princess Young arrived at Bernadine "Bernie" Petersen's (Doris' daughter, David's stepdaughter) in Cokeville, Wyoming.

12:30 a.m. —David arrived in Des Moines, Iowa to pick up Deppe. Both men left together in the rented Toyota van.

May 13, 1986 7:30 a.m. —David and Deppe arrived in Cokeville, Wyoming. David telephoned Doris from a local restaurant and Doris arrived in approximately fifteen minutes. After getting acquainted,

Doris and Deppe went to Preston, Idaho, to pick up Doyle Mendenhall.

May 13, 1986, 3:15 p.m. —Deppe and Doris picked up Mendenhall and returned to Cokeville, arriving at approximately 5:00 p.m.

David rented Room 26 at the Lazy T Motel in Cokeville. Deppe and Mendenhall shared this room while Doris and David went to Bernadine Peterson's residence to spend the night.

May 14, 1986, after breakfast—Doris, Princess, Mendenhall, and Deppe went sightseeing and got acquainted while David drove to Jackson, Wyoming, to meet Robert Harrison (another investor in David's theory) at the airport.

5:00 p.m. —David returned to Cokeville and rented Room 35 at the Lazy T Motel. The rest of the evening was spent getting acquainted. David passed out copies of the "0 = oo" (*Zero Equals Infinity*) letters for everyone to read.

7:00 p.m. —David and Princess left to go to Montpelier, Idaho, and Doris went to Petersen's residence to get her clothing.

David rented Room 6 at the Sunset Motel in Montpelier for himself and Princess. In the Sunset Motel parking lot, Princess painted the van windows white. David instructed her to do this "for our protection and security." Princess carried all of the firearms, wires, a can of aluminum, tuna fish cans, and wooden boxes from the van into the motel room.

David manufactured the bomb in the bathroom of the motel room. After completion, Princess thought he might be making a bomb and asked about the device. David stated, "You're scaring me. Quit." Princess helped cut down one of the wooden boxes so it would fit into the shopping cart.

May 15, 1986, Early morning—Princess helped reload all of their belongings and the bomb into the van. The shopping cart with the bomb was placed in the rear of the van.

5:45 a.m. —Princess mailed "0=oo" letters to President Reagan and to news agencies, including the *Des Moines Register.*

David purchased a half-gallon of milk. (Later the carton was used to contain gasoline for the bomb.)

Items that were to be left to Princess by David and Doris were transferred from the van to Young's Subaru, which was left at the motel.

7:30 am. —Princess and David arrived in Cokeville and everyone had breakfast together. At that time, it was noticed that the windows of the van had been painted white. The only window not painted white was the windshield.

8:15 a.m. —Everyone returned to the motel and placed their personal belongings in David and Doris's Subaru. Initially, the plan was for the Subaru to be left in Cokeville while the party took the van into the country where David would tell them about his "formula." Because of protests by Harrison, David decided to take both vehicles.

David drove to a place near the ski area in Pine Creek. David had group photographs taken and stretched their legs for a while. David said if any of them wanted out now, he would take them back. In response to this statement, Harrison stated "I like to control my own destiny, and I'm not in control now and I want out." David then instructed Doris to take Harrison back into town and make arrangements for his return to Jackson. Doris took Harrison to Cokeville and made arrangements for his return travel.

10:00 a.m. —Doris returned to the area near Pine Creek where everyone was waiting for her. David said he was too tired to get into the formula that day and said they would do it tomorrow.

11:00 a.m. —Everyone arrived in Montpelier and checked into the Best Western Motel. The remainder of the day was spent lounging around while David slept.

Evening—David, Doris, and Princess occupied Room 131 while Mendenhall and Deppe occupied Room 130.

May 16, 1986, Morning—Everyone placed their personal property in the Subaru, which was to remain at the motel. Everyone then got into the van and started toward Cokeville.

Approximately four to five miles out of Montpelier, David stopped the van on the old highway, and everyone got out for another group photograph.

After stretching their legs for a few minutes, David told everyone to get back into the van. David then gave seating assignments. Mendenhall was in the back seat. Doris was on the driver's side middle seat, Deppe was in the passenger side middle seat, and Princess was in the driver's seat. David was in the front passenger's seat.

David then stated, "I am going to take over the elementary school in Cokeville. In the back of the van are several bombs with deadman switches to be strapped to myself. I have sent letters to President Reagan and others. I will secure the school and tell the government I want two million dollars per child." David said the reason he chose the Cokeville school was because if the government refused to pay the ransom, the "Mormon Church" would. David stated he was planning on a ten to thirty day siege. David then asked each person, individually, if he or she was in or out. With the exception of Doris, each stated they would not go along with such a proposal. Doris stated, without hesitation, that she would go with him.

David gave Doris a handgun and then handcuffed Deppe and Mendenhall to the frame of the back seat of the van. Princess was moved to the center seat and Doris drove.

11:00 a.m. —The group arrived in Cokeville. The school children were outside at that time. David said, "I want them all inside." They then left and parked for a period of time on a trail off of Smith's Fork Road, east of Cokeville. David allowed everyone to stretch their legs, but threatened to shoot anyone who tried to flee. He said Princess would have to help them unload the van and when everything was in the school and the building was secure, he would give her the ignition keys.

12:52 p.m. —David noted the time and said it was time to go. He then drove by the school. On that occasion, additional children were outside. David backed out of the school parking lot and drove to a remote area west of Cokeville.

1:13 p.m. —David stated the time again and said the kids should be inside by now. He drove by the school again. The children were still outside and so he drove on through town to a hillside near the town elementary where he could watch the school with a pair of binoculars. By the time David got the binoculars out, the children had gone inside and he got back into the van and proceeded to the school.

1:30 p.m. —David backed the van up to the south door of the elementary school. David got the shopping cart out of the rear of the van and proceeded to the school office. Doris, armed with a revolver, walked the halls, assisting in grouping all of the occupants into the one classroom. Princess unloaded the van into the south end of the hallway. When the building was secure, David threw Princess the keys to the van and told her, "Get the hell out of here."

Princess drove the van, with Deppe and Mendenhall still handcuffed to the backseat, to the city hall where she summoned help and reported the situation.

The entire 154 present student body and faculty, (with the exception of one "excluded hostage," the janitor), were placed in a classroom which measured approximately 30 feet by 32 feet. Doris remained near the main door of the classroom while David stood in the front of the classroom. The children were forced to remain there; however, some of the faculty were allowed to come and go. The faculty was advised that, if they failed to return to the classroom, he would kill all of the children. When all of the building's occupants were in the classroom, David described how the bomb worked and announced that if anything happened to him the bomb would go off, killing everyone in the room. David also threatened that if anyone tried to escape, he would kill everyone.

Three rifles, two .22 caliber and one Mini 14, a .223 caliber, as well as a wooden military style munitions box were placed near the main door of the classroom. This box contained components for the manufacture of an additional destructive device.

Additionally, several firearms, ammunition and personal records were placed under a bench along the west wall near the south end of the north/south hallway.

Approximately 2:30 p.m. —David expressed fear that one of the children would bump him, causing him to accidentally detonate the device. David then instructed the teachers to construct, with tape, a neutral zone in the middle of the classroom. The neutral zone was approximately 9'2" by 9'8." Inside of this neutral zone David placed the shopping cart with device and a small student desk upon which he could sit. (Teachers called the area the "magic square" and instructed the children to stay away from it).

3:40 p.m. —David told Doris to hold the lanyard to the firing device while he went to the bathroom, that adjoined the classroom. While holding the lanyard in one hand, Doris told one of the teachers to keep the children quiet. Doris then turned to look behind where she was sitting on the table. In that instant, the bomb detonated with a large fireball filling the room and engulfing Doris. At the sound of the explosion, David opened the bathroom door in time to see a male faculty member attempting to flee. David, armed at that time with a handgun in each hand, shot the faculty member in the back with a .22 caliber revolver and shot and killed Doris, who was burning. David then stepped back into the bathroom. The teachers and rescue personnel evacuated the children through the windows and the two classroom doors.

Witnesses were unable to provide any additional information concerning the activities of either of the suspects. David and Doris both died at the scene. They were the only fatalities.

Personal History as I Remember It

Through the investigation of this incident and my family's involvement in this horrific crime, I have had the unique opportunity to witness what I now know to be a true miracle. This is a summary of my personal experience.

Two days before this incident I made arrangements with Rob Erickson, (a long time friend and oil field construction associate), to go with him to look at a possible job opportunity in southern Utah.

On the way home Rob was driving. As we approached the Sage Junction intersection, there were three ambulances with their emergency lights on going toward Kemmerer. I don't remember our remarks about them, but I expected to see a major accident before we arrived at Cokeville. We continued on north to Cokeville and never happened upon any accident. Near Thompson's Ranch I could see unusually large aircraft at the little Cokeville airport. I also saw a helicopter approaching the airport. As we turned down toward Main Street, all we could see were fire trucks, ambulances, law enforcement vehicles and hundreds of people. The entire street was full.

We went as far down Main Street as we could and suddenly drove next to where Kathy Davidson was swiftly walking. I rolled down the window and asked, "Kathy, what is going on? Do you have a mock disaster in operation or what?"

She then gravely answered, "A man and woman took the whole elementary school hostage and they had a bomb and it has gone off! I have to go!"

I couldn't believe what I'd just heard. I grabbed the door handle and jumped out of the truck and told Rob, "I have to go!" as I ran for the school. I don't think I took a breath. All I wanted to know was, are my children in there? Are they OK? Who in the hell did this?!

As I ran I saw children crying. They had clean tear tracks down blackened little faces. Parents were crying for their children and the children were crying for their parents. EMTs were holding children down to keep them from running to wherever.

I finally came to the barricaded police line. I went through. I could see Sheriff Wolfley talking on a patrol car radio. I ran up to him. "Are my kids OK? Are they in there? Where are they? Is Claudia with them? What happened?"

Sheriff Wolfley answered, "Your kids are OK, and Claudia is with them. They are on the way to the Kemmerer hospital. They're OK. I need you to help me. I need you here."

"What do you mean, they're on the way to the hospital? What is wrong with them?" I persisted.

"They are OK. They are just being checked for smoke inhalation," the sheriff continued, "I need you to get the background on these two and find out if there are more. Get with Earl Carroll and interview David's daughter and the two guys. You get on David's and Doris's motives for doing this and see if there is anyone else out there involved!"

I then left the sheriff and went toward the school. One of the deputies gave me his portable radio so I would have radio contact. I headed toward the south entrance where there was a truck from the Sweetwater County Sheriff's Office. I knew the truck and the deputy who drove it. He was a bomb technician for bomb disposal and investigation. As I neared the entrance I asked Rich Haskell what happened.

He replied, "You've got a miracle here. If this bomb had functioned as it was designed, this part of the wing of the school wouldn't be here and there would be a lot more death and injury." He explained what he knew so far. Then Earl Carroll, the other Lincoln County Sheriff investigator, came out the door.

Earl said, "Come in and I'll bring you up to speed."

Earl showed me the boxes of diaries, ammunition, guns and the bodies. I also learned that a teacher had been shot. I saw the extensive damage to the room by heat, smoke and the pockmarked walls from the ammunition detonating in the bomb. Suddenly, I had to check on my kids again. I couldn't believe my kids were OK. I heard a Diamondville police officer in the Kemmerer hospital on the radio reporting he would be in the hospital assisting where he could. I knew him and called him on the radio. I asked him to check on my wife and kids and see personally if they were OK. It seemed like forever, but he finally called back and said he had personally seen them. They were OK. They would return on a bus later that night.

I could now focus more. I took a box of the most recent diaries after they had been logged in for evidence. I took them to my office at the city hall so I could focus on them and avoid the reporters and the confusion of the emergency and I began to read them. I looked for and found the most recent one. The first page read:

1986 Year of the BIGGIE

1-1-86
WED

81 Subaru   216595
72 BMW   46490

55 =   27785
(I later discovered this meant David owned 55 guns
with an approximate value of $27, 785)

BIGGIE (BNW)

The following are excerpts from that diary:

1-2--86 ....
....*BIGGIE always on mind as I work out problems*
that   come   to   mind   and   havin   trouble   sleepin.   Did   however
manage...
...................................I off on scoot & to MHSH (after goin to Cortaro P.O. &

mailin ZEN of MM to SOB & orderin a chart of Halleys Comet whereabouts [an advantage of big city. I merely called U of A Planeteriam}] BlowHole. Evc of CdeO & theryde gettin over 100 rds(4-of em unfired .22's RFS)

None of this made much sense. His handwriting in his diaries was extremely difficult to read. He used abbreviations and codes throughout all of them. It was evident that this was going to take an enormous amount of time. I skipped toward the end of the diary and went backwards to get his recent entries that ended before his and his wife's death and the various injuries of 154 adults and children.

I found this:

4-30-86WED
And it comes down some 12 yrs + & 5 yrs + later. BIGGIE BNW. Got little zzz's waitin for alarm. Then it too dark & waited near another hour. Then off with Subaru & out on desert for crucial experiment that did just as it was supposed to do. Excitedly came home and gave 'D' notice
Back home I fidgeted and tried to call Gerald (no answer) SOB (got his wife who was excited it was me callin) & Bob got him @ his office & after tellin him he'd get back with me @ twenty:00 to fine tune (and freely talk). After a while I gave P notice (assuming 2 wks but hurring it a bit I think)
.....'D" also v. excited & we yak seriously a lot. I got brief nap. On phone a lot & off on scoot tryin to run down a shopping cart.
Bob called @ twenty:00. Seems he's wholley busted & doesn't want to take but minimum time off his job. Maybe have to fly him to Wyo   Finally I ran down a shopping cart & off to Safeway on West Valencia twenty m' distant & got one for $10.50..........
22:30 call Gerald (just back from Germany) and make plans to get him & D.M. 12:30 12th @ 1228 Grinell. He seemed real excited. Got a hold of S.O.B. @ 17:30 & he was excited, ready to go, last wk, last mo., last yr. I so excited it long time till I wind down.

I knew after talking with Sheriff Wolfley, Earl Carroll and other agency investigators that they were conducting interviews with all of these individuals who were listed in David's diary. It appeared we had all the suspects involved in this incident and the interviews gathered by Detective Carroll, the FBI, and the ATF proved it beyond doubt.

At approximately this point in the investigation, I received a radio call informing me that the buses were arriving from Kemmerer Hospital. I drove up to where the buses were. I saw Claudia and my kids for the first time since I had gone to Utah two days before the bombing. It was the most emotional moment of my life. I picked them up, examined, hugged and kissed each of them. I took them home and then returned to the investigation.

For the next several weeks, I lived, ate, and dreamed those diaries. I knew who was involved in the incident but I didn't know *why*. I did know David wasn't planning on coming out and neither he nor Doris were going to live through this. There were two separate pieces of physical evidence stating that fact.

1. David often referred to the abbreviation "BNW." During the examination of the diaries it was discovered it stood for *Brave New World*. In one of the diaries David made the statement, "I wonder what we'll be called in the New World." There were other references in both David's and Doris's diaries about their relations as husband and wife being over. Doris stated "friends from now on....changes." (Doris' diary 5-7-86).

2. The second and the most descriptive physical evidence was copies of notes that Doris left for her children.

David had also left evidence that they were going somewhere else after the incident. It didn't appear to be any particular place, as we know it. He had taken only the items that documented his life thus far: his diaries (47 of them), his guns, and two metal boxes of photographic slides. These slides had been cataloged, categorized and alphabetized and reflected most of the important times of David's life.

So where was David going? David made multiple statements

about discovering and believing in reincarnation throughout the diaries he had written while attending Chadron State University and in the diaries thereafter. He had on several occasions sent the book *Zen and The Art of Motor Cycle Maintenance* to individuals who wanted to know what new theory he was working on. No one ever figured out what he was alluding to.

Why Cokeville?

During interviews conducted by various agencies it was reported that David thought that if the government didn't pay the ransom then the "Mormon Church," which placed so much emphasis upon families, would. There are two additional possible reasons on why David chose Cokeville:

1. September 14, 1977, the Town of Cokeville terminated David's employment as the Town Marshal. The letter stated, "...due to decline in your job performance..."

2. David wrote a letter while employed by the Town of Cokeville where he stated the following:

I accepted a position here in Cokeville, Wyoming as Town Marshall. A town of 600 at an altitude of 6200 feet and the mountains go up in all directions around. A wonderful place to raise children. The school system is fabulous, having 170 students in grades kindergarten thru twelfth & top scholastically adept students.

David was always critical of the education system and how poorly the system prepared the students in the "important things" as he saw them. (David was intelligent and possibly only wanted to bring intelligent people with him to the BNW).

In David's personal copy of *Zen and the Art of Motorcycle Maintenance*, he underlined part of a page and he referred to this phrase on several occasions in his writings. The underlined portion: *...him as a prototype for the many millions of self-satisfied and truly ignorant teachers throughout history who have smugly and callously killed the creative spirit of their students with this dumb ritual of analysis, this blind, rote, eternal naming of things.*

These few examples of evidence are a small part of the evidence examined and used to determine, as best as possible, the motives of the two hostage takers. As a result of their deaths they were unable to provide their motives personally. David was obsessed with record keeping and documenting his thoughts and actions. He gave us an intimate portrait of his life and his distorted way of thinking.

During the week of the bombing there were thousands of letters to the children and citizens of Cokeville. With them came a lot of donations and support both in money and expressions of sympathy and encouragement. The federal and state organizations worked closely with the community to offer psychological support for the children, parents and any other individuals who were trying to cope with the horrendous experience that fell upon that rural farm community.

As with the rest of the community, some of our children were demonstrating symptoms that they, too, were having difficulty coping with the experience. The two girls, Cynthia and Brenda, sometimes cried easily and sometimes tempers flared among all of them. Jason would startle easily with an exaggerated jump. Nathan was having nightmares and a high fever continually. None of the kids who were in the bombing wanted to go shopping or anywhere where there were crowds of people. Nathan would even hide on the floor in the car while Claudia would go into the post office or a store. I would sometimes have tears surface while driving home from Kemmerer where I would discover a little more about the intentions of David Young and how close we all came to losing our families.

Our oldest daughter, Diana, and the youngest, Sabrina, were not students in the elementary school. Diana became a lot more protective of the younger ones, which irritated them, and caused them to tell her she wasn't the boss on several occasions. Claudia resorted to comforting everyone else and used writing and anything else she could do to keep busy. After a few weeks we were doing well and working our way back into normal life. Except for Nathan who continued to have a fever, sometimes 103 degrees, in spite of the fever reducer medication that was prescribed by the Montpelier doctor.

As the officers' reports came in from various agencies, the information became a massive case file. Many of the interviews used the same unusual statements and phrases such as, "it sure was lucky that this didn't...," or "it could have been a lot worse if...," or "it's a miracle that this didn't do what it was supposed to do," and others. All of these phrases were used continuously and by some who are experts in their fields. These statements later caused me to examine my beliefs and attitude about being a father and a cop.

I had been scrutinizing the diaries and interviews and trying to decipher the man's abbreviations for so long, it seemed to me I was living the life of David Young. I could not, however, understand even one paragraph of the 0=oo letter. I took headache medicine like candy and drank Cokes by the quart.

Then one day I received a telephone call from Claudia about 2:00 p.m. She indicated that she was downtown and one of the mental health associates, Dr. Ford, happened to ask her how well she thought her children were coping. She told him they were doing fine but that Nathan was running a fever and she couldn't seem to get it to stay down, despite of the medication. He indicated if she would like, he could see Nathan and maybe see how he was doing.

She made the appointment and brought Nate in to visit with him. Claudia then told me that after Dr. Ford had spent nearly an hour with Nathan, he came out of the interview and asked her if she believed in angels. She told him her religion said there are such things but she hadn't personally seen them. Dr. Ford then said, "You should talk to Nathan." Claudia then told me how Nathan had told her he had seen angels at the bombing and particular his great great grandma. She was "his" angel.

At that time I was very angry that the psychologist had even met with Nathan because I had a very low opinion of their capabilities due to my law enforcement experience with them in the court system. I also didn't want my son going around saying he had seen angels. He had enough issues with other kids because he was a cop's son. I told Claudia that I was going to come home right then and straighten him out. I needed a break anyway because I had been working late every night since the bombing.

When I got home, I talked to Claudia some more about what Nate had said. I then sat Nate down at the table and began to interview him like I did any other person I needed to get information from. I will forever regret my attitude that "interrogation." I asked Nate if he actually had seen angels like he told the doctor and his mom. He said, "Yes." I then asked him what he had seen. He told me he had seen this angel and she was very white and stood by him. She told him he needed to go to the window and that what they (David and Doris) were doing was very bad and that the bomb was going to go off. She said he needed to go now.

I asked if he knew her name. He said she never told him, but said, "I think it was grandma Meister." This was just what I was just looking for to prove to him that he hadn't seen an angel. Grandma Meister was still alive and living in a rest home in Pinedale, Wyoming.

I said, "Nate, grandma Meister is living in Pinedale so she couldn't be an angel. Are you sure you saw an angel?"

"Well, she didn't tell me her name, but she said she was my great, great, grandma," Nate replied.

I then did what every investigator would do in that situation; I asked Claudia to get the photographs. We would see if he could pick the "angel" out of all the pictures in the album. She got the photo album. I set it on the table in front of him and began to turn the pages.

The photo album was a large one and it took a long time to get through. Suddenly, Nate put his little hand on a photo that had both of his great great grandmothers in it.

"That is my angel!" His finger didn't point to Grandma Meister, but was right on my Grandmother Elliott. There was no pause in his words. It was a statement of fact. His countenance even seemed to brighten. He was sure.

I then began to realize that what he said he saw, he *had* seen. I then asked him to tell me exactly what he had seen. He told us of many angels coming down through the ceiling just before the bomb went off and that there were angels holding hands around the bomb and as the bomb went off, the angels went up through the ceiling.

Immediately, I recalled the statement that was made by the bomb technicians Ron Norda and Rich Haskell, when they described the unusual way the explosion just seemed to "go straight up" causing fewer injuries to the children than what there should have been. Rich and I had been friends for several years. When I first arrived at the scene of the bombing, Rich said, "Hartley, when this went off, there should not have been any survivors. It appears the explosion went straight into the air. There was not the big explosion there should have been."

After the examination of the site by the bomb technicians, they discovered that there were two blasting caps that failed to go off. Both of these blasting caps were inserted into the explosive powders that would have caused the explosion to be catastrophic. They also found that the milk carton had a leak in it and the gasoline was leaking into the explosive powder in the cans. It had soaked the explosive powder making an incendiary bomb instead of an explosive shock. The explosion was a low-order explosion instead of going high order as it was designed to do.

I continued to talk with Nate about the incident and what he had seen. He told of how there were a lot of angels, one for everyone, except for the lady, her angel "was leaving." I listened to him and was amazed at the detailed account given by this six year old child. I then asked the question that has haunted me ever since: "Why didn't you tell me about the angels, Nate?"

He looked up at me and looked me right in the eyes and said, "Because you wouldn't believe me." Nate's fevers never returned.

As time went on, I thought how amazing it was that all the law enforcement officers who lived there (4), happened to be out of the area at the same time and that the emergency management officer *was* there. Kathy Davison, who happened to be there for flood evaluation, handled the initial report with courage and professionalism. She initiated the response needed and isolated the incident. I can only hope that I would have responded as professionally and appropriately, knowing four of my children were being held hostage by someone with the profile of the most dangerous hostage taker—the one that is not planning on coming out alive.

Incident Summary

As a result of exhaustive investigative research, intense scrutiny of the evidence and the psychological profiling of David, it has been determined that David had planned since the early '60s to take advantage of the reincarnation principle and take with him his most important possessions, the records of his current mundane life, whatever amount of money he could extort from any source, and the children of Cokeville and, through the explosion of a homemade bomb, enter into the "Brave New World" where he would be set as the empirical leader. He would control this group and those who wanted to go with him and be subject to him, and be totally in control of the proper training of the "top scholastically adept students."

The case was closed out and the personal property of David and Doris was returned to their surviving family.

The educational staff of Cokeville Elementary was, and will forever be, heroes for facing certain death to evacuate the children. The parents, with their hearts full of prayer and self-control, waited while at the same time the angels stood suspended, blanketing the children and surrounding the bomb.

Photo by Rick Sorenson
Courtesy of the Casper Star Tribune Collection, Casper College Library

Survivors
and
School Stories

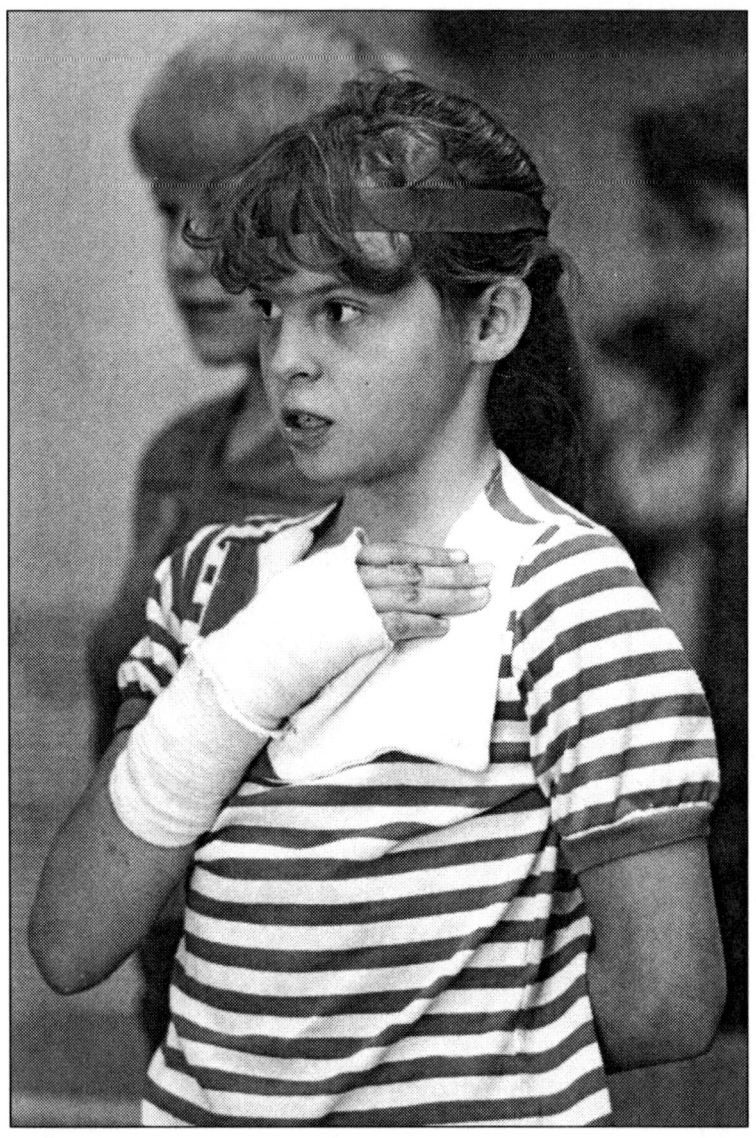

Third grade survivor Jamie Buckley pledges allegience to the flag.
Photo by Bill Wilcox
Courtesy of the Casper Star Tribune Collection, Casper College Library

Kim Kasper
Kindergarten Teacher Survivor
(Email Submission)

I rarely think of the actual event, possibly because it took place at the end of my kindergarten teaching career in Cokeville. My husband, Kris, was just finishing his student teaching in Rocky Moore's fifth grade classroom and our goal was to move to a warmer climate. Maybe distance and change make it easier to forget. Or it could be because I made a point, during the ordeal and in the days afterward, of avoiding anything that might leave a lasting impression. I did not look at our assailant's face. Even if I try, I cannot recall his name or what he looked like. I did not read the news reports. I was not interested in the ensuing investigation.

I do recall the look of fear on my father's face as he rushed me from the school grounds. I remember thanking God that it was me inside that classroom and not my own two children. I think of the courage of my kindergarten students who went on to perform our end of the year circus program, especially the tightrope walkers with burned arms wrapped in bandages, holding umbrellas above their heads and balancing delicately as they tip-toed along the imaginary tightrope.

As much as I may have tried to block things out that day, God must have had other plans. Shortly after I was out of the building, I was met by Judy Himmerich, my children's babysitter. In desperation she said, "Kim, I can't find Trini." I don't know who else I pushed out of the classroom window, but in the blackness I can still see a pair of turquoise blue, flower print pants going out the window. Was that God's purpose for me there that day? To be able to say, "Judy, she's OK?" I don't know. I don't need to know. I've come to realize that on that day and every day, God is in control. That has been and will be a comfort to me for the rest of my life.

Heather Cory Joy
Kindergarten Student Survivor
(Typed Submission)

May 16, 1986 is not a day that I will ever forget. It is probably the most vivid of all my childhood memories; I can even remember the clothes I was wearing on that day.

As I think back to that day, I am thankful that I had my sister and my cousin there to help calm me. As a young kindergartner I really did not understand fully what was going on around me and it was comforting to have them there by my side. I am also thankful for my grandma; she was the first person I saw as I climbed out the window. I was confused, and without her, I may not have known what to do from there. She took me to the car and home to my mom. From there I remember going to the hospital and all the time there, I had my mom and my dad by my side. I recall having my mom come back to school with me when we did go back. The events of that day made me realize at a very young age that family is very important.

Now, nearly twenty years later, I am still grateful for the loving family I have, and as I start my own family, I hope that they will never have to have something so drastic happen to make them realize how important a loving family is. The realization of the importance of a loving family is a great blessing that I received through the events that took place on that day.

Jody DaLyn Pope Keetch
Kindergarten Student Survivor
(Typed Submission)

May 16, 1986 will never be forgotten in my mind and heart. I have very mixed feelings, but the most important is how I feel now after it is all over and I can look back on it. People think I am crazy when I tell them that I am glad now because I know that we were blessed and I saw God's hand in our protection that day. There are so many little miracles that happened for all of us that day and I will just share a few of my most memorable ones.

I had afternoon kindergarten and my mom and I were out at Cheryl and Joe Buckley's doing gold leafing. Well, I was mostly playing with the kids. When we got home I was too late for the beginning of school. I loved school. Mom kept telling me she did not think it was a good idea for me to go, but I was a stubborn six year old who knew better than my mom. Finally, I convinced her to let me go and that I could wear my favorite outfit.

I was walking up the sidewalk backwards, on the south side of the elementary, blowing kisses to my mom, little sister Lacy, and little brother Jade as they drove away. Everything looked normal as I hung up my backpack, then I looked into my classroom through the window on the door. It was dark, I tried to open the door but it was locked. As I turned around a lady asked me if I was looking for my class. Not liking to be alone, I told her yes. She said that they were in an assembly and to follow her. We headed to my brother Shiloh's classroom. I was comforted by that until she opened the door into the room, I instantly felt my heart fall and knew that something was wrong. The only person in the room I wanted was Shiloh. Though he was not much bigger or older than me, I knew that he loved me and that he would protect me. Shiloh and I were close before then but after that day we had an unspoken bond that would never be broken.

I was not afraid of guns until that day but to see them all lined up along the chalkboard was very intimidating. The worst part of those few hours was the smell. It was not quite a gas smell, close but unidentifiable. I can smell it now. Even when I just think of the scent and all the memories of that day come back. It is a smell that makes me nauseous and not just because of the way it smells but the feeling it brings with it.

I did not know at first what was going on, but I did know that something was wrong. To see the starkness of the faces and the trust that was put into the hands of our teachers, friends, parents, but most of all our Heavenly Father. There were so many silent prayers; many prayers were whispered. We tried to do anything we could to get our minds off of the reality. We sang primary songs, played games, watched movies, and just listened very intently while pretending to block it all out.

When David Young taped the square around him I was close to that line. I remember trying so hard not to touch it because of the threat of shooting us and carving us out like canoes. I did touch the line a little and just hoped that he did not see me. I knew he was serious or he would not have been there.

Meanwhile at home, my mom had just put Lacy and Jade down for a nap. She looked out the window to see the school bus stop. She looked at the clock thinking it is early for school to be out. Then looked back out the window to see my big brother Justin, who was in Junior high, running up the lane alone. Instant fear came over her as she wondered where Shiloh and I were. She met him at the front door, frantically asking where the kids were.

Justin said, "You haven't heard—there is a crazy man holding them hostage at the school. They are telling about it on the radio and everything."

That was the first day ever that my mom did not turn the radio on. She feels it is blessing that she did not hear it on the radio before she heard it from Justin because she knows she would have gone in and fought to get us out of there. In fact, she was going to go as soon as she heard the news if Justin hadn't stopped her and told her she was to just listen to the radio for further word and to stay off of the phone lines. These were the instructions he was given at school.

I have always known that Justin has a very big heart and that he loves his family with all of that heart. When he heard the news he asked one of the teachers if they thought that the crazy man would trade him for his little brother and sister. He would not have asked if he did not mean it, and for this Justin has always been one of my greatest heroes. He was willing to sacrifice himself for the safety of his brother and sister.

My mom called my sister, Lorie, in Swan Lake, Idaho, and told her to get a hold of all the kids and especially Dad and let them know what was going on. She told her to have everyone pray for the children. Dad was in Blackfoot, Idaho, at a cattle auction. Lorie called up the auction office and told the lady what was going on and asked if she could please try to find Evan Pope, and let him know what was going on, the kids were OK, and to hurry home. The lady got on the loudspeaker and paged Evan Pope to come to the office, but he never came. She decided that she would go outside and see if anybody knew who or where he was. She drove downtown after having no luck in the parking lot at the auction.

When she saw a man wearing a cowboy hat, about to get into his truck with Wyoming license plates, she said, "Excuse me, Sir, you don't happen to be Evan Pope, do you?"

Dad said, "Yes I am, and how can I help you today?"

She told him everything she knew and sent him on his way. With a knot in the pit of his stomach, Dad offered many prayers that all would be well as he sped toward home.

Shane, my brother, and his wife, Laura, were in Logan, Utah in the mall. They could not believe what they heard, "Cokeville, Wyoming—there is a hostage situation in Cokeville." They immediately tried to call Mom, but all the circuits were busy.

Lisa, my oldest sister, was at BYU in Provo, Utah, when she heard the news. She immediately started to ask Heavenly Father to bless all of us who were in the school and headed for home.

Linda, my last sister, was in Casper, Wyoming, at the state track meet. She and most of the track team went into one of the rooms and cried and prayed that their brothers, sisters, parents, and friends,would all be safe. These were a few of the prayers that I knew of, but I know that all of the prayers that were offered on our behalf were answered. Heavenly Father was watching over us that day.

As the bomb went off so did the pushing, shoving, screaming, we were all searching for fresh air. I went out the window with help from the teachers lifting us up and out. Mr. Moore got his belt buckle stuck when he went out the window and then he helped us get out. He told me, "When your feet hit the ground, run." I did run, as fast as I could, to Steve Taylor's house. There we were welcomed with open arms, tears, smiles, blankets, and water.

Mom and Justin were listening to the radio at home, three miles south of Cokeville, when they heard, "The bomb has gone off, the bomb has gone off!" Justin grabbed a child under each arm, (Jade, 1, and Lacy, 3,) and ran to the car. When they got to town, they saw children, adults, ambulances, and fire trucks all around. They found Shiloh shortly after arriving. No one could find me, not even Shiloh knew where I was. Finally, someone told Mom I was in an ambulance.

After searching through several ambulances she peeked her head around the corner as they were closing the doors to head to Star Valley. I saw her and waved for her to come with us. The rest of my family wanted her to stay with them, but I was the lucky one who got to have her come with me.

We were on our way to Star Valley to the hospital, me with a burnt arm and eyes and Mom with an answer to prayers. All was not exactly well, but better than expected. I was not the only one injured in the ambulance, but I do not remember who else rode up with us.

One more miracle or answer to prayer happened. The fan belt

on the ambulance went out, so we were stopped along the side of the road when two truck drivers stopped to help. Amazingly enough, one of the drivers had a fan belt that fit perfectly. What are the chances of one miracle after another? As he left and went on his way, he opened the door to the back and said, "God bless you all!"

When we arrived in Star Valley we were greeted very lovingly. They cut the dead skin off my arm and my favorite shirt off my back. They wrapped up my arm and put me in a room to recuperate.

Dad was rushing home when he heard, "The bomb has gone off, the bomb has gone off!" He did not know if his kids were OK. He dropped his horse trailer off in Bennington, Idaho, so he could make better time, wherever he needed to go. He had heard that there were ambulances from Montpelier, Kemmerer, and Star Valley. He did not know which direction to go, so he stopped in Montpelier, Idaho, to see what he could find out. He got word that Shiloh was OK and that I had some minor injuries but that I had gone to Star Valley.

After getting the news that I had gone to Star Valley Hospital, and would stay overnight, my dad came to my room. He and Mom both stayed with me through the night. Leon, my oldest brother, and his wife, Lynne, stayed and took care of the rest of the family for my mom and dad.

When I look back on everything that happened—that with a bomb that was to clear a mile radius and leave nothing of Cokeville, we had only burns and bad memories—I see how blessed we were to have only two fatalities: David and Doris Young. We were definitely blessed that day, and to be able to say I was one of those chosen to be saved and looked down upon by Heavenly Father's grace and touched by His mercy, is truly a miracle.

Britney Swensen Knight
Absent Afternoon Kindergarten Student
(Oral History)

I was only five so I don't remember a lot about that day, but looking back now I am very lucky that I wasn't at the school. There were some days afterward when I wondered what it would have been like to have been there. I never had any stories to share about the "Bombing." Just because I wasn't there doesn't mean that I was never afraid to enter the elementary school again. It was tough dealing with the scary feelings of returning to where something bad happened. The only consolation for me was knowing that I was saved from having to deal with the bad memories and that I could focus on getting past what happened that day.

Today I enjoy working for a successful dentist in Logan, Utah, as his dental assistant. I love to spend time with my husband, Brett, and dog, Kasa, play volleyball, water sports, snowboard, hang out with family and friends and just enjoy the good things life has to offer. There are many miracles in my life, but avoiding that dreadful day on May 16, 1986 was definitely one I will remember.

Bret Taylor
Kindergarten Student Survivor
(Typed Mailed Submission)

I was a kindergartner at Cokeville Elementary at the time of the school bombing, but I remember it as if I were much older.

I remember feeling scared and confused as to what was going on. Through it all I know one thing for sure: There was a higher power looking down on us all. And because of a loving Heavenly Father, a modern day miracle was performed. Many times I run into people who associate the "little" town of Cokeville, Wyoming, with the "big" miracle that happened that spring afternoon. Through the years it has definitely been a testimony builder for me that there is a God, and He loves me.

Joshua Wiscombe
Kindergarten Student Survivor
(Email Submission)

The day of the bomb had many moments that still stand out in my mind to this day, whereas other things have faded away. I think for some reason I was supposed to be in the bombing situation. As a kindergartner, I remember getting ready for the afternoon school session, that day as I had not done something my mother told me I should do. I remember she said that I wouldn't be going to school if I didn't clean up. For some, not going to school would be a punishment. I decided to obey, clean up, and go to school. Being a kid who did anything to get out of school, that was an unusual punishment. But, even more unusual is that I would choose to go to school that day.

As a kindergartner, I remember bits and pieces from the day the bomb went off. I remember doing our schoolwork and looking up to see a gun pointed at my teacher Mrs. Kasper's chest and my teacher calmly telling us that we were going to have an assembly and that we needed to follow her. I remember thinking how strange it was that the assembly was in a regular classroom and that there were guns all along the wall.

Some kids were crying and I remember thinking something was wrong. I remember sitting with my class for awhile, until my older sister, Stephanie, came over and asked if my brother, Byron, and I could move over closer to her, right by the door. The feeling of comfort returned. Steph has always been the "mother hen" type, the one to look out for us and to say things we weren't able to voice for ourselves.

The man with reddish brown hair (David Young) with the grocery cart asked that there be an outline of tape placed on the floor around him in the shape of a box. I remember Steph keeping us busy by playing with Lite Brite. Then the man left and the woman took his place.

We had just finished a smiley face on the "Lite Brite," when I looked at my brother and sister, smiled, and then, "Boom." The bomb had gone off. I immediately leaped for the door, tripping over a chair that was placed right next to the door. I was trampled by others. Every time I tried to get up, I was pushed back down. I looked down toward my feet seeing nothing but black and flames. I remember thinking I wasn't going to see my mom again. The next thing I remember, I was running through a hall toward light. I hit the door, pushed the metal handle, and ran toward my bike. I saw men in black with guns and firemen jumping the fence. I remember them saying, "Get out of here. Don't get your bike," as I ran to my red bike, jumped on and rode toward the street.

I remember being in the street and seeing kids with black soot all over them and some of the kids being watered down with hoses. I was met in the street by my mother, who was six months pregnant, and by my sister. Shortly after, Byron came running over. From the innocence of my youth, this is what I remember of the "Bomb."

After the bomb my teacher, Mrs. Kasper, had us draw a picture of our experience. I remember drawing circles for all the children and the man with red hair and a beard in the middle. We also had trips to Lagoon and a circus came to town to help us, I suppose, to not be afraid of school. We were also able to go back through the school and see the room. The smell of the place still lingered like the smell of wet damp cave, a sulfur smell.

I still have a hard time with loud noises and guns. I appreciated the money from the foundation after graduating high school.

The memories of Cokeville and the incident of the bomb will forever remain. The events created an unbreakable bond with my siblings. We have had many wonderful memories, trials, challenges and experiences. We were taught early on by my sister, that if we stick together we will be OK. And as we three have done this, we have been able to make it through the hard times. We were some of the lucky ones.

Some of my friends who were sitting on the other side of the room, where I was sitting before my sister came to get me, were burned badly. I only came away with singed hair and scars on my hands. I'm grateful for my sister and brother and how they have always looked out for me.

Since then I have had opportunities to serve others, to grow, to learn new things and meet many people. We moved to about eight other small towns since leaving Cokeville. None of these places have ever had the same feelings or memories as Cokeville. Some of my happiest childhood memories come from Cokeville, from the friends I had to the tree forts and penny candy. Great people made the town of Cokeville.

I married Shanna Priest on March 22, 2002. We have a son, Samuel Porter Wiscombe, who was born July 31, 2003 (named after my friend, Sam Bennion, of Cokeville) and a daughter, Emma Wiscombe, who was born December 20, 2005. I'm grateful for my wife, Shanna, my kids, and my parents, Steve and Joanna Wiscombe, for their neverending faith in me to succeed, and also for my sisters and brothers.

The coldest storms of our lives eventually bring greater understanding. As I came through this storm, I feel my life has been the better for it. I remember meeting people from Cokeville in different places over years and feeling almost related. I'm grateful for the unheard prayers of that day by people of all faiths on our behalf. I'm grateful that my Heavenly Father answered the prayers of our parents and the prophet.

Janel Dayton
First Grade Teacher Survivor
(Typed Submission)

The bell calling all of the elementary children in from noon recess had just rung, and I settled down at my desk in one of the two first grade rooms to catch up on some book work and prepare for the last few days of school. Normally I would have had about sixteen first graders in my classroom, but that had been a year where the number of first graders warranted two classes. Jean Mitchell, the other first grade teacher, had taken all of the children because we felt that it would be a good idea to put them together a few times before they all became classmates in second grade. I was totally unaware of the white van that pulled up outside the first grade classroom window.

Before I settled in to the work for the afternoon, I ran down to the office to get the mail. As I rounded the corner, I saw a man and woman walking toward the office. The man was pulling a grocery cart filled with what I thought were cleaning supplies, gallon jugs of a pale yellow liquid partially concealed by coats. I thought, "Uh oh!" But then I realized that they had seen me, so I thought I'd better proceed on my errand with an air of nonchalance, which I did. I entered the office and walked to my mailbox. The man, who I soon learned was named David Young, spoke to me, calling me by name.

"This is a revolution," he said.

I asked him who they represented.

"Ourselves," he replied.

I had read of a group of dissidents who were coming from the south, but Wyoming was not a state that they had planned to visit.

David showed me the bomb, explained that it had the capability of doing extensive damage to the school, and indicated that it would not be wise to try to harm either David or Doris, his wife. At that point a young woman came to the office looking for the principal, Max

Excell. She was applying for a job. Doris put Cindy Cowden, the applicant, and me into the conference room. Cindy, whom I had never seen before, suggested we go out the open window. I didn't think that would be a good idea, because in the few minutes that I had associated with David and Doris, I had a healthy respect for the seriousness of their plan. Within minutes, Doris came to get us. She walked us down the hall toward the south door. As we passed the intersection of the hallway, I saw Delbert Rentfro, the custodian, coming toward us. I motioned for him to go back. Doris said, "We'll have none of that." They made no attempt to bring him with us, perhaps because of his size and gender. We continued on down the hall. As we approached the second grade room, a young woman, David Young's daughter, came flying through the doors and screamed, "I can't believe you're going through with this." David tossed her the keys to the van and told her to get the h*@! out of there, which she did.

We went into the room, which is now the computer lab but then was being used as the other first grade room. There were not many people in there at that point. David Young was talking to me. That is the first time I felt fear, and it went clear to my bones. He explained that the children were valuable, but the teachers, the adults were highly expendable. He had exposed an arsenal of guns, some from the cart and some concealed on his person. He assigned me to watch the exit, which passed the bathroom door. The bathroom served both classrooms then, first grade and second grade rooms. A barricade was put up to keep children from going out of the building through the second grade door.

Doris went from room to room gathering up all of the classes in the school and bringing them for an "assembly." When all 154 people were assembled in the room, it became hot and stuffy. As many windows as possible were opened. Still, with the heat and the fear, some of the children became nauseated. Doris didn't want the children to get drinks because that would increase the traffic to the bathroom. It would increase the confusion and lessen the control the two of them had over the group.

Furniture was moved to make room for the children. A masking tape rectangle was taped on the floor to keep David's victims away from him and his bomb. Coloring sheets were passed out to entertain the children. The afternoon moved on, and things were fairly peaceful, until David Young came to the bathroom line. I told him that someone was in there, and he would have to wait. As he turned to look at me again, there was obviously no one home. The light had gone out of his eyes as he had submitted to a darker power's rule. Jean Mitchell and I tried to lighten the situation.

"You'll just die when you go in there," (the bathroom) one of us said.

"Yes, the potty's only a foot high," the other one said. He didn't think we were funny. He went in.

David had turned the bomb over to Doris in his absence. It was now attached to her wrist.

I turned to Tina Cook, our school secretary. I said, "I don't think she would blow these children up."

Tina's reply was, "Don't be too sure."

I turned my head back to look at Doris. I heard nothing, but I saw a huge fireball hit the ceiling. Children started rushing toward every exit as they had been trained to do a few weeks before when someone had suggested we have a fire drill from one room in case we should ever all be in one room and have to exit.

Jean was sitting on the floor across the doorway from me. I grabbed her arm and started pulling. I don't know what happened. The next thing I remember I was clearing the barricade from the second grade side of the bathroom hallway. Children were streaming through the doorway. John Miller fell at my feet. He regained his stance and ran.

There were no more children coming out, so I went back past the bathroom door to check the classroom where seconds earlier there had been seven years worth of Cokeville's future plus parents and teachers. I tried to look into the classroom, but saw only black smoke which seemed as thick as black cotton. I saw a glow on the floor. I tried to go around to the other entrance to the classroom. Jack Mitchell said, "Have you seen Jean?" I said no, even though seconds earlier I had been tugging on her arm. Hysteria had set in and had suppressed reason. A little farther down the hall, firemen told me to get out of the building.

I heard nothing as I ran down to the main street. I saw John Miller lying on the grass. I thought he had merely tripped in the hallway, but I later learned he had been shot. I saw nothing of the first graders who were my responsibility. I ran down to Russell Thornock's home. The children weren't there. I only saw a little girl whose face was stark white from the burns, sitting all alone. I never saw her again. I ran to the lawn where everyone was congregating. They weren't there.

A car came by. They had just come into town and had no idea why the town had gone berserk. One lady stuck her head out the window and told me to "Get the h*@! out of the middle of the road."

Ambulances began arriving. Children were loaded and taken to hospitals, thirty-five, forty-five or fifty-five miles away. People reluctantly drifted home, though some lingered, feeling the safety of numbers.

College students raced home to see for themselves the condition of family and friends. One friend whose family had a motel called from our home to his home, the motel. He asked, "Who's up there?" The reply was, "ABC, CBS, and NBC." The news media from many news stations and newspapers seemed to appear out of nowhere. A reporter from a Denver newspaper was at our home when I got there.

Three things have stayed with me. Plan your escape route when you are in a crowd and know where the exits are. Second, during our ordeal a little child asked me, "Are we going to be all right?" My spontaneous reply was, "We're all right right now," and maybe that's all we can expect out of life. Third, miracles do happen. I think we all had our own personal miracle. Mine was that I didn't see the elements of the "bombing" that nightmares are made of. I think as I stepped back to clear the barricade out of the doorway, I missed seeing David Young come out of the bathroom, shoot John Miller and then turn the gun on his wife and then himself. I was just a few feet away from all of that, but I was spared a personal view of that carnage. I am very grateful for that. I am very grateful for the Savior Who saved us and for the little children who had the faith that He would if they prayed to Him.

Jolene Buckley Bradshaw
First Grade Student Survivor
(Email Submission)

I remember I was sitting at a round table in my classroom with my classmates playing with play dough or coloring (I can't remember what I was doing) when a man walked in with a cart full of smelly stuff and lots of guns. I remember how bad it smelled. At the time I don't think I knew it was gas, I was only in first grade. The whole school was gathered into my classroom and I had no idea why. Someone told us at one time we were going to have an assembly, but that really didn't happen.

David Young was the man holding us hostage. He had a woman with him, too, but I don't really remember much about her. Mr. Excell, our principal, sat next to David and seemed nervous. I remember them talking to us a little. At one time David put a square in the middle of the floor with tape and he sat in the middle of it. He told us not to cross it. I sat right by the line. I have no idea why. I remember looking up at him and thinking, "What is he doing?" David told us that he was going to take us to another world and that he was ruler of it. He told us what a wonderful place it was going to be. I remember thinking, that is not true, that is not what my mom and dad had taught me. I knew that when I died I was going to go to my Heavenly Father.

At one time they brought a TV in and I went and lay by Mr. Moore. I don't think I watched anything, I was too busy thinking about what was going on. I stood by my teacher Mrs. Petersen some of the time. For some reason I don't remember being with my two sisters, Jamie and Jennie. Maybe I just was looking for someone older to help me out. My band teacher, Mr. Miller, stood up and started talking to David. David seemed upset with him and I was saying to myself, "Please, please just sit down so nothing bad happens." David shot him in the shoulder, but I don't remember seeing him getting shot or hearing the gun.

There are some things I don't recall or remember and I'm so grateful for that. I decided in my mind I was going to go right by the door and get ready to escape. The door was right by a bathroom so I was going to ask to go to the bathroom and then sneak out the door and run as fast as I could go. David told us if we tried to get out, that there were men outside with guns. I pictured them on top of the building for some reason. Who knows if David told us that or I just thought that. I thought to myself, is that really true or is he just trying to keep us in? So I continued to think of a way out.

The next thing I remember is the bomb going off and it was pitch black. I ran as fast as I could go out the door screaming. I was one of the first ones out because I was standing right by the door ready to run. If I remember right my cousin Meaghan was right next to me running also. Outside I saw my sisters Jamie and Jennie and they had burns on their arms. I didn't have any burns at all. I was very blessed.

I think of my classmate, Billy Jo Hutchinson, and how she was burned all over her body and how bad I felt for her. When we were back in school I remember seeing her in a wheelchair covered with white bandages. We were all so glad she was still here with us. It was a complete miracle that any of us are still here. Later, I learned that only half the bomb went off and that if the whole bomb had exploded, we would, of course, be gone.

I know for a fact that we were being watched over. Some people say they saw angels, I didn't, but I know we were blessed. Some days I think about the bomb and how I am so grateful that I have been able to have the life I've had. David Young sure had a lot of guts to try and take all our lives, but there is someone more powerful than him and I'm sure glad.

Ever since that day I know for a fact that our loving Heavenly Father is ALWAYS watching over us.

I have a wonderful life!! I married the man of my dreams,

Brad Bradshaw. We live in Lyman, Wyoming and just moved into a beautiful home my husband and I built. We have three beautiful children: McKailey, 4, Braxton, 3, and Braydon, 1. What a blessing they are in my life. They bring me so much joy. I am so grateful for the wonderful life that I have been able to live.

Fawna Eastman Cook
First Grade Student Survivor
(Email Submission)

May 16th is a day that I honor every year. Although I was only seven at the time, I remember the events of that day very clearly. My story of survival is a story that I share with the students in my high school English classes each year. I tell them about the scary man with the shopping cart, the square made of tape in the middle of the room, the mushroom cloud of smoke, the run home to my mother with my two older brothers.

From there my story changes from those of other survivors. I talk about the two-month stay in the Salt Lake City Burn Center. I talk about my brave mother, who, although miserably pregnant with twins at the time, never left my side. My students laugh when I describe the horrible food at the center. They get tears in their eyes when I discuss the nightmares of a confused seven year old girl, who cannot get out of bed because of the skin grafting surgeries. Every time I tell the story they ask me if I am bitter toward David and Doris Young, and I always tell them that I am not. I was too young, and that experience helped mold me into a strong woman who has since survived more terrible tragedies than the memories of that day. Without that experience, I don't think I would be able to handle the events that have transpired in my life. That day shaped me into someone who can survive, no matter what comes my way.

Jennifer Cory Dwinell
First Grade Student Survivor
(Typed Submission)

May 16, 1986 was a day many of us will never forget. I have many memories of that day. I remember the exact felt board story the teacher was reading to us, when the strangers and principal came in. I remember the room rearranged with a rectangle taped off in the middle. I remember crying with some of the others, scared and yet not really knowing why. I remember staying close to my sister as we colored together. And I sure remember the blackness that followed.

In the smoky darkness I saw someone (at the time, I thought was the second grade teacher) counting us as we tried to scurry out of the door. I remember feeling confused and somewhat upset, I thought she had counted me as a second grader, and I was only in first. I remember running out the doors into the sunlight. The first person I saw was my grandma, running across the schoolyard. I later found out she had jumped the six foot fence to get to the school to find her three granddaughters. And I remember the hospital stay afterward, our mom by our sides.

When people ask where I am from and I reply Cokeville. A usual response is, "Isn't that where that bombing was?" And as I reply, "Yes, I was there." These are the memories that come to my mind.

I sometimes wonder what the effects of that day have meant to me now. And I do think there are a few things that come to mind.

One is that I realized that there could not have been a teacher counting us as we ran out of the door. I know our Heavenly Father had angels there that day to watch over us. Was it one of those angels? I don't know.

Next, I have often wondered at my various jobs over the years, what other people think about at work. I have often found my mind going through the scenario, *if someone were to walk in with guns right now, what would I do?* I am always taking in the "safe places" around me. I know that sounds crazy.

Probably the hardest thing has been sending my little ones to school. Parents always think their children are safe at school. I know anything can happen in this unpredictable world. I will never forget how my heart dropped the first time the school called to tell me they were in lockdown, with my first grader inside. I wanted to scream and cry, but as calmly as I could I asked, "What do you mean by that?" I was told it was a safety precaution. When there is ever a threat in the area of the school, they go into lockdown. They lock the doors and no kids go in or out without a parent. What a relief. Yet as I hung up the phone, I wept a little.

In the end I know we are survivors. We are really strong spirits and there is a great plan for us. I believe in some ways we were weakened by the incident of that dreadful day. But I also believe that we were strengthened somehow, as well.

Nathan Hartley
First Grade Student Survivor
(Email Submission)

How do you compare your life to one you have not lived? It seems nearly impossible to measure the impact of one experience when compared to the complexity of an entire life. Is it true that a person can be no more than the sum of their experiences, or does a person's perspective of and reaction to those occurrences play a more intricate role? Throughout the years, I've shared with many people my thoughts and experiences of that day. Their reactions vary, but there seems to be a common strain. Inevitably, they will remark, "I can't even imagine..." Each time that statement is made, I try once again to fathom what my life would be like *without* that experience, an attempt I fail at even now. All I can really do at this point is examine some of my more conscious decisions and thoughts I have in this regard.

For me, the time is long past when I would look at my experience as detrimental to my life's progression. Many times, it has served only to strengthen my resolve to make things better. I can't change what others have done to me, but I *can* change my reaction to it. The experiences I had during, as well as after the bombing, have made me what I am. More importantly, they impact what I will one day be. Whether that is for good or ill, at least to a certain extent, is of my own making.

For years, I lived in a household that had constant reminders of that day. My father had been the head investigator, and still owns many artifacts and mementos of what happened. We had more and more access as years went by to the various documents and items that he had pored over for countless hours to obtain an understanding of David Young and what led up to that infamous day. In later years, I occasionally found myself rifling through those pages and examining those items myself.

I soon discovered something that my younger mind had failed to grasp: David Young was as human as anybody else I had ever known (albeit not normal). I came to the realization that I had demonized him for a long time. I made him a thing of nightmares and fear, when he was nothing more than a man pretending to be a god.

This seems to me to be one of the most important perspectives I could have learned. It's taught me to look at people with the realization that they are all human, and therefore subject to the same strengths and weakness that I am. David Young's reasoning stemmed from a failing of the mind. It was a failing that ended with dire and drastic consequences, but it was a human failing, nevertheless. The example in this has given me pause before I assumed somebody has wronged me out of spite. I've often realized that others have not wronged me at all, from their viewpoint. They just did what they saw as right and just from their perspective. The amazing thing is how often that viewpoint has helped me resolve the perceived issue.

It's difficult to say how many of these lessons I would have grasped now if I had not had the opportunity to experience the bombing as I did. How different would my life have been, had I not seen the angels? Not long ago, my wife (apparently very bored) happened to type my name into an internet search engine. It wasn't long before she found references to my story, as well as commentary on it. On another occasion, I remember walking into a pawn shop and having a man recognize me from a rerun of a TV show he had seen just the night before. He thanked me for sharing my opinion, and shared with me his opinions of the afterlife. We differed on many nuances, but I walked away with another experience, as well as another perspective.

In the end, I think that none of life's occurrences can be dismissed. No person can hope to become what they will be without the ups and downs that a walk through life entails. Even though some of these may have more of an effect than others, a person is a complex structure of body and mind. Who's to say what we would be without the scars of the past? Sometimes large amounts of sorrow or joy only serve to make a more colorful tapestry when your life's weaving is at an end.

Jennie Sorensen Johnson
First Grade Student Survivor
(Typed Submission)

It is amazing to me as I look back over the last twenty years of my life and realize what I could have missed if David Young had succeeded with his ludicrous plan of terrorism. I was only seven years old at the time of the hostage situation. Being that young, I was easily persuaded that it was only a gun assembly in my classroom. At first, everything seemed normal to me. I caught on early to the fact that the apparatus in the middle of the room was going to hurt everyone if he wanted it to. When the time to go home came and went, I was wondering if I was really going away with this man forever. I wondered if I would ever tease my grandpa, cuddle with my grandma, wrestle and tease my little brother or enjoy my mom and dad's vacations ever again. I remember the feeling of fear and deceit. How could anyone steal me away from my family who loves me? That was just not understandable to a child of my age. I sat in fear among many others who were feeling the same way.

As the clock slowly ticked on and the smell of gas became nauseously strong, I was with my teacher and tried my very hardest to be brave. Doris Young, David's wife, was very kind and tried to carry on cordial conversations with the teachers. David turned the bomb over to Doris and placed the firing device around her wrist secured with a rubber band. Unexpectedly, Doris turned too far as she rotated to talk to a teacher and the most dreaded moment in the afternoon happened. The bomb went off, but not in the way it was intended to, that's for sure! David never planned on angel intervention. In that moment of chaos, there were at least three times as many personages in my classroom that helped diffuse the flames.

I was sitting just outside of the taped off square David had made to keep us away from the bomb. My aunt Ruth, who died before

I was born and whom I later pointed out to my Grandma as the person who helped me out of the school, was there to protect me as I crawled on the floor through many shocked students and teachers, flames and rages of gunfire. I was filled with horror as I watched David shoot aimlessly into the crowd of panicked children to make one last attempt to take any and all of us with him to his world. He luckily didn't succeed. One teacher was shot, but survived.

I remember seeing Doris in a ball of flames and hearing the shot of death ring out as her husband took her life. He knew his plan had failed. I will never forget the sick feeling of dread that will always be associated with that memory. One of my good friends, Angie, tried to find me in the chaos. I will be forever grateful to her for caring for me enough to search me out in the flames and smoke. Crawling on my hands and knees in the madness for escape, I remember being enveloped by black and seeing the light from the little bathroom between classrooms, where David had taken his own life in defeat, and thinking, "go toward the light. You will make it." There is no doubt in my mind that there was another force in that room besides evil helping us survive.

I pushed on and remember the envelopment of warmth and love as my Grandpa Toomer scooped me up in his caring grasp. After that terrifying day, I never needed to question my purpose on this earth. I learned that my family loves and cares about me so much. My dad "flew" home from Kemmerer, where he was working at the time, to be with me. My whole family gathered securely around me for the remainder of the day to help soothe and comfort me. I escaped with only minor bruises and burns. Some of my close friends weren't as lucky, but I am so grateful we all escaped with our lives.

Forgiveness helped me overcome the outrageous nightmares I suffered into my teenage years. I could finally look back and actually forgive the man who tried to take me away from my mortal existence and ever-caring family. Forgiveness was the key to end all my suffering.

I have since come to learn that we cannot prevent bad things in the world from happening, but how we deal with the bad things and overcome them in our own way is what makes us stronger. I have achieved my goals. I was Valedictorian of my Cokeville High School graduating class. I attended and completed Bridgerland Applied Technology College. I was married in the Salt Lake Temple to my wonderful husband, Jared Johnson. I have two beautiful girls; Kirina Lee, 5, and Kysa Christine, 3, and I have a wonderful and fulfilling career in accounting. I know I am a survivor for these reasons.

As the time approaches for my children to begin their elementary education, I struggle with letting go. I hope and pray every day that they will not have to endure any hostage situations. I don't consider myself a paranoid mother, but it will always haunt me.

There are many thank you's to be said for the miracle that May day in 1986 and the internal turmoil that others helped me survive over the last twenty years. Dr. Sandall, my mom, my dad, my grandparents, my aunts, my uncles, my friends, my teachers, the doctors, my husband, my children, and last but by far not least, my Savior, Jesus Christ.

I support the Cokeville Miracle Foundation and proudly serve as a board member in hopes that our stories in this book will leave a legacy that is never forgotten but remembered for the miracle it was.

Jay Metcalfe
First Grade Student Survivor
(Email Submission from Iraq)

There really wasn't anything memorable that happened or any one thing that sticks out in my mind about the morning of May 16th 1986. I woke up, got dressed, ate, and then caught the bus to school with some of my brothers and sisters.

The first part of the school day went by much like the morning did. Nothing really worth mentioning happened. You see, I was a tall, extremely shy, imaginative (a bit of a day dreamer), seven year old kid. I never did like school all that much, so I probably spent most of that morning by myself, dreaming of how someday I was going to become a hero like Spiderman or He-Man. I was going to save the world.

That afternoon Mrs. Mitchell, our first grade teacher, told us that we were going to have a combined activity with Mrs. Dayton's first grade class after lunch. We were going to get to listen to the story of *Goldielocks and the Three Bears*. I was pretty excited because I always loved listening when the teachers read stories.

After lunch we all filed back into our classroom. Mrs. Dayton's class came into our room and they sat with us as Mrs. Mitchell brought out the flannel board and the story book and proceeded to tell the story by reading out of the book and then putting the characters on the flannel board. We were about halfway through the story when the classroom door opened and into the room walked David and Doris Young. I think there were two other men who came in with them but my attention was focused solely upon David and Doris, the shopping cart that he was pushing into our room and the handgun that was in his hip holster. I didn't know exactly what was in that shopping cart, I just knew that something bad was going to happen.

I remember David and Doris very well. She was wearing jeans and a green coat. She had shoulder length black hair and glasses. She spent most of the first few minutes trying her best to calm us down while the other men placed high powered rifles next to the door. She would tell us things like, "If you guys behave yourselves, nothing bad will happen to you." David, on the other hand, didn't say a whole lot. He was tall and skinny, he had curly brown hair with a beard and mustache. The thing that I remember most about him was that his face was stone cold. I always felt like he was the type of person who could have taken all of our young lives and it wouldn't have bothered him at all because he had no soul. As Mrs. Young was trying to calm us down, I looked over at one of my classmates who was sitting in the desk right next to mine, and she was crying. Then I thought to myself, why am I not crying? Maybe I should be crying, too.

So for the first and last time in my life I tried to cry. It didn't work, but nonetheless I was scared. After a few minutes, all of the other classes from kindergarten to the 6th grade started to file into our little first grade room. All in all there were about 140 kids in that room. It became so crowded that David had some of the teachers take all of the desks and tables out, but he let them know that if they tried to do anything he didn't like, he would hurt the children.

At first all we had to do was just sit there and stare at Mr. and Mrs. Young which I'm sure is what prompted him to do what he did next. David had the substitute third grade teacher take a roll of tape and make a square that surrounded David and the bomb. Then we were told that if any of us touched any piece of that square, we would get shot! That was about the same time David and Doris said that it would be all right if the teachers got us crayons, markers, and coloring books to use. They also brought in a TV and let us watch cartoons like *Transformers*. I think they allowed this because David was starting to feel uneasy with all of us just staring at him, so he gave us something to distract us.

It was at this time that I decided that I wanted to get some crayons and a coloring book. It just so happened that the only way that I could see to get to where these items were, meant that I had to pass right by where David Young was sitting. There was a rather large group that was trying to get to the same area, and they were moving around quite a bit. All of the sudden, by complete accident, someone bumped into me, which forced me to take a step to the side to catch my balance.

The moment I caught my balance I froze completely because I knew that my left foot was touching the square tape that was surrounding David Young. As quick as I could I moved my foot and I tried to act as though nothing had happened by grabbing a coloring book and crayons and going to a corner of the room where I would not be noticed.

It was around that time that I noticed one of our teachers, Mr. Moore, and our principal, Mr. Excel, were trying to talk to David. I didn't know what they were saying to him, but I later found out that they were trying bargain with David to get the children released by offering themselves up in our place. But David wasn't having any of it.

All that I was trying to do was focus on coloring and trying not to think about what was going on all around me. I was sitting on the ground only about five feet away from Doris Young, in a corner of the room. I had just finished coloring the picture of a cougar coming down the side of a mountain. I looked over my shoulder to see what was happening behind me when POOF the bomb went off.

I saw this big cloud of black smoke quickly cover the room. Now I don't remember what happened right after that because I must have gone into shock, when the back of my shirt caught on fire. Luckily, one of our teachers, Mrs. Sparks, had been watching me and quickly came over and put the fire out. The first thing that I remember is one of the other teachers, Mr. Mitchell, running to the door and yelling, "All of you kids get out! Get out! Get out!"

At that moment I made a mad dash for the door and ran out the side entrance to the building. As soon as I got outside I started to frantically look for my two older sisters, Joanna and Jaime. While searching for my family, I looked at my elbow on my right arm and saw that I had a little black bubble and a tiny scab. I wandered around for a few minutes, scared and burned. I saw a lot of my other schoolmates and they were covered in black smoke.

A few minutes later Jaime found me. When she tried to hug me, I yelled out, "Don't touch my back! Don't touch my back." Joanna then found us and we went to one of the nearby homes that was being used for helping the children who had been burned.

My mother and my brother, Aaron, were there. They sat me down and started placing a lot of cold wet rags on my back. All the while I was screaming in pain, and the rags would only help for a second or two because they would get warm quickly. After awhile they put me in an ambulance with some EMTs and sent me to the hospital in Montpelier, Idaho. My sister, Andrea, came with me to try to help calm me down.

On the trip to the hospital, I continued to feel a tremendous amount of pain, and I wasn't at all cooperative with the EMTs. They kept trying to stick me with a needle, but I didn't let them. When I got to the hospital, they put me to sleep and did what they needed to do.

The next thing that I remember was waking up and noticing that my face was wrapped up like a mummy. That night my brother Aaron came and stayed with me in the hospital for as long as they allowed him to stay. The next evening I was sent home.

I don't remember much of what happened that first night I was home, but my mother and other family members told me that all I did was go and sit in a corner of the room. I didn't say a word to anybody, and she knew that there was something wrong because it still hurt when people tried to hug me.

The next day someone took a look at me and told my mother that I needed to see a burn specialist. So I was taken to Logan, Utah, where I spent the next week or two. I spent a good amount of time in a whirlpool, and I underwent a skin graft surgery for my elbow. That was the last time that I had to go to the hospital for any of the injuries that I received that day. All of my scars, except for the one on my elbow, have fully healed.

As for the emotional scars that came from the bombing, those healed a little slower. It took three years for me to be able to open up and talk to anybody about what had happened. I have had nightmares, and trouble speaking to people I don't know. I have always been a little shy, but I think the bombing made it harder for me to be with people I didn't know very well. As with most things it has gotten a lot better as time has passed. As I have gotten older I've thought less and less about it. Occasionally, I will tell someone the story because it doesn't bother me anymore to talk about what happened.

Katie Walker Payne
First Grade Student Survivor
(Typed Submission)

I would like to tell my story, one that I hold very sacred. It is one of terror, prayer, the faith of little children, and a testimony that God lives and hears and answers our prayers. When I was a child seven years of age, a man, David Young, came into our 1st grade classroom pushing a cart and carrying several guns. The woman he had with him soon gathered all the other classes into our one small classroom and then David Young told us of his evil plan. He explained he had a bomb in his cart and that with the flick of the hand we would all die. He also explained that there was a price to pay for each child and teacher in the classroom, which would total a lot of money.

The teachers tried to tell him to let us children go and keep them. His reply was, "the people of Cokeville love their children and they will do anything to get them back." When the teacher tried a second time to ask him to let us go, he pulled a pistol out of his vest and told him to stop or he would shoot.

I was terrified. I didn't totally understand what he wanted, but I just wanted to go home. I was told by a teacher that everything would be OK and to sit down for a while. When I sat down with other students and friends, the teacher told us that we all needed to pray and ask our Heavenly Father to help us. We all held hands and each of us took a turn praying. I can't tell you what I prayed for that day, but I do know it was answered.

As David Young began to get a little irritated, he said that he needed some space. He then taped a "magic square" in the middle of the floor, a square that was made of masking tape with a desk in the middle. We were told that we had to stay out of the area because if we stepped inside it, we would be shot.

As I sat there coloring a picture on the floor, I suddenly looked up. Standing there was a woman dressed in white with little slippers on her feet. She told me that she loved me very much, that I needed to listen to my brother and everything would be OK. She told me to always remember that she loved me. I looked back down for a second and when I looked up again, she was gone. I did not know who she was, but I knew she loved me and that I was going to be OK.

It wasn't long after that my brother came and got me and told me to come with him. He took me and my sister and sat us down behind the bookshelves by the window. He said to stay there and he would be right back. He walked across the room as the bomb exploded. The room was instantly black, and when I looked toward the center of the room, I saw flames. Smoke started to fill the room, teachers and children were screaming. Someone was yelling for everyone to get down. I was scared to death. The next thing I remember is running across the lawn, seeing my cousin, and her picking me up and carrying me to the yard of a house nearby and telling me how she loved me.

When my mom found me, I told her we "prayed and they saved us." I testify to you that I know that God hears and answers our prayers and that if we ask, He will help us. I know that it is a miracle that not one student or teacher was killed that day. I know that miracles do still happen today and that all of us children of Cokeville are proof of that.

Shawn David Stahl
First Grade Student Survivor
(Typed Submission)

My family had just moved to Cokeville the month before from Monteview, Idaho. I remember thinking what a big town Cokeville was compared to Monteview.

The events of that day have stayed with me. I remember listening to David Young tell Mr. Excell how he (David) was going to kill all of the adults using his .357. Then he was going to wound all of the children with his .22 and hang us still alive on nails on the classroom walls by the backs of our collars.

I remember the sound of the bomb going off and watching the smoke fall like a curtain of blackness over the room.

I will never forget Rocky Moore picking me up by the back of my shirt and pants and throwing me out of a broken window yelling at me to run. Neither will I forget the look on my father's face as he met me on the front lawn of the school, picked me up, and ran as fast as he could.

I am told that I became a more serious child after that, always watching the news with my father.

People have asked me if the experience affected how I grew up and if it influenced the person I have become. I am sure that it has, but as to how, I cannot tell them. I have no other life to compare this one to.

I do know that a miracle occurred that day in Cokeville. I know that every May 16th I can expect a call from my mother to tell me how much she loves me and to make sure that I am OK.

Every May 16th I take the day off from work, go out, and have a day filled with nothing but fun. For me it is now a day of celebration and a chance to celebrate the time, which has been granted to me by my Heavenly Father. I look at my wife and son and am so thankful for the life that I am blessed to have.

Ryan Taylor
First Grade Student Survivor
(Email Submission)

It's been twenty years since the bombing at Cokeville Elementary School. I am now twenty-seven years old and can still remember much of that day. It began with my mother, Racheal, and my sister, Mandi, getting ready to go to Logan for my sister's appointment. I begged my mother to let me go with them but she said no, that I should stay and go to school. I ended up going to school on that dreadful day.

I remember that there where two 1st grades because of how many kids there were in that year. Our teacher told us we were going to be combined for the day. I was excited because we'd all get to hang out together. When it came time to go into the classroom, I remember going in and starting to do an activity. This was just shortly after lunch break.

All of a sudden and man and a woman walked into the classroom and said to be quiet and nothing would happen. One of the teachers asked what was going on. I remember the man pushing a cart and carrying guns on his shoulder and at his waist. The lady had some guns in her arms. She stacked them up against the wall. The man told everyone that he was going to hold the school hostage and that our parents were going to give him money to get us back.

I remember that lady (Doris) leaving and going to the other classrooms, telling everyone to come to this certain classroom because there was an assembly going on. After a while the room began to fill up with the whole school. When everyone was in the room, the man said he was holding the school hostage and that if anyone did anything stupid he would harm us. The teachers were trying to calm down the kids and tell them that everything was going to be all right. The man passed out a letter for all to read explaining his "master" plan for us.

After a while the room began to fill up with the smell of

gasoline. The teachers asked if they could open the windows and door to ventilate the room. They stacked desks and chairs in the hallway between the two classrooms so no one would escape. The man taped a square in the middle of the room to keep everyone away from the bomb. It was tied to his arm with two clothespins with screws and wires connected to it and a half of a pin in the middle for keeping the metal from touching.

The next thing I remember is coloring a picture when all of a sudden I heard a big explosion and the room turned red and orange. It began to get really hot. Then I realized the bomb had gone off. I remember one person in white picking me up and carrying me out the door. I remember running down the road not realizing what had happened. Then someone was patting my head and squirting me with water. I realized later that they were putting the fire out in my hair and cooling off my burns. I was put into an ambulance and taken to the hospital.

I remember getting to the hospital and all the doctors bandaging me up and making sure I was taken care of. I was in the hospital for a while and remember all the family, friends, and strangers coming and making sure that my family and I were OK. I got lots of letters from people throughout the country wishing me well. I still have all those letters to this day.

I returned to school after a while and remember walking into the room and seeing the shape of a figure on the wall. To this day I believe it was an angel watching over the kids and making sure that no one was killed. I also remember that the man was not going to let us go but kill us all and take us to his new world where he believed he would be our god.

Twenty years ago I could have died along with 153 other people, but I was given a second chance at life. This made me strong and made me become the person I am today. To this day I am still not able to walk into that classroom. When I get to the door I instantly freeze and can go no farther. Maybe it's fear still inside me and maybe one day I will be able to go back into there and sit where I was and remember the day that a madman took over our school.

Carol Petersen
Second Grade Teacher Survivor
(Typed Submission)

It was an ordinary Friday morning. I arrived at school early because there were a lot of things I needed to prepare. We were going to have a program for our parents, kindergartners and the first graders as a culmination of our Teddy Bear Week. We'd studied the habitat of different kinds of bears. We'd learned poems and songs about bears. Thursday, I had taken my little second graders to the City Park for a "Teddy Bear Picnic." Our program took most of the morning, rehearsing, presenting and cleaning up afterward. The children performed well, reciting their parts and singing their songs. I was proud of them.

During lunch break I ran home to eat and Robert drove me back to school. He was home recovering from a broken leg. A horse had fallen on him while working cows. I asked if he would pick me up after school. I usually walked home but the week had been busy and quite stressful.

The bell rang for the children to come in. I took them to get drinks and to use the restroom. When we came back into the room I read a chapter of *Charlotte's Web* then went into reading groups. I was sitting at the back of the room with eight students around the reading table when I looked up and saw a strange woman walking toward me. She was already part way across the room. She approached me and said, "There is an emergency in classroom two. Bring your children and come quickly."

My first thought was, why would I take my little children into a room where there was an emergency? I should take them away from danger. The next thought was, she sure is bossy and sober, why should I do what she demanded? She was not well groomed and was wearing an old pair of blue slacks and faded blouse. For some reason I did not have a very good feeling about her. Something was just not right. I hesitated, but again she made the same demand. I reluctantly lined up my twenty-four students and followed her. She led us down the hallway to the next classroom.

Upon entering the room, I observed four or five guns lined up against the chalkboard. The smell of gas was strong and nauseating. My eyes moved to a strange man holding onto a cart, similar to a grocery cart. On the top shelf were two bottles. One I assumed to be gas, the bottle next to it was blue. I had no notion as to its contents. The other shelves had several boxes stacked on top of each other.

The sinister looking man wore a western shirt, old Levis that were frayed around the bottom, boots and a gold windbreaker. His eyes were deep set and piercing. Curly, matted brown hair framed his face with long strands falling on his neck. He was tall with drooping shoulders. I felt fear, a fear that I had never experienced before. Even then, I did not know the magnitude of the situation we were in. Nothing was said. I looked at Tina our school secretary and then Janel my sister-in-law, the first grade teacher. They both gave me a look of fear and despair. My attention was then drawn to Mr. Moore, the fifth grade teacher. He was talking to the strange man, and what I heard next chilled my blood. I don't know what the conversation was but I did hear him say to Mr. Moore, "stand back or I'll shoot."

Several other classes were led into the room. Expressions of anxiety and bewilderment and panic were on their faces. Some little children began to cry. When all one hundred fifty three elementary students, teachers, and support staff were gathered in the room. The man said, "I am a revolutionist. I'm the most wanted man in the country right now." He pointed to the guns and said, "These .22s are for the children. They are precious and we don't want to hurt them, but we will use them if we need to." He next pointed to the rifles and said, "These are for the teachers. Their lives don't mean a thing to me. But if you all do what I say, you won't get hurt."

The woman then told the children how precious they were and

this experience would be something they could tell their children about. It would be history and they would be famous. I remember feeling such anger toward her. Then he asked each teacher how many students were in his/her class, and demanded two million dollars for each child.

Now let me go back to tell about when my students and I entered the room. I walked directly to the back of the room and stood by the bathroom door. The children followed me silently. I don't know if he thought I would try to escape through the little hallway that led to the bathroom and my classroom but Young's deep-set eyes kept staring at me. I began to tremble and wondered what his plans were for me.

I tried to get the children to sing *Teddy Bear's Picnic.* They started to sing, soon one by one their singing faded away. They were clinging to me, looking up at me and saying, "What is he going to do with us? Is he going to shoot us?" That is my nightmare today: the expressions of fear and anxiety in their innocent little faces. I could not assure them that all would be well. Again my feelings of anger surfaced, how could these two people do this to these precious children?

David Young pointed to me and said, "Come up here." My heart started to pound so hard I thought it would burst. I had cottonmouth and could hardly talk. I wondered, would I be the first to be shot? The children followed me and we went to the front of the classroom in the northeast corner. We sat on the floor because many pieces of furniture had been moved into the hallway to make room for everyone. I tried to find books to read, but the children were not interested. One of my students had been sick all day and we hadn't been able to get in contact with her mother. She said she needed to throw up. I took her over to the wastepaper basket. She was very miserable and started to cry.

The Youngs allowed the TV to be brought into the room to play a video, but again the children were not interested. As I sat in the room, wondering if I would ever wake up from this terrible nightmare, my thoughts were of Robert. How could I signal to him not to come into the school when he came to pick me up? Then the thought went through my mind; does anyone else know about us? What are they doing to help us? Would he shoot the teachers one by one when his demands were not met? Could I be brave facing death? Why he had me come to the front of the room I do not know. Because from then on he hardly spoke a word and I tried to avoid his piercing eyes.

Mr. Excell, our principal, was getting the mail while this was all happening. When he got back from the post office and walked back into the deserted school, he wondered where everyone was. Finally, he looked through the small window on the door where we were all being held hostage. Mr. Mitchell motioned to him to not come into the classroom. But Mr. Excell wanted to know what was happening. As he stepped into the room and he identified himself, Mr. Young told him to go call the authorities and make the demand of two million dollars for each child. He was allowed to leave for only ten minutes at a time. He pled with Mr. Young to keep him and let the children go.

Much of my time was occupied taking care of the children, as did every other teacher. At one point he instructed Kris Casper to make a square in the middle of the room with masking tape. Then he instructed us all to not take one step into this "magic" square. He moved a desk and the bomb into this square and sat on the desk. I could tell he was getting very nervous and irritated. He took off his windbreaker and wrapped it around his wrist that held the detonator.

Many conversations were going on around the room. As I conversed with my children, we talked about freedom. A week prior to this experience I asked the children to write a paper about "Why I love Living in America." They did not know why we were so blessed. I began to question them. Could we leave this room? Could we say and do whatever we wanted? Were they frightened because of the guns in the room? I told the children Mr. Young was just like a dictator. He told us everything to do and if we didn't do it he would shoot us. We talked about many people in the world who were living in fear and did not know what freedom was. Then I said, "Are we free?" In unison they all said, "No!"

We talked about praying and asking the Lord to help us through this difficult situation. I'm sure it was because of the faith of these little ones we were able to remain calm and be sustained. At one point I looked up and saw a little group of children in a circle taking turns saying a prayer.

Pages could be written describing what went on in that classroom—each one from a different perspective. All I know is what happened in my little corner.

After about two hours and forty minutes, I saw Mr. Young take the cord that was wrapped around his wrist (which was connected to the detonator) and give it to Doris to put it around her wrist. He walked to the back of the room by the bathroom and leaned against the casing. He looked directly at me again. I quickly turned away. He went into the bathroom. I found out later he was waiting for one of the children to get out of the bathroom.

I watched Doris as she now had control of the bomb. She took David's gold windbreaker and wrapped it around her hand also. Within the next few minutes the bomb went off accidentally. I think she forgot about the cord on her wrist. There was a deafening explosion. The smoke mushroomed and flames filled the room, and yet a thick blackness hovered such as I have never experienced before.

At first everyone was stunned, the fire alarm went off and this brought us to action. I couldn't believe it! I was still alive! Could we escape without getting shot? The room filled with terrifying screams. Mr. Mitchell was at the door motioning everyone to get out. I was reluctant to leave because I couldn't see my children. He shouted, "Get out." I followed his command and ran out of the hostage room and down the hall, looking over my shoulder wondering if Young would come out of the bathroom and shoot me.

I don't remember a lot until I got out on the lawn. I saw only one child crying on the south lawn. I went over to comfort him, put my arms around him, and he began to scream louder. I discovered he was badly burned. I saw the Swat Team in camouflage suits running across the lawn with guns positioned, cautiously approaching the school. Was this really happening to me or was it a dream? I heard children screaming, teachers and parents looking for their children, the fire engine was racing toward the school. The whole scene was pandemonium.

Out on the main street were crying children, news media all over, EMTs trying to take care of the children, ambulances, and parents still frantically searching for their child/children, not able to recognize them because of their black faces. Over seventy-five children were taken in ambulances to Afton, Montpelier, Kemmerer and Logan. The community was in a state of shock and disbelief. Things like this don't happen in Cokeville! But most stopped to pause and express deep feelings of gratitude that we were all alive. Only the two perpetrators were dead.

When I ran out of the burning classroom and onto the lawn, I saw Robert hobbling along on his crutches and Julie our youngest daughter running toward me. I could see the expression of anxiety and relief on their faces. We embraced and all wept.

Only time and the Lord can heal. I am grateful for each new day.

Words cannot express the gratitude I feel for the many miracles that happened that beautiful spring day. I know our Heavenly Father intervened and protected His children in that room.

I took a sabbatical leave in 1997-1999 to serve a mission for our church. I came back and taught for two more years, then retired in 2001. I am presently serving on the Lincoln County School Board #2 and am still involved with children. I have thirty grandchildren, and continue to reside in Cokeville, Wyoming.

Wendy Bartschi
Second Grade Absent Student
(Email Submission)

I'm not sure my story would be of much interest to you, as it's really one of those things that didn't affect me as strongly as it may have for others, but here you go...

I remember waking up that day feeling a spirit of defiance and I just knew I wasn't going to school. I got up and lounged on the couch in my pj's while explaining this to my mother, who was getting ready for work. It wasn't a matter of "could I" stay home; I just simply told her that I wasn't going. It was the first time I had ever rebelled. My mom tried everything to persuade me to go to school and, in her last effort, told me if I didn't go to school, I'd have to go with her to work and help her. She was cleaning motel rooms at the time.

There was no swaying my decision and much to her dismay I happily agreed to go to work with her. (And strangely enough the guy who brought the bomb to our school happened to be staying at that very motel, we cleaned his room that day.) So we set off for the motel and returned after a hard day's work. As our house has a good view of the school, we could see the fire trucks and police cars and found out shortly thereafter what was going on.

My biggest concerns were; first, I was worried about my best friend, Nancy Bennion and, second, I was worried about my teddy bear which happened to be in our classroom in preparation for the Teddy Bear Picnic Mrs. Petersen does for her students. I don't remember if my teddy survived, but, like all of the students that day, Nancy did. We watched from our living room window as the bomb went off and smoke came billowing out of the windows. And well, you know the rest of the story. I've always had this funny feeling that if I had been there that day I wouldn't have made it out alive.

Clark Walton Bedell
Second Grade Student Survivor
(Handwritten Submission)

I was not feeling well that day, and my mother (Sue Bedell) was thinking about letting me stay home. I wanted to participate in a class activity so I decided to go to school. I had no idea that terrible things would happen that day.

The school day started as it normally did. We had the "Teddy Bear Picnic," and we ate lunch in the park. We came back to class in the afternoon, and started some class work. Soon after someone knocked on the door of my classroom. Mrs. Petersen went to answer it. There was a strange lady at the door. She told Mrs. Petersen there was an assembly in the classroom next door. We lined up single file. I was at the front of the line so when the door to the classroom we were going to was opened I could smell gasoline. It was then I knew something could be very wrong, and that this was no ordinary assembly.

After we entered the room I saw all sorts of guns lined up against the wall, and a man (David Young) with a pistol in his hand. He was standing in the middle of the room. He told one of the teachers to tape a square around him on the floor. After that he said, "If anybody crosses this line I will shoot you." All grades, kindergarten through sixth, were huddled in this small classroom. It was very hot and we were very scared and bored. David Young brought in some toys and a TV set.

He went to use the restroom so he switched with his wife (the strange lady), and she took over the trigger to the bomb. She turned around to tell one of the kids to be quiet. I was playing in the corner by the window and I was looking down. Suddenly there was an explosion and black smoke. The room was becoming very hot. I got close to the floor and covered my face so I wouldn't get burned. I was so afraid I yelled for my mother and then my teacher. I was so hot I felt like I was burning up.

Another memory I have is seeing Mrs. Young (the strange lady) burning alive and crawling on the ground to the bathroom. I heard gunfire and I saw Mrs. Young's body drop. I started looking around and I saw a window and saw kids being carried out. Mr. Moore picked me up and handed me to a fireman. The fireman told me to run away. My cousin Judy grabbed my arm and ran with me. I heard bullets firing. We ran to Main Street. I saw my aunt, Emma Walton, and wrapped my arms around her. I also ran to my mom, but she didn't recognize me because of my black face.

There were angels there that day protecting us kids and teachers. By rights we should all have been dead, but we were saved by grace from above. It has been twenty years since that day and I'm grateful for my life, and to still be living today. You could also say I'm a firm believer in miracles.

Michael Brandon Brooks

Second Grade Survivor
(Oral History—Telephone)

I don't really even think about it. It doesn't bother me at all. I'm glad I lived. I am so glad I got married and had kids. I love my wife.

Tareesa Covert
Second Grade Student Survivor
(Typed Letter Submission)

Even though I was only eight at the time I still remember all the little details. Like the line of kids to the bathroom, the smell of gasoline, (which was making everyone sick), kids vomiting in the sink, and the angels all around the room. I knew they were angels because they were all white, and brighter then the rest of the room.

I remember being very scared and just wishing I would wake up in bed. It was like a bad dream and I still have that dream. I'm twenty-seven now and have been diagnosed with post traumatic stress syndrome. I can't watch fireworks without flashes of that bomb going off in my head. It is a very scary feeling.

I do know we were all saved for a reason. I think mine was to make a difference in other people's lives and to be their helping hand. I am a CNA and work at Caribou Memorial Hospital and Living Center. Every time a resident smiles at me and tells me thank you I know that is why I am still here. Even though each and every one of us carries scars, we can still live and help others to live, as well.

That Day

It is hard for me to say,
The things that happened on that day.
Kids all sick and scared,
With an Angel we were paired.
The Angels were like a guiding light,
Protecting us from death's sight.
There are scars in each our souls,
Eating us up like Black Holes.
Those scars may never go away,
All because of the events on that day.
Even though some of us still have nightmares
We know that for each of us God cares.

Jason Hartley
Second Grade Student Survivor
(Email Submission)

My experience in the Cokeville bombing was not one of particular interest or concern. I am one of the many children that this incident did not affect so traumatically as perhaps people expected and certainly not as much as some of the others involved. Being in the 2nd grade I had little grasp of the reality and depth of the situation, thus it did not register at the time as such a life changing event.

Thanks to my mother I was "encouraged" to write a journal entry of the experience. Due to the fact that I was more interested in other things and the nature of the things I did during the siege, I intentionally left the entry incomplete so as not to be in trouble with my parents. This is the entry I wrote shortly after the bombing. I submit it this way so my maturity level at the time may show through. This I think will help the reader connect more with the thinking processes and feelings of such a young hostage. Any editing I did is noted and is added solely for the purpose of including facts and experiences previously left out. The entry portion is in italics, the misspelling and punctuation mistakes I have left in to preserve the purity of the entry:

I was in 2 grade Friday May16 1968 (1986, I'm not dyslexic, just not too bright.) *working on our math when this ugly woman with brown curled hair and glasses steped in. she told us to go to the first grade room. When she told us this everybody shouted for joy because we didn't have to do math.*

Actually I don't think anybody shouted for joy but in my mind I was really excited, not that I did not love doing math, I was just excited to be doing something new and unexpected. I also really hated Math, odd for a future major in Mechanical Engineering.

But we thout it was a assembly about guns. But when Kristy Moore was crying I knew something was wrong. So other little kids started crying to.

If my memory serves me correctly, we were then briefed by Rocky Moore on the situation.

I wondered if I could help.

I would love to say I was really that concerned for others but let's face it, when you're eight years old there is really not much else on your mind other than what is going to entertain you for the next thirty seconds. I'm sure my mother was very impressed when she read that, though. Sorry mom.

At the time I figured that I should be ready for this where my dad was a cop. I found a nearby table and told my buddy Clark Bedell that we should stay under the table because the bomb would blow up and the debris would fall on us. Pretty deep thinking for a 2nd grader, but that is exactly what happened. Unfortunately the table was taken away sometime during the crisis.

We were later given the instructions of the taped off square around David Young. We were told if we entered the square we would be shot.

I felt horrible.

This feeling only lasted for a few seconds. What I really felt was boredom. About this time Billy King and I started to compete to see who could cross the taped perimeter around David Young and touch his desk without being killed. Like I said, not too bright.

They started to bring books from the library. They also turned on the T.V. I watched T.V.

This is when I noticed that we should be out of school by now. Impatience set in and I was getting rather irritable. The volume on the TV was turned down so low that I was unable to hear the *Transformer* cartoon.

Then David Young went to the bathroom. Then somebody tapped Doris Young's shoulder and she turned and the bomb accidentally went off.

This was all from rumors that were circulating at the time.

I didn't see any of it.

I never knew it until there were screaming.

This was accurate. I don't remember a huge blast, just a small pop. In the time it took me to turn around the room was already pitch black. I put my hand no more than an inch in front of face to try the ol' couldn't see my hand in front of my face bit. I moved it closer to my face until I touched my nose and I couldn't see a thing.

The whole room was filled with smoke. I was right by Clark Bedell. He was screaming in my ear and when I got out I couldn't hear.

I was pretty much emotionless thus far. No fear, no panic, just astonishment.

My eyes began to burn and I was choking with smoke. I heard some one saying "cover your mouth and nose." I covered my mouth and nose with my hands. I was very relieved to receive this instruction. I had been trying to breathe by covering just my nose, then just my mouth, neither worked. When she yelled to cover the mouth AND nose I was finally able to somewhat breathe.

It stunk like gasoline very bad. I crouched in the (corner) *trying to figure out what that black burning thing was.*

I was able to keep my eyes open long enough to see a burning ball (Doris) falling from the desk in the middle of the room.

I felt Clarks hair it was hot and soppin wet. I didn't feel anyone by me in the corner so I moved over to the window where someone was saying "Quickly get out the window."

I am not sure on the chronological order of this event but at one point Clark and I were grabbed by one of the female teachers. We were held and rocked back and forth while she was sobbing uncontrollably. I think it was she who told us to go to the window.

Then I saw 5 men. The first one pulled me out the window by my hands. The others told me to run far away where the rest of the people were. I found my mom. I looked back at the school and was glad that I was out of there. The End

But it wasn't the end. The scene outside was almost more

traumatic than the scene inside. As I ran in the direction everyone else was running, I ran into my sister Cindy, who was crying. At first she did not seem to recognize me, but quickly caught on. She was very confused and asked if I had seen my little brother Nathan. She had found our older sister Brenda, but was frightened, actually panicked about not finding Nathan. I replied that I hadn't seen him and she walked hastily away in a random pattern as if she was in shock. I was confused as to why she seemed not to recognize me. I looked at my clothes and my once white stripe was pure black as were my hands. Later I found my face to be black, as well. I continued in the direction I was going. There were large trucks and vehicles crowding the entrance to the school limiting my view. Once past the vehicles, I saw the entire town crowded across the street in one collective panic. Parents were grabbing their kids, kids were running and screaming back and forth.

I looked to my left and saw my little brother Nathan held by three adults, one of whom was my mother. He was screaming and shook vigorously with pain as water was poured over a burn on his lower back. I did not immediately go over because I did not want to interrupt, so I looked around for Cindy to tell her I had found Nathan. I couldn't find her so I began to go toward my mother. Cindy was already there.

That is about as much as I can recall. I remember being in a hospital for smoke inhalation and reuniting with my father, who had been away on business during the incident. I have been told by my parents of nightmares I had on occasion, but it is all in the past now. For years a day would not go by that I did not think of that day. Now it is months.

Tina Morfeld Helenske
Second Grade Student Survivor
(Email Submission)

I remember we all had just come in from recess. We were in our classroom when a lady ran into our room and said, "One of the students broke her leg you all have to come quick." I remember being confused about why we all had to go but our teacher had us do it. Once the whole school was in the little classroom I remember all of us seeing guns around the classroom and thinking it was an assembly on gun safety.

I have no idea when we realized we were being held hostage but we figured it out eventually. It was a very tense atmosphere once we all understood. There was also the smell of gasoline coming from the bomb that was making some of the students sick. Some of the students killed time by playing games, some by coloring, others by talking amongst themselves, and the rest just sitting around. They put a square of tape around the bomb because too many students were walking too close to the bomb and it was irritating David Young. He said if anyone walked into the square he would shoot them. I remember there were rumors around about which kids David just didn't like.

I remember when David got up to go use the restroom. I felt relief because Doris was so nice to all of us. Little did any of us know it was going to be her who blew us all up. She was talking to one of the teachers and next thing I remember everything was dark. Somehow I was one of the very first ones out of the building but I'm not sure how. I don't know if someone helped me out or if it was my instincts that got me out. I remember getting to the corner and a lady holding me close to her chest, which hurt like crazy because I was burned on the cheek.

Then I remember talking to the paramedics and the first thing I asked them is if my hair was burned. I remember the guy laughing and saying, "Yes, but it will grow back and right now you have more serious things to worry about." Then I was in a lady's house, sitting under a table and I remember being upset. I kept asking people where my mom wa at and nobody would talk to me. I ran into Monica at some point and I remember the look of shock on her face because I had a chunk of skin hanging off my face from being burned. Then we were separated. At some point I finally got to Mom and I remember feeling so upset because she was helping other kids (more serious ones), instead of me. I didn't comprehend that was her job, I suppose.

The next thing I remember is being in Montpelier and the doctors trying to shove a tube down my throat. I was so humiliated because all I had on in front of all those people was my underwear. Then I remember my dad coming into the room and again they were trying to shove a tube down my throat and I was kicking my dad in the stomach but he just stood there and wouldn't move. Then I was sent to Logan.

I don't remember much about being in Logan but I remember that when I was airlifted to Salt Lake I was freezing cold. Then I was in Salt Lake for a week. I remember watching *The Neverending Story* a zillion times but that is really about it. When I got home, I got to go see my classmates which was nice.

Melanie Chadwick Luthi
Second Grade Student Survivor
(Handwritten Mailed Submission)

May 16, 1986 will always be a day that I will remember. I was in the 2nd grade when the Cokeville elementary was bombed. I remember almost everything from that day: what I wore, how it started, the looks on the teachers' faces and knowing something was not right and also being very scared.

I don't think of it often, and when I do, I try to forget. My mother and brother were in that room with me that day. I still can remember everything that I saw and how I felt. I remember how scared, very scared, I was when that bomb went off. I was told to run and I did.

Every teacher would have given his or her life to save us, many teachers saved a lot of students from getting burned. I remember that I could not believe how many people were in Cokeville that day to help. I would rather not share all the details, but it is an experience that an eight year old doesn't forget.

When I was a senior in high school, it was the ten year anniversary of the bombing. I don't think there was a week that went by that a reporter would not ask us to share our story about what happened. I was interviewed on *Unsolved Mysteries* that year. People could not believe we all survived, and that was the "unsolved mystery." The bomb should have killed us all.

I know what happened that day and know that there are a lot of people who have made their mark in the world because they are still here. Some of my classmates are very successful and some are like me; after college I got married and had children. In this world today, that is a great success. I now stay at home with my two beautiful little boys. I am thankful for what I went through. I say that now.

I came home to Cokeville to raise my children. I still believe that it is the safest place on earth. What happened to us made us stronger and more determined to become great people in this world. We are having our ten year class reunion this next year and I think that this experience has not held us back. This reunion would be a whole lot different if the bomb had worked right. I have only been in that room a few times since then and never in the bathroom. I don't care to go there any time soon. My children will learn of what happened that day and know we are to be grateful for each day together.

I am glad that I could share my story with you. I just hope by still being here I can touch someone's life with my experiences. Thank you.

Kellie Jo Miller-Hite
Second Grade Student Survivor
(Typed Submission)

I was in second grade the year of the bomb. I was also one of the new kids, having just moved to Cokeville to start the new school year in 1985.

I've often thought what a "Welcome" my sister and I got. Then I chuckle to myself.

That morning I went to my mother complaining of a stomachache. She gave me some Pepto-Bismol and sent me on my way to school.

I can still remember sitting on that bottom table right in front of the bomb with nothing between us except the line for the square around the bomb for David Young's "comfort and safety zone," and looking at her (Doris), wondering what was going to happen.

As the bomb went off I covered my eyes and then ran from the room. As I hit the hallway I looked both directions, seeing some older kids headed toward the front office. I figured I'd follow. As I ran out the doors, I stopped to look around to see if I could find Bobbie, my sister. She had gone out one of the side doors. We ran to each other and then got told by the military men to run.

As we ran in the direction of everyone else, the only thought then in my head was to find Mom and Dad.

That day will always linger in my mind, as I know it will for everyone who was there or who had someone in there.

I'm beyond thankful to be alive and still have my family.

I take nothing for granted and live every day to the fullest.

I remember going back into the school and the room before they fixed it for two reasons: one, to get my teddy bear (it was "Teddy Bear Week."), and two, to look at the room.

As I looked around I could see shoes where they had gotten

lost and a very burnt room, with no lighting because of them all being broken out from the blast.

Then I came upon the burnt image in the corner on the wall. It looked like a giant figure wearing a hooded cloak. At that moment I knew God had been there with us and wanted us all to live for some reason or other. I just knew we all must be very special.

I work at the Flying J and to this day people come in and ask about the bomb. I point across the field to the school and say, "That's where it happened."

I am now twenty-eight years old and newly married with a new four year old son, both of which I'm thankful for.

Ryan Thornock
Second Grade Student Survivor
(Typed Submission)

As I reflect upon the events of May 16, 1986, it seems natural to wonder why we were spared when so many others in similar situations were/are not. My mind has rested on a few conclusions. First, in the words of Nephi, I *know that He loveth His children, nevertheless, I do not know the meaning of all things.* (1 Nephi 11:17) Second, *God has not ceased to be a God of miracles.* (Mormon 9:15)

As I think about the mothers and grandmothers with children and grandchildren in the school that day, I wish there were some way to quantify the power of their collective faith and prayers. I'm grateful to mothers and fathers who taught their children, *that if they did not doubt, God would deliver them.* And, *we do not doubt our mothers knew it.* (Alma 56:47-48) Consequently, *...there was not one soul of them who did perish...and their preservation was astonishing...and we do justly ascribe it to the miraculous power of God.* (Alma 57:25-26)

I pray that I can be like the Nephites in the time of Moroni who, *...were not slow to remember the Lord their God,* (Alma 55:31) and always *...confess His hand.* I appreciate the opportunity to record my gratitude so that my children might, *...remember the great things that the Lord has done for [their] fathers.* (Ether 7:27)

And behold, we are again delivered out of the hands of our enemies. And blessed is the name of our God; for behold, it is He that has delivered us; yea, that has done this great thing for us. (Alma 57:35)

Jennie Lee Buckley Walker
Second Grade Student Survivor
(Mother recorded shortly after incident)

It was Friday afternoon sometime after lunch. I was putting on earphones at the Hoffman so I could listen to a story on tape. A lady came walking in very rudely. She made a lot of noise and everybody looked at her. She said, "There is an emergency in the 1st grade classroom. Please come now." Almost everybody yelled out, "Can we take our teddy bears?" It was Teddy Bear Week. I didn't get to take mine, but a few did. My teacher, Mrs. Petersen, asked if her kids could get out of going so they wouldn't be harmed. The lady said, "You need to come now." We lined up and went into the room.

At first we thought it was going to be an adventure, that we were going for a walk or something. When I walked into the room and saw guns lined up against the chalkboard, I thought we were going to have an assembly on guns but I didn't want to attend.

When everybody got into the room, she said we were going to have an adventure that we could tell our grandkids. It felt scary to me in the room. I went into the room and walked over by the cupboards, past the bathroom, and stood by Mr. Miller, holding his hand.

I asked Mr. Miller and Mrs. Cook if it was going to be OK. I also asked Mrs. Chadwick. They said, "I do not know, Sweetie." I started to cry when they said that. I looked down the middle of the room and down the sides to see if there was a place I wouldn't get harmed.

The man said, "Please do not get by the windows," in a rough voice. I tried to scoot over into a corner by Mr. Miller and Mrs. Chadwick. When I was sitting by Mr. Miller and Mrs. Chadwick, I saw some chains. I thought they were going to tie us to the bomb with the chains.

I tried to watch TV, but I couldn't. Then after that Mrs.

Chadwick was reading us stories, but I couldn't listen to them either. It bothered me very much. Then I wanted to go over to my teacher. She was in a corner by the man. I started crawling to her and I asked Mrs. Dayton if I could go over to my teacher. She said, "I think it would be all right." So I started crawling over to her in a little corner over by the windows.

Mr. Moore asked the man if he could go get the TV in the library. The man said he could go if the lady went with him. When he came back, the man pointed his gun at Mr. Moore and Mr. Moore said, "What is the matter?" He did not answer. I felt nervous about the man pointing the gun at him. Then Mr. Excell said, "Can I get these precious children out of here and you can keep me?" That was nice of him, but the man said, "No, you cannot." Then Mr. Excell said, "Can I move these kids to a bigger room?" The man said, "I'll kill you if you say one more word." When I got over to my teacher, I started to cry and said, "Teacher," but she didn't hear me the first time so I said it again louder. She said, "What's the matter, Sweetie? Are you scared?"

Then the lady told us to get a napkin wet and put it on our forehead and then we wouldn't have to go to the bathroom or get drinks. I laid on head on my teacher's shoulder and cried. I wished I was home giving my mother a love. The bell had rung for us to go home so every minute after that seemed like forever.

I worried he might give me and my friends a gun and tell me to shoot my mother to keep him safe. I worried he might tell us all to go to sleep and he would let the bomb off while we were asleep and we'd all be dead. When I was by my teacher I prayed that we'd be safe.

The man ran to the bathroom and Mrs. Dayton moved over because she thought she had done something wrong. The lady said, "Let's all be quiet now." I must have been asleep or something because I don't even remember her saying this. When the bomb went off, I started to roll back and fell down and bumped my face. I kept rolling. The room was pitch red and orange and I saw a huge glob of fire in the middle of the room. My teacher was dragging me. I was hanging onto her skirt, but I kept on rolling. I was always taught that in a fire you stop, drop and roll so that's what I was doing. Mr. Mitchell said, "Hurry, get out of the school."

When I got to the double doors, I bumped my head and looked up and saw it was the doors, so I jumped up and pushed them open. I ran and then I saw the cops and they scared me because I didn't know if they were the bad guys. Then I saw Mr. Fredrickson and I knew I was safe. I was screaming all the time. I was standing in the middle of the road and a high school girl came up and hugged me and took me out of the road. I don't know who she was. I got several hugs from all kinds of people.

When I hugged my teacher, I couldn't believe I was alive. Dad was there and asked my teacher if he could take a turn hugging me and my teacher said, "Yes, you sure can!" Then I walked with Meaghan, Mike, Jolene, and Norene. I saw Jay getting his back wet because he was burned. Then someone hugged me again. We went to Norene's and watched the news. Norene did my hair and almost all the words I heard on the news were wrong. I told Norene I didn't know so many people loved me.

One of the special memories I have is of the Sunday we went to church after the bomb. I remember in sacrament meeting that many testimonies were given and I remember bearing mine. I expressed to my Heavenly Father that I was so thankful to still be alive and that I knew He was the one who stopped the whole bomb from going off and that we were all saved because we all had special missions still to accomplish here on the earth. All of us who were in the bomb event stood and sang, *We'll Bring the World His Truth*. The verse that I remember singing, even with more meaning now, was verse two: *We have been saved for these latter days to build the kingdom in righteous ways*. My testimony was strengthened then and I knew that I had been saved for a reason and had an important mission to accomplish.

Even though it will be twenty years since this miracle happened in my life and to so many others, a year never goes by that on

May 16th I don't stop to think about the miraculous event of that day and thank my Heavenly Father for my wonderful life. I was able to serve an LDS Mission to Louisville, Kentucky and almost ten months after being home I got married in the Logan Temple to my best friend, Jeff Walker.

We have been blessed with two handsome boys; Bryson will be three on June 24th and Braden turned one April 26th. We are expecting another new baby in April 2006. I remember Doris telling us that day as we were all cooped up in that room that "this will be an experience you will be able to tell your children and grandchildren about." That was definitely true. I want my children to know that we have a Father in Heaven Who knows us, loves us, and is always watching over us. He performed a huge miracle in my life that day and He can and will perform miracles in their lives, as well.

Byron D. Wiscombe
Second Grade Student Survivor
(Email Submission)

I was an eight year-old second grader in Mrs. Petersen's class on May 16, 1986. I suppose I was too young at the time to recognize how terrible the setting really was as we walked next door to Mrs. Mitchell's first grade classroom. The guns lined up against the wall in an orderly fashion provoked a question to a fellow classmate, "Why aren't we having the assembly in the gym?"

During the next two to three hours my naiveté was tempered as I saw real concern on teachers' faces and some of my older peers began to cry. I smelled gas and heard low voices whisper "bomb" and the unfamiliar word; "hostage."

I was sitting on the floor with my back to a square that had been taped off around the homemade bomb when it went off. There was a loud noise and everything went dark. The next thing I remember was running down the hall toward the outside light coming through the exterior metal doors. I don't know how I got out of the room. I don't remember standing up, walking or running out, being pushed or herded through the door which was the only exit from the room besides the window. I didn't see anything in the room after it went dark. One moment I was sitting crosslegged on the floor and the next moment I was running down the hall to the sound of the fire alarm. The ringing of fire alarms and the occasional ringing in my ear still reminds me of the Cokeville bomb and I take a moment to say a silent prayer of gratitude.

If there is one word to express my thoughts about the Cokeville bomb it is gratitude. Gratitude for life, for family, for memories since and for the future. I'm grateful for the protecting hand of a loving Heavenly Father. Although I never remember doubting the existence of God, my assurance of His involvement in our lives began to grow as I heard principal Max Excell in church the following Sunday use the words "divine intervention." I've come to know since then that life is not always protected in such a miraculous manner. Living life requires faith.

I'm grateful for the good memories and the wonderful teachers during my time in Cokeville. Since leaving there, I've moved eight times and have learned that there are good and bad people everywhere, regardless of the size of the community.

I'm grateful for and have a firm belief in the power of prayer. Truly, many prayers were offered during those few intense hours both inside and outside the classroom, throughout the community and beyond as the word of children being held hostage spread.

Finally, I'm grateful to the Cokeville Miracle Foundation for their work to preserve the modern day miracle of May 16, 1986. For many years afterward my family took the day off from school and work on May 16th to share feelings and write in our journals. In writing a history of one's life or an event like this we "remember" which is a commandment in all Holy Writ. This remembering shows gratitude to the Giver and Keeper of Life and preserves for future generations a record to remind, reflect, give thanks and help others in similar circumstances. I look forward to reading the stories and thoughts of my fellow survivors, their families and others involved.

Pat Bennion
Third Grade Substitute Teacher Survivor
(Email Submission)

Only two more weeks of school left and I was again on my way to the elementary school to substitute third grade for Briant Teichert, who was away with the track team. I had often substituted for him and felt comfortable in his classroom.

I followed the routine and the children knew what to expect. It was after lunch and I was reading to them from a novel they had started a week ago. My reading was interrupted by a middle aged woman who said we needed to meet in the classroom next to us. I was surprised. I hadn't been told by the principal of this meeting. But I was a substitute and not always aware of everything going on at school.

The children followed me into the classroom, a crowded room of children and teachers and guns. It didn't seem right. I regretted bringing the children into this situation, but what were my options?

Disbelief was the emotion I was feeling. Many of the children quickly felt the fear of the situation and began crying. Teachers were comforting them, knowing that their crying would only make the situation worse.

The room was crowded, hot, and the smell of gas permeated the air. I knew the conditions would deteriorate as the hours wore on. How would the children handle this?

I never felt fear. I am not sure why. Was it the disbelief that this was actually happening? I was still in a state of shock from a younger brother's death three months prior. I had so much at stake in this room. Not only was I the substitute teacher and felt responsibility for the third grade children, but I was a mother of three of the children there. My mother-in-law was also in the room. My husband would lose all of us if something did happen. It would be very hard on my mother to lose another child and grandchildren.

I was calm. This would work out. It is not meant to be.

As I was passing out crayons to comfort the children, I saw a flash, heard the explosion and felt the sting on my arms and neck. My thought was we were promised this would not happen.

There was a lot of commotion in the dark, smoke-filled room. We were alive. It was difficult to breathe. This alone motivated everyone to evacuate the room any way it was possible. I helped children exit through the window, hoping that my children would be among them.

Outside of the school I could see two of my children. Later, down the road I met up with my husband who had our third child and his mother with him. I was badly burned but again I was numb to pain. But I did feel love and gratitude that we were together and safe. So grateful that this ordeal didn't drag out any longer.

Twenty years have passed. Our children have grown up and married. It was a deeply spiritual experience for all of us to know that we have good things yet to do and the Lord spared our lives and continues to bless us daily.

Briant B. Teichert
Absent Third Grade Teacher
(Typed Submission)

The Missing Teacher's Perspective

It was a cold track meet in Casper, Wyoming on May 16, 1986. It was snowing and several kids had fallen in the hurdle events. Finally they delayed the event to wait for better weather. After about an hour and no change, the meet was postponed until the next day when they would try to combine two days worth of events into one day with better weather.

My brother Chad, Kurt Robinson and I went back to our motel. Later that afternoon Chad had a meeting with some people in another motel where the Cokeville track team was staying. When we entered their motel we saw quite a few Cokeville people in the lobby. They asked me if I had heard what had happened in Cokeville. I hadn't and I couldn't believe it when they told me. We hurried to someone's room to watch a report on TV.

I became more sick with each unfolding minute of the story. Here I was, the third grade teacher and so far away. The reports let us know that none of the Cokeville adults or children had been killed. A wave of relief swept over me. At the same time I was wondering how many of my third graders were hospitalized with severe burns. It was an agonizing time. As contact was made with Cokeville, it was decided that we couldn't do anything if we came home. It was determined that the kids should stay and participate in the state meet.

When we arrived home late Saturday night, my wife Clyda tried to fill me in on all the latest situations. Sunday didn't come soon enough. I tried to make contact with all of my third graders that day to see how they were. On Monday, no school was held but the teachers all came to school to try to come up with a plan about finishing the school year.

I wanted to have the kids come back immediately so I could be with them. However, the other teachers weren't feeling that way. I had to sit back and listen. They had been through the ordeal. They had had the traumatic experience, not me. Here was a group whom I greatly admired and loved. I was more than willing to relinquish my wishes to theirs. I don't believe I ever stated how I felt because it was evident that they didn't want to be in that building any more than they had to, or require the kids to come back until they felt like it. Here I was, wanting us to all be together at school and they didn't want to be at school. I'm not saying they didn't want to be together, they just didn't want to be at the school right then. A plan was finally made for how to finish the school year. It was one made out of love and concern for the kids. We finished the year and the kids did admirably well. The staff was remarkable.

I have always been grateful to my Father in Heaven for His protection of this wonderful staff and these magnificent children. Many of the staff have moved on with only a few of them still in Cokeville and only a couple of them still teaching. I still admire all of them for their heroic actions in helping to save our children.

Matthew William Buckley
Third Grade Student Survivor
(Email Submission)

May 16, 1986 will always be on the front of my mind. I remember that day like it was yesterday. It happens to be the day after my birthday. So every birthday I have had since 1986, has been a great day but I always know that the next day is the anniversary of that frightening day that has left an impression on my life. I look back to May 16, 1986 and I remember while being trapped in a classroom with hundreds of students. David Young let them sing Happy Birthday to me and one other child, but I was still pretty scared.

Moments before the bomb went off I was standing by the sink, throwing up. I was sick from the smell of gasoline. I put water on my face. David put the string that was attached to the bomb around his wife's arm and walked to the back of the classroom to use the restroom. While I was standing at the sink I heard a voice say "Matthew, go over by the window." I didn't think much of it, but I heard it again. "Matthew, go over by the window." Still I ignored the command. And then a third time, I heard the same voice say "Matthew William! Go over by the window!" When I heard Matthew William I knew I was in trouble and I better do what I was told. So I went over to the window. I was only there long enough to sit on the windowsill and look outside for a second and then the bomb went off.

The pressure from the blast pushed me out the window and I landed in a pokey bush. I lay there thinking, I need to get out of here! So I ran toward home. I remember seeing John Miller coming out of the back door of the school and he ran toward Main Street. He had been shot and he was in front of me. I didn't realize his blood was all over my face and my shirt and I didn't think twice about the paramedics chasing me. Out of nowhere my dad grabbed me. I kept telling them, "I am OK, I am OK." Just like today, I am OK.

Every year, I think of that day and I thank God that I am OK. Every now and then when I share my story I can tell people that I know that there is a God and He knows about what is going on in this world. He and His angels know me by my name. I have an amazing story just like a hundred other kids who survived that day. I am grateful that there is good that can come from such a horrible thing. I can live a normal life, with a wife and a child and learn from the events that I will never forget. This experience in my life has obviously had a long lasting affect on me, some things for the worse but some things for the better. I am so grateful we all made it out alive and that we can share our stories!!!

H.J. Esterholdt
Third Grade Student Survivor
(Email Submission)

The thing I remember the most about that day was the unflappable strength that the adults showed in that room. As children we look at adults for guidance and comfort. That day there was no one better to handle the events than those adults. The first face I remember seeing when we were brought into the room was Rocky Moore. Rocky's face was stern and composed, as I began to look around the room all the teachers were that way. Even though I had no idea what was going to take place that day. I knew that we were in the best hands that we could be in. From a teacher comforting someone with a nervous stomach, to turning the school bells off to prevent upsetting us, their actions are appreciated. Each of these things was equally important in controlling the emotions in that room. Now, twenty years later, I would like to thank each of them for doing everything that they did on that day.

Mandi Taylor Hall
Absent Third Grade Student
(Email Submission)

May 16, 1986, I was in Logan with my mom at the dentist getting some teeth pulled. While we were there my aunt, Ida Romero, called to tell us what had happened and that Ryan was OK. I remember that after talking to Ida on the phone my mom fainted. When she had recovered we left the dentist to head home, but stopped at the mall and ran into some people from Cokeville. I can't now recall who it was. On the way home we went by the hospital in Montpelier to see if there was anyone that we knew. When we drove into the parking lot we saw my grandparent's car. They were supposed to be on their way to California, so that was a red flag. So we stopped and as we walked into the hospital my dad met us and told us what had happened and that Ryan wasn't that bad. Turned out that he was one of the worst ones. Ryan was in the hospital for several days and there were several others from Cokeville there as well. While I wasn't there for the bombing, it is still a day I will remember for the rest of my life. It was truly a miracle what happened that day. Someone definitely had a hand in saving everyone.

Cindy Hartley Allred
Third Grade Student Survivor
(Email Submission)

This was written April 28, 1995, a day or so after the Oklahoma City bombing. I was having a hard time with it because of all the memories it brought back of the Cokeville bombing. So my mom told me to write everything down that I could remember. It helped me a lot because once it was recorded, it felt like I didn't have to remember it anymore.

May 16, 1986 was a Friday. It was a bright day and pretty warm. It showed all the signs of spring coming. That day was also the parade of the bears day. In the younger classes, such as first and kindergarten, the children had all brought their teddy bears. Early that morning my third grade class went to the 2nd grade classroom. They did a little presentation of the numbers from 1-15 in Spanish. Then we went back to our class in the same hall on the same right hand side as the first grade classes.

Later, after lunch, everyone was outside playing soccer as everyone did. My team was losing so I turned to my best friend Jamie Buckley and I said, "This is gonna be a bad day." Little did I know that day would affect me for the rest of my life. A few seconds later the bell rang, so I went back into my classroom. My third grade teacher was Briant Teichert but he was gone that day so we had a substitute who was Pat Bennion. After recess, she began to read us a story. In the middle of the story a dark short curly haired lady who was kinda heavy set peeked into the door and said, "We need you to go to the 2nd grade room." We all groaned and said, "Again?" and the lady said, "Well it's just next door." We said, "Oh, that's the first grade room." We all got up and started going to the first grade class taught by Mrs. Mitchell.

When we walked in a man was standing against the wall to the left of us, right directly by the door. He was tall (but anybody is tall to a third grader) and skinny. He had dark curly hair. He wasn't really old looking, probably in his thirties. He had real nervous eyes. There were already quite a few classes already there. I heard whispers, here and there, that this guy had a bomb. I immediately thought this was some kind of assembly and that this guy had found a bomb in the school and was teaching us to not play with bombs.

He began talking to us. He said things about this being a revolution. He kept talking for a little bit and one of my classmates, Kristi Moore, started crying. Her uncle, Rocky Moore, who was also the fifth grade teacher, took her and held her. She still cried. I think that is when the atmosphere changed a little. Some people were starting to understand what was going on. And those of us who still didn't understand were alarmed because of Kristy's crying. After that all us kids just basically began to do our own thing. There was a feeling of nervous anxiety with the teachers. They looked at us like they were hoping we didn't know something.

At one point I was standing behind fifth grade teacher, Rocky Moore, as he approached David Young. Rocky said, "Can we get the children out of here? We'll stay, but we just want the children safe." David pulled out his gun and said, "You come any closer and I'll shoot you down." Rocky put his hands up and backed away saying, "OK, OK." I didn't wait around behind him because it scared me a little. I think I went and told my best friend about what I had just seen.

Meanwhile, they (the teachers) had cleared the desks out into the hallway and stacked some tables on top of each other. On one of the tables they set up a fun thing with magnets. I remember playing with the iron filings. They were pretty cool. At one point Kliss Sparks, the 4th grade teacher, began reading to our class *The Adventures of Tom Sawyer.* They brought in the TV from the library and other things to keep us busy. You couldn't walk around the room very well because there were so many bodies spread out. Mr. Mitchell (the 6th grade teacher) quieted us and told us about the "magic square." We were playing a game and no one was allowed to go into the "magic square." What it was, was tape that had been put in a square in the center of the room around David Young. All that was in the square was a desk that David sat on and the bomb, which was in a hand pulled shopping cart. From what I could see of the bomb there were milk jugs filled with gasoline and a big Duracell battery with wires hooked to it. There was a little square open container filled with white powder. And a wire that followed up to his wrist.

While we were in the room our music teacher led us in songs. We sang *Happy Birthday* to Jeremiah Moore also. David sang that song with us. I remember him sitting on that desk mumbling the words kinda looking off into space. This whole time David's wife had been gathering other people into the room and she was now standing by the door. There were several of the older kids standing around her. Heidi Roberts was talking to her. She seemed to be crying also. I walked over there and noticed how everyone was crying so I began to cry.

I think I was a little scared at this point. This was the only time I remember being scared. (Actually what happened was Jamie had started crying and we were all trying to comfort her. So I left and started crying, partly because I was scared and partly because I wanted someone to comfort me.) But all of a sudden I just stopped and I got up and the feeling was gone. I believe someone comforted me then but there was no one around me. I don't remember exactly about it so I won't claim it for sure.

As I was walking toward the square to get to the other side of the room, Billy King tapped me on the shoulder and said, "Watch this," and he jumped across the corner of the square. David had his back to us and I don't think he saw. If he had seen it, I don't know what he would have done. Billy started laughing and I told him to stop it. As I continued to go over to where my best friend was, I heard somewhere from somebody along the way that we might have to stay there a week. As I began to tell this to Jamie (when I told her this she looked up at me and she was really scared) a teacher who was applying for the kindergarten teacher job was there and she shook her head "no" and said, "Don't!" I was kinda scared by that because I began to think about what it would be like to stay there for a week.

As I began to think about this the thought was swept away and I was comforted again. That is one of the great miracles of this incident. The fear was taken away from us and I remember feeling unthreatened and secure.

At this time I remember the sixth grade class in a circle having a prayer together. I think they were holding hands. My sister was in that circle. So by seeing this, someone suggested that the little group I was with say a prayer so we got together and had one. Everyone was coloring or playing with clay. Everybody was pretty content and everyone was busy. That teacher applying for the job was named Cindy. She was very young and pretty. She had long brownish blondish hair. She really comforted us. One of these days I would like to thank her.

The fumes from the gasoline jugs were starting to affect everyone so the teachers opened the little windows. At that time we were watching TV. The cartoon *Transformers* was on. A commercial came on and then the news. Celeste Excell started telling everyone to be quiet because she wanted to see if we were on the news. The picture came on and it was a picture of the Kremlin at night in Russia. There was a dark haired lady talking. I had my back to the bomb.

Suddenly there was the great sound. It sounded like a sonic boom yet you could feel it. But the sound seemed removed from me— like it happened far away. I don't remember how I ended up on the floor but I was completely turned around on my knees, crouched in a little ball on the floor. The heat was so intense everyone was screaming. Things were blowing up and glass was breaking. It was pitch black. The heat was unbearable and it was burning my skin. The worst part was that I couldn't breathe. The smoke was so thick you couldn't see your hand in front of your face. While I was huddled there, trying to breathe, I became severely scared. I immediately said out loud, "Oh God, don't let me die. Don't let me die."

There was a big sound of crashing glass and I looked up and I could see the light from the window shining in. My mind saw it as ivory columns that I had seen fall over in the old movies. Then my mind brought back the picture of a huge skyscraper that was on fire. People were on the very top of the building jumping off to their deaths. This video had been shown to me when I was in kindergarten or first grade in the gym of the high school by the firefighters. After I thought of all of this I turned my head to the left and looked at where the bomb had been. All I could see was a strip of fire about two or three feet high from the center of the square to about the back wall.

This whole time I hadn't moved. I was so terrified I couldn't get out. Then I heard a woman say, "Who's in here?" I reached out my arm and said, "I am." I couldn't see her or anything else but she found my arm and pulled me to the windows. Immediately firefighters from outside the room grabbed me roughly and yanked me out. I cut myself (not badly) on the glass from the broken window.

I never got to look back and see who it was that saved me but we believe that it was Verlene Bennion, Pat Bennion's mother-in-law, who also worked at the school. She ended up getting pneumonia from being in the smoke. Once I got out I just ran, following the direction of all the other children.

The first people I met were my other friend, Kara Thornock, and her mom. I began to walk around and I saw Brenda and Jason (2nd grade). He was one of those who earlier that morning told us the numbers in Spanish but Nathan wasn't with him. I was scared for him and kept asking about him. Somehow, someone grabbed me and laid me on the grass right next to my brother Nathan and Jamie. Jamie was screaming and I tried to tell her that I was OK. Her dad came to her and picked her up and carried her away. I later found out that she had been burned on her forearm, badly. At that time I finally saw my mom. She came up to both of us and started crying, "Oh, my babies, my babies," while holding us and rocking us, but then she left.

Later I got up and my friend Kara and I were on our way to

her house. There was crying and screaming and a mass confusion everywhere. As Kara and I were leaving, Kliss Sparks yelled to us to come over and be counted. She was very frantic looking because they were trying to see if everyone was out of the room yet. Kara and I ended up at her house and her mother told us to be on the bed with our feet up. As we were lying there I remember saying to Kara, "I can't believe that just happened to us." My mom then came and she took me, Kara, and Kara's mom, Dana Thornock, in the station wagon to the Kemmerer hospital. Before going, my mom bought me a 7up because my stomach was so upset.

When we got to the hospital, the halls were just full on both sides of people and kids being helped. I remember passing Brenda and she had an oxygen tube up her nose. I was scared for her and I thought those tubes up her nose were hurting her. We all had to see the doctor and be generally checked over. While waiting there I asked Mrs. Mitchell, "What did we do wrong?" I was referring to why had the bomb been set off. I believed that David was mad because we were watching the news. She told me that it wasn't our fault and that Doris had accidentally set it off. I went in to see the doctor and he asked about the sore I had under my lip. A little while before that I had put my top teeth through my bottom lip while jumping on the trampoline. The only injury that I had was smoke inhalation. We then went home on the bus.

Back in Cokeville there was a Channel Five helicopter parked on our football field and I also saw my Aunt Sandy waiting for us. We went to Thornock's to get our car and we drove toward Main Street. There we saw my dad for the first time. All of the kids were there and I remember my dad coming and picking us up individually—just crying. He just let out a big sigh with a bunch of tears.

The next things I remember were on Sunday we all went to church and we had a testimony meeting. I remember Brent Petersen standing and saying how sorry he was that it had happened because David Young was his father-in-law. My dad next stood and said how he knew it wasn't the Petersen's fault and that they shouldn't feel bad because they didn't know anything about it. After church we went to the school to go through the room. As we entered, Mr. Mitchell was there and he asked if I understood that it wasn't our fault. As we went in the room, the once white walls were black. The carpet had blood on it from Doris's body and a lot of things were melted. I put an X on a map of the room to represent where I was. And then I signed my name in the soot on the wall.

Rachel Walker Hollibaugh
Third Grade Student Survivor
(Oral History)

There are things that I learned throughout this whole process. It just didn't stop in 3rd grade. There's just so much that I've learned and different steps that I've had to take and... I remember the day of the bombing. I remember the clothes that I was wearing. They were ruined and they had to take them off of me. They were these cute little overalls, they were red. Three friends and I asked the teacher to go to the restroom as recess ended. He said, "You just went." We said, "Please, please, please." He let us go.

The first recognition I had was smelling gas. To me every time I smell gas there is a flashback and I remember that day. One of my best friends got sick from the smell and actually asked to go home. Our teacher took us into the room.

I remember seeing guns, not really understanding what they were doing, I knew what guns were but there were so many. The things I try to remember are things pertaining to me and things that pertain to my life. I'm not going to go minute to minute as it all muddles together in my mind. As they separated us and gave us activities to do, I remember one of the teachers asking us if we wanted to pray. I was with one of my friends and remember praying that we would be safe. I was sitting by the far window and I remember coloring a picture. I remember David Young getting very nervous.

In my heart I know it was from the prayers that we said. I know that Heavenly Father was protecting us at the time. They put tape around the room, and as I was coloring, I looked up and there were angels around every single part of that tape. And this is where it gets very personal to me, because as I looked at those faces...I knew every single one of those faces. One stood out to me. As I looked at her, I was very happy to see her. There were not just adults but kids there which made a huge impression on me—I will talk about that later. My brother came to me and told me to stand by the window.

I remember turning to one of my teachers who had been an aid there and asked her for a piece of paper. She gave it to me and right then is when the bomb went off. I remember hearing gunshots. I still flinch at those. The paper that I was holding came and burnt my arms and I remember that hurting. I remember someone grabbing me and pulling me out the window. I was so happy to see Mr. Moore outside the window, to see a familiar face. I was so happy to see him. I remember sitting in a teacher's home, because my mother and father were part of the emergency help, they got me stable and put me somewhere safe. They had to put oxygen on me, I went into shock. I remember that cold feeling and not really understanding what was going on.

My next memory is of riding over in the ambulance to Montpelier. My mother was in front with my sister. I was in the back with a couple of very critical children. I can still in my mind hear their screams as they were screaming the whole ride over there. When we got to the hospital I remember some men coming and giving me a priesthood blessing and the calmness that I felt when that happened. Because my grandparents lived in Paris, Idaho, and my sister had smoke inhalation, we were able to just go to their home and stay there that night.

As far as my burns go, they were very, very painful. Through the summer I had to wear long sleeve shirts. I still have scars on my arms from those. I remember sitting in the hot-pool and them having to pop blisters when they got too big and then they had to scrub them. I know I wasn't near as bad as some others but I still remember that. Throughout the process of this healing we realized that the person that I had first seen that I had recognized was my Grandma Ruth. She died when my mom was sixteen but I've always felt a kinship with her. She will always be my guardian angel.

As far as how my life is doing now, I've had to take certain steps. About four years ago I had a child that had some medical problems. I'm not exactly for sure why it happened then or what started it but the feelings came back about, "Why did this have to happen? Why do bad things have to happen to good people? Me? My children?"

While I was in Primary Children's Hospital in Salt Lake City, with a sick child, I was struggling with this a lot. I went to see a friend, and as I talked to her, I saw the vision again of what I had seen when I was in the bombing. But as I saw this vision open, I saw people both young and small. My grandma stood out to me again and surrounding her was every one of my kids. I know without a doubt that my kids were there that day, also letting me know that they were waiting for me. That there was a purpose that I needed to go on.

After talking and having this experience, it opened up a brand new perspective on all that happened because I know that in times of struggle I am not alone. It doesn't have to be some huge thing like the bombing, it can be the everyday things. I know that Heavenly Father and my ancestors and my posterity are aware of me. Another thing that I have learned and tried to teach my children is how powerful prayer is. I learned at a very young age that I am not alone and that I can pray whenever I need that assurance.

I know my story is different than those of others and I know that there is not a lot of the little tiny things that happened, but this is my story and this is what I remember and these are the things that I have learned. I pray every time I send a child to school that they will be safe because they are going to the same school that the hostage and bombing happened in. The only protection is that I taught them how to pray so they can be protected from things, just like I was.

I am proud to say that I have five children. I have a wonderful husband whom I married nine years ago in the Logan Temple. I enjoy life and I'm aware of how short it can be but I am also aware of the wonderful people that are just beyond the veil. When I've had children sick, when I've had trials in my life, they have shown themselves again. They have shown me and taught me that families are forever. I know that they are there supporting me, cheering for me, and wanting me to succeed.

This year I had the opportunity to go do a fireside at the place where David Young was from. Before I went through the experience with my own children, there were still some feelings that I didn't understand, that didn't make sense to people when I did tell them. So because of that I did not talk. I was not one of the ones that did firesides like my mom and my sister did. This fireside was a very spiritual experience for me and there were things I needed to learn from the experience.

Unless you have the Spirit to understand the things that happened to me, it doesn't make sense. It's unbelievable. There were times I would see that doubt creep into people's faces and I didn't like that. Because of that, I didn't share much. My testimony now is that it doesn't matter what other people think of my story. This is what happened to me and it's personal. It will be something that I will be able to be honest and open with my kids about and in turn I hope that they have the testimony of prayer that I do. I want them to know how special their Grandma Ruth is to me. I didn't grow up with her here on earth but I know that she is aware of me. I know that I can pray to my Heavenly Father and he will protect me. And it's not because I have faith, it's because I *know*.

There is a part of me that, each time my child has a birthday, and they get closer to the age that I was, my heart breaks a little bit. And I hope that they realize and understand the things that I have taught them. Would I be as strong as my mother was then if this happened to me? And would my kids know what to do in that kind of situation? My children know my story and as they get older they will learn more.

I hope as a mother I can be as strong for my kids as they were for me on May 16th.

Jamie Buckley King
Third Grade Student Survivor
(Oral History)

It all started at lunch recess when we were coming in from playing a soccer game and we had lost, I turned to my friend and said this is going to be a really bad day. We went into the classroom and sat down for our afternoon story. I was resting my head on my desk when there was a knock at the door. The teacher went and answered it and it was a dark haired lady with a big smile on her face. She came into our room and told us that there was going to be an assembly next door.

Of course as a third grader I was very excited about an assembly. I looked at my teacher and she looked puzzled because she didn't know about an assembly. I've always pictured in my mind that Mr. Teichert was there that day. But, I found out when I wrote this that Mrs. Bennion was our substitute.

Despite her hesitation she lined us up and Doris, still having a smile on her face, led us into the room next door. I immediately knew when we walked in that no assembly was going to be taking place. It seemed very dark. I got very scared. I looked over at David and saw him sitting in the center of the room with guns surrounding him and it looked like a grocery cart full of, I think, explosives. Would I have known that? Or was it just "things?" As we were walking in, David turned to us and told us to be very quiet. Doris told us the whole time to be quiet. He seemed very nervous. I don't know what I did except I wandered around to the southeast corner of the room. I hung out there, in the corner and colored.

I remember when he put the tape around the bomb because the kids were getting too close. He said, "DO NOT GO PAST THIS TAPE." The children's chairs were sitting right up to the edge of that tape. I remember all the legs of the chairs. I remember David saying he wanted tape around the bomb. They (the children) were getting too close to him. He was just sweating. I remember Doris asking if he needed something and teachers asking him, too. He was so nervous. I remember him saying, "QUIET! It's getting too loud in here." I don't know if I heard this in the room or later, his plan was he wanted two million dollars a kid to let us go. If he was the one to kill us, he would be the God over us. We would go to this island and he would rule over us because he would own us since he was the one to take our lives. He was so uptight and nervous, not sure what to do next. I remember him saying he needed to go to the restroom. I remember her putting on the wrist thing and there was like a clothespin or something. If you bumped that, it would trigger the bomb.

I hung out there, in the corner, and colored. The next thing that I remember is the teachers were trying really hard to keep us entertained. They brought in a TV. I wasn't interested in watching a movie. They had this table where you could color and I was coloring a rock on this picture. The room turned black and the bomb had gone off. I looked up and saw Doris with her arms straight out and she was on fire. I was told that somebody from behind had distracted her and she turned to the side and she just pulled it and that's when it exploded. That's what I was told. I haven't read the book. I'm just trying to think and remember details in the room.

I remember the smell of gas. I was one of the last ones out. I was not running to escape. I ran into the corner where I had spent time and put my arms over my face and curled up in the corner and prepared to die. I was not voluntarily running or going anywhere. Someone had to pick me up and throw me out the window. I was in *my* corner. There was no one behind me. I saw kids in front of me. I was there, for what seemed like an eternity, when someone grabbed me from behind and threw me through the window. It surprised me that I was alive.

I ran toward the main street and I was met by my dad and he had a gun in his hand, ready to go kill David. The cops had stopped him and told him that he couldn't enter. I looked up to my dad and I was scared to tell him I had lost my shoes in the room. When he looked down, he saw that my right arm was severely burned. He wanted to get me to the hospital. I wanted to go get my shoes. We went to Mr. Taylor's lawn where they had blankets to put on us. We were all going into shock. I was cold. They were trying to put us in the ambulance, I absolutely refused.

This is a funny part. I looked on Main Street and I saw this lady in hot pink flowered bell bottom pants with bare feet, and it was MY MOTHER! I was embarrassed. My mom put us in someone's car and we went to the hospital in Montpelier to have my arm looked at. I remember going back quite a few times and they had to scrape my dead skin off and they put ointment on. I had to keep it wrapped because it was summertime. They said if I didn't keep it wrapped, I would be scarred for life. That summer, whenever my sisters wanted to run through the sprinklers, I had to be careful not to get it wet. Thank goodness that was all I was burned, unlike some of the other victims.

I feel like I went back into the room way too soon. I also struggled with all of the reporters around town because I felt like they were only after a story. They didn't care what happened, they only wanted the story and the money that came with it. I would run from them. There was just no feeling there. When they would approach me, there was just nothing there from them.

I never shared my story. I am very grateful that they are doing this book because it will be the first time I will hear my sisters' stories. I also had a really hard time with people who shared their stories of angels and ancestors. I didn't see any angels. I felt like I had done something wrong. I felt like I was naughty so I wasn't able to have protectors like others had. I was later told it was because I didn't need to see them. I didn't need to see because I knew in my heart that they were there. I believe we did have angels there with us, protecting us. Just with the scientific viewpoint of it and the way the bomb was made, we should have been dead. I believe we were saved for a reason. But I still have insecurities and I'm twenty-eight.

I still feel like I go back to that day. I don't trust people because Doris opened the door with a big smile on her face and told us that we were going to an assembly and then lured us into this room, knowing that we were probably going to die. I find myself not trusting people, even kind people. I feel like they are going to lure me into another trap. There are kind people out there, but it takes me a long time to trust.

I didn't get better all of a sudden. For one reason, I was running from it for many years and then realized that I had this trusting problem and this fear of death. I didn't know where it had come from.

It was nineteen years later in front of the Country Shopper that a friend who had moved to Cokeville, who had not lived here during this time, told me that I did die in that corner. I was telling her my experience, because I was talking about wanting to write about it for this book. It was fresh on my mind and her viewpoints, not having been a part of the experience, changed my life. I was telling her about putting my arms over my face and going back into a corner and preparing to die. She told me that I *did* die back in that corner. She told me that it was time to live again.

I had no idea it had affected me that deeply. That was the first time I had put it together, that it had really happened to me and that was where the fear had come from, from a little third grade mind. It was one of those experiences in your life where time stops, and you are healed. The Savior healed me. The woman was a spokesperson.

I have had many fears for the past ten or fifteen years about dying. I have died over and over again. I have not gone places, fearing I was going to die and leave my children behind. An answer to my prayer came to me that day when my friend spoke from the outside and told me that it was time to start living. I guess I've had insecurities come from it but because of prayer and the Savior intervening, I have been able to overcome one of these insecurities, which is the fear of death.

Through the years I would talk to my mother about having this fear, constantly in my life, and my mom always says to me, "Faith and fear don't coexist." I turned to the Savior because I knew that if I had fear, it was because I wasn't going to the Savior for help. I didn't want to talk about it.

Every year my mom calls me on May 16th. My mom would say, "Jamie, it's the day of miracles." Then she would go on about how grateful she is that I am alive and that her daughters are alive. She's never missed a year. She called me this past May and said, "Jamie, do you know what day it is?" I am so involved with my children that I never know what day it is anyway. It catches me off guard every year.

I don't think that most people are grateful for the trial when they are going through it, but it is only through trials that we go to the Savior and humble ourselves for answers. We find that He has always been there and that He will always help us through when we ask. He never left us in the first place. Sometimes I think that people think He doesn't love us or we have done something wrong, like I felt when I didn't see the angels. I am grateful for people that help us see that, yes, He was there, He is there, and He will continue to be there.

I am grateful that David Young did not get the chance to take my life away that day because it would have taken away the experiences I've had of being a mother, a sister, a wife, a daughter and a friend. Because of this experience I have gained a stronger testimony that I have a Savior that loves me. Believe me, since that day I have backed myself up into many corners wanting all the pain to go away. Because that person grabbed me from behind on May 16, they told me that I was worth saving. Don't run to the corner and hide when you need help. Run to your knees. Prayers are answered! MIRACLES HAPPEN!!!!!

Kristi Moore Nelson
Third Grade Student Survivor
(Typed Submission)

I remember the day before that I was sick and so my mom didn't want me to go to school that day. But as a kid I loved going to school, so I went. After lunch I started feeling sick again, but I thought it was from being sick the day before. (Little did I know that it was Heavenly Father trying to help get me out sooner). So I decided to tough it out. When we got back in from lunch I felt even sicker and that I should call my mom, but I decided I would wait until our substitute teacher was finished reading a book.

I remember feeling a sudden heavy weight on me. A woman came in and said that there was a surprise in the next room. The substitute asked if she could finish reading the book and that we would be right there. The lady said that would be all right, but just to make sure that we came right in. After she finished reading we all lined up and went out into the hall and into the next room.

You could feel the presence of evil. I remember going in and seeing guns everywhere and kids all around the room. It felt like something you can't really explain, but evil. I ran to my Uncle Rocky and he picked me up. I told him that I didn't feel well and wanted to call my mom to come and get me. Uncle Rocky told me to wait and see if I felt any better later. Little did I know that there was no going home anytime soon.

I remember looking at the guy and his wife (I still have a hard time saying their names), and just feeling even sicker. I remember him pointing a gun. I also remember him telling everyone to stay off the white line around him or they would be shot. (Man, I didn't think this would be so hard, but I'm really having a hard time writing this. It is as though I'm almost reliving it.)

I remember him letting someone bring in a TV that we could

watch. The rest is just kind of a blur until toward the end.

I remember sitting by my cousin Jeremiah. It was his birthday that day and we started singing *Happy Birthday* to him, and the man and his wife even joined in. (I just don't understand their thinking). Anyway, I remember sitting by Jeremiah by the door near the bathroom that led to the other room. He (David) had desks stacked up so that you couldn't get to the other room, but you could go to the restroom. I remember the man handing his wife the string around his wrist and he went into the bathroom. All of a sudden there was a loud noise. I remember looking up and seeing orange shooting straight up into the air. It didn't go out like in the movies. It went straight up. Then I remember turning toward the bathroom door just as the man opened the door. I remember he looked at me. It was a look of confusion.

Then, he shut himself back in the bathroom. Then I think instinct took over. I jumped over the desks and into the other room and out the doors into the hall and out to the outside doors.

When I got outside I remember seeing kids running and guys jumping out of helicopters and I swear it seemed like they were coming out of the ground. They were everywhere. (Now that *was* just like in the movies).

Then I realized I had lost my shoe. I remember thinking, my mom's gonna be so mad, so I turned around and went running back to go get my shoe. (Yeah, I was really smart!) Mrs. Mitchell stopped me and asked me what I was doing. When I told her, she told me that my mom wouldn't care about my shoe, just to run over to where all the other kids were. So I did.

On my way over there, I saw Mr. Miller and he was hunched over by the grass and I saw blood on his shirt. I asked him what happened and he said he had been shot. The weird thing is that I ran out the same way he did, and I was the first one out because the guy was in the bathroom. The only thing I can think of is that it happened while I was on my way back in to get my shoe and Mrs. Mitchell stopped me. So maybe in a way Mrs. Mitchell saved my life in more than one way.

So THANK YOU Mrs. Mitchell.

When I got to where everyone was headed I saw my uncle Wayne. He came running toward me and picked me up and gave me a hug and asked if I was all right. Then I remember my grandpa Harmon coming down the street with a rifle. He stopped and asked me if I was all right. He had tears in his eyes. My uncle Wayne asked him what he was going to do with that gun. My grandpa went storming toward the school and said, "I'm going to make sure that *@!# is dead!"

One of the police or FBI stopped him and said that he was already dead. After that it is pretty much another blur. I remember having to share a blanket with Mike Thompson and I was embarrassed because I had to share with a boy. Then I remember my aunt Pixie coming to pick me up. I remember walking into the house and my mom was sitting on the rocking chair and my aunt Doris and cousin Lenita were behind her. My mom came over to me and gave me a big hug. (I even got to sleep with one of them that night. I felt pretty special).

I also remember them taking my uncle Rocky and me to the Kemmerer hospital for smoke inhalation. A little something else that I like to let people know about is that when the bomb went off my dad, who was a firefighter at the time, didn't see me come out and so he broke the window (which is supposed to be unbreakable) with his bare hand. Now that is a VERY TOUGH DAD!

I listen to the Holy Ghost a lot now. Whenever I get even the slightest feeling that something is wrong, I listen. I know that we're not in a safe protected place. Bad things do happen and it's how we live with it and learn from it that counts. I know that every time I go into a store or anywhere where there are a lot of people, I am very aware of what is going on around me and I ask myself "what if" and "what would I do if?"

I know the hardest thing for me was sending my son, Payson, to school. That was very, very hard. I was a total wreck. I had dreams of things happening to him at school and just terrible thoughts of things like that happening to him. But over time things have calmed down a little. I think that has helped me. It's amazing how this experience still affects me to this day.

I'm married and have two children, Payson, 4, Brodie, 2, and another on the way. I used to work as an office manager of the Flying J corporate office and then at Frontier BioMedical. Now I am a stay at home mom which I love and wouldn't change. I love spending time with my two boys and my husband. I also sell *Salt City Candles* and *Close to my Heart Scrapbooking*. We live in Nibley, Utah. We built our home there almost three years ago. We like to go camping, 4-wheeling (especially my boys), going to grandparents for the weekends, anything we can do together. I love my family for everything they have had to put up with and I want to thank them. THANK YOU ALL FOR EVERYTHING!!!!

Kara Thornock Titensor
Third Grade Student Survivor
(Email Submission)

I was young enough at the time to have been spared the terror that preceded the explosion. I was not oblivious to the seriousness of the situation, but the magnitude of what was happening could not have entered my nine year old mind. I can close my eyes and still see that wall of fire shoot right over my head.

I was sitting maybe six feet away from the bomb when it detonated and yet I have no physical scars from that day. I saw no angels but know that I had some help getting to the window. All of my memories from that day give my adult life purpose, remind me that every person is precious and prove that there is a plan for our lives. The miracle of the bombing was no random act of luck. It is by the grace of God that Cokeville, Wyoming, did not lose a generation of children that day.

My future husband grew up eighty miles from Cokeville. He remembers his parents discussing the events of that day over dinner. He became so intrigued by the bombing that he saved the front page of the local newspaper detailing the events. He had numerous opportunities to throw it away yet, time after time, he saved it. It was not until he met and married me that it became clear to him why he felt so drawn to a now tattered and yellowed piece of newspaper.

Kliss Sparks

Fourth Grade Teacher Survivor
(Handwritten Photocopy Submission)

It was Friday afternoon May 16, 1986. Only two weeks until school would be out for the summer and the students were ready. I'd probably have to read a little longer to them that day. I was reading them *Tom Sawyer*. Tom and Becky were in the cave. The children liked this part of the story. A knock came on the door and I called, "Come in." Nothing happened so I stood up—still reading—and went to the door. A dark-haired woman with streaks of grey in her hair was standing outside the door. I continued reading as I was in an exciting part of the story.

I opened the door and the lady said, "We'd like you to come down the hall, please." She turned and left.

I lined the children up at the door. I hadn't remembered any assembly. The children asked me to keep reading as we walked down the hall. I didn't see anyone in the gym where I thought an assembly would be held. I saw some guns sitting against the hall benches but I didn't see anyone else. I decided to take my students on outside to the grass and finish the exciting part of the chapter. It wasn't too much longer—only two or three more pages.

We went out the south door and sat in a circle on the grass. I had read about two pages when the lady came to the door and asked us to come in to the second grade room. As we came in the door, I saw a gun in her hand.

We entered the room and she told the man (David Young) that "everyone was here now." He walked to the center of the room and told us that he was holding us hostage because he wanted our parents to pay for our freedom. He told us that he knew most of us were Mormons and they loved their children so they would pay a million dollars apiece for every child or adult in the room (he later changed it to three million each). He sent Max Excell, our principal, to the office to call anyone and everyone, including the U.S. President, to raise the money for the ransom payment.

There were close to 160 people in that room which was probably only 27' by 27'. It started with the afternoon kindergarten and included each grade through the sixth grade. We also had quite a few adults besides the teachers Kris and Kim Kasper. He was student teaching and she was the kindergarten teacher. There was also a young woman, Cynthia Cowden, who was applying for the kindergarten job because Kris and Kim were leaving so he could find a job. There was a mother whose kindergarten child had missed the bus, Eva Clark. She had left a young child alone in her car. There was also a young UPS. delivery driver, who just happened to make a delivery of school supplies for the next year.

Pat Bennion was substituting for the third grade teacher that day. The music teacher, John Miller, was there. Verlene Bennion, an aid, was there as well as the special ed teacher (I can't remember her name), the librarian, Gayle Chadwick, and the secretary Tina Cook. The regular teachers were there; Janel Dayton 1st grade, Jean Mitchell, 1st grade, Carol Petersen, 2nd grade, Rocky Moore, 5th grade, Jack Mitchell, 6th grade and me, Kliss Sparks, 4th grade.

All during the year we'd had had the fire alarms go off. Each time we had one, we exited the building. We went out at all times of the school day and from everywhere in the building. When the firemen came to the school or the electrician came to check out the alarms, they could never find anything wrong. We got so we could exit the school quite quickly.

David Young told our principal, Max Excell, to go to the telephone at the office and begin to call people to arrange for ransom. Mr. Excell was to ask for a million for each child. Mr. Young said that he was sure the parents would pay because Cokeville was a Mormon town and Mormons loved their children.

Mr. Excell received a telephone call telling him that the Civil

Defense Committee for Lincoln County was meeting in the basement of our city hall. Kathy Davison, the coordinator of the committee, told us she would get ambulances here in town, ready for whatever was needed.

As we were finding places to sit in the room, Dustin Eastman came up to me and said, "Mrs. Sparks, I don't want to be here."

"Neither do I Dustin, but we have to stay because he has a gun," I told him.

Adam Hymas told me he didn't like it and was afraid. I told both Dustin and Adam that I was afraid, too, but we had to do what he told us to do. I hoped that would keep us safe.

Just then, Melanie Chadwick came to the sink on the west side of the room. She was so frightened she was throwing up. I bent her over the sink, got some paper towels, wet them and patted her face. I hugged her and was wetting her face again when her mother, Gayle Chadwick, the librarian, came to her as soon as she saw that she was sick.

Mr. Young was sitting on one of the tables on the north side of the room with a bomb in a grocery cart. There were several guns, mostly rifles, leaning against the table he was sitting on them. I walked in front of Mr. Young to get some paper and crayons for the children to have something to do to pass the time. They were fairly quiet—from fright, I suppose. Mr. Young asked me where I was going and I told him that I needed to take care of the children so I was getting paper and crayons for them to be entertained. "Oh yes," he answered. "We need to protect the children," and let me go. I brought back lots of crayons and paper to the west side of the room where my fourth graders were sitting.

Mr. Young seemed to be much more antagonistic to the men in the room, rather than the women. Most of the adults were sitting around the edge of the room. He was very upset with Rocky Moore and threatened him with his gun unless he got into a corner. Rocky gathered his students around him and they sat in the southeast corner of the room.

About that time Mr. Young became concerned because he was afraid that a child would bump his arm and set the bomb off. Mr. Young made us carry all the desks and tables out into the hall so the center of the room would be clear. He then had Kris Casper and Jack Mitchell take tape and put it in a square on the floor. The men called it a magic square and told us to have a contest to see which group could stay outside the magic square the best.

Mr. Young had unwittingly helped to make our children safe. If the tables and desks had been in the room our youngsters could not have gotten out of the classroom safely. Someone would have been killed. The children could not see because the smoke was so heavy and they would have inhaled those toxic fumes and perhaps died. Those who were burned would have had more serious burns because they would have been in the room longer.

I asked the children if they would like to listen to another chapter of *Tom Sawyer*. I began to read to them but they could not maintain interest in the story. They were talking amongst themselves and Mr. Young was telling them to be quiet. I stopped reading and asked the kids if they'd like to sing a little. We sang a couple of songs, very half-heartedly. We sang *Happy Birthday* to Jeremiah Moore. He said afterward that he never liked that song again.

I went up to Mr. Young and asked him if we could let Dustin E. go free because he was diabetic. He looked at me and said, "I might change one ten for two twenties," but he didn't move to let him go.

The students gathered their younger brothers and sisters so they could sit together. Those who were sitting together took turns saying a prayer for their safety. It didn't matter what religion they were, they were united in asking their Father in Heaven to protect them.

I went up to Mr. Young and told him that the children needed something to do so could I walk to the school library and bring back a portable bookcase so the kids could read. He looked at me, pointed his finger at me, shook it in my face and said, "You can go but if you don't come back one of these kids is dead."

He meant it and I knew he meant it. I walked down the hall, went into the library, and carried the bookrack back down the hall to the second grade room. When I got back to the room the kids came and got books. A few tried to read but most of them looked at the books for a few minutes then put them back.

Rocky Moore asked if he could go the library and bring back a television on a high cart with some tapes so the children would be able to watch some of our National Geographic tapes, some short story tales, and other tapes.

Most of us were trying to talk to our students to help keep them calm and help them to be less afraid. It seemed that the time was going very slowly. Some of the children had put their heads down in their hands and seemed to be praying.

Jack Mitchell was sitting at the door where Mr. Young had told him to sit to keep the children in the room. Along the south wall of the room many of the adults were sitting on the floor (especially those who did not already work at the school). Mrs. Young would tell some of the children how well they were behaving.

I thought "oh yeah" when I heard her comments.

The bomb had a trigger device which was made with a clothespin with some kind of metal wrapped around the bottom of the pin. Between the metal bases was another clothespin attached to Mr. Young's wrist. If anyone bumped his arm it would put enough tension on the pin without the metal to pull it out of its position. That would allow the two metal clad clothespin points to make contact and that would set the bomb off.

The room was quite warm and you could smell the fuel mixture in the gallon bottle on the top shelf of the bomb.

Occasionally a child had to go to the bathroom and so Mr. Young would have Mrs. Dayton, the first grade teacher, accompany them to the door of the bathroom then wait for them to come out so she could take them back to where they were sitting. He had piled desks at the door to the extra room so no one could sneak out and get away.

It was getting close to three o'clock and school let out at 3:15 p.m. The children were beginning to get more restless. They seemed to know when it was time to go home. The noise level was beginning to rise. It looked like Mr. Young was sweating. None of us knew that he was diabetic and it was beginning to affect him. He decided he needed to go to the bathroom so he called his wife over and attached the trigger to her wrist. Then he left to go to the restroom.

After a few minutes Mrs. Young commented that the children were too noisy. She asked Mrs. Mitchell if she could get them to quiet down. Jean Mitchell told her that it was time for school to be out but that she would try.

She stepped to the corner of the magic square, being careful not to get too close to Mrs. Young. She called out, 'Kids, it's getting too loud in here. Let's play a game to see which class can be the quietest. It's called "Quaker Meeting" and you can make movements with your hands but if you talk, your group loses."

Mrs. Young turned to Jean and said, "What a good..." As she turned, she pulled the half clothespin out and the two metal ends of the pins made contact.

There was a sound like a large firecracker exploding.

Instantly the room was filled with heavy black smoke and tongues of flames were flying everywhere. The flames looked like arrows to me. I began to scream, "Run kids run." Jack was yelling, "Get down. Get out!" Someone ran to the east window to open it. It only had an opening of about 10 inches, but the teachers were pushing kids out the window. Rocky Moore climbed out the window and began pulling kids out the window. Kris was yelling for kids to come to his voice.

Mr. Miller ran to the hall and pushed the desks out of the way. Mrs. Dayton was taking children to the hall, then to the main hall so they could run outside. Then she came back to get more children. Mr. Miller was also helping the children run past the bathroom to the outer hall. Just then Mr. Young came out of the bathroom and shot John in the back. The bullet went in quite close to his spine and stopped on the other side of his spinal column.

Jack and I were still calling kids to come to us! I could tell that most of the children were gone because I couldn't hear or feel them going past me. I ran out into the hall where I rubbed fire out of the hair of three boys; Ryan Taylor, Jay Metcalfe, and I can't remember who the third boy was.

I couldn't see Jack so I ran out the south door and went to the east window to help pull children out. One father, Frank Lazcanotegui, was trying to break the window so we could get more children out. Rocky told me to check to see if any other children were still in the room.

We had practiced gathering at the south end of the school grounds but there were no children there so I ran to look for them.

At the corner of the school street and Main Street were ambulances from Kemmerer (2), Afton (3), and Montpelier, (3). They were already treating burned children and those who needed to be hospitalized were being sent to the hospitals.

As I looked at the children, most of them had black faces from the smoke. Some were coughing and many were inhaling oxygen.

Some of the children were looking for their brothers and sisters to see if they were safe.

We had completely exited the building in about forty-five seconds—no longer than a minute at most.

I ran to Steve Taylor's yard to see if I could account for all of our children, to be sure no one was left in the schoolroom. The children who lived in town had run home and many many of the townspeople were there to love, comfort, and ease the pain of the children as they came running from the school. Many people told me where the different children had gone. Slowly I accounted for all of them. It was then I realized how great our little town was.

I went back to the school to try to find all the people I worked with. Rocky told me, "I know I told you I wouldn't believe unless I saw a burning bush, but this is ridiculous." I hugged him and told him I was glad he was all right. I found each of the other people and hugged them, told them I loved them, and was glad they were alive.

I then heard that Mr. Young had shot Mrs. Young in the back of the head and then had gone back into the bathroom and shot himself. We stayed on the school grounds for a long time talking and hugging one another. The police from Cokeville, the bomb experts, and the FBI, wouldn't let us go back into the school that night.

The next morning I went back to school—I couldn't stay away. I asked the bomb expert if they had found anything and he told me they had indeed. The bomb didn't explode the way it was set up to do. Only two of the ten percussion caps had gone off—there was no reason for that. The gallon of fuel (gas and fuel oil) had evaporated or leaked so that the aluminum powder did not become an incendiary device and yet the powder was not wet. The bomb was set up so well that it should have leveled the school, but it did not. The chain link could not explode into shrapnel because the explosive force was not strong enough. The power of the explosion was absorbed into the acoustic ceiling tiles. They were blown into the attic area of the room.

On the wall of the room in the smoke covered wall was an outline which looked like the shadow of an angel.

I don't know who the Lord wanted in that room, but I do know that Mr. Young did the worst thing he could do to us and Heavenly Father protected us.

At no time was I afraid. I had a sweet peaceful feeling and I have always believed that it was because I had taken out my endowments in the Idaho Falls Temple on May 10 and this incident took place May 16, 1986. I didn't see any angels, but they must have been there because of the way we were protected.

If I close my eyes and think about that day I can see curved orange tongues of flame in the black smoke. I can see little black faces of children looking for family. I can see Mr. Miller in the hall with his shirt off showing children his back where the bullet hole was and hearing him tell the kids to look at the hole because he was healing so fast that his wound would soon be gone—healed.

Some children looked at pictures in family albums and recognized ancestors as being those they saw in the room telling them they would be fine—safe and sound.

Did I see angels? No, but they must have been there and I'm going to try to repay my Father in Heaven by serving Him faithfully for the rest of my life.

You're looking at an ex-Relief Society president because of that bomb. I never would have accepted that calling before the bombing. Now I'll do anything, I can't say no to anything Heavenly Father wants me to do. I'm just trying to repay for that day.

Rusty Birch
Fourth Grade Student Survivor
(Email Submission)

I haven't talked much about the hostage ordeal over the years. My wife and I have talked about it off and on, mostly because many of her relatives are from Cokeville, and what she knows about it came from her family and the TV news. However, I have never really gone into great detail when we've talked about it. When we were notified about the book project, she really started to grill me about details. I hope no one who reads this will be offended by my take on some of the events. I was a boy in fourth grade at the time. This is just what I remember about my own experience.

My wife asked me if I was scared during the hostage situation. When we were first taken into Mrs. Mitchell's room, the whole thing was scary. After a while, though, it turned into wondering what was going to happen. As a fourth-grade boy, I started planning my escape, fantasizing about how to get away, assemble my sniper team and come back to save my friends.

When the bomb went off, I was standing about ten feet away from Mrs. Young. She turned toward me, enveloped in flames, and all I could think was, "She's comin' right at me!" I wasn't sticking around for that! I turned to run out the bathroom hallway. There were desks and chairs everywhere. Katie Walker was on the floor among the desks and chairs. I tried to help her get up, but someone pushed me from behind, so I had to jump over her. Someone obviously helped her because she got out.

David Young was standing in the bathroom doorway to my right. I ran right past him, so close I could have kicked him. I realize now that it's probably a good thing I didn't. At first, I didn't understand why I didn't get shot. I was sort of expecting a bullet as I ran. My head was right at barrel level; that's how tall I was. If he had been shooting straight in front of him, every one of us that went past him would have been shot. Because he was shooting to his right and left, he missed all of us kids. I ran into the first grade room, out into the hallway, and out the south doors of the school toward my home.

That run across the grass was the fastest I'd ever gone home in my life! Uncle John (Bird) was at the fence catching the kids the firemen tossed over. I think Doug Prows was the one who tossed me over the fence. Uncle John helped me get steady on my feet as I landed. I ran in my house, but no one was home. That kind of scared me, so I ran outside and over to Grandpa (Russell) Thornock's. Grandpa was out on his lawn making a head count of his grandkids, and Grandma was inside taking care of some kids who were burned. We headed over to the Taylors' to assemble in classes to make sure everyone was out of the school.

I heard that Uncle Ernie (Thornock) and several others showed up at the police line with their guns. I'm sure part of the law enforcement officers' work that day was trying to keep the citizens from shooting the guy if he made it out of the building. Over the years, I've thought that Cokeville was the wrong town for David Young to try pulling a stunt like this. A small town in rural Wyoming with close-knit families—yeah, those people aren't going to have guns or be willing to use them, are they? How did that guy think he was going to make it out alive?

One thing I've wondered about is why there was no video or TV camera on the school when all of us came rushing out. That would have been quite a sight!

Another memory I have came after that day. Billie Jo Hutchinson was badly burned and had to do a lot of physical therapy. My mom was one of the many people in town who helped her with it. I remember riding my bike over to Hutchinsons' to get her so that she would have someone with her on her way to my house when she came for physical therapy.

Over the years, people have talked a lot about angels being

present in the classroom that day. My wife asked me if I saw angels, as some people did. My response was, "I was running too fast to worry about angels. I figured the angels could take care of themselves."

No, I didn't see angels, but looking back now, I'm sure they were there.

Jaime Metcalfe Connor
Fourth Grade Student Survivor
(Email Submission)

I have been putting this off for months. Ever since I heard that the Cokeville Miracle Foundation wanted survivor stories from those of us in the bombing, I felt like I should write something, and yet I kept putting it off. As another deadline approached, I was tempted to just let it go. No one really needed to hear what happened to me that day, they had other accounts to read that were far more eloquent than anything I could share. But, try as I might, I just couldn't let it go and I realized that I owed it to myself and to my children to write about what happened that day in May. So here I sit, already on the verge of tears and I have barely even started writing.

Lunch recess was the longest of our three breaks. My mother always packed a good lunch for me and it was nice to have extra time to run around and play and get the kinks out before returning to the classroom. After recess came one of my favorite activities in the fourth grade: It was story time. Fourth grade story time was different from any other I had experienced up to that point in my elementary school experience. It wasn't that the stories were better, the difference was Mrs. Sparks. She would read the stories in a wonderfully expressive way and she used different voices for different characters. It made the stories come alive for me.

At that time, if I am not mistaken, we were in the middle of reading *Tom Sawyer*. We were all sitting very quietly, listening raptly when there was a knock on the door and a strange woman poked her head in. Mrs. Sparks stood up to talk to her for a few minutes and then the woman left. Mrs. Sparks then had us all line up and we began to walk in the direction of the first grade room, then we walked past the first grade room and out the door at the end of the hall. It was a beautifully sunny day and Mrs. Sparks arranged us on the ground in a circle, gave the book to Jerry Dayton, who was one of the best readers in the class, and told him to read the story to us while she went in to find out what was going on.

I often marvel at the fact that if we had only known what was happening inside, we could have just walked away and avoided it all. I believe that Mrs. Sparks must have had some feeling that all was not right and that was why she took us outside. Unfortunately, they did not let her return to warn us and instead, the strange woman, who turned out to be Doris Young, came out after about ten minutes and brought us into the room with the rest of the school.

I think that we were the last class to enter, although I can't be certain. Once we were all settled, I remember looking around at the guns and the strange device in the center of the room and thinking that we must be having a gun safety assembly. Then Mr. Excell stood up and proceeded to explain to us that we were being held hostage by this man David Young. He told us that Young had a bomb and that we had to stay in the school until he said we could leave.

I was nine years old at the time. I had no idea what he was talking about at first. I just knew that kids were crying and teachers looked concerned so this was obviously a bad situation. I got scared, too.

At first I just wandered around seeking some kind of comfort. I really just wanted my mom and there was no substitute that was satisfying to me. Finally I heard someone suggest prayer. That made sense to me so I knelt in a corner of the room and offered my own little prayer. Immediately after saying that prayer I felt better. I felt as though I had received an embrace that was so comforting that I was no longer afraid. I knew that, somehow, things were going to work out and we were all going to get out of that room alive. Looking back, I remember seeing many small groups of students praying together. I think that there was no way that the Lord could ignore so many prayers from so many children.

Now that I was calm and unafraid, I was also bored. We had been in the room for some time at this point and I think that most of us had overcome our fears and were looking for something to do. All the restlessness in the room was making David Young nervous and the "magic square" was introduced. Mr. Mitchell stood up and got our attention. He told us that we were going to play a game. They were putting down tape to make a square in the middle of the room. Mr. Young and his bomb were going to sit in the middle of the square. If we crossed the line, then we would be "out." Luckily, we never found out what he meant by "out."

The teachers gained permission to go to the media center and get books, coloring pages and a TV and bring them into the room to keep us busy. They also got permission to open the windows and the doors (although the doors were blocked by desks) because the stench of the gasoline on the bomb cart was making everyone sick. I remember that before that day, I thought that gasoline smelled good and loved to have my window down while my dad filled up the car. Since that day, the smell of gas makes me sick and it is a trial to fill up my own car.

By this time my older sister Joanna had gathered me and our younger brother, Jay, together so we could look out for each other. Joanna and I played various games. One in particular was a color peg game where you used different colored pegs to make pictures. Jay was coloring paper pictures with crayons. We also watched TV for awhile. I specifically remember watching the *Transformers*.

At one point I remember approaching Doris Young with a group of other students. We asked her what we were going to eat. She said that our parents would bring us food. Someone asked her how we would brush our teeth. She looked in her purse and found a toothbrush and said that we could pass it around. I thought that she must be more than a little crazy.

We were there until after five. *The Five O'clock News* started and Joanna and I told Jay to stay where he was because we were going to see if we were on the news and that we would be right back. We ran over to the television which was situated in the back corner of the room along the wall with the windows. We were listening intently to the newscaster when suddenly the room went black, there was a huge booming sound, intense heat and the sound of high pitched children's screams. I turned around and found myself gazing into a huge fireball in the center of the room. Although I know it was only a few seconds, it seemed I stood for many minutes trying to comprehend what had happened. Then I saw a smaller ball of fire in the shape of a person detach itself from the main fire and run toward the drinking fountain.

This sight jarred me into action. It was as though my brain stopped thinking. I forgot everything except for the overwhelming need to get out of that room and avoid that fate. I looked around and saw the light from the windows. I ran toward them in a panic. Everything and everyone I touched was so hot they burned my hands. Somehow I got to the window and joined the crowd of kids already there. I would like to say that I waited my turn like a good little girl, but that would be a lie. I pushed my way to the front and flung myself out the window. Mr. Moore was already outside and was pulling kids out of the windows as fast as he could. He grabbed my hands and pulled me so fast I had scrapes on my stomach but I didn't even feel it. He told me to run for the street and I ran as fast as I could.

When I got to the street that leads out to Main Street, my senses came back to me and I realized that I had left my sister and my brother behind. I started screaming their names hysterically and turned to run back to the building when Mrs. Sparks caught me and slapped me across the face. This snapped me out of my hysteria and I calmed down enough to hear my name being called. To my relief, it was Joanna. We grabbed each other and started looking for Jay, then found him seconds later behind us. We ran over to him and grabbed him in tight embraces, only to have him scream in pain. He had been sitting by the "magic square" and when the bomb exploded, he caught on fire. Luckily, Mrs. Sparks saw him and patted out the flames before too much damage was done, but he was in a lot of pain and in for a long recovery. I remember him being very upset by the fact that his picture had burned and that his favorite shirt was ruined. We have pictures of him sitting at a school desk with a sign on his shirt that read, "Please do not touch my back."

Minutes later we heard our names again and turned to see our oldest sister, Andrea. She had raced over from the high school and when she grabbed Joanna and me in an embrace I remember that she smelled so good. She then turned to grab Jay and both Joanna and I screamed "NO!!" We told her that he was hurt and we began to make our way toward Main Street to get help. I remember seeing Mr. Miller lying on the ground and I was afraid he was dead.

We made it to the ambulances and we got separated. Although I was not badly burned, the blast had blackened me from head to toe and when the paramedics saw me they thought I was burned badly. Someone from the town took my glasses and before I could get them back the paramedics from Afton bundled me up in their ambulance and took me away. This convinced me that I must be dying and I kept asking the nice lady if I was going to die. I often lament that they took me instead of Jay who really needed the attention.

When I got to the hospital they put me in a room, gave me some food and tried to get hold of my mother. I didn't have my glasses and was quite blind without them. After several hours, my mom came to get me and together we went to Montpelier, Idaho, where Jay, Andrea and Joanna were waiting for us. While we were at the hospital, I went to see my best friend, Amy, who had been burned and was being treated. She was so upset because her eyelashes had been burned off.

When we finally returned home my parents let us all sleep in the roll out couch together, as no one wanted to sleep alone. I don't remember having bad dreams, but I do remember climbing into my parents' bed early in the morning, crying. For several days, I had to wear an old pair of my sister Andrea's glasses so I could at least partly see. I can't remember how many days I had to wait to get my glasses back, but to me it seemed like forever.

It has now been almost twenty years since that day. After all the time that has passed I still cried like a baby during parts of this narrative. Mostly, I think that it does not affect my everyday life, although the smell of gas still gives me a headache and I still cringe every time I light my grill.

I had an interesting experience this year as it is my son's first year in school. He is only four and goes for only three hours, but on that first day when I dropped him off, I almost had a panic attack. I was leaving the building and I was suddenly terrified that someone would try to hurt my son the way that David Young tried to hurt us. It took all I had to leave him there and not snatch him up and run from the building.

The week after the bombing, my mother took me and Joanna back to the room. Jay could not come because he was in the Logan hospital being treated for his burns. We walked into the ruined room and faced our ghosts. We found the colored peg picture we had made all melted and blistered from the heat. We saw and felt the hand of Divine Providence that had saved everyone except the two terrorists. I hope that my life has been and will continue to be worth the miracle that happened to me in my childhood.

Dustin Eastman
Fourth Grade Student Survivor
(Oral Histoy—Telephone)

The bomb is something I don't think about anymore. I feel it made me pretty hateful about people with the same look as them and that try to control me. I have had to overcome some issues and have learned to be controlled to a certain point. I have had to learn that all people are not mean and not out to get me. I have realized my life has been a big test since then, more in the last two years, and now I hope it all will make me stronger.

Stephanie Wiscombe Frew
Fourth Grade Student Survivor
(Email Submission)

I was ten years old when we moved to Cokeville, Wyoming and eleven years old when we moved away. Of all the places my family lived while I was growing up (and there were many) Cokeville was my favorite! Perhaps it was the wide open spaces or the freedom to run barefoot with my siblings and friends down to Cokeville Mercantile to buy penny candy. Or maybe it was playing at Grandpa Dayton's old barn, (affectionately known as the "fort") or even the lazy summer we spent there as kids catching crawdads and floating our innertubes down the river. Perhaps there is more to it than just this.

It is a bit ironic that, as my brother Joshua always says, "Cokeville is a happy place in my heart," when the most traumatic event that has happened in my life took place there. Even so I believe the real reason I love Cokeville is because of this almost tragic and certainly traumatic day.

May 16, 1986 brought great change and realization in my life. I learned about shock, fear and repression far beyond any feeling of this kind that I had ever known.

There was one particular moment during that three to four hour experience when for me, time is still frozen. I remember the smell of gas, sweat, the musty pages of old books. I sat in a corner of the room, my knees curled up under my arms. The chaos had subsided and most everyone was calm and engaged in one activity or another. Some were reading, coloring, and making crafts, others were watching TV. It was right after we sang *Happy Birthday* to Mr. Moore's nephew. Sitting there in the corner of that room, the reality and gravity of the situation sank deep into my heart and weighed dark and heavy on my mind. I could not leave, ever! I had no choice that would not threaten or take my life or another's. There was no longer FREEDOM! The repression was suffocating.

I felt nauseated and sick. I left the spot in the corner of the room next to the orange closets and went into the little bathroom attached to Mrs. Mitchell's first grade classroom where we were being held. I wiped my sweaty face with a damp paper towel and stared at myself in the mirror. I wondered if I would survive and how I might die. Resigned to this unknown fate, I saw through the mirror behind me a toilet and a tall garbage can with a swinging lid. I immediately decided I could fit inside and that I could quietly hide myself under the trash! At the same moment that I found a way to escape and save myself, my mind caught a glimpse of my two brothers in the room just outside the bathroom, also being held hostage. Immediately my thoughts turned away from saving myself to them; to what I could do to protect and comfort them, even if it was just until we all died. I left the bathroom, gathered my two brothers—Byron, 8, and Joshua, 6,—and brought them over from the other side of the room to be close to some of our friends, the Jamisons and the McNamaras. This brought me comfort and peace even though I could not change the danger we were in.

Less than one hour later the bomb was accidentally triggered by Doris Young and exploded. Somehow, miraculously, we were all able to escape. Seeing that he had lost control, David Young shot himself in the same bathroom in which I was going to hide. I don't know what could have happened to me. I can only speculate and recognize this small and great miracle in my life!

It is interesting to note that as we turn away from ourselves and our needs and turn our concern to others, we are empowered with courage and determination to do what is right regardless of the outcome.

No one exemplified this greater than our teachers and administrators. Mrs. Cook was the first to be taken hostage by David and Doris Young and told to help gather the teachers and students. This all happened at gunpoint. I can still see Mr. Excell, our principal, standing before us, after we were all gathered, calmly and bravely informing us that we were being held hostage and must listen and do whatever this man asked of us, reassuring us with his tone and courage that somehow we would be OK. I can only imagine the stunned fear and terror in Mr. Moore's face as he stared down the barrel of David Young's gun. He had bravely requested to be able to gather some things for us kids, to help calm and distract us. He was told that he must return quickly or some of us kids would be shot.

I'm sure today Mrs. Sparks' hands still bear the scars from burning children's hair and clothing. In the black and the smoke we couldn't see but I could hear Mrs. Sparks voice and that help guide me to the exit. The list goes on and on. We are forever indebted to them. They truly set their lives aside to protect, prolong and save ours. The way in which they each responded when they were totally unprepared, preserved our security despite the situation. From them I learned that ordinary people are life's heroes! Thank you for being my heroes!

None the less heroic were the EMTs, firefighters, police officers, army personnel, government officials, counselors, therapists, doctors and nurses, who worked behind the scenes to try to free us and to help us overcome the personal challenges we were left with after our initial survival took place. Thank you!

In the days and months that followed this incident we all tried to come to grips with what had happened to us and somehow make sense of it all. It was a different kind of challenge. It was a time of helping, healing and supporting—a time of forgiving and letting go. Some of this healing is still taking place.

I remember one specific example of this aftermath. A group of people, mostly elementary students, were gathered at the corner where you enter the school grounds. Exactly one week before, this corner had been our "safety net." This was where we ran to meet the arms of our parents, family members, friends and medical personnel as we fled the horror of the bomb room. Perhaps because it had been our "safety net" here is where we all gathered; kindergartners to sixth graders, hanging out talking about it all. Was Billie Jo Hutchinson going to make it? How were Mr. Miller and Tina Morfeld Were they going to be OK? Where were you burned? Did you have to go to the hospital? What did you see when the bomb exploded? How did you get out?" Each had their own story. I think it was a sixth grader that summed up the change that had happened in our little town when she said, "I don't know what will happen when we go back to school but I know it will be OK because we have each other."

Things had changed. The town gossip was no longer about who's made the high school sports team or who was driving the fanciest truck in town. It was still about people but it was no longer trivial. We had been through something significant together and it had made us one! I felt that even at the age of ten. From this I learned that adversity can make us stronger and can bring those who suffer together. TOGETHER.

To the parents and family members and all the others who were made aware by the media or other sources of what was happening to us and prayed for us, thank you. I learned that prayers and faith precede miracles.

In conclusion, I wish to add that I know we are not unique in our experience. Many have experienced this and much more. Throughout time man has suffered for the mistakes and ill will of others. This will always be so, as long as evil exists.

The light in all of this and probably the greatest lesson for me, personally, was that God is real and aware of each of us and is involved in each of our lives, more than we take time to notice. Sometimes it's not until something traumatic happens that we see His hand in all! I know that there was divine intervention that day. I am alive today because of Him.

I have shared some of the lessons I learned from the Cokeville incident but the greatest blessing for me is that I am alive today. I am now thirty, married to the love of my life, David Frew, and we have three darling children: Hannah, 6, Jonathan, 4, and Rebekah, 2. I have experienced many of life's ups and downs over the last twenty years and I am grateful for every day of it!

Jamie Taylor Hillyard
Fourth Grade Student Survivor
(Oral History -Telephone)

I remember coming in from lunch recess and Mrs. Sparks was reading to us when a lady came and knocked on our classroom door. She asked Mrs. Sparks to talk to her out in the hall. Mrs. Sparks came back in and told us to line up and go down to Mrs. Mitchell's classroom. When we entered the room, I remember one of the kids saying that we were being held "hostage." I didn't know what that word meant. I asked Mrs. Sparks what "hostage" meant and she explained it to me. I remember that I understood and sat down on her lap and cried because I was scared. Eventually I quit crying and got up and went and sat by my friends.

At this time the Young's didn't realize that they did not have the kindergarten class that my brother, Bret, was in. Young's realized they were missing a class and went and got them. We had to move more desks out of the room to make room for the kindergartners. I went over to my brother and moved him over into a corner of the room and got him a coloring book and some crayons. I told him not to move but to stay in that corner and color. About this time they put the square on the floor with masking tape and told us not to go into that square. I don't remember David Young talking to us very much. Sometimes he would wink at us, but the lady did most of the talking. He seemed kind of nervous. Kids were getting sick from the gas fumes. They brought in a TV and VCR and I remember the news was on and it seemed like they were talking about what was going on there at our school and so they made us turn it off. I went over and sat down against the wall.

Mrs. Mitchell was talking to Doris Young and asked Doris a question. Doris turned to answer her and that's when the bomb went off. Everything went pitch black. I remember it felt like my clothes were so hot they would melt right onto me. The room was cut in half with fire. I was on the side of the room by the window so that was the only way I could get out. I ran pushing my way to the window. I was halfway out the window when I remembered my little brother. I tried to go back in and get him but of course they wouldn't let me. They told me to run. I felt bad about that for a long time afterward, forgetting my brother like that. Mr. Miller was running ahead of me and fell just in front of me. I didn't know that he had been shot. I remember thinking something was wrong with him and wondering if he just got tired.

My dad was a firefighter at the time and walked right past me a couple of times looking for me. I finally said, "Dad, I'm right here." My brother had gotten out and my mom had him. He was one of the last kids out and he was pitch black from head to toe except for his white teeth and the whites of his eyes. My parents loaded us on a bus and they put an oxygen mask on me and we went to the hospital in Kemmerer where they treated me for smoke inhalation. When we got home my mom put us in the tub because we were still so dirty from the smoke. I think the power went out that night for a little while because I remember we were taking a bath by flashlight. I was in the middle of washing my hair and couldn't see a thing and someone let the toilet seat fall and it made me jump. I slept with my mom that night and my dad slept with my brother. I shook all night. I don't think I slept a wink.

The Sunday after the bombing they let us go back to the school if we wanted to because they thought it would be helpful to us. I found my glasses still in the room and not a thing was wrong with them. They were perfectly in one piece and I continued to wear them. The only thing was that they smelled smoky. I remember that there were A, B, C cards with pictures on them all around the room. The only one still on the wall was the letter "C" and it had a picture of a church on it.

At that age I just appreciated the fact that no one was killed except the people that held us hostage. Last year, as my little girl and little boy went to school, I realized that one was in 4th grade and the other was in kindergarten, just the same age as my brother and me at the time of the bombing. As a mother now, I don't think I could handle my kids having to go through something like that at their age. It was a miracle and we obviously all had a purpose on earth still yet to fulfill because it wasn't our time to go that day. I have learned that our Heavenly Father loves us and has a purpose for each of us. We need to live every day to the fullest because you never know when it might be your last.

Julie Anderson Hunting
Absent Fourth Grade Student
(Oral History—Telephone)

I was there half a day and I ate lunch. Mom drove the bus. We left and went to get Wendy from the high school. I forgot my books and went back to the elementary school. I couldn't get in, the doors were locked. I could see my class lined up. They were the last class to go in, I think. I asked Mom if I should go around. She said, "just get in." So I did and we left.

My sister Debbie and Renae Teichert (now) were good friends and I was tending Renae's two older kids, Brooke and Brandon. Debbie was moving to St. George and they lived in the same apartment building. I watched it on TV. I was scared. I was in 4th grade. My biggest thing was I wanted to go home. You know, you think if you could just be there you could make it better.

Lea Kae Roberts Weston
Absent Fourth Grade Student
(Email Submission)

Nervous anticipation filled the air. It seemed as though every living creature knew of the difficult circumstances. I glanced up toward the clear blue sky. Pillars of sunlight faintly made their way through the leaves of the tree that stood in front of my grandma Jennie Robert's white house. My mind was racing with many unorganized thoughts; *What is happening? Can it be as serious as my sister made it sound? Why did mom have to go shopping in Evanston on a day like this? How did I luck out? I wonder if everyone's OK?*

The sound of a passing police car interrupted my thoughts. I looked ahead and realized more people had gathered on the street. Some were crying, upset and distraught and others were busy comforting and consoling. Many police cars passed, followed by ambulances and fire trucks. Every community nearby sent help. News reporters were gathering trying to catch all the latest details. One of their helicopters landed in the middle of the football field southeast of where I was standing. Our little town had never had so much excitement.

Grandma's old hinged door creaked. I glanced over and my older brother Denton approached me. I could tell he was very upset from the nervous energy he portrayed. His voice cracked as he said, "Lea you stay right here, I'm going to see if I can help."

Being extremely bored, my thoughts began to wander. *The guy I had passed in the hall...is he the one? I did have a horrible, sick feeling as he waved and smiled at me when mom and I were leaving the building. If mom had been just a few minutes later in picking me up...*

My sister Cheree's sharp voice startled me, "Lea, it is your turn to watch Nathan!" Cheree was in the eighth grade so she usually had the chore of watching our little brother Nathan.

Nathan was born with cerebral palsy, so he required constant supervision. I had been babysitting him since Mom left so I found it a relief not to worry about him. I quickly replied a firm "No! I'm not going to. I've been watching him all afternoon, it is your turn." She knew how stubborn I could be so she stomped in the house letting the screen door slam behind her.

I wondered, *What is going to happen? Is everyone going to be all right? I can't believe my two brothers are in there. I sure hope nothing happens to them. Our family would never be the same without them. Cameron, being a sixth grader, probably feels responsible for all the others younger than him. Collin, only a first grader, probably doesn't have the faintest idea what is happening.*

The minutes seemed like hours. It was about 3:45 and school should have been out at 3:20. Then for a moment the world seemed to stop turning, time stood still. I heard a big explosion. Black smoke quickly filled the air...it had happened. I suddenly felt weak and a cold sweat beaded on my forehead as I thought about my brothers and classmates. Everything became a blur, it was as if I was under water.

The crowd of people on Main Street had become one big mass. Everyone was frantic. Kids were screaming with a horror in their voices that can't be described. This wasn't a dream, the bomb had gone off.

The next thing I noticed was Cameron on my mom's bike, pedaling furiously toward home. Collin was in the baby seat, clinging to the sides. Their white hair glistened in the sun, but spots of black covered their bodies.

"We are over here!" I yelled, waving my arms. With terrified faces they hopped off the bike and ran into the outstretched arms of Grandma. Collin crouched in a corner of the entryway and sat shaking, with his knees pulled tightly to his chest. Cameron sat on the couch with a blank stare on his face. They were alive! Grandma was shedding tears of joy as she wiped off the black smoke that covered their arms and faces. They were safe for now. We all gave our hugs with words that we only hoped would give them comfort.

Minutes later my mother arrived, unsure of what she would

find. Overcome with joy and relief. she gathered me and my brothers in her arms, holding us closer than ever before.

This senseless act had immediate and long-term effects on my family. Collin couldn't sleep through the night, so his bed was moved beside my parents so he could relax and rest. All of us struggled when nighttime came, even Cheree and Denton at times. The nightmares continued for years but decreased in their frequency and intensity as we got older. Collin and Cameron would never talk about that day and would become very upset when it was mentioned. I had to visit with Dr. Sandall because of all my confusion and curiosity about what had happened in that room. We lost our trust that day, we lost part of ourselves. We were psychologically scarred, never to be the same. I was always looking over my shoulder, scanning crowds, wondering if and when evil would unveil itself again. I seemed to gain a greater appreciation for life at the tender age of nine. Life was precious, never to be taken for granted again.

I soon began to realize the magnitude of the event and God's hand in preserving the life of my brothers and all the others who were trapped in that room. He had His tender, merciful hands outstretched on our behalf that day. Not only were lives preserved, but many were comforted and given peace in time of need. He watched over us, not only on that dreadful day, but the many days, months and years that followed. He has healed my broken heart, rebuilt my trust and love of mankind. Little did I know that His miracle performed that day was just the beginning; the beginning of many more miracles that would become a part of my life.

Lori Nate Conger
Fifth Grade Student Survivor
(Email Submission)

I was in the fifth grade, barely eleven years old, on May 16, 1986. Having grown up in a small town, I felt sheltered and secure. Nothing tragic had ever happened to anyone I knew, and I thought that scary things only happened somewhere else. I never dreamed that I would ever experience such a terrifying, life-changing event, but my life was changed that day in many ways. I don't think a person can go through a life-threatening experience and not be impacted, and as the years go by I continue to learn and grow from the miracles of that day. I hope to be able to share in a few short paragraphs what May 16th has come to mean to me and some important truths that I hope to never forget.

First, having had the privilege of growing up in a home where God was at the center of our lives, a home of prayer and scripture study and church attendance, I had a strong knowledge that God was real, I knew that He was my Heavenly Father and that He loved me more than I could know, even as an eleven-year-old child. I knew He heard and answered the prayers of His children, and that He was always there when I needed Him. I believed in miracles and had faith that with God nothing was impossible; what I didn't really understand or consider was that God is absolutely aware and in charge. The reason no one but our captors lost their lives that day is because God didn't allow it. He was in charge, not David and Doris Young.

I remember sitting in that classroom wondering what our fate would be, wondering if any of us would die, wondering if it would be my two brothers or me. At that time it seemed that David Young had a lot of power over our destiny, that our lives were in his hands, but they never were; they were in the Lord's, and He said, "No." "No, you cannot take the lives of these children; no, their time is not yet; no, I still need them to fulfill their roles on earth." If any one of us had would have lost our life that day it would have been because it was the Lord's will, not David Young's. I truly believe in the scripture that states, ...*fear not what man can do, for God shall be with you forever and ever.* (D&C 122:9)

Next, that day has brought to me the realization that life is indeed fragile. I went from thinking that the scary stuff we hear on the news every day only happens to someone else, somewhere else, to thinking it has just as good of a chance of happening to me or my family, right here. There is seldom a day that goes by that I don't find myself thanking the Lord for the opportunity of living that day.

It is not a light thing to me that I am married to an incredibly good man and am a mother to three amazing children. I am truly living my dream, and so I thank God daily for my life, knowing that it, or the lives of my family, could be over in an instant. I tell my children each day, every moment I can, that I love them. At times when I am tempted to spend my time selfishly when a family member needs me, I remember that they could be gone tomorrow and then my priorities change. I try to not worry incessantly about losing someone I love, only to take full advantage of each teaching and loving moment, knowing it may not always be there.

I will always be grateful to my mother for sending us off to school that day as prepared for the events that took place as we could be. We had read scriptures, had prayed together, and she had kissed each of us and told us she loved us. Of course she would never have believed what we would be facing that day, but she'd done all she could to send us out the door with faith and a sense of security. That lesson has stuck with me, and so I try now each day to do the most important things first, like studying scriptures, having prayer, hugging and kissing my husband and children. Who knows what the day will bring? I hope to do all I can to prepare them to face whatever may come with faith and courage, just as our mother prepared us.

Lastly, I have learned undeniably that God is truly an unchanging God of miracles. May 16th, 1986 was a day of miracles—

miracles of all magnitudes. Of course the preservation of 154 lives was the most obvious, but I believe there were miracles of all forms that day: families became united, angels intervened, hearts were changed, prayers were answered. That is the way God has worked since the beginning of time, and that is how He will always work.

I think each individual had their own miracle that day; for me, it was the knowledge I gained of how close God really is to His children. I know the Lord knew me individually and blessed me because there is a block of time that I have never been able to remember, and I believe it was His way of protecting me emotionally. I didn't see angels that day, but I do remember being directed and guided by someone. Maybe some day I'll know who.

The miracles of that event extended far past May 16th. The months and years that followed required continued faith and answered prayers as families and individuals united to try to heal—physically and emotionally. Perhaps in these personal stories of healing the greatest miracles occurred. It wasn't easy for me; my scars were not from burns but from the emotional trauma of experiencing such an event. I was old enough to understand how serious our situation was, and to worry, not only for my own life, but for the lives of my friends, teachers, and my two brothers who were also there, and for my family that we would leave behind. But with counseling and time and faith, my fear turned into profound trust and a testimony of the reality of the nearness of God to His children. I have learned what a wonderful gift life is. May 16th never passes for me without spending time on my knees in gratitude to my Father in Heaven for the miracles of that day, for the miracle of life itself.

I feel a tremendous responsibility as a survivor, not only to value my life, but to live it the best way I can. I also feel a responsibility to share my experiences of that day and my testimony. I appreciate others who have shared so that I could learn from them. I think it is important that we never forget. If there is any way that I can possibly show gratitude for all that happened it is to always remember what the Lord did for us that day. Some of the memories are painful and scary, but the outcome was truly miraculous and one I hope to never forget.

The Youngs told us that this would be an experience we could tell our children and grandchildren about—they were right. I hope to tell them over and over of the miracles of that day and to pass on the knowledge that I have gained that the heavens are open, prayers are answered, and God loves His children.

Janaan Bennion Lake
Fifth Grade Student Survivor
(Email Submission)

I was kneeling by a chair, coloring a picture when the bomb went off. The room went pitch black and then filled with orange flames. I was surprised that the bomb went off, and as I tried to escape I wondered if I was dying. I instinctively knew that I was closer to the window than the door, and I ran to the light coming from the window. When I reached the window, my fifth-grade teacher pulled me out. I looked all over my body to see if I was on fire or hurt. As far as I could tell, I didn't think so. But I still wasn't sure that I was OK.

Outside the school was chaos: kids screaming and crying, parents frantically searching for their children, emergency personnel yelling at us to come down the street and general confusion. Most of my memories after the explosion are quite blurry. I do remember running, just running anywhere until I found someone from my family. My entire family except for my father but including my mother, grandmother, brother and sister were all in that classroom with me. My mother happened to be substitute teaching that day, and I was glad she was with me. Her presence was comforting, and when she told me we would be OK I believed her.

I found my brother first. We then kept running and yelling until we found my mother and sister. My father soon found us. He searched for the last family member missing, my grandmother. She was one of the last people out of the school and was quite unrecognizable from the smoke and dirt. My mother was badly burned on her arm and neck, and my grandmother wasn't breathing well, so my father took them to the nearest hospital. My siblings and I walked out of that classroom without any physical harm.

The next days, weeks, and even months were rather surreal in many ways as our small town dealt with the aftermath of the bombing.

Miraculously everyone lived except our captors. Gradually, though, my life got back to normal as my mother and grandmother recovered and returned home and as I settled into another school year.

Twenty years later I don't really think much about that day. I am fortunate that I don't have any physical or emotional scars that cause me to think of it often. I am grateful that our town can slip into anonymity again and not be associated with other horrific school tragedies like Columbine or Beslan. Once in a while, though, I remind myself that I am lucky God has allowed me to still be on this journey.

Colton T. McDermott
5th grade Student Survivor
(Email Submission)

May 16 1986 was a day that you really have to give to the teachers and the Principal, Max Excell. They did an outstanding job of trying to take all of our minds off of what was really going on that day. We sang songs to try to lighten the mood a little. I specifically remember the 10' x 10' box they made around the bomb to protect us just in case, then they finally got the Youngs to let them open windows to let the gas fumes out.

I'm not a religious person but I do know God was there that day protecting us, He knew that it wasn't time for any of us to go yet. Now I am just thankful to be here and to have a beautiful wife and a handsome son. I would like to give a Big Thanks to all the teachers and, of course the principal, Max Excell.

Brad Shane Nate
Fifth Grade Student Survivor
(Oral History –Telephone)

The basics from what I remember—I have to mention what came before. I remember there was a play the night before, isn't that crazy? It was in the old auditorium. I remember studying about Christa McAuliff, we were talking about the explosion of the Challenger—it was weeks before.

But anyway, I remember it was lunch and the recess bell rang to come in from recess. We all headed in to Mr. Miller's music department. It also doubled as the art department. I played the percussion. It also was the storage department for a lot of the art. Mr. Miller was one of the first taken, actually before class even started, so we were waiting for him. And, as kids do, we started playing World War II or some kind of game and I remember shooting rubber bands and just playing around and I was with Colten McDermott because he was a percussionist, too. We got bored and went into the percussion area and we were playing around with the clay. Meanwhile, she came in, Doris Young, and she had collected everybody and we were still in that room. We were throwing the clay around and somehow, between playing, part of the clay hit the base drum and she heard it and she came in and got us. She probably would not have ever known we were there.

So, she started walking us down. Most of our class was way ahead of us. Even when she came in to talk to us, we weren't really interested in leaving. On our way down to the room, I had to go to the bathroom and we were passing the main bathroom area, and I didn't tell her I just went in. I was very surprised. She came in to get me. She just walked in. I had to go. I did get to go, but I had stage fright. She said, "Fine, I'll wait outside." She told me I had a very short time to go.

She was getting perturbed with us. I believe Colten even went into the bathroom. We were taking our time. We passed the drinking fountain. Of course, we had to get a drink. I think she was stressed out. We were kids and we weren't in a hurry. We were taking our time. She grabbed us and dragged us in.

I didn't think much about it. As we entered the room, first thing I noticed was the guns. I was very interested because growing up on the ranch and being around guns, it was very interesting. She did tell us, "You have to come down. It's an assembly." So I thought it was a gun assembly of some sort.

As I walked in I thought it was odd to have an assembly there but I didn't disbelieve it. Meanwhile, there was a gentleman, Kris Casper, and he was just a good guy who took the boys in and was kind of a big brother. But he was a very big man. He pretty much stayed to himself in the room. Meanwhile I went over to Mr. Moore and I sat close to him and he was my main teacher even though Mr. Miller was supposed to be in charge of our class during that period. Being as old as I was, after Mr. Moore explained what was going on, I knew it wasn't good and understood the severity. A lot of younger kids might not have understood as much it seemed.

I remember David Young getting tired and wanting to move forward and put that square around him. Tape the square. I remember later, Mr. Moore lying there on the floor after we got the TV in, I remember my head was on his belly and he joked with me saying, I always knew how to find Mr. Moore's soft spot. I remember watching *GI Joe* and *Transformers* on the TV. Before the TV had my attention, I wondered if I ever would see my mom and dad. I don't know if I believed it could really happen, it was just a "routine wonder" kind of thing and it repeated a few times.

I remember actually before I laid on Mr. Moore's belly, back to Kris Casper. I felt like I had a good relationship with him. I walked over and talked to him. I believe Mr. Young told him he would hurt him or kill him if he tried anything. Kris was a very big man. Especially for me, I was a little kid. He said everything will be fine. He kind of stayed around the 5th graders, I believe. I just remember I liked him very much and he seemed to like me or the boys in our class as well, we just did a lot of stuff together.

So anyway, I'm on Mr. Moore's belly and I heard someone ask me to leave, to go over to the window. So I sat up and kind of looked around. Then I laid back down. Now this wasn't like a still, small voice. It was like a person talking and I knew it wasn't in my head. Then remember the voice again, asking me to go to the window. And I remember looking around, it was definitely an adult voice. And I ignored it again.

Meanwhile, Mr. Moore got up around this time and shortly thereafter the voice came again and so I went over to the window. The voice actually said, "Go over to the window." Colten was by the window so I went on over. We were friends. So we started playing games. I sat up on the windowsill on the far right windowsill. Actually it would be far left if you were looking out the window. We were playing many different games, but the game I remember was this wood block puzzle game. I remember as we were playing I had a really good hold of this piece of wood puzzle. It was knocked out of my hand but yet it wasn't knocked out of my hand for I just knew I had a firm hold of it and was dumbfounded by it being dropped. I looked down to see it, and I was kind of puzzled and the bomb went off.

The blast was very powerful. I weighed very little, sixty-five pounds or less. It actually sucked me into the window, behind first. I was stuck in that window bent over. My head was near my feet. My rear end was out the window. I was kind of wedged. The handle on the window was in my back. When it went off—the bomb—it was the loudest boom; even today I think I can remember it. It hurt my ears. It was as if you had turned the sound completely off after the explosion. Then it got dark very, very fast.

It seemed forever in my mind, but very short. As I remember looking up, I could see someone on fire, which turned out to be Doris. I couldn't see clearly, just someone or something on fire that was moving. I didn't know it was her at the time. Many hands on my face and all were pushing on me, which was scratching my back real bad with the handle, and I fell out the window. I remember someone, and I'm assuming an adult, yelling "RUN! Run fast!"

Meanwhile, as crazy as it seems or sounds while this was happening, in my mind I was wondering, "Is this how she died?" Thinking of Christa McAuliff. It was dark and I was thinking I was dead. It was dark and then I got pushed into the light. So I thought I was in heaven. I had died. And then I remember the sound being turned up, being turned up very fast, like the crescendo from nothing to very loud, very fast. Then there was a lot of high screaming. And that's about the time the sound came up. I remember thinking when I was in heaven, there wasn't any sound. I remember ringing in my ears, like after gunshot going off too close to one's ear. I remember being short of breath from the initial blow into the window.

And then the voice that was telling me to run made me realize, "Hey, I AM ALIVE!" I stood up and I could see kids coming out the window. Some head first, some feet first. Some anyway they could. I wanted to run and yet I was scared because I was told that other people outside were with David and they had guns. The helicopters would be with him. I don't remember seeing a helicopter at the time but I remember hearing him saying something about it. So I took off and I started to run. I was passing people, kids. I was running really good actually. I got around the corner. I didn't go over any fences. I ran around the corner and saw cops with guns; I remember seeing a lot of parents. I stopped by the ambulance that was on the corner by Main Street, I just knew I was the first kid on that corner. I don't remember any kids, just adults and then someone saying, "Stay here, you're OK." I didn't believe him because I had gone into a very hyper and overly excited state.

I remember seeing Mr. Miller kneeling on the left of me saying, "My back. My back" and the EMTs were pulling on his shirt and I just saw blood. It didn't seem like an extreme amount but it was coming out of his back. At that point I turned into a Ferrari and I was heading to my grandma's house and the peddle was on the floor. Parents later said they were trying to chase me down, but there was just no way they were going to catch me, I was going too fast. I still don't remember any kids. There was no one on the road except some parents out on their lawns but no one on the road. I was cruising. It just seemed really quick. The adults on the lawns were trying to catch me, to comfort me or whatever. I would actually zigzag away and I could only think about my grandma Alva Nate. It was the only place I could think of that I considered "safe." It was close and always safe. I assumed people would be there, family or whatever.

So I came around the back, as that was the way to enter. I remember kicking that door open so wide, I didn't touch it I just kicked it wide open. I came barreling up the stairs. My grandma had the biggest surprised face I could think of. It took me only two steps from the door to her arms. I almost knocked her over, to be honest. Even then, she was still frail. At that point, I think I just started to sob. It was over and I emotionally let go. I remember Grandma was very good, She was getting my mind off what was going on. She got out color crayons and books. Kevin Thornock was in the house, he was in high school at the time. I remember him asking, how did you get here so fast? It just came on the radio. I remember the radio being so wrong. Saying there was bodies, like everyone was dead. I remember thinking everyone was fine. I do remember thinking Mr. Miller was going to die. But I knew everyone else was going to be OK.

I also remember praying. I remember singing *Happy Birthday*. Sorry, this is looking back. To whom we were singing *Happy Birthday*, I don't remember. And I remember praying. Personal and in a group. But not really out loud. Even the group one. I don't remember anyone out loud. It was almost like we prayed individually in a group.

I also remember not actually seeing a person, but seeing while we were praying and stuff, it was like someone was there, but they were invisible. But yet not totally invisible. You could see an outline. You could see the background moving. You knew they were there. Like how a movie portrays invisibility. I don't remember many people. Just one particular person. The way I...it's kind of hard and spiritual...I just remember my honest feeling was...I honestly thought it was Christ. This person was very powerful and you could tell He was there. I remember thinking, later when I was asked if I saw anybody, it was calming to know that a powerful person was there. It was like viewing and feeling the person at the same time. But it wasn't someone you could just say that's a person...sort of like invisible, but not. But yet it moved, it didn't stay in one spot in the room.

From the moment we prayed, I don't remember a time NOT seeing it. At first, I was getting my mind off of the bombing. I was playing games, watching movies, laying on Mr. Moore. It wasn't until we got together and we said, "You know we should be praying." Praying was second nature to me. Everything spiritual was what I knew internally. I knew it. Like going to church wasn't just because your mom tells you to, it followed my own inner conscience. So at the point when people said we should be praying I just thought OK, and once we started doing spiritual things, then I saw it. HIM!

I talked to my brother Greg, but I don't remember what about. I probably told him that I was scared. I prayed right before I was watching TV. And then I remember thinking, when that voice was going on, I remember thinking, "Who was that?" and, "Was that Chris or who?" I wanted it to be someone in the room, a real person. Then I realized it was that powerful being. Let me put it this way, nothing has ever come close to it ever. I would say in my mind, if it wasn't Jesus, it was someone really powerful high up. I just remember how powerful it was, I could feel the power of Him. First I was playing to not feel scared, and then later I was just playing because I wasn't scared.

On the spiritual side, I didn't see a person, person. It was a being and it wasn't like a mist. I could tell it was living, walking, moving. It was not an unnatural thing, though. It was like...I knew. At first it was startling, and I was surprised, curious, very curious. I actually caught myself watching it. It seemed a lot of time had passed by, but all this was very, very short. This was at the very end. And then, like I said, back to the part where I was holding that puzzle piece, literally it was like it was knocked out of my hand. I remember feeling peaceful when I was thinking about Christa McAuliff, like it was a relief it was all over. And then I think the whole getting out and then realizing I was alive and getting to my grandma's, I had to release again.

My mom wasn't around for quite a while. No one showed up for quite a while, my brother or my cousins. Then they did show up. My parents still weren't there. They were not around. My mom was out of town. I don't know where my dad was. My security was with my grandma. I remember it was later in the day when my parents finally were there to comfort me.

I remember my Grandma Nate saying, "Brad, your hair." My hair just fell off into her hands, it was burnt. My face would have been really burnt if I hadn't dropped that piece of wood and looked down. My head was down and away. Colten may have partially blocked it away. Obviously there was a lot of heat. Almost all the hair on the back of my head was gone or singed badly. That piece of wood had to have been dropped or knocked on purpose or I would have been worse off.

I guess everyone was looking for me. They were doing a head count. I guess no one knew where I was. Aunt Linda told them I was at Grandma's, I'm told. I believe she was on the steps of Art Robinson's house. She saw me run by, I think. I remember everyone looking at me as I ran by. They seemed confused like they had to count to ten before they realized I was real and alive and could say, "OK, you're OK now."

I did go to the hospital in Kemmerer for smoke inhalation. They wanted to check to see if my head was burnt. They said my hair would grow back. I have a birthmark on the side of my face and no one remembers it being visible until after the bombing. It was never noticeable before. It covers my whole left side of my face. It is very light.

I do remember since then, my mom tells me this story, I don't remember as much as she does. She says almost exactly a year later to the day I had a nightmare of it. I remember having a nightmare. It was almost like I was reliving the day. My mission call, years later, came the day of or the day after the anniversary of the bombing.

I have always hated that school, before the bombing until even now. I don't go in that school alone. My only memories of that school aren't very good. I remember moving into it from the old school after it was built. I remember many fire alarms, false fire alarms. They actually sent us home, they thought they were fires. They thought once there was a fire upstairs. I always thought something was amiss with the building. I was only in there 4th, 5th, and 6th grade, I think. I remember at least four occasions where they actually sent us home because it had gone off enough that they weren't sure that there wasn't a fire.

I'm rarely in that school after hours. I don't like to be in there. I do sometimes have to go. They have dinners. They have fundraisers. But I don't like to go in there. I don't like to use the bathroom.

The main thing I want to close with, is just that I know that it was a special event that many people ponder over... this could have happened or that could have happened...I felt this part of the spirit or I saw a person, but all in all, we all knew something very special happened there, and I personally cannot deny a Supreme Being, or Christ, being there. I want people to know that there is a God and He was with us all. For those that believe, I want them to know He was there. For those that don't believe in God, I have to tell you, this happened, this is real and I did see what I saw. It was so physically *there*, that I cannot ever deny it.

I cannot say, "What a coincidence everyone got out." It was a miracle, all the way from the littlest thing to the most amazing thing. I was lucky enough to see the things I saw, as well as I was not lucky enough to see some things that other's had seen. One of the greatest things I think of the most is, "What happened with that piece of wood?" How simple this was and how much it made a difference in the outcome in my mind.

Now, twenty years later I am happily married to a lovely gal. Her name is Stephanie. I'm living my life, enjoying the friendships I had back then and now and the opportunity I have to continue on.

The other thing is, most people can't imagine that this can happen to them. I say, it can happen to you. Not the bombing, or some kind of tragedy, but the "miracle!"

BranDee Hess Prows
Fifth Grade Student Survivor
(Oral History)

I am now married and I have a boy and a girl. They are in the same school that I was in when it happened. The main thing is that it's in the past and I'm alive today.

Joanna Metcalfe Stowell
Fifth Grade Student Survivor
(Typed Submission)

I'll never forget the feelings of that day, even if some of the particular details are no longer as clear. I do remember that the weather was beautiful, the kind of late spring brightness that, as a child, I longed for. I mark that day as the one in which I grew up, for those events brought on a level of maturity some never reach.

Not everyone faces their own mortality at eleven years of age. I remember David Young's face now as a bearded blur with cold eyes. Doris is even fuzzier, I recall simply a mousy woman with glasses. The faces that stand out sharply are the ones I have known and loved...and still do. They are heroes, all of them. I see Max Excell, who with great kindness and without patronizing me, explained the perilous circumstances we were in. There is Rocky Moore, who comforted me while I cried. I can still see Kliss Sparks, whose bravery is a marvel. After the bomb went off my brother's shirt caught fire. She put it out with her bare hands. And I can still hear Jack Mitchell's call, "Get down! Get out! Get down! Get out!" It is the voice that guided me to safety.

And so I ran, bursting through the double doors of the school into the clear air and sunshine, into the loving arms of family and an entire community anxious to help and comfort. In the years that followed I tried to put the bombing behind me, it was a nightmare I didn't want to remember. Little things, however, would call it back: the day the back window of our van exploded because of heat, or the roaring grease fire at my first job. After each incident I would pull myself together and move on, but May 16th lurked inside me, a wound that never really healed. I finally came face to face with my buried feelings while serving a mission for The Church of Jesus Christ of Latter-day Saints.

My first area in Arkansas was a military town called Jacksonville and I worked there in the spring of 1996, almost ten years after the bombing. Raised, as I was, by a news hound, I found the requirement to leave the world behind hard at times. At a dinner appointment one night I found myself overwhelmed with curiosity about world events. A newspaper was close at hand, and I guiltily opened it to see some of the headlines. The first one my eyes fell upon was about a school shooting in Scotland. A man walked past a school playground, pulled out a gun, opened fire on the children there, and then shot himself. I remember feeling absolutely horrified as I read the number of the dead. I hid in a corner, shaking and crying, completely overwhelmed with pity for the victims and their families, and all the while thinking, *why am I alive?* Why did that particular violent episode end with so many dead, while the Cokeville bombing ended with a miracle? We, as children, were certainly no better than they. Why was I alive?

There came, at that moment, the clear and unmistakable answer: *You have work to do.* I realized that I have a purpose to fulfill in life and that my time on earth is sacred. It is a gift given by a merciful Father in Heaven. I give meaning to that gift as I do my best to fill each day with goodness. I now understand that the events of May 16, 1986 are not a nightmare to be forgotten, but a miracle to be celebrated. Thus, my New Year's Day comes every May. That is my time to look back on the past, make plans for the future, resolve to do better, and rejoice in the gift of my life.

Travis Walker
Fifth Grade Student Survivor
(Email Submission)

The thought of having my words on paper is a little daunting. I would rather talk to everyone than have them read my jumbled words, but as I thought about this opportunity, I wanted to take it so I could relay some thoughts of how the bombing has through the years changed my perception of life and what is important. I know that some who read this will judge and possibly ridicule, but for the survivors, I think there is a connection and an understanding, so I will share a few thoughts that if, in some way, make someone think or smile, it was worth it.

To all who has been involved in this experience and the Cokeville Miracle Foundation I say THANK YOU. I think that one of the best things that has happened through the compilation of this book was the quiet moments the writers would have had, thinking about the experience and thinking about how their experience, unique as they all are, shaped their lives.

I know that was my experience. Thinking about what I would say has been a great opportunity for me to reflect on how it changed my life and what I would say to the world, my friends, and my family. How has it changed me? First of all, I believe that the things we go through in life make us into who we are but more important is how we react to those experiences. I think how we react shapes us into who we can become and who we will be tomorrow. So I think that the events on May 16, 1986 changed all of us and we will someday understand all that it did to shape and mold us. How we reacted to the event has shaped who we are and helped those around us and I think that is a miracle in itself. We could have just forgotten or hidden what happened but we didn't. We chose to share and in that sharing others have been touched and experienced miracles.

As I thought about my experience, I didn't want to share my

story. I save my story for those times when I am prompted to share it with an individual or a group that possibly needs it. But I wanted to share some advice and things I have learned from this experience:

To the World:

I would say that God is real and that He is aware of your needs, not your *wants,* but your *needs,* and that if you open your heart and go to Him, He will protect and heal you. God knows you better than you know yourself and is willing to help with any concern or heartache that you have. I have seen His protection and His hand of comfort in my life and in the lives of others around me and I know that you're a child of God and that He will help you, too.

To my Friends:

I would say life is short, enjoy the world around you. I would say that out of this experience I have learned that life isn't perfect but life is what we make it. We can look down and think about all the bad things that happen or we can look up and see all the great things that the world has to offer. It is easy to take for granted all the blessings that we have, but in the quiet moments, take the time to be grateful.

Be willing to share. God made enough for everyone but it is up to us to share it.

To my Family:

I know that families can be together forever and I would say THANK YOU for all the good times. I am looking forward to many more. Out of this experience I have become so grateful for a family that I can talk to and rely on for any need that I have. I have an amazing family and I would let them know that they're the most important thing in my life and that "family is worth fighting for." Having a strong family is worth all the hurt feelings, all the sleepless nights, and all the worry. I would let my lovely sisters know I was there for them in that room and that I will be there for them forever. There is no mountain too high to climb as long as you have a family member to lean on. Love ya heaps!

To my lovely wife and kids:

Out of my experience I think I have learned to look for the good things, and so should they. I would tell them to enjoy every sunrise and every sunset because with the coming of each there is something new and exciting that will need to be explored or enjoyed. I have also learned that there are a lot of great things in life if we will only take the chance to experience them. They can enhance our lives for the better and will strengthen not only us, but those around us.

I would tell my wife Katherine that she is everything to me and I am excited to spend forever with her. I would tell my kids that not only do they have a daddy who loves them more than life itself, but that they have a Heavenly Father Who loves them even more than I can imagine and Who will protect and help them through life. I would tell my kids to look out for each other and be willing to make whatever sacrifice is needed to help each other and keep each other close through life.

I would tell my wife and kids thank you for the opportunity to know you and to be a part of your life. I love you.

Thank you again for letting me share my thoughts. I know that my life has been shaped by the challenges that I have had, but they have made me into what I am today, so for that I am grateful. I hope that these words will help someone, or possibly be a reminder of what is important in life. If no one gets anything out of this, that will be fine because it has been a great cleansing for me and an opportunity to reflect on what is the most priceless in my life. I am truly blessed and need to be grateful everyday for the things that I have been given.

Angie Nostaja Weston
Fifth Grade Student Survivor
(Typed Submission)

I can vividly remember the details of that day, as if it were yesterday. When I'm reminded of it, or someone starts talking about it, a flood of feelings and emotions come pouring in. I knew that we had witnessed a miracle and I knew that for some reason I was given a second chance, I truly was given the gift of life.

Through the years my heart has healed and as crazy as it sounds I am glad to have gone through such a tragic ordeal because even today it makes me want to be a better person. As I watched the people run from those burning buildings on September 11th, I knew what they were feeling. I know the feeling of desperately running for your life. I remember the feeling of chaos being everywhere. I went out the classroom window that day, but I remember even after I had gotten out, I still wasn't sure that I was safe and that it was over. I remember how crazy it all was with paramedics everywhere and parents searching for their children, burned victims crying out in pain.

I know that I will never forget what I went through and witnessed that day, but I hope I will always be a better person because of it. Really great things can come from tragic events. I remember a community coming together as one. Enemies became friends, people forgot their troubles one with another. Strangers were willing to help out in any way they could. Everyone realized just how fragile life was and how a whole town could have been drastically changed had the outcome been different. It didn't matter what religious background we came from or what we believed, we all knew that the reason we got out of that building that day was from power from a higher source.

I can't believe twenty years have come and gone since that bittersweet day, but I'm very thankful that I have had that many years to reflect on a wonderful miracle that I was given.

Amy Bagaso Williams
Fifth Grade Student Survivor
(Email Submission)

Refined by Fire

Each year I celebrate two birthdays. The first is August 16th, the day of my physical birth, and the second is the day I call my spiritual birth, it is the day I truly celebrate my life, and it is May 16th.

On that day so many years ago in a small classroom, as a frightened ten year old girl, I faced my mortality. For the first time in my young life I exercised faith in a God I did not know. I found Him as I knelt to pray with a young kindergarten teacher and a small group of children. I felt His love as warm and strong as the sun on my face, and His peace as safe and secure as the arms of my mother. I knew from the moment I felt His presence that He was aware of my situation and no matter how that day would turn out, He would always be there. His grace and love gave me the courage and the strength to endure that day and the difficult hardships I faced during the months that followed.

The true miracle of my experience was not only that I survived, or that the severe third degree burns I suffered healed without a trace, it was that I learned I was not alone in this world. I was a daughter of God and He knew me and loved me. My life was not chance. I had a specific purpose. My prayer was answered that day by a merciful and gracious Father in Heaven who granted me the gift of a second chance.

I remember the events of that day, vivid and clear, as if it happened yesterday. Every second of every moment is locked in my memory; the nauseating smell of gas, the distant hum of a helicopter, the soft sound of weeping children, the high pitched sound of the explosion, the choking smoke, the bright red and orange flames, and the strange tingling sensation of my skin burning, and the sight of John Miller as he lay lifeless on the sidewalk, his white shirt covered in dark red blood.

I have not forgotten because I choose to remember. The bravery of Rocky Moore and Jack Mitchell as they slapped the fire out of my clothing with their bare hands, the courage of my eight year old brother, Andy, who was burned while coming to my rescue, the hug of comfort from Delbert Rentfro as he guided me to safety, the compassion of Glenna Walker as she carried me to an ambulance, the shouts of excitement and happiness as everyone celebrated that no one perished, the joy of being with my family again, and finally, the hope of tomorrow—I will always remember.

A seed of faith was planted deep within my heart that day, and it continues to grow. I have often thought about that innocent, loving and spirited little girl who entered that classroom. I know she is not forgotten, or lost. She has become my hope, faith, aspirations and all I believe to be pure and good in this world. She continues to teach the woman I have become as I am reminded daily of my many blessings. I still believe, as I did with all my young girl's heart, that humanity is great and full of love, grace, and goodness.

In many ways I have found myself in that small room again on different occasions in my life as I have faced great sorrows and overcome difficult challenges. Each time I have been through the "Refiners Fire," my character has been strengthened and molded and I have been given a deeper understanding and appreciation for my life. I believe that our lives are not our own nor do they belong to us. They are borrowed. By turning my life over to God I have been completely healed and have done more with my life than I ever could have done on my own. I have been changed by His love in ways I never could have imagined. This knowledge has empowered me. It has given me the strength, courage, comfort and determination to live my life the best way I can. This is the gift I give back to my Heavenly Father for my second chance.

I treasure every experience I have had over the last twenty years and often think about the life I almost missed. I compare my life to the parable of the ten talents in the New Testament. Like the talents,

I am responsible for the sacred gift of time I have been given as it will one day be accounted for. It is precious and can never be relived. What I do with this time is my choice, so it must be used carefully. I do not take it for granted. Every laugh, every hug, every tear, and every moment is cherished.

I have stood at the top of the Eiffel Tower and watched the sun set over Paris just as I dreamt about in Mr. Metcalfe's history class. I have seen the Stratford Upon Avon I read about as I learned Shakespeare from Mr. Birch's eighth grade literature class. I have had the chance to attend college, experience new adventures, meet new friends, travel, find the love of my life and know the joy of motherhood and I have felt the presence of heaven while rocking my son to sleep at night.

I know my priorities and I choose wisely. I tell my husband I love him every day and spend as much time with him as possible. I choose to play with my son instead of doing housework and hold him just a little longer. I am slow to anger and quick to forgive and have learned to live my life without regrets. I am a more compassionate woman, a more loving wife, a more patient and devoted mother, a more understanding daughter, a more accepting sister, a more dependable friend and a more considerate human being than I ever could have been without this experience.

There is a poem that has become the theme of my life. The author is unknown and the title is *The Plan of the Master Weaver*. In short, our lives are each a weaving in progress, and every moment, every choice, every experience represents a colorful thread that is delicately interwoven into the tapestry of our lives creating a unique and beautiful pattern. I am grateful for the chance I have had to sit at the loom and I can't wait to see this masterpiece I am making. Each of us who survived that day, in our own way, resembles the ancient and legendary Chinese Phoenix that rose from the ashes, born anew. We are as unique and different as our experience, and each of was given a new tapestry. This experience has given me a deeper appreciation for the atonement of my Savior, Jesus Christ. I have experienced, firsthand, His unconditional love and have felt the healing power of granting complete forgiveness to a man I had never met before May, 16, 1986. I will never forget the miracle of that day or the blessing of being strengthened by the "Refiners Fire."

Brenda Hartley Bateman
Sixth Grade Student Survivor
(Email Submission)

Nightmares

For awhile after the bombing I would have nightmares. I moved a lot when I was younger, so in my dreams I would be pedaling my bike with my little sister on the handlebars, from one residence to another, trying to find my family. But the thing was, all the houses would be on fire. I dreamed that all of the people in Cokeville were lined up on the main street and a truck full of terrorists would ride down the middle and shoot everyone. I dreamed that my family was taken hostage in a house by someone from my past.

You know what's interesting? David Young was never a figure in those nightmares.

My Heavenly Father blessed me on that day, May 16, 1986. As a mover, I knew what it was to not fit in. I knew what it was to not have friends and to not feel understood. With a child's naiveté, I looked at David Young in one of the most frightening situations possible, and said to myself, *I bet that he doesn't have any friends. I bet that if someone would talk to him or try to understand him, he would be OK."* I smiled at David Young.

I say that I was blessed because I never really thought of him again for quite some time. I didn't watch for him in crowds, I didn't think of him and I especially didn't hate him. Hate can be a very hard thing to carry around. I was blessed with a child's forgiveness, a type of forgiveness that didn't have to be asked for. I am very thankful for this blessing.

I would like to say that I have never had any bad experiences because of the Cokeville bombing but it would be untrue. It wasn't until ten years later when a situation happened that made me realize that there were some deeper scars to deal with.

I was married and pregnant with my first child. We were in a school library at a town water meeting. I don't know if you have ever dealt with water issues but it can get really ugly, really fast. In this meeting there was a man who was beginning to behave in a way that seemed too familiar. He was very intelligent. He had lawyers' books he was quoting from and was acting very erratically. He would nervously pace back and forth and was getting frustrated because nobody was listening to him. I kept thinking, *Somebody listen to him. Somebody try to appease him. Don't make him so mad.*

Everyone else was focused on the central debate. Not me, I was focused on him. I saw him get up and leave the room. I told my husband that I would be right back and I followed him. I tried to be stealthy (as stealthy as my seven months pregnant body would allow!) I followed him at a distance and watched him turn a corner and enter the men's bathroom (that's probably why he was pacing!)

As I was sitting there waiting for him to exit the bathroom, it dawned on me what I was doing. I was making sure that he was not going to get a gun. The situation was all too familiar to me. There was a large crowd stuffed in a small schoolroom with a personality that I had seen before. My heart jumped to my throat. I was getting out of there. I went back into the library and told my husband that it was time to leave. He said to go ahead and he would catch a ride. I said, "We are leaving. Nobody that I love is staying in this room with that lunatic." I'm sure my husband wondered what lunatic he had married, but he left with me and was very understanding later on. That was my first comprehension of the terror that must have been felt by the parents outside of the school on that terrible Friday.

I now have five children and I am still very cautious around people who have mental psychosis that causes them to be agitated. Putting my family at risk is just not something that I am willing to chance.

After the bombing I remember saying to my mom, "I will

never be bad again." I don't know if it was because I was so thankful at the time and I wanted to please Heavenly Father, or if it was because I just didn't want to be like David Young. I think it was a little of both.

Needless to say I have certainly not chosen the right in everything, and in some cases I have been very wrong. But I am improving, and I know beyond a shadow of a doubt that my Heavenly Father and Savior love me and are always willing to work with me as I continue to repent. That was the miracle for me; the *knowing*—the knowing that Heavenly Father and Jesus Christ were there and are still there, the knowing that we all have angels who watch us and protect us every day.

I am also glad to know that our ancestors are the angels that are assigned to us. It makes me feel like they have a vested interest in our lives and love us and want us to do well. I know that our prayers are answered. I am thankful for living in an area where we were taught to pray as children. We prayed individually and together and we knew that there was a God and I knew deep down that we were going to be OK.

I have found that two people in the same situation can have two totally different experiences. Our views are not necessarily right or wrong, just different. These are my experiences and I don't expect anyone else to feel the same way. I am grateful for the understandings that I have. I am thankful that our lives were preserved. But, I am also grateful that I don't have nightmares anymore.

Brandi Himmerich Bell
Sixth Grade Student Survivor
(Email Submission)

May 16th, 1986 is a day I can remember as clearly as if it were yesterday. I can testify that a miracle took place that day. I have no doubt in my mind that our Heavenly Father was watching over us and angels were placed there for our protection. Although I will always remember most of what happened that day, there are two memories which stand out.

My memories take me back to the sixth grade. We had been in the room for some time and realized how serious and real our situation was. My class gathered together to offer a prayer. I remember feeling nervous about what would happen if he, David, saw us praying. However, after the prayer I felt comforted and knew everything would be all right.

My second distinct memory is right after the bomb went off. I have a very vivid image of, not my sister Trini herself, but her blue pants with big pink flowers going out the window. I knew she was safe. After I finally got out the window, I started running down the sidewalk and ran into my mom on the corner. She told me she had found my other brother and sister, but couldn't find Trini. I told her I knew she was out and safe. Then I hugged my mom and jumped up and down crying, "We're all out! We're all out!" Even today, thinking of that moment brings tears to my eyes and gratitude to my heart. It was such a relief to know my family was safe.

To this day, there are many things that cause me to reflect back on that day. I have had the opportunity to share this experience with others and bear testimony of a Heavenly Father who watches over and loves each one of us. We are all here today because of a miracle.

Tammy Coates Christian
Sixth Grade Student Survivor
(Email Submission)

Many moments of that spring day back in 1986 are etched forever in my mind. I remember the strong smell of gasoline and the dampened paper towel I used to filter the odor. I can still see the "magic square" of tape fastened to the floor around David Young and the bomb and remember the panic I felt as I saw my sister Michelle, a second grader, sitting inches from the tape. When I realized some kids were crying and saw another child being held and consoled by a teacher in the corner, having been sickened by the fumes, I realized how serious this was and I said the most heartfelt prayer I could.

It wasn't long after that a group of the sixth graders huddled together for a prayer that we hoped the Youngs would not catch us participating in. I remember walking over to the TV to see if we were on the news and just moments later the bomb being detonated.

There are many other moments that I recall, but one stands out in my mind and has been the cause of much reflection over the years. It was a conversation that I held with Doris Young. As she guarded the door leading to the hallway, I remember asking her why they were doing this to us. Her answer was in essence that they were going to take the ransom money they received and give it to the hospital where her brother was very sick to help save his life. In my young mind, though it didn't make complete sense to me, somehow her words seemed to soften my heart and give me a sense of trust in her.

Since that day, trusting the various people I come in contact with does not come easily for me; yet, from that day was born a knowledge and a full trust in God that He does hear and answer even the most simple of prayers. For this blessing and miracle will I always be thankful.

Celeste Excell Jackman
Sixth Grade Student Survivor
Daughter of Principal
(Oral History—Telephone)

I don't know where to start. I was in 6th grade and our afternoon routine was to go to the bathroom after reading or whatever. I came out of the bathroom and our teacher and class were just sitting there. A lady came up and said there was an assembly. Mr. Mitchell, my teacher, said, "What assembly? I don't know of one." He was assistant principal. The principal was out getting the mail so Mr. Mitchell was in charge of the school as well as his class. The lady said there was an assembly in room 4. We headed down to the room. We found out later the lady was Mrs. Young.

I remember looking in and seeing the guns along the chalkboard and it looked like the whole student body was in there. A man was sitting on a desk in the middle and he had a little square grocery cart sitting there, like the little old ladies used to pull around. We knew that the circus was coming to town the following Friday, the 23rd, and we had to sell tickets and we thought it had to do with selling tickets. It was the first circus in like fifty years to come to town and everyone was really pumped about it.

We went in and found a place to sit. Mr. Mitchell went up and found out what was going on, and learned about the "New Revolution" that David Young was talking about. We learned we couldn't leave. Things kind of blurred a little bit. I remember when my dad came into the doorway. I wanted to tell him to run. But, I didn't want to get in trouble or be in more danger because my dad was the principal. He didn't want to get me in trouble by showing that I was his daughter, so we kind of ignored each other. But we kept an eye on each other.

So he came in and sat down on the desk next to the guy and I thought, *Dad, you idiot! He's going to blow you up.* It might sound stupid that I thought that, but I was in sixth grade.

I remember getting nauseated from the gasoline fumes, and the little windows just weren't doing it. The windows were open but people were still getting sick. I was starting to feel sick. People were going into the bathroom and throwing up. There was a bathroom monitor, maybe Janel Dayton or Jean Mitchell. Only one person could be in at a time. The bathroom monitor made sure that when one person came out, then one could go in.

At some time they had all the men who were there move all the desks and tables out so there was more space. The other door was barricaded so there was only one exit. My dad kept leaving the room and I wondered where he was going. He was working as a go-between. He was relaying messages from David Young to the outside world. I didn't know that then. He just kept coming in and out. He was told if he wasn't back in the room in five minutes David would start shooting kids. Dad says he has never run so fast in his whole life to make sure he got back to the classroom in time. They were also trying to get medicine in to kids who needed it.

About this time, my class decided we were going to have a prayer. So my class just went off to a corner together to say a prayer except one girl who didn't want to join because she was not LDS. She chose not to but the rest of us did.

I remember after the prayer feeling calm and peaceful that things would be OK. Some of the stress had left. When they moved everything out, they brought in some coloring papers for the little kids and a TV. We had the TV on.

The next thing I remember was trying to read Young's paper that talked about his "Brave New World." It made no sense at all to me. Total craziness. The next thing, I was kind of walking over to where the TV was, I think it was on CNN. The headline came on that a school in Wyoming was being held hostage. It was kind of chaotic in the room, people talking. They tried to make it as normal as they could.

David Young had a square marked off, he called it the "magic square." The goal was not to get into the magic square. I remember big circles of sweat under his arms. His face had sweat running down it. He handed a string that went into the cart to his wife. Then he went to the bathroom. When the Youngs were in their square they were facing north. The bathroom was southwest. The TV was southeast. He went to the bathroom and the headline came on TV, and one of the teachers who was monitoring the bathroom said, "Let's listen to the news," and Doris said, "Shhh, let's listen to the news," and that's when the bomb went off.

My back was to Doris when the bomb went off.

She was very nice. She was singing the little songs with us. I was not scared of her at all. I was scared of him because he looked like a "cuckoo bird." I didn't know her name, I don't think.

I remember kind of a muted sound that sounded a lot like a sonic boom, like when they are doing surveying. I turned around and saw flames and smoke. I had actually been feeling nauseated enough that I had gone over and got a paper towel with some water on it just before the bomb went off. I dove into the southeast corner of the room and put that towel over my face and mouth. Little kids all around me, they were screaming and crying. I was pulling little kids down under the smoke.

A voice was yelling, "Get over to the window, get over to the window!" It was the firemen. "We'll get you out."

Mr. Moore was one of the first faces that I saw. He was already out. He was crouching there by the window yelling in and helping pull kids out. So I got over to the window and was pushing the little kids in front of me. I lifted them up out the window. They were just standing there. They were scared and they didn't know what to do.

Then I climbed up and they pulled me through. We were so shocked we just huddled by the window once we were out. We didn't know what to do. We had seen the ambulances pulling into town. We saw the fire trucks. We heard helicopters coming over. We knew people were on the corner by Art Robinson's house. The police had them barricaded off.

I was looking for my class because you know we were trained to find members of our class. I was panicking because I couldn't see all the members of my class. I found my teacher and he was doing a quick count. Other kids had headed home. I started looking for my family. I was scared. I didn't know where my dad was. He was out of the classroom when the bomb went off. I didn't see my dad leave the room, I just knew he was gone when the bomb went off. Rick and Bob, my brothers, passed me two or three different times and they didn't recognize me because I was so black. Then they recognized the braces on my teeth and my mouth. And then I went home.

I did have to go to the hospital later. It probably took three or four different baths to get the soot off of me. That's when Steve, my oldest brother, called.

They took buses to several hospitals. I had a cut on my elbow, from shrapnel. I got on the bus to go to Kemmerer and my brother Rick went with me. I went to Kemmerer Hospital and when I got there, the stress and the gas fumes made me throw up all over. They put two stitches in my elbow and then I went home.

That's basically the events of that day as I can remember them. I can't remember what has been filled in from doing so many firesides with my dad or what I knew then.

Geraldo Rivera was doing a thing on crisis trauma in schools. He called and paid for my family to go to New York City to do the show. My dad and I were on the stage. My mom was in the audience. He interviewed her at the end. The same or next summer, my dad and I were called to Washington, D.C. to testify before a Judiciary Committee. We were on C-SPAN. The government paid our way, I think. I can't remember what that was all about. I think it had to do with crime in schools.

I did look at it then as a miracle. And I do now. My dad was privy to things and I knew that there were miracles that happened. I saw the place where the pictures were burned off the wall. I saw the image of Christ with his arms out-stretched—it looked that way to me. Rick and Bob helped with the bomb as squad scribes and they heard if that bomb had gone off correctly, the whole wing should have been gone. Flattened.

I would just say that I believe that things happen for a reason. I believe at the time it was very traumatic and very trying. I still have adverse effects. I hate thunder, that muffled loud sound that takes you by surprise. I can't stand it, although I know things happen for a reason they and are there to help us to grow, not there to hurt us. It's like a learning experience.

I want to add, when I was out walking and trying to find my family, I remember seeing groups of people, very non-denominational, everyone taking care of everyone else's kids. It was the whole community gathering together to gather children and saying prayers, heads bowed. The community really came together and really came together quickly. It didn't matter who you were. They came together, people put aside their differences in the face of tragedy and really took care of each other. It was a real testimony building experience for me at the time, and it still is.

Greg Nate
Sixth Grade Survivor
(Typed Mailed Submission)

I can't believe it has been almost twenty years ago that the Cokeville bombing took place. It's amazing how fast time flies. I can't remember a lot about the bombing, but this is the journal entry that I wrote a few days after the event.

I woke up and went to school. It was just an ordinary day until after free reading time, which was right after lunch. We always went to the bathroom after reading time which was around 1:30. When we came out of the bathrooms this lady (Doris Young) asked my teacher (Mr. Mitchell) if he was the 6th grade teacher. He said yes, and then she asked him if he could take the class to the first grade room. I remember Mr. Mitchell was a little bit confused why we should go to the 1st grade classroom, but we ended up going. As I entered the classroom I noticed guns everywhere and a guy (David Young) with a bomb. Mr. Moore (5th grade teacher) motioned us over to him. He told us that we were being held hostage for two million dollars each. I got a little scared and started to cry wondering if I would ever see my family again. Our teachers got books, games, and a TV to keep us calm. I started to play a game with my cousin Kyle.

It was about 3:45 when the bomb went off and Mrs. Bennion fell towards Kyle and me. The room went completely black and the flames were going everywhere. Kids were screaming and the teachers were helping everyone out of the windows and doors. I remember wanting out of there more than anything and pushing Allison Cornia out of the way and going out of the window. I was one of the first kids out.

There were policemen and SWAT teams everywhere. I remember running to Main Street and trying to find my brother Brad, who was also in the bombing. I couldn't find him at first and thought he was dead. My Aunt Linda finally told me that he was OK and that he had run all the way to my grandma's house. Everyone ended up making it out alive except for the two terrorists, David and Doris Young.

My parents were out of town and I couldn't wait to see them again. My Aunt Linda ended up taking us to Kemmerer to the hospital to get checked out. We were really lucky because neither Brad or I had any injuries, just a little smoke inhalation. When we got back to Cokeville I met my parents and started to cry. I was happy to see them again. I could not sleep at all that night.

When you are older, you are more aware of the miracle that happened that day. I'm one of those who didn't see or hear any angels, but know without a doubt that angels were watching over us that day. I know that the bomb didn't go completely off or it would have killed everyone in the building and God's hand was involved. I am very thankful to a Heavenly Father that has allowed me to live and experience all that life has to offer. That is one "blessing" that I will never take for granted.

I am now married to my beautiful wife Chynell and we have two boys, Tristan and Trey, and a girl, Jordyn. We live in Mountain Green, Utah, and are doing well.

Heidi Roberts Rausch
Sixth Grade Student Survivor
(Email Submission)

Throughout my life the bombing experience has brought out many different feelings.

Being the oldest class in the room that day we probably understood more of the danger we were in than the younger classes. But looking back I have realized how little I really understood about how horrible the outcome could have been or was supposed to be.

I think the next few years were probably the years that I didn't have a lot of fear or thoughts of that day. My little brother, Aaron, on the other hand, couldn't sleep at night, and was having a lot of nightmares. I didn't experience any of this that I remember. For me, I remember taking a shower later that night and wondering why I wasn't scared or having any feelings of fear. But we had just knelt down and had family prayer and my dad, of course, thanked Heavenly Father for sparing our lives and asked for Him to comfort us. And I know that the peace I felt as a child was an answer to my father's and mother's prayers.

It wasn't until I was in my college days, up at Ricks College, that I had a client who was a news reporter for a local Idaho channel. She asked me to tell my story on the ten o'clock news after the show, *To Save the Children,* aired for the first time. I thought nothing of it until after watching the show. I, of course, didn't want to be on TV alone so I had Brandi Himmerich and Michael Taylor, who were also going to school at Ricks, come with me. I don't know how watching the show affected them. But for me, for the first time I finally got it. It hit me that we all could have died that day. I was so humbled. I haven't looked at that day the same since. As an adult I realize the fear the teachers must have been going through, wondering how they were going protect us all. I thank them for being our strength that day.

I'm grateful for my husband who understands my fear of being in public places and wanting to get out quick if something a little abnormal starts to happen.

I'm grateful for the many opportunities I had on my mission and throughout my life to share my testimony of that day, to testify that our Savior lives and that He loves us and was watching over us that day!

Allyson Cornia Risenmay
Sixth Grade Student Survivor
(Email Submission)

It was interesting to me that I received the letter from the Cokeville Miracle Foundation just last weekend, right after I got back from helping out at a church girls' camp for a week. Two nights before I had told some of the girls about my elementary school being held hostage and what I learned from it. It's not a story I tell often, so it seemed coincidental that I received the letter requesting my thoughts about that day shortly after I returned.

Anyway, I think it's great that you are compiling these stories. I would love to hear other people's recollections of that day We moved to Washington the summer of 1986 so I haven't seen very many people from Cokeville since then.

There are a few things that stand out in my mind when I think about what happened on May 16, 1986. I remember when I walked into that classroom, Mr. Moore was the one who told us what was going on and I didn't believe him at first because I was so used to him teasing us all the time. Even after I realized what was happening, I still took comfort from the fact that I knew all the teachers in the room and I knew they had our best interests at heart and would do anything they could to keep us safe. Living in bigger cities since then has made me understand what a blessing that was to have such a personal relationship with all my teachers.

Another thing I remember was the opportunity I had to say a prayer for my friends and me. I don't recall how long we had been there when a group of other sixth graders approached me and asked if we could all say a prayer together. I remember the feeling of peace that came over me as we knelt together with arms folded and asked Heavenly Father to bless us and keep us safe. I didn't know if we would all get out of that classroom alive, I just knew I wasn't worried anymore.

Whatever happened, it would be OK.

I know that it was a miracle that we all came out of that room alive and I know Heavenly Father answers our prayers.

Kamron Wixom
Sixth Grade Student Survivor
(Typed Submission)

My thoughts twenty ears later...

At twelve years of age, I was one of the older kids the day he wheeled that bomb into our school. It happened on May 16, 1986. During the summer that followed I remember tasting and smelling that burned out classroom. I can't really remember the smell now. It took about a year of listening to soft music at night to get myself to nod off to sleep at night. Now I turn on soft music for my seven month old son, just as I did for my daughter when she was that young. I sit in the room and listen to the music, watch them sleep, and think of where I am now. I'm very happy where I am now, but twenty years ago, did I think of where I might be by this time?

What does it mean twenty years later? Should my life be something more spectacular because I know it was spared so miraculously when I was younger? What about the other 150 kids that were in that room that day whose lives were also spared? Where are they now and what do their lives mean to them? What do our lives mean to the people around us because we were spared that day? Have we returned the grace to others as the angels did for us, or have we grown proud and stubborn in our own little "big ideas" like David Young? Have we magnified the role of God in our lives and those around us? Or have we diminished Him to "Zero equals Infinity?"

Some saw angels. Some heard voices. Some even recognized their angels months later when looking through old family photo albums... "That's my angel right there, Mommy, only without the glasses!" What about those who didn't see angels? What should we think? Obviously we are here...saved along with the rest of those who did see and hear.

Even if I haven't thought about it for a while, I know what

happened that day, even if the only flash of light I saw was from the exploding bomb.

What saved us that day? The thought that God would not let anything bad happen to us when we knew we'd done nothing wrong. Childlike faith saved us. The minute our minds and our hearts took hold of the idea that "only Heavenly Father can help us now," we simply bowed our heads and asked for that help. It was a matter of fact. It wasn't just "positive thinking." It was faith because there was no doubt what would happen to us after that prayer. There was no negative outcome in view. *We'll be OK now,* is how I felt.

Pure, childlike faith was the first step toward deliverance from that room of terror. Deliverance and salvation did come to that room... but not immediately. It built slowly, preparing the children— whispering to an older brother to get his sisters near the window— revealed itself calmly but majestically to others, and acted as a shield between bomb and child.

I didn't have to see angels, hear them, or even think that their presence might be required that day. I did not have to imagine how God would move in His majesty that day when I'd said my little prayer just hours before, I simply knew He would. He did deliver our salvation that day. That much I know. I'm living proof of it.

Verlene P. Bennion
Teacher's Aid Survivor
(Oral History as told by son Samuel O. Bennion, Jr.—Telephone)

Mother had climbed out the window and she always teased Rocky Moore afterward that both of them ought to lose a little weight. She teased Rocky that she got out a little easier. They really liked to tease each other.

I know that she was the last one out. The reason I know that is just as I came, the kids were all coming out. I saw Pat and she said, "I haven't seen your mother." I had to find mother. Of course she had white hair and it was coal black when I got her rounded up.

There was one little girl—she was down on her hands and knees, there on the east side, inside the room by the windows. She was on her hands and knees in front of that window. The kids were stepping on this little girl as they were getting out. Mother was still inside and when the other kids were out, mother picked the girl up and handed her outside. Then she climbed out herself, after all the kids were out. She noted that after the bomb had gone off, there was quite a little fire and Doris Young was on fire. She saw that.

Mother's prayer had been that if anybody passed away it would be her because she was old.

Then I took her and Pat to the Montpelier hospital. Pat was burned on the arm and back. Mother couldn't breathe. She got pneumonia from smoke inhalation. They took her to Logan. She went to her grave with that cough that she got from that smoke.

She came home quickly. We laughed, too, because in the Logan hospital the nurse asked her if she would like her hair washed. The nurse was very surprised, she didn't know mother had white hair.

She was grateful that none of the kids lost their lives.

Verlene P. Bennion died June 4, 2001 at her home on the Ranch near Cokeville, Wyoming.

Christine "Tina" Cook
Cokeville Elementary School Secretary, Then and Now
(Typed Submission)

Oh, what is true? How do you put into words, the feelings in your heart, about the most terrible yet spiritual experience of your life? I have read some accounts of others' stories and realize that we each have our own story and it isn't necessarily the same story because of what happened to each of us as individuals that day.

I have gone back so many times and reread what I wrote that night and several days later. I can still feel the fear and smell the fumes of the gas and the fire. I can still remember knowing how real it all was and that I would never get to see my two precious children or my wonderful husband to say goodbye. (A word I never use by the way, I just say "so long" or mostly, "see ya later!")

I was the first hostage taken and was in it alone for a very short time before others were caught up in it. I suppose the question I have been asked the most is, "Did you think it was for real?" I have to say, "Yes, I knew he was serious right from the first moment." You only had to look into his eyes and see the empty look, the coldness and the feeling that there just really wasn't anyone in there. I have never before seen—and pray I never do again—the look I saw that day.

It was hard for me to look people in the eyes for so long afterward. In fact, I notice I still have a tendency to look away often as I talk with people. I also know that I am still always aware of where I am in a room or building and where the exit is. I never like to sit with my back to an exit and mostly want to sit with my back to a wall with a view of the room. Other things that I am always aware of are the smell of gasoline, smoke, dark rooms, large groups of people and young children when they cry in fear.

Like others, I have gone through the agony of wondering what I could have done that day to make a difference for my children. (All those in the building I considered my children). I dealt with a lot of guilt for not grabbing the intercom and yelling for everyone to get out. I was told many times that it would have made it so much worse and many would have died if I had tried that, and yet we always feel we should have been able to stop something that can hurt those we love. I am so glad a kind Father in Heaven knows the best way to handle these things because as humans, we can't see the full picture.

I could give you a full account of that day and my story would be similar to many, but I have such sacred feelings that are too hard to express on paper so you could truly understand the miracle of that day. Yes, we were taken hostage, yes we were scared and most of us have lived with nightmares and had a very profound change in our way of thinking. Some of them have been good changes, like the witness we are able to bear of a loving Father in Heaven Who loves us and watches over us, and how things don't always go the way we would want but we can always feel His spirit if we remember to search it out in prayer. Of course the other changes are harder to deal with like the distrust of people with a look similar to the Youngs, the smell of gasoline, the sound of fireworks, especially the Grand Finale on the 4th of July. Also the fear of being closed in and dark rooms can take me back to May 16, 1986 in a flash.

I am so grateful to live in a small town that is filled with loving and giving people. Our students were exceptional in the way they hugged us often during the school days. It changed for a while after the bombing and we were so sad for the trust that was lost. However, children are amazing and the trust for those they knew cared about them returned for most. It is amazing to me that things on the surface really didn't change much afterward. Most of us still live here or have family here. Children grew up and went off to school, missions or work but not many families moved away.

I still sit at the same desk in the front office as I did that day. I still tease the children and still think of them all as my own. I did find out one other important thing that day; I loved everyone of those children and would have done anything possible to save them from the agony of the next few hours and then the nightmare of years that followed, if it had been in my power. I know this is true of every adult in that room. We had a very caring and close faculty and still do and that is why I am still here. Some places are so much better to work than others and I think I still have the best job in the universe!

I will never forget the look on my own children's faces as they saw me for the first time afterward. They were 8th and 11th graders at the time and I am so thankful they were not part of the hostage situation. My daughter says she thinks it would have been easier to be with me, so she knew what was happening, than it was to listen to people talk about what probably would happen, and know her mom was in there. She said she was so terrified for me and wanted to be reassured it would be OK and she would see me again soon. She just could not hug me enough and tell me how much she loved me for a long time afterward, in fact she still does, often, even today.

My son was on a school trip and heard it on the way home. He says the radio said the bomb went off just as they were getting close to Cokeville. He said the announcer said, "The bomb has gone off, people are flying out the windows!" When he finally got to where I was standing, he just ran into my arms and hugged me so tight. He asked several times if I was sure I was alright. I have always had such a close relationship with my children but I am sure this intensified the strength of it even more. We are able to talk and get those feelings out in the open whenever we feel the need.

What can I say about the man I am married to? He has been there for me when I've needed him, every minute of every day before and since. He has held me close in a protective way and helped heal the fear when nightmares rocked my world. He has let me talk and cry and laugh but never questioned my actions as I waded through the hard times.

Like I say, my story of the events is all written down in my journal and I have read it often. I saw many of the same things others saw. I did not see the angels but I do testify to a shift from fear to calmness that came over me not long before the bomb went off. I know with all my heart and soul that we were not alone, we had help from the other side and a miracle did indeed happen that day, a miracle that we relive every May 16th and I'm sure we will as long as we live.

I have a wonderful husband of thirty-seven years, two children and ten wonderful grandchildren who help me realize what I could have missed out on if we hadn't been so protected.

The true story here is not the psychopaths that did this terrible thing, but the story of survival, courage and spiritual experiences (for each person that is different), and knowing the meaning of a second chance. I am grateful for that second chance and pray that I might live to be worthy of the many blessings in my life!

Max T. Excell
Cokeville Elementary School Principal Survivor
Father of One Student Survivor
(Personal Journal Entry Photocopy Submission)

May 16, 1986, Friday, 26° F—60° F Cloudy, Page No. 136

"A day that will live in infamy" for Cokeville, Wyoming. David Young, a former Police Officer—he was when we moved here— and his wife Doris, who is the mother of Bernie Petersen, entered our school at about 1:20 p.m. and started a siege that will trigger nightmares for many people for the rest of their lives.

The Youngs held our children hostage for nearly two and a half hours in Mrs. Mitchell's classroom. They had a homemade bomb in a wire cart. The bomb was made up of gasoline, powder, blasting caps, ammunition and other ingredients which if they had combined as they were intended to do would have killed everyone in the nine hundred square foot classroom.

I had been for the mail and returned for a prospective teacher interview at 1:35. As I entered the rear hall, Delbert Rentfro, the custodian, met me to say that the 5th grade was in the music room without a teacher. So I went looking for Mr. Miller. As I looked down the South hallway, I was taken hostage along with about 160 students and staff members. The UPS lady, Sandy Gonzales, and Eva and Cathy Clark were there along with prospective teacher Cindy Cowden, and Pat Bennion who was substituting for Briant Teichert.

When questioned, Young told me it was a revolution and we were being held hostage so the government would listen to him. I asked him if he would please release the children and keep me as a hostage and he said "no" that they were his bargaining power. He said our school was chosen because of "the love people in Cokeville have for their children and because of the strong Mormon influence here and that everyone knows that Mormons love their families; that pressure would therefore be exerted on the government to listen to his demands." He said he wanted two million each for every person in the room and that the government would pay it.

I tried to get him to release three student hostages. He would exchange them for more hostages with a formula for exchange. He allowed me to leave the classroom periodically to procure certain items: Kleenex, Tylenol, paper towels, and mop bucket, but each time I was on a time limit, that if I was not back within ten minutes (later it was fifteen minutes) he would start shooting people.

After that, I was told to call the authorities. When I asked which, I was told "the sheriff's department." So, I spent the rest of the time as intermediary from Young to the telephone. I relayed his demands and kept one line open. On the other line, I answered calls from Joanne Metcalfe, UPI, AP and TV stations in Denver.

It was while I was talking to one of those that the bomb exploded. I said, "It just exploded, I have to go," dropped the receiver and ran to the classroom. As I came around the corner by the drinking fountains, I saw smoke and students coming out of the room. I think before I ran through, I went back into the office to tell Earl Carroll, deputy sheriff, the bomb had exploded—(I told him sometime.)

As I approached the classroom, I met Jack Mitchell coming out. He said, "We have to get fire extinguishers," so I ran to the gym hall for one. When I returned, I couldn't go in because I heard popping sounds like shooting and ran to the door to shout for officers to come quickly, "I think he's shooting the kids in the classroom." I learned later that the "shots" were actually ammunition exploding.

As I went outside again, I saw Tess running across the lawn and knew she was safe. Her face was as black as coal. I had been told that Mrs. Young had been given control of the bomb while he went to the restroom and had triggered it accidentally.

The officers were directed to the restroom where Young was last seen and I went around to the window to help with survivors. None were coming out a few minutes later, we were told Mr. Young was found dead in the restroom having shot himself, so we were free to start searching for bodies. I helped them remove Mrs. Young by way of the window. There was no one else in the building so all of the children survived.

Ambulances from Rich County, Kemmerer, Afton and Montpelier joined our own to take kids and staff to area hospitals. Art Robinson also loaded his bus with the least injured to go to Kemmerer. Tess was checked for smoke inhalation and had a cut on her arm sewn up. John Miller had a gunshot wound in the right shoulder. He was sent to Montpelier, then transferred to Pocatello for treatment.

After coming home to show the family I was all right, I went back and answered media questions and police inquiries until 9:00 p.m. Then I came home to return phone calls and answer questions until very late when I retired for the night.

May 17, 1986 Saturday

I called the area hospitals to get a condition report on our injured. We have twenty-one who were hospitalized overnight. Another fifty-five or so were treated and released. John Miller was released from Pocatello this morning with a .22 slug lodged in his left shoulder blade.

May 18, 1986 Sunday

Deb Wolfley told me they are now studying a theory that David Young left the restroom after the bomb exploded, and shot his wife in the head to stop her agony, then shot himself!!

Sandy Gonzales
UPS Driver Survivor
(Oral History—Telephone)

I was delivering a package that day and went in to the desk to get a signature from the secretary, Tina Cook. Rocky Moore was at the desk and so was David Young with his bomb. I remember thinking it was some kind of an exercise for the kids but then he was pointing his gun and I looked at Tina and realized yeah, this is serious.

I remember that we were some of the first people taken into the classroom. There were a bunch of kids already in the classroom and more coming in. They seemed excited at first but then they began to realize what was really going on. I remember one little girl was crying because she wanted her teddy bear. I had on a brown down-vest so I took it off and gave it to the little girl so she at least had something to hold on to. I thought of my own two little children at home and felt sad that I might not have the chance to talk to them again.

I was worried because we were out in the middle of nowhere and people on the outside wouldn't care, wouldn't take this all seriously. I didn't see how we could get out of it.

It seemed like it wasn't that long before suddenly the bomb went off. I was sitting by the bathroom door. My first instinct was to get out of there as fast as possible. I remember that I went to Town Hall and stayed there until everything was pretty much over. I remember going back over to the school to get my UPS van and seeing Doris Young's body laying on the ground covered with a green blanket. I had lost my glasses in the explosion and so I couldn't drive. I had to call the supervisor to come and get me to drive the van home.

For a while after that I felt guilty that I had just run out of there without stopping to make sure everyone else was OK. That bothered me for quite a while. I had lost my mom the year before the bombing and had been feeling pretty sorry for myself. This experience helped me realize just how precious life is and that we take too many things for granted. I know God doesn't throw anything at us that we cannot handle.

Gloria T. Mower
Special Education Teacher Survivor
(Oral History—Telephone)

Some time before the bombing incident I was in the teacher's workroom and I remember Rocky Moore kind of heckling Carol Petersen saying, "If you want me to believe, just show me a miracle." She just kind of ignored him and went about doing her work. Finally, I said to Rocky, "That's not true. You either believe or you don't."

I liked Rocky, very likeable guy. Very outspoken. You knew where you stood with him.

My room had a window in the door. I was over in a corner with my student where I couldn't be seen. My after lunch student was brushing his teeth. If Doris Young came by my room, it looked like it was empty. I had to ask Tina something so I went to the office and no one was around. I saw the custodian and said, "Where is everyone?" He said, "They are down in Mrs. Mitchell's room for some reason or other."

Doris came up to me in the hallway and said, "Who are you?" She said, "you need to be in here." I said, "I have a student in my room." She said, "You go in and I'll go get him." I went in and thought it was a demonstration on what to do if a terrorist ever comes into the school. Guns were all lined up on the wall. Students were crying. There *were* terrorists in the school. I was out long enough that Rocky had already been threatened with being shot and everyone was scared.

I remember they had masking tape fixed in a square, and David Young was in the middle, sitting on the desk. He only let the principal get near. The rest of us were around the edge. I remember the smell of gas, quite strong. The windows were open. I remember talking to my son (Scott) who was in the third grade and I asked him if he wanted to go with his friends or stay with me. He wanted to stay with me. The kids settled down and were watching TV. My student was with me, too.

I remember it as being about 4:30 but maybe it was 3:30, school was supposed to be out. Tina said it was about time for her Pepsi break, would he let us go have our Pepsi break. I asked her if there would be enough for all of us. We were kind of joking.

The bomb went off. All of a sudden my son and I were on our faces in the hallway between the two classrooms, by the bathroom where the guy had gone. People must have run over us. I'm not conscious of that. I remember thinking that people die like this. I remember that Scott was out and I thought, *good, he was out.* I got on my feet and was standing face to face with the guy in the bathroom doorway and his gun. I got pushed out. Scott came running to me crying, arms outstretched. The custodian came and handed me my student and asked me if I was OK.

Police and firemen were running toward the school saying "Run, run, run!" Our music teacher was lying on the ground and I asked what was wrong and he said he was shot. I didn't hear anything.

The principal later asked if anyone knew if the fire alarms went off and I said yes. I was going to take the kids on the grass like we do for a fire alarm but we were told to run, so we did and ended up over on the Taylors' lawn where many people were congregating.

A long line of ambulances and EMTs was there. We weren't burned. We were fine. There were teachers wringing their hands saying, "I can't find my students, I don't know if my students all got out." Parents would come up and shake you and ask if we saw so and so and they wouldn't give you a chance to answer and they'd run up to the next person. It wasn't until the firemen came out and said none of the students or teachers were in there that we knew everyone got out.

After everyone was taken care of, about 5:30, Scott and I went home and got on our knees and gave thanks for our lives and everyone else's. We were supposed to go to Logan that weekend but my car, purse and car keys were at the school and they wouldn't let us get them. They wanted to check all the cars and make sure there were no bombs in them.

Saturday morning someone called and said we could go get our cars. I had to go into the school to get my keys. A man led me in and told me not to touch anything. He had to check my purse and make sure no one had put anything in there. Then I went to Logan like we had planned.

We left Cokeville that summer. I had already given my notice.

We just handled it. We had to talk about it an awful lot. We talked about it all night long. We certainly couldn't sleep. We talked about it as much as needed, then put it behind us.

We knew a miracle had happened. I've talked about it quite a bit. After the event, I said to Rocky, "Did you see a miracle? Rocky said, "Yeah. I even saw a burning bush."

Delbert Rentfro
Cokeville Elementary School Custodian
Excluded from Being a Hostage
(Oral History—Telephone)

Well, I had been over to the high school. I can't tell you for what reason now. When I came back that outfit was backed into that south door. That was weird but I just assumed there was a show or something. Sometimes people parked there so I didn't think too much about it. I parked and went in and went down the hall. I saw the door closed and I looked in. I assumed they were talking to the kids. I went back up the hall.

About that time I met Kliss Sparks. She said, "Where is everyone?" I said, "In Jean Mitchell's room." We went back and knocked. Kliss said, "Do you want me in here?" Kliss's class was already in there. She was a little bit late or something. They didn't want me. I walked back down the hall to where I had my little office. I did some paperwork.

Kris Casper, he was a student teacher and he was Allan Burton's brother-in-law. They were at the intersection of the two halls. The lady was with him. I said, "What's going on down there?" The lady said, "You never mind." I had had some problems in the kitchens, a leak from a steam table, so I went down to take care of it. I still didn't think too much about it.

Finally, Max came down. He looked kind of pale and kind of serious. We were always joking with each other. He started telling me this tale about the school being held hostage and them wanting all these millions of dollars. I didn't believe him. He told me about the guns and the bombs. I really didn't believe him for a bit. He told me I had to get to the city hall and let people know. I didn't know there was already someone down there and they were aware of the situation. The daughter was already down there but I didn't know that.

I expected someone to take a shot at me as I left the building. Max had told me they were well armed.

When I got to the city hall, they had everything sitting outside. I said, "We need to get it up there. We need to barricade that street off." Our local police were there and I think a SWAT team was there. A little time had passed. I told them that if we passed a certain spot they would start shooting kids. So we got everything up there and blocked off the streets. We hadn't been there too long when that bomb went off.

The first kid I saw—you wouldn't believe how fast he was going or how fast he got out of there—he was taking steps ten feet wide. It was Brad Shane Nate. He went zooming past us like you wouldn't believe. He ran by me and his eyes were huge. The second kid was Craig Taylor's kid. I thought, what had they done to that kid? His hair was green and slick and shiny. I came to find out it was all singed off. He was the second one.

Then John Miller came stumbling down the fence to where we were. I said, "Are you OK?" He said, "No, I've been shot." Betty Allen was sitting a little way down there with an ambulance. I motioned for her to come down.

I remember Frank Lazcanotegui more than anyone. He got a bar or a piece of pipe or something and he started beating on the window. Somehow he got that window open and off that wall. I don't know how. Frank got that window open. He started getting kids out.

They got a body out to us. I thought it was Heidi Roberts. She was a sixth grader. I helped pack the body over and lay it on the lawn. It was the woman. Her body was like a bowl of jello. I don't think there was a bone in her body that wasn't broken.

I couldn't go in, I just could not go in that building alone. I made Cal Fredrickson go in with me. We went through every piece of duct work up in the attic. Who knew what was up there? Young could have buried things anywhere. It was the next day.

Bob Dayton and Allan Burton came over and cleaned up the

blood in that restroom. I passed that door three different times. They never opened the door for me or let me in or anything. I just couldn't clean up that bathroom. "You never mind." I still remember them saying that.

After visiting with all the psychologists or psychiatrists, they said I must have intimidated the Youngs. They took Kris Casper. Eva Clark was there for some reason or other. The UPS lad was also there. They took everyone.

Then we had to put up with the press. We finally had the halls cleaned up and the tiles down and replaced. We got the carpet scrubbed. We'd just gotten them done, the floors were wet and then this lady had to go see the room. So she tromped through our clean floors. She just had to go see.

Max Excell wanted to get those kids back in. I thought, boy, I wouldn't let those kids back in the school for a while.

I can remember Marlene Hess, she was dragging that kid of hers, that youngest girl, back into that school. She was screaming at the top of her lungs, "I don't want to go in." Marlene was literally dragging her. Now I think Max made a wise decision to make those kids go back. It was really good to get them back in.

Cynthia Cowden Triplett
Job Interviewee—Survivor
(Email Submission)

Lessons Learned

On May 16, 1986, many lives were changed forever. Everyone who was involved in the events of that day learned something whether we wanted to or not. This is what I learned from my experience when I went in for my job interview and was taken hostage:

1. Life isn't fair. (I already knew that but this was a nasty reminder.)
2. No matter how in control we think we are, we aren't.
3. Bad things happen to good people (and innocent children.)
4. David Young took two hours and forty minutes of my life ... I made a conscious decision to not give him anymore of it.
5. God gives you peace, even in the most unimaginable circumstances.
6. In times of crisis, pray, and when you're done, pray some more.
7. When feeling nervous or afraid, I compare the current problem with the ones we faced that day and immediately feel better.
8. No matter how much time passes, it still hurts when there are reports of violence in a school setting.
9. It is necessary to forgive the perpetrators of the crime, because through Jesus we are forgiven for our sins.
10. If the guy that looks like the janitor has a gun, skip the interview.

Many people carry physical as well as emotional scars from this event, but more importantly, we all took valuable life lessons with us. God Bless.

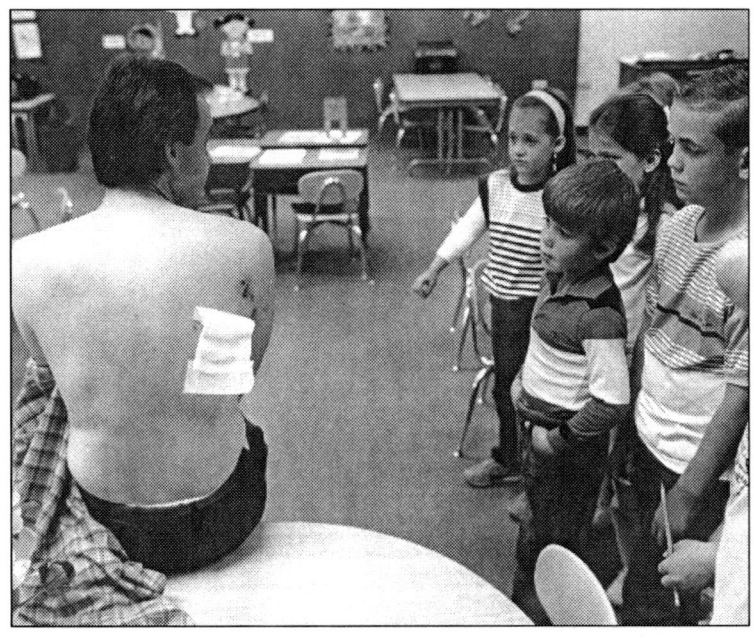

John Miller shows some students his gunshot wound.
Photo by Bill Wilcox
Courtesy of the Casper Star Tribune Collection, Casper College Library

Emergency Workers

T. Deb Wolfley, Lincoln Country Sheriff, talks to reporters.
Photo by Rick Sorensen
Courtesy of the Casper Star Tribune Collection, Casper College Library

Gregg M. Athay

Bear Lake County Sheriff's Department
(Email Submission)

May 16, 1986 is a day that I will never forget. This is the day that evil took over a small western town in Wyoming. It was very hard to imagine that something of that nature would happen so close to home. The thought of a hostage situation involving young children and a bomb just didn't seem possible.

When the bomb was detonated and I responded to the scene with the Lincoln County officers, what I saw there will never leave my mind. I watched as young children were handed out the windows of the school, some with burns and others just scared. I watched as parents frantically searched through the children to locate their own.

Entering the school through the thick smoke, attempting to locate the suspects and making sure that everything was secure was also devastating. I think all the officers there were hoping that all the children were out and none were seriously injured.

That day was also a day that I witnessed an entire community as well as three states come together to handle the situation. There were law enforcement, fire departments, and ambulance personnel from Wyoming, Idaho, and Utah as well as federal agencies en route to assist in any way possible. I was also very impressed by the way that everyone involved acted as one to take care of the injured and secure the scene.

It has been twenty years now and I have lost track of most of the officers that I was involved with, but I will never forget them. As I write this, I also hope that all the children have been able to deal with the mental as well as the physical trauma that they went through that day.

Brad Anderson
Wyoming Highway Patrol
(Email Submission)

I was a five and a half year veteran of the Wyoming Highway Patrol and was living in Cokeville, Wyoming at the time of this incident. To date this is the most powerful event of my career.

The sixteenth of May, 1986 was a blustery day with a strong wind blowing from the west to the east. I was working a day shift and was thinking about the following day when my younger brother was going to be married in the Salt Lake Temple. We were planning to travel to Utah after my shift had ended.

I had worked the morning and ended up in Kemmerer and had sat down for lunch with a friend at the Pizza Hut. This was close to eleven o'clock. It seemed that I had just ordered my meal when I received a phone call from the Wyoming Highway Patrol dispatch center. I made the comment to my friend that "I can never sit down without being called to something." This was made in a joking fashion. Little did I know that this call was going to change the lives of nearly 180 people.

As I answered the phone by the cash register, I identified myself to my dispatcher. She started to speak and she seemed very serious. She said, "At the Cokeville Elementary School there is a hostage situation going on." My first thought was that someone was having a domestic problem with their spouse and that it had gotten out of hand.

I asked my dispatcher why was she calling me on something like this as my duties were dealing with traffic problems, not domestic? She responded that the county was unable to contact the Cokeville City police officer (he was out of town), and that the county officers were busy doing something else.

I then asked her, "How many people are involved?" still

thinking maybe only two. She said, "Brad, you don't understand, all of them are being held hostage. I then asked her to clarify this, and she repeated and added, "All of the people in the school are being held and they have guns and possibly a homemade bomb."

I then went to my car and started toward Cokeville which is approximately forty miles from Kemmerer. While en route, I continued my conversation with my dispatcher and was giving her information on who to contact (fire, ambulance, etc.) and I then had her contact my wife and only ask her if my son had arrived home from morning kindergarten.

When contacting my wife, my dispatcher said, "Kayleen, Brad wants to know if Josh is at home? Kayleen answered "yes" and asked why I wanted to know. My dispatcher said that she was not able to give her any more information but to make sure that she kept Joshua at home. She then hung up. This left my wife (who is very curious, anyway) with a lot of questions unanswered.

I then continued to Cokeville with the winds hitting my windshield. It felt to me that it was really holding me back but after everything was over I found out that it only took me eighteen minutes to go that distance.

When I arrived at the entrance of the elementary school, I placed my patrol car across the driveway so that no one could enter. I was informed that if the assailant saw any law enforcement he would retaliate on the hostages. I then instructed the firefighters and EMTs to control traffic and not to let anyone enter the schoolyard.

It was at this time I realized that I was not wearing my bulletproof vest. My wife would always remind me to wear it, but I thought that I knew better than she did. I then approached one of the EMTs and asked if they would contact Kayleen and have her bring my vest to me.

I then moved to different view areas of the school and would report my finding (by portable radio) to Deputy Earl Carroll. He had set up a command center in the town hall. At one point, as I was positioned at an area where I could see down the south hallway (the hall that ran past the classroom where all of the hostages were located). I noticed a man that was walking down the hall. I noticed that this man was in light clothing and I reported this to Deputy Carroll. As soon as I had reported this, I was told by Deputy Carroll that I was being monitored by the assailant and that he had heard all of my radio traffic. He said that the assailant stated, "Tell Anderson to get off the radio. I know where he is and I will retaliate."

Now our hands were even more tied.

With limited personnel and no communication there was little to do but to sit back and pray that everything went well.

Another problem was growing. Some of the townspeople (mostly parents of the children) were gathering on the road where my car was blocking the school entrance. There was talk that some were going to go in and get their children out themselves. Of course I could not allow this to happen due to the many lives that were at risk. For some time it was very tense, but everyone (but one man) calmed down and let the situation play itself out.

One person (whom I won't name) was determined to go in. I had to threaten to arrest him for interference if he continued. Later, after the bomb had gone off and when I entered the school to apprehend the assailant, I met this same person crawling down the smoke filled hall. Ironically this person matched the description of the assailant and he met me with my handgun pointing at his head. I think that he now realizes how serious and difficult a position he'd placed me in.

As the day continued and became closer to the time when the closing bells were to ring (normally to let the children out) everyone outside seemed to become more anxious. By this time many law enforcement personnel from numerous agencies (including a Jackson SWAT team, a Rock Springs SWAT team, the Wyoming Highway Patrol and the Lincoln County Sheriff's Office) were arriving.

At this time I was carrying my patrol issued shotgun. While watching my position at the entrance to the school, Deputy Greg

Goodman pulled up to me in his patrol car and was discussing the situation with me. It seemed only a few minutes had passed before I heard the explosion and the screaming of children. I couldn't believe, or I didn't want to believe that Young would have carried out his threat.

I immediately charged toward the south doors of the school. I had given my shotgun to another officer and pulled my service handgun. As I ran through the children that were exiting the school, I noticed that most were covered with black smoke and most were crying in terror. My biggest concern was that the assailant would follow the children out of the school and start spraying the crowd with gunfire. So as I was running through the crowd, I was looking for him and telling the children to get down. However, the assailant stayed in the school.

I noticed that the principal of the school (Mr. Excel) was at the door, waving and yelling for me. When I arrived at his location he informed me that he (the assailant) was still in the school and was "shooting the kids." I entered the hallway at the south door and had to go to my hands and knees due to the thick black smoke that was in the hall. I remember the fire alarm ringing and that I had a difficult time communicating with Deputy Goodman because of how loud it was.

As we made our way down the hallway I could hear gunfire. Deputy Goodman and I hurried to the classroom door where we heard the gunfire. We came up with a quick plan and decided that Deputy Goodman would open the door and, at that same time, I would charge to the center of the classroom and "take out" the assailant.

At this time Deputy Goodman and I noticed someone moving north of us. It was very difficult to identify who this was (he was in street clothes and we were looking through thick smoke) and we both had drawn down on him. For just a quick moment I realized who it was and I lowered my handgun. I informed Deputy Goodman who it was but he was not sure that I'd really identified him. I called out several times for this person (Cal Fredrickson, Cokeville City police officer) but he was not able to hear or see us. I felt that Deputy Goodman was about to shoot him and I grabbed his weapon and forced it down. Later, after recounting this event, Deputy Goodman said that when I pulled the gun down he was pulling the trigger.

As we carried out our plan of attack, Deputy Goodman pulled the door open and I charged into the classroom. Immediately I went down to my knees due to the heat of the fire and smoke that filled the room. I had to retreat and regroup. It was at this time we heard larger caliber gunfire. I made the comment to Deputy Goodman "he is trying to kill us." I felt that he was trying to shoot through the door at us. Then we heard a second round.

When I entered the classroom the second time, I entered the small restroom and found the assailant lying on the floor, dead.

At this time it became a rescue of any children/persons that still may have been in the school. I searched with many others through closets, cupboards and furniture and never found anyone.

I guess that I may have been in the school for nearly an hour and I felt someone come up to me who told me that I needed to get out of the school. I guess that I was feeling the effects of smoke inhalation and didn't realize what was happening to me. I told them that I wasn't going to leave until we had all the children accounted for. Then I felt more than one person force me out of the school and into the fresh air. I fell to my knees and the EMTs placed oxygen on me. I was unable to move for some time and the medical staff wanted to transport me to the Montpelier hospital for observation. I told them that I could not do that because I had to get home and pack for our trip to Salt Lake (brother's wedding).

After a short time I was able to get up and went to the crowd of children, teachers, school staff and parents. After what seemed like hundreds of hugs and tears a teacher who I was friends with came up to me and hugged me. While she held me she was crying and asked me, "Why didn't you come in and save us?" I am not sure if this was in jest or if she was disappointed with me for not protecting her from the assailant. I still don't know the answer.

LaRee Baker
RN, Bear Lake Memorial Hospital
(Typed Journal Submission)

My name is LaRee Baker and I have been a registered nurse at Bear Lake Memorial Hospital for twenty-four years. I will never forget the afternoon/evening of the Cokeville bombing incident. I hope to never see anything like it again. I've told several people, after the fact, that it was the closest thing to "war" I have ever seen. This is an entry taken straight from my personal journal. (I never name patient names in my journal because of confidentiality.) I suspect several of our patients or their families may remember me.

May 17, 1986
(This is about yesterday, May 16th, but it is now after midnight)

Dear Journal,

May 16th is a day I will never forget.

After working a midnight shift and getting a nap, I decided to take my boys fishing—because the weather was gorgeous. We had poles and bait in the car and were ready to go for a couple of hours when it started snowing! (That's Bear Lake for ya!) Then, it started sleeting and the wind was whipping around like crazy. So back into the house with two very disappointed boys and I went. (They insisted they didn't mind fishing in the snow!) Anyway, instead of relaxing on the reservoir bank, I was busily helping the boys clean their bedroom.

I knew nothing of what was going on over in the town of Cokeville, Wyoming. Sheila Tueller called me from the hospital and said, "LaRee, we have a disaster and need you to come now! A bomb has gone off in the Cokeville school and we have many burn victims coming in. Can you come?" Of course, I said, "yes."

I told Marty to make sure his fire department pager was on.

He walked over and the pager was off. He flipped it on and we heard the urgent message, "The bomb HAS gone off!" Very shortly, engine 10 (Bennington) was called out. I explained to Angie, as I was throwing on a uniform and grabbing some essentials, that I had been called in for an emergency and what to do until I could get home or call her. Of course, I did not have any idea how many hours I would be gone. Leaving an almost thirteen year old in charge of three younger siblings, we both got out the door as quickly as was physically possible. Angeline did a very responsible job with supper, bedtime and all.

I headed into Montpelier in my little Ford Escort, praying for things not to be as serious as they sounded. I turned on KVSI radio and midway through a news brief, I heard Jay Martindale announcing that "Keith Martindale is at the Cokeville Elementary School scene and reports that two perpetrators of the incident are dead—the man holding the bomb and his "accompanist" (he really DID say that!) and that the others injured had minor burns and cuts. I was somewhat relieved after hearing this news report. It sounded as if our patients would be less serious than the scenarios I was imagining. I was still very much in the dark as to what this was all about and who the people were that had done this.

I learned later the correct details of what had happened and who they were. (I'm sure Jay meant to say "accomplice," but at a time like this, everyone is entitled to get a little rattled. Anyway, it gave people something to chuckle about.)

Entering the hospital, I got nervous all over again. I was briefed on what we knew at that point, what my assignment was and started setting up for the patients. Two doctors, Dr. Noall Wolff and Dr. Paul Daines, and as many of the hospital personnel as could be summoned, were awaiting the arrival of incoming ambulances with teachers and children.

Though there is no such thing as a "calm disaster," I feel things were handled very smoothly, professionally and efficiently throughout the next several hours. Thirty-seven patients were seen through our emergency department and eleven of those were admitted to the hospital floor. Four patients were transferred to Logan per ambulance and one was Life Flighted to Pocatello. Ambulances from surrounding communities helped with the transport and Kemmerer and Star Valley hospitals also received patients.

A total of seventy-four patients were initially treated for burns and/or smoke inhalation through the course of the afternoon and evening—at several different hospitals. ALL hospital employees pitched in together to help—doctors, nurses, office workers, kitchen workers, housekeepers—everyone who was there or could get there was part of this. I remember the kitchen went the extra mile by fixing up many guest trays for the patients' hungry parents. For the staff that had been called in and were working hard, they furnished French dip sandwiches—on the house.

Tension ran high through the ordeal, but I personally never saw or heard of one argument or disagreement among the staff. Logan sent one doctor and four nurses to offer help to us. At one time, fourteen of our twenty-one nursing staff were there helping. I worked from about 4:00 p.m. to midnight.

At first, I worked in a "makeshift ER," set up in the cast room, assisting the doctors as they examined and evaluated patients coming in. Much later in the evening, Cleone Cochran, my boss, gave me the job of assigning beds and starting the admission procedures for those who would be staying at least overnight. It was quite an undertaking to get the patients all physically settled in bed and all the doctor's orders, admission forms and all the admitting paperwork properly done.

A system I have never seen used in the hospital setting before or since was used that day for admitting all these patients. A number was written right on the patient's hand as they came through the ER doors, with that same number on their chart. None of the traditional demographic questions were collected initially. That was a true time saving method. Of course, later it had to be done, but NOT in those first precious minutes of triage.)

I tried to accommodate siblings, friends, and other preferences as I assigned beds. I tried to make it as easy as I could on parents and grandparents with more than one child to be with. It was 10 p.m. before we got some of these kids bedded down. Most of these kids had come in cold and shivering from the wet compresses to their burns, shocky and very emotionally upset by the whole ordeal they had lived through. It was so good to see most of them perking up toward the end of the night and giggling over the "funny gowns" and the little tubes of toothpaste. I gave one little boy a washcloth and towel to wash up for bedtime and he said, "I don't know were you want me to wash—I don't have any skin!" He was referring to the fact that his hands, arms and some of his head were covered with dressings. I suggested he wash all the black off his face, but even with my help, it would not all come off.

The 10:00 p.m. news was on in every patient's room with parents, other family members and friends huddled around to hear what the rest of the world knew of "their tragedy." Reporters and camera crews from many stations—both TV and radio, had been and were at the hospital all evening trying to get headlines and stories that was tonight's biggest news story in the nation. Marty taped what he could for me—realizing I would not be able to watch it and would be interested in what was said.

I went home with a very tired body and mind that was spinning and not ready to sleep. I watched the taped news portions and listened to a bit of update on live news. My mind kept going over the night again—hearing the children crying, smelling the singed-hair burn smell and seeing the many varieties of burns in my mind—black, blistered, peeling and missing skin on various parts of their bodies.

Some of the children and many of the parents are people I know from prior hospital stays, Cub Scouts or other connections. I remember constantly thinking through all this, "This could have been any school, any day and it could have been my own kids!"

I guess the only thing I was unhappy about was that I felt the news media really played down the injuries. Yes, the kids were lucky to be alive, but there were very serious burns—many on particularly vulnerable problem areas such as the face, ears and hands that would take months and years to heal properly—if ever. Many came in trembling in pain and fright and cried with excruciating pain as the burns were dressed. Many of the patients had to come in for daily treatments—debridement and dressings. I'm certain that these little victims and their parents are feeling that the injuries are more than minor.

Two girls ended up on the University of Utah intensive care— one in critical and the one in serious condition. I will say it again. The best thing I witnessed through all this, was that everyone in the hospital and community worked together, pulled together working side by side without bickering or contention. That was really great.

After the fact notes:

I learned after the fact that not only were my husband and I both called to help with this emergency, but my brother-in-law Randy White, had been called to Cokeville and played a key role with law enforcement.

We did see the patients for a long while after their initial treatment for dressing changes and evaluation of the healing process. I will honestly say that I have only heard good reports of how the hospital handled this emergency. Reed Dayton, an ex-officio hospital board member from Cokeville, commented that he had received many favorable comments from Cokeville patients and families who had expressed appreciation for the care and service received at the Bear Lake Memorial Hospital following the bombing incident.

This nice and complementary letter came later to Bear Lake Memorial Hospital:

Dear Nursing Staff:
We, as the staff of Logan Regional Hospital, would like to

express our appreciation for being called to assist you in the disaster in Cokeville. We were and still are very impressed with the expert care given by all of you, especially in a crisis situation. We feel you all handled the multiple cases with skill and expertise. We wonder how well we would have maintained, as you did, if the injured had been our own children. Parents, EMTs, and medical staff were well organized and in control, so the injured were cared for very well. Our hats off to you for a very impressive and "well done" job!

Sincerely,

> *Lori Daines, R.N.*
> *Nancy Stiles, R.N.*
> *Peggy Wolfley, R.N.*
> *Lelan Dainew, R.N.*
> *Carol Smith, R.N.*

John D. Bowers
Lincoln County Deputy Sheriff
(Typed Submission)

The following is a summary of my involvement in the unfortunate Cokeville bombing that took place years ago:

On the day of the attack on the Cokeville elementary school, I was employed as a deputy sheriff for the Lincoln County Sheriff's Office. In 1984 I began my employment with Lincoln County as a jailer in Kemmerer, Wyoming. When I started with Lincoln County, my wife, two small children and I rented a lot in Cokeville for our mobile home and lived across the street from Craig Chadwick. After nine months working as a jailer, I was promoted to a road deputy and worked for a short time in Kemmerer. I was then transferred to Star Valley as a deputy sheriff and on May 16, 1986, was living in Star Valley and working as a deputy sheriff.

On the day of the attack, I was off duty, spending time with my family at my father-in-law's. We had been outside most of the day with the kids and later, went in the house to visit. My father-in-law turned on the TV and was watching a program. The program was interrupted when a banner ran across the TV about the hostage situation in Cokeville. I called the sheriff's office. They told me they had been trying to locate the deputies to respond, however, they had not been able to locate me and I was then asked to respond to Cokeville. I notified dispatch that I was responding to Cokeville and I was able to hear the busy radio traffic from the other officers already at the scene as I drove toward Cokeville.

As I neared the Canyon Club, I heard the radio traffic indicating that the bomb had gone off and that officers were entering the school. The radio noise then became a blur with emergency personnel and officers attempting to coordinate the evacuation of the children. I felt my adrenaline rushing through my body as I was trying to understand from the radio traffic where the hostage takers were at in the school. At some point, just before I arrived in Cokeville, there was radio traffic indicating that the hostage takers had been killed in the bombing.

When I pulled into the school parking lot, my first observation was the stunned and scared look on the on-lookers faces and those people who were now walking away from the school. I contacted one of my supervisors who directed me to help with the removal of the hostage takers' bodies. I became sick inside when I viewed the bodies of the hostage takers with their charred skin and the smell. My job was to help the coroner's office load the bodies. I was dreading the task of touching the bodies and being in the proximity of the smell of the charred flesh.

There was a delay while the coroner's assistants obtained the necessary equipment to load the bodies. During the short delay, I was asked by some other officers to help in the measurement and diagram of the crime scene. As we walked around the premises and inside the school, I came in contact with numerous people who were at the school during the bombing. There were so many there that I can't remember all of their names, but I do remember their scared expressions and the tears that ran down their faces. I tried to comfort them the best I could and help them find other friends or loved ones that they could be with.

When I walked back to where the bodies were, I found that other officers had helped the coroner's office load the bodies so I was free to go back to assisting with the other people at the scene.

The most vivid memory I have of the incident that day was when I walked into the classroom where the bomb had gone off. It was like walking into a black hole with a terrible smell from the burnt flesh. I remember looking at the walls, thinking to myself, there must have been children that had been killed during the blast. At that point, it wasn't clear if children had been killed during the explosion and in my mind, I was sure that there were numerous children who were seriously injured or killed because of damage to the room. When I later found out that no children had been killed, I was amazed. The explosion had been so great and hot that it had actually melted items in the room that were across from where the bomb had been set off. From a law enforcement perspective, it makes no sense that those children were not killed or injured worse than they were. From a personal standpoint, it is obvious to me that those children were protected.

Ultimately, when the majority had left the scene and the school was sealed off, my thoughts were that I wished I could have done more. As I reflect upon that day, I am thankful for all of those people who worked so hard to help those around them. There were so many people that arrived at the scene who were able to comfort and help their families, neighbors and loved ones. I believe that these acts of kindness from all of the people played a great role in helping those people involved in the trauma get through it.

The experience has not had a terribly adverse effect on my life. Because I arrived after the bomb had gone off, I was spared the trauma of seeing the little injured children. However, the experience has made me appreciate what a wonderful place we live in. The kindness and love that was shown by everyone after the bombing to the victims and to the victims' families is a wonderful reflection upon our communities. I, like many, am just hopeful that those people that were victimized by the evil acts of the two hostage takers, may be able to deal with this traumatic past.

Allen D. Carter, M.D.
Afton, Wyoming ER
(Typed Submission)

Thank you for your inquiry regarding the Cokeville bombing of 1986. I do have some recollections from that day as it was my first day on the job in Afton, fresh out of my residency training. I was scheduled to begin my practice July 1. Dr. Morgan had become fatigued and asked me to come up (since I already had a Wyoming license) and cover the medical services in Afton for a few days. I had been in Star Valley for a couple of hours when news of the bombing came in. At first I thought that perhaps it was some sort of a joke or hoax, but we soon learned otherwise.

We received eight patients, as I recall, into our emergency room from the bombing. Most of them had burns over somewhat limited areas of the body involving extremities. One little girl had some facial and extremity burns and on examination we noticed soot in her airway and kept her in the hospital overnight. She did go on to develop fever and mild complications relating to her lungs, but did recover adequately to be discharged from the hospital after a day or two, as I remember. They were a very pleasant family to deal with.

One of the notable things that happened that day is that a number of physicians from Jackson received word of the bombing and got in private airplanes owned by one or more of the doctors and flew to Afton to stand by and assist. This included general surgeons and orthopedic surgeons from Jackson. In fact, we had, I think, as many doctors as we had patients by the time the ambulances began arriving.

This put me in an awkward situation as a brand new physician trying to supervise a group of experienced surgeons, none of whom I had ever met before, but they were very helpful and very gracious to use their personal aircraft and the time and means to get down and assist.

Thanks for your inquiry. I wish you success in your endeavor to commemorate this infamous day.

Craig L. Chadwick
Cokeville Fire Chief
Husband of One Staff Member Survivor
Father of Two Student Survivors
(Mailed Submission)

Regarding the Cokeville bombing of May 16, 1986, I was a coal miner and was working for Gulf Oil (of which P&M was a subsidiary). The day this occurred was different for me because at the mine on what we call the floor underneath the number 1 seam of coal in the Big Pit of 1UD, the floor was sliding. A large chunk of material thirteen to fifteen feet thick, five hundred feet wide and about two thousand feet long, which lies on a seventeen degree angle, was moving.

I was operating a D9 Cat that day, and was going as fast as I could up and down the slope to retrieve twenty foot sections of eight inch Victaulic water pipe. I would make a trip to the bottom with a couple of lengths and by the time I went back up to get some more the gap had widened ten to fifteen feet and I would have to build a quick bridge with dirt to get back up and get more pipe.

I was just about done when my supervisor John Hunzie called on the radio and said I needed to come down as fast as I could. He told me there was a hostage situation at the elementary school in Cokeville and that I had better head home. My wife Gayle was the librarian and my two kids, Justin and Melanie, attended school there.

Cem Mackey and I started home and were listening to KMER radio. Just as we rounded Sage Junction, about twenty minutes from home, the announcer came on and said a bomb had just gone off inside the school and it was total chaos outside. Cem (who had several kids in that school) and I didn't know what to think at this point and headed for town as fast as we could.

I was currently the fire chief and training officer for the EMTs and trying to run things through my mind about family and also helping the fire department and EMS was difficult. I had countless hours of training for both, but nothing prepares you for the scene we witnessed as we pulled into town. It was total chaos. My first priority was Gayle and my kids. I remember Ron Hartley (deputy sheriff) telling me he had seen Gayle and Melanie and they were OK. I caught someone else and they happened to say they had seen Justin running down the street.

My initial thought was that my family was not seriously hurt, so I had better go help the firemen. I got to the school at the same time Lyle Forrest was lifting a lady's body out a window. The smoke was still very thick and I could not see into the room. After another search of the building, it was determined there was no fire and a man's body was found in a small bathroom. The scene was taken over by law enforcement to start their investigations.

The town was still in a frenzy and the media had showed up and tried to talk with anyone they could. Now I was determined to go home and see how my family really was. I found Gayle, Justin and Melanie home and physically they were fine. They were pretty shaken up emotionally. We learned Jenny Ferrin (Gayle's sister's daughter), had been burned, and was headed for the hospital. There was no telephone service because of the overload to the system, so letting our outside family know our family was OK was virtually impossible.

Now, twenty years later, as I reflect back on the events I can remember, I know that a higher power definitely was in control. Through all the investigation and research that I was a part of, the mechanics and velocity of the potential of the bomb that was used should have destroyed at least a quarter of the entire building. Many things can never be explained and are part of the mysteries of God.

A few months later, I was asked by the International Association of Fire Chiefs to speak along with T. Deb Wolfley (Lincoln County Sheriff), at their convention in Dallas, Texas. Deb and I flew to Dallas and I discovered that somehow I had left my prepared speech at home. I was scheduled to talk for about forty-five minutes to six thousand fire chiefs from all over the world. Amazingly, I sat down for a few minutes and made some notes. Everything went well and I talked with several people after that who wanted to know more.

Robert Cory
Cokeville EMT
Father of Two Student Survivors
(Typed Submission)

I had been a volunteer on the Cokeville ambulance for several years when the Cokeville bombing incident occurred. That particular day I was working at my job on the Union Pacific Railroad inspecting track on a motor car between Cokeville and Montpelier. We only had one vehicle at the time so on Fridays, when I ended my inspection of the tracks in Montpelier, my wife and kids would come and pick me up from work and we would go and visit my wife's parents and have dinner and then head for home.

This day, however, would be different. I had heard on the radio that the children and teachers were being held hostage in the school. I phoned my wife to see if she knew what was happening as we had two daughters in the school, one in kindergarten and one in first grade. I told her that I would find a way home and not to worry about coming to Montpelier to pick me up—just stay there for the kids. I called the railroad dispatcher and explained what was going on and they got me a straight shot into Montpelier on my motor car. I then contacted my friend Murray Sneddon who owns the Ford dealership in Montpelier and he said he would have a car outside the dealership waiting for me. I hurried down to the dealership and found an LTD in front of the dealership with the door open and engine running—waiting for me. I got in the car and headed for Cokeville.

As I reached the highway to head home the radio announced that the bomb had gone off. I put the car in high gear and headed home, not knowing what I would find. It took me twenty minutes at the max to get to Cokeville. As I neared Todd Dayton's house there was an ambulance on the side of the road that had overheated. I stopped to see if everything was OK. They got it restarted so I continued on into town.

The roads were closed going down Main Street so I parked at the church and walked down toward the school.

Several children were in different people's homes on Main Street and they were loading others who were burned onto buses to take to the different hospitals. One of the EMTs told me that my mother had taken my two daughters and my niece home and that they were OK. They needed EMTs to go on the buses with the burned children and teachers. One bus was going to Kemmerer and one to Montpelier. Craig Taylor, who was also an EMT at the time, asked if he could go on the bus to Montpelier as that is where his son had been taken, so I volunteered to go on the bus to Kemmerer. It wasn't until I got home that night at around 10:00 p.m. that I discovered the note my wife had left me telling me she had taken my daughters to the hospital in Montpelier. The phone lines were all busy so I headed back to Montpelier and found my daughters admitted as patients in the hospital.

I think the incident made me more cautious about things and people. I watch and pay closer attention to people—especially strangers in town. When my children were younger I didn't like to let them out of my sight.

Paul Daines, M.D.
Bear Lake Memorial Hospital
Montpelier, Idaho
(Interviewed by LaRee Baker)

Dr. Paul Daines, now retired from Bear Lake Memorial Hospital, remembers being out at his ranch and on a 2-way radio the day of the Cokeville disaster. He got a request to get to a landline phone ASAP. He went immediately to Lee Rigby's home and called in to the hospital. He learned of the Cokeville hostage situation and was told that David Young knew him (Dr. Daines) and wanted to negotiate with him. This message was relayed: "I'll talk to you if you will come in unarmed. "Dr. Daines remembers feeling the gravity and weight of this request, but agreed to go to the Cokeville school. However, before Dr. Daines could even get out of Lee's home, the word came that the bomb had gone off. He was now needed at the hospital to prepare for an unknown number of incoming patients.

Dr. Daines recalled that things ran very well. "Of course, the first priority was to sort out the 2nd degree burns from the 1st degree burns." He recalled that there were not many 3rd degree burns. The treatment of the day was evaluation, Silvadine ointment and dressings. "We went through a ton of Silvadine at the time and in the weeks ahead." A very important decision on Dr. Daines' part was to make a call to friends at Stanford University where he had connections from past plastic surgery training and work.

Advice was obtained and actually some initial rehabilitation steps were instigated from that initial call. Permission was obtained from Dr. Laub, the head of the Plastic and Reconstructive Surgery Department, for a team to come to Bear Lake Memorial. The team of five burn specialists was headed by Dr. Ronald Sato, burn unit director at Santa Clara Valley Medical Center, which is part of Stanford University. Dr. Daines remembers meeting the team at the Salt Lake

Airport and bringing them to Montpelier the next day. All the burn victims were invited back to be seen by the specialists.

In an article in the *News Examiner* dated June 19, 1986, Rod Jacobson, administrator of the hospital, was quoted as saying, "The team spent two days seeing the patients and going through the ABC's of burn care and making recommendations for burn treatment." It ended up being a learning opportunity for many. Doctors from outside the area also came and it was reported that it became an excellent training opportunity for burn care."

Dr. Daines recalls the Stanford team being very complimentary of the care that had been and was being given to these patients. The care for many was ongoing—requiring soaking in the Hubbard tanks, debridement of the burns and redressing. Many required the ongoing care of compression stockings. Dr. Daines remembered that the physical therapist from Caribou Memorial Hospital came to help with some of the follow up treatment and lent us Hubbard tanks. Dr. Daines marvels that things went as well as they did. It was such a huge calamity for such a small community to sustain. Dr. Daines said, "We shouldn't brag, but we felt these patients got excellent care."

Thanks to Dr. Paul Daines who allowed me this interview with him about the Cokeville bomb incident. I hope to have captured the essence of his story in this writing.—LaRee Baker

NaDene Dana
Town Clerk
Mother of Two Student Survivors
(Interview)

Basically I did not work on Fridays at the time. I just felt like I needed to come over to the office that day and I don't know why and so I was over there and I was just working along. I was here about half an hour and Princess came bursting through the door, saying that her dad had taken the elementary school hostage.

Kathy Davison and the state guy for emergency management were over in DeMont's office. Kathy came over to my office and we questioned Princess and tried to calm her down a little bit. We questioned her and found out that two guys were in the white van and handcuffed to the seats. They were in on the project with her dad and at the last minute they backed out so he handcuffed them to the seats.

Kathy hurried and called the dispatch. And at the time, our police officer was in Logan getting his car worked on. They had it all torn apart. I called him and he told them to put his car back together. They must have, because he was home in nothing flat. Earl Carroll was also a county deputy who lived here at that time. He was in Kemmerer and he was here within twenty minutes The mayor was in Montpelier and came as fast as he could. I didn't know where he was. I just knew he was in Montpelier. He heard it on the radio.

By the time the police officers got here, Princess Young came in and explained that there was a bomb so I called all the hospitals and EMTs from the surrounding area and had them on alert and had the fire departments come. By that time, I had telephone calls from Tom Brokaw and a bunch of others. It did not take very long for it to go out in the news and to be disseminated. Our two lines rang off the hook.

It was pretty warm outside. We went out and took the men out of the van and put them in the conference room. John Teichert came in and sat in the room with them. One thing I will always remember: I went downstairs to ask John something and he was on his knees in the middle of his office. This was a little later when someone else was with the two men.

David Young would call and of course wanted to talk to the police officers. Sometimes Max Excell would call and give the police officers information that David Young wanted them to know. He wanted, (I think) a million and a half dollars. Russ Thornock was ready and prepared to sell his place. At the time, I think he was County commissioner. As things went on, we saw roadblocks, fire trucks, and ambulances where Young couldn't see them. Main Street, clear to my house, was blocked. I couldn't go home. The high school kids couldn't go home from school. A lot of them were here in the senior center.

The community pulled together very well. I just heard the police people in the police offices, jam packed with people, and then I heard, "The bomb went off! The bomb went off!" There was such a mass exodus out the door. I had two kids down there. Where am I supposed to be? Here? Down there with our kids?

Bob (my husband) was there, he said, "I'll go that way and you stay here because someone has to be here for the calls." I said a quick little prayer and kept going. Mrs. Excell was there and saw the kids and grabbed them. Bob walked by them and did not recognize them. They were just black and all you could see was the whites of their eyes. They had smoke inhalation. Bob took them to the Star Valley hospital. They were OK. Some of them that were worse were transferred to Logan from Montpelier. I remember Gina Taylor went there.

You can't believe the outpouring of money, $35,000-$40,000 came in. My job was increased by three times, right there. We set up a fund and it took care of the travel expenses to and from doctors. Some of it helped pay for the treatment the children received. We had money left over afterward. We had a board that approved the expenditures and we now have some tables over in the school library that were purchased with final expenses in memory of the bombing. We opened a checking account with the bank and that's how we dealt with it. Every year for each kid that was in the bombing situation, they received a check upon graduation. The bank figured it out, so each graduating Senior involved in the bombing received $108 from the Cokeville Children's Fund. Tina Cook would give me their addresses if they had moved. She kept track of all that. The town withstood the expenses of the postage for the whole thing. We sent thank you letters back to those people who contributed. It was a lot. The town had a lot of extra expense back then. We had many counselors who volunteered to come from all over the United States. All were willing to help.

The one thing that was the hardest of all for me was afterward when it was time to debrief. That was hard. You go in a room and you have to talk to them about what you felt and how you handled it. That was when I broke down. I felt like maybe I should have been there for my kids but I needed to be here because I would be more use here. I've had to put it out of my head. My kids still, today, cannot fill up their cars. The smell of gasoline makes them sick. They can do it, they just don't like to. They prefer not to dwell on it.

We asked them what they were doing while they were in the room. We asked, "Why didn't you get together?" They just said, "We knew we would be OK." It was just a feeling. They were in third grade. When the bomb went off, Frank Lazcanotegui went over to the school and pulled one of the windows right out of the frame so the kids could get out. He is very strong.

It was a day to remember and be thankful for all the blessings our community received.

Kathy Davison
Lincoln County Emergency Coordinator
(Handwritten Submission)

Little did I know when I rose that day that it would be the longest day of my life.

I had been the emergency coordinator for about six weeks and still had little idea of what my job was. I had been called to Cokeville, Wyoming, a little town about forty-five miles from Kemmerer. With me were Grant Sorenson from the state office in Cheyenne and Bob Looney, our area Coordinator.

We had met along the river with the Army Corps of Engineers all morning to look at the flood situation and planned on building a dike along the river.

As we finished our meeting at the town hall and were getting ready to leave the building, a young girl came running in and right into me. She was very agitated and started talking about her dad being in the school and people were going to get killed. I asked her to explain and she said her dad had taken the school hostage. I asked the town clerk to call the town marshal and the resident deputy.

In the meantime, I asked the girl to explain to me. She said her dad had taken guns and a bomb into the elementary school. I asked why and she said her stepmother was with him. From my training as a dispatcher I assumed it must be a domestic situation and they were fighting. Then I asked and she said no, her stepmother was helping her father.

About this time the clerk told me that neither of her officers were in town. I told her to call and get the sheriff. When she did, the dispatcher had a hard time believing what was going on, so because I knew the dispatcher, I took the phone and told her to get everyone headed to Cokeville, knowing then that we had two armed people in the school.

I then asked the girl, Princess Young was her name, to tell me what was going on and she informed me that she didn't want to tell her dad's name, but that he was going to ask for money and hold the school hostage until he got it. I explained that if we could find someone who knew him, we might be able to help him, but we needed his name. She then told me his name was David Young and there were two other guys who were going to help but they decided they did not want to be any part of it and her dad had handcuffed them and put them into the back of the van—the same van that she had driven to the town hall.

I quickly sent someone out to bring them into the town hall and started asking them questions. They said they had nothing to do with this plan, that David Young had told them and one other guy, a few years before, that he had a big business deal going and asked if they wanted to invest in it. They had been sending him money and finally he had called them and said it was time to come out, it was ready.

When they'd arrived a few days earlier, he wouldn't tell them what it was, so the third guy had left and they'd stayed. When Young finally told them that morning, they refused to help. David told them that he planned to ask for two million dollars for each child in the school. Princess had also helped her dad until she heard this. When she got scared her father had gotten angry and told her to take the van, along with the two guys and get out. She had come straight to the town hall. At this time I was trying to keep the sheriff informed as I talked to Princess.

There were a lot of people starting to come into the town hall and Princess told me that her dad had said if anyone tried to get into the school, he would start shooting the kids. I immediately realized that I needed to do something with the people, so I asked them to go downstairs to the senior center and make sandwiches and coffee for the responders. They did this. At some point someone came over and asked what to do as they were out of sandwich stuff and I told them to get all that the little store had and keep making sandwiches. The sheriff asked me at some point what I was going to do with them as the kitchen was full and I told him I didn't know but I guess freeze them and the seniors would eat them. We ended up feeding the first responders all weekend as the cafes filled with the media.

The state guy, Grant, and I went toward the school to stop anyone from going into the school. We put Grant's little red car across the road and right away a lady came up and I told her she couldn't go into the school. She said her children were in there. I told her I couldn't let her go and would arrest her if she tried. She then left. Then a fireman came up and was angry because he thought it was a drill. When I explained, he asked what needed to be done. We replaced the car with a fire engine and started to set up a perimeter around the school.

The sheriff arrived about that time and I was relieved thinking my job now would be to just work on resources. But he told me to help with the evacuation. So a patrolman and I started evacuating the homes near the school. At the first home I went to a lady who told me that her husband had a gun and wouldn't leave. I went in and talked to him and explained that we needed him to go to the town hall. He didn't want his home looted and I explained that if the bomb went off his home might be ruined and that if everyone had a gun, some innocent people would get hurt or killed and that we had people coming to prevent any looting. He gave me the gun and left. We finally had the houses evacuated, so I went back to the town hall and started lining people up. We had a SWAT team and bomb squad on the way. We were working on getting other ambulances and fire equipment from nearby areas.

I had just stopped to talk to the sheriff and I heard the fire alarm go off at the school. The sheriff said the bomb went off. I didn't believe it and told him no, someone just pulled the fire alarm. He said no, it was the bomb. All I could do at this time was pray. Then the sheriff and I ran toward the school and I could see smoke coming out everywhere.

We quickly set up a triage. Right away I could see firemen getting children out the window. I will never forget those little black tear-stained faces and when they hit the ground they would take off running. It looked like popcorn popping out those windows. We didn't understand why the kids were running away, until later we learned that they had been told if they got out of the school, people would be waiting to shoot them. I remember thinking, *what will we do if any child doesn't come out with all of these parents around?*

There were many heroes in Cokeville that day, all of the responders, the dispatchers, the parents and especially the children. Everyone did their jobs, even knowing that one of their loved ones might not come out.

This incident affected all of us. When I finally got home, I had two scared little girls. All they knew was that I was in Cokeville and this awful thing was going on. They had no idea if I was in the school or where. It took all summer before they were OK with me leaving them.

The miracles that day cannot be counted. The angels were there protecting everyone. I know that I was led by the Heavenly Spirit.

Gail Dayton
Head of Purchasing, Bear Lake Memorial Hospital
(Interviewed by LaRee Baker)

Gail Dayton was the head of purchasing at the time of the incident. She remembered the day well. She had relatives involved as patients and was very involved in the disaster as a hospital employee. She opened up the basement as additional supplies were needed, helped with the numbering system at the ER door as the patients came in and anything else that she was asked to do or that she saw needed to be done. She recalled how well organized everything seemed to be. One thing that stood out for her was that the children were so calm as they came in.

Ron Douglas
Lincoln County Sheriff's Office
(Email Submission)

The Beginning

It was a nice (rare) spring early afternoon in south Lincoln County. A lot of white cumulus clouds blew by. I was at the Lincoln County Jail, getting ready to transport some Uinta County inmates to the county line for transfer to a Uinta County deputy. As I pushed the doorbell to the sally port jail door, Maggie informed me through the intercom that there was a hostage situation at Cokeville Elementary School.

I immediately headed out of Kemmerer and west on Highway 30 toward Cokeville. Lincoln County Detective Earl Carroll was also dispatched and we were in contact with each other via radio. Lincoln County dispatch would provide us with updated information as they received it.

Earl would take on the role of on-scene commander because of his position within the department. Come to find out we were the only two peace officers available at the time in the entire county. Cal Frederickson, Cokeville police chief was away, other Lincoln County deputies were either on days off or in some type of training. Kathy Davison happened to be in Cokeville that day doing emergency preparedness duties at the Cokeville Town Hall when Princess Young (daughter of David and Doris Young) drove up in a van with two men handcuffed behind each other.

As Earl and I approached Cokeville, he instructed me to take the intersection of Main Street and the access road into the elementary school while he proceeded to the Cokeville Town Hall to get briefed by Kathy and start collecting intelligence. I positioned the patrol car with the front facing northeast and the rear facing southwest. This allowed for optimal protection from gunfire, for traffic and crowd control and created a great observation position for intelligence gathering. I drew my shotgun. When I first looked through my binoculars, I observed the south entrance of the school and a man was propping open doors with chairs (later I found out that this was the janitor for the school). Unfortunately I do not remember any time frames while piecing this story together.

Over the course of the hour to hour and a half, crowds started forming so crowd control was an issue. The local radio newsman approached and asked where the press tent was setup. I deterred him for quite a while until I talked to the sheriff and he had established a room in the Cokeville Town Hall. During this time more law enforcement help started showing up. Brad Anderson from the Wyoming Highway Patrol arrived along with ambulance and fire. During a quiet moment there was a gentleman standing next me. He had a sad look on his face and in his eyes. I asked him if he needed any help. He said that he was from the Cokeville Fire Department and the situation would not be so hard if his five year old son was not one of the hostages. That really put a lump in my throat and made me realize the magnitude of this situation.

As the afternoon wore on, more deputies arrived to include Corporal Greg Goodman and Sheriff T. Deb Wolfley, who set up a command post at the Cokeville Town Hall. This helped strengthen the perimeter and provided better crowd control. Large news trucks started to show up from Salt Lake City. Lincoln County Communications Center was extremely busy. I sure take my hat off to all of the dispatchers for handling the situation that day.

We would receive periodic updates from Lincoln County Communication Center and from the sheriff as the information became available. Two pieces of information received really concerned me: One piece of information revealed was that David Young was the Cokeville Town Marshal back in 1976, which meant he had a law enforcement background and knew law enforcement tactics, and the other was that there were two EMT volunteers in the school and they had their radios with them, which meant that Young could monitor our channel and know what is going on. I remember that intelligence information was being passed by word of mouth after this information had been revealed. At this point, I also learned that the Jackson Hole, Wyoming Sheriff's Office SWAT team was in the air and headed our way.

Demands of the Hostage Takers

At first there was no contact with David or Doris Young. But then a series of demands started to roll out of the school. At this point I was wondering if David himself was calling in the demands from the school, but I later found out that the principal was released from the classroom to go to the office and call the command post and release the information to Deb. The first demand was that Young wanted to speak with the president of the United States, Ronald Reagan. That was denied. The second request was a ransom of two million dollars per child, totaling 320 million dollars (this is significant later on). All went quiet after this.

Boom

It was getting late in the afternoon. I think three hours had passed. Corporal Greg Goodman had driven up in his car. I leaned over and was talking with Greg on the driver's side when a thunderous boom erupted. Everything around me went into slow motion. I turned and started running for the school as did Greg (we were on Main Street at the time). As we headed up the access road, pandemonium had erupted.

Children started running out of the south end of the school, and others were being handed out of the classroom window where they had been held hostage. I remember at some point that Patrolman Brad Anderson had joined us. Parents and the fire department were also running and driving toward the school. From what I remember, Greg,

Brad and I headed for the south side of the school. While running we were turning parents back and trying to control the situation as quickly as possible. Children were streaming out of the south end of the school, as we were turning the parents around and getting the children running toward Main Street. I remember seeing "snapshots" of these people as we made contact. I remember three or four kids that were black with soot and one little girl that had skin hanging from her face and hands. I remember a man staggering out (he looked drunk) and his back was all bloody. I found out later that this was the music teacher, John Miller, who had been shot in the back by a .22 (more about this later).

A fire truck was at the south entrance and I remember Deputy Randy White getting a Scotts air pack and there were no more. I cannot remember who, but one of the deputies told the fire crew to get out of the area and go back to the perimeter until we had a chance to clear the school. The truck started pulling back. When Greg, Brad and I got to the south entrance, both doors had been propped open by the janitor earlier. I found this to be a godsend because it helped ventilate and clear some of the dark, thick smoke and provide some light in the hallway. The electricity had been knocked out by the bomb going off.

Somewhere during all of the confusion, another deputy or city police officer from Idaho (I think he was from Bear Lake County) joined us, so we had four of us for the entry into the school. At this point I had no idea who was at the north end of the school, if any of the terrorists were holed up in the classroom, if they were dead or alive, how much fire power they had, if all of the children and adults where out, if we had more hostages, or if any of the children were dead.

I remember Greg was on the east side of the south entrance, I was on the west side. But I do not remember what side Brad was on or the police officer from Idaho. Greg was the first to enter, traversing the east side of the wall, at this point, I do not remember if Brad went in next or if I did. Brad (I think) was on the east side of the hallway, behind Greg, and I was on the west side. I had my shotgun. I had never been in the school before, so it was like going into a cave with only scant light.

The first human contact we made almost got shot. The male subject was head down in the south hallway. I remember Greg yelling something and I put the barrel of the shotgun right in his face. The gentleman identified himself as either a parent or firefighter (I cannot remember) and he had run into the school after the bomb went off. He was instructed to leave the building and go back to the perimeter. I heard Greg yell halt again, identify himself or he would be shot.

As I moved up the west side of the wall, I came upon a classroom door, checked it and it was locked. On the east side of the hallway, I remember seeing several rifles, clips and canisters of ammo. On the east wall, the first classroom door (solid) became visible through the dark, smoky air. Greg had moved beyond it and to the second door where all of the hostages were held. Not being familiar with the layout of the school, there was no telling what was beyond. In retrospect, part of the intelligence gathering should have been getting the layout of the school. I remember that there were three of us around the door, I think it was Brad, the peace officer from Idaho and myself. At this point, my memory is a little sketchy, but I do remember handing my shotgun to the Idaho officer.

Someone propped the door open and I remember entering the southeast classroom first. I entered by scanning the room from north to south and placing my back up against the west wall and moving down about half way. What I remember is the classroom being filled with thick black smoke and I was having trouble breathing because of it. I did a quick sweep of the room with my gun and flashlight and determined that no one was in the room. I moved north to a small hallway that separated the classrooms and noticed two doors. The north door separated the classrooms and it was closed. I was relying on my fellow officers at this point to secure the classroom where all of the hostages were held.

I noticed there was water running from underneath the door on the west wall of the classroom and surmised it was a bathroom. As far as I can remember, there was another officer behind me, but I do not know who it was. At this point, not knowing if any of the terrorists were holed up in the room, I swung the door open with my gun ready. In the northwest corner of the room, lay David Young. He was in a seated position with his back in the northwest corner and his legs sprawled and facing the southeast corner of the room.

I walked out of the bathroom and into the next classroom.

What I walked into was disbelief; I wonder how any child or adult could have survived the explosion. I observed a grocery basket that was mangled and on the floor, a taped off square in the middle of the room, ceiling tiles missing. Most of all I wondered how one hundred fifty people fit into that small classroom.

After talking with all of the deputies and ensuring that end of the school wing was secure, I noticed that I was really having a hard time breathing now that I was coming down from the adrenaline high. I made my way out of the classroom and to the south entrance and to the sunlight. Brad Anderson, the highway patrolman was ahead of me. I watched Brad go down to the ground and he appeared to be in some type of distress. I went to his aid and the last thing I remember is when I stepped out into the fresh air, my lungs started burning and I went down to the ground, too.

The next thing I remember is being on an ambulance stretcher surrounded by children and headed toward Kemmerer. All I can remember about the ride is hearing some of the children screaming, crying and saying how scared they were. I remember being on oxygen and it burned my lungs on every inhale and exhale.

The next event I am going to describe impacted my very soul and to this day I will never forget the feeling or image engraved in my memory. I felt the ambulance stop and start backing up. When the doors opened, my wife was standing there with the most horrid look on her face I had ever seen and I felt bad for putting her through this. Once I spoke to her and let her know that I was all right, she relaxed.

I was wheeled out of the ambulance and the hospital had set up a triage center in the parking lot. I remember telling the nurses and doctors to take care of the kids first. When I met with the nurses and doctors, I was still on oxygen and each breath burned, when they added moisture to the oxygen, it seemed to help, but the burning never went away. I was at the hospital for about an hour and was feeling better.

My wife told me that Cindy Miller, Deputy Scott Miller's wife, came to the Ben Franklin store and told her that she had picked up our two sons from daycare and that I was on the way in from the bombing scene in an unknown condition. That is why she had such a horrid look on her face when they opened up the ambulance doors. Cindy, thanks for all of your help!

After I was released from the hospital, I wanted to go back to the school and help with the processing of the scene. Since there were no deputies in the area, my wife took me up in her car. That was one of the nicest rides I ever had with my wife. As we drove by Cokeville airport, I had never seen so many aircraft parked there. There were helicopters and different sizes of planes. The only time I had seen activity at the airport while on patrol was when an aircraft flying overhead would trip the light via radio frequency.

After returning to the scene, all of the chaos had subsided and all of the major news channels from Salt Lake City had their big satellite trucks parked around the school. The sheriff took command along with Earl and Ron Hartley, Lincoln County's other detective (Side Note: Ron Hartley had children in the school at the time and our hearts went out to them that day). I heard a siren blaring; it was Deputy Scott Miller escorting the ATF out of Salt Lake City.

When I walked back into the school, a spooky feeling came over me. The entire day's events seemed surreal. I walked into the first classroom I had entered earlier and checked the bathroom. The only things left were blood and water. Then I entered the classroom where the hostages had been held. I am still amazed to this day that 154 people were in that room; it must have been horrid for them.

I noticed that the ceiling tiles were blown out and there were what appeared to be brains lodged on the ceiling. I walked out of the classroom and down the hall (north) and through the remainder of the school. It was late then and the sheriff had gathered all us deputies up to tell us we were done for the evening. Rod Norton (who is a lieutenant at a sheriff's office in the state of Utah) drew the first watch.

We all headed over to the local café to have some dinner. I remember chatting with one of the Jackson Hole SWAT team members who I had been to the academy with on several occasions. We chatted about some of his "cop stories" from his time with the LAPD. I remember seeing Terry Drinkwater from CBS news.

We Were Lucky

In the following weeks, stories were starting to filter out from the hostages and other people who were involved with the scene. I found out that David had rigged a triggering device from the bomb to his person using a piece of string, a clothespin and a piece of conduit. David had wired the connection points to each side of the clothespin that closes. He pinched the felt conduit between the two ends of the clothespin and tied one end of the string to the felt conduit and the other to his wrist.

Doris was the one who set the bomb off, but there was some confusion for many years as to what happened. One report from a student states that Doris said, "What would happen if I did this?" making a pulling motion with her arm, placing tension on the string and releasing the felt conduit from between the clothespin and allowing the contacts to connect, setting the bomb off. The second scenario was that she was startled, which caused her to turn, setting the bomb off. (I found out years later from Celeste Jackman that Doris was startled, setting the bomb off).

We were lucky in the sense that Greg did not shoot John during the entry and clearing of the building, but most of all, the children and adult hostages were lucky because when the bomb went off, it only ignited the gas bottle and not the bottle full of metal shards and bb's. When the bomb went off, it exploded up in the air, flash burning the children sitting around the bomb. If the bomb had exploded properly, it would have leveled the south wing of the school, killing everyone.

Why?

For several months, many unanswered questions loomed. Why did David ask for ransom totaling $320 million dollars? When John Miller went running by, why did David shoot him in the back with his .22 cal gun and kill his wife with the .44 cal? The answers soon came.

David Young kept meticulous journals of his life. I remember boxes and boxes of notebooks and photos. The starting date of one notebook was October 1956. I remember reading a few pages of Young's writing. It appeared that he was trying to mimic Zen, but he did a horrible job of it. It took Ron Hartley about six months to go through everything, but the answer as to *why* the bombing took place was written in a red, 8 1/2" x 11" spiral notebook titled *The Year of the Biggie,* written in black ink.

To this day, just thinking about this brings chills to my soul. In short, the reason why David and Doris Young took the school hostage was to collect a $320 million dollar ransom, kill all of the adult hostages and then blow them and all of the new children into the "new world" where they all could live in peace.

Demon Slaying and Healing

Months after the bombing of Cokeville Elementary School, I had a hard time driving through the school parking lot on patrol, but did it anyway. In May of 1988, my family and I left Kemmerer, Wyoming and moved back home to Sacramento, California, where my wife and I finished raising our boys. In 1995, we took a family vacation through

Cokeville, headed to Kemmerer to see old friends. Headed south on Highway 30, you could see the school from the road off to the left. I just looked straight ahead and drove on. I had buried the incident and did not want to deal with it.

In 2004, my wife and I moved back to the Ogden, Utah area. On April 29, 2005, Robin and I took a weekend trip to Wyoming for the first time in years that put us in close proximity to Cokeville. It was coming up on nineteen years since the bombing and time to put it behind and move on into life. My wife and I arrived that Friday afternoon at the elementary school. It had been the first time I had returned in eighteen years. The school was locked and a bus was loading children for swim lessons. We contacted the only adult there and her name was Celeste. We explained the circumstances of our visit. Celeste said that she was married to the chief of police and also explained that there were only four-day school weeks so the school was locked up on Fridays. Celeste tried to get hold of school officials and have them respond to open up the school so we could visit the room. Celeste was unable to reach anyone so she invited us to her home and got her husband involved.

Meeting John and Celeste Jackman was a godsend that day and I cannot express in words how these two individuals helped with my healing process. They went out of their way to get someone to open the school so we could visit the classrooms. John drove us around Cokeville and we visited with folks we had not seen in many years. We found out some more information about the bombing. Celeste was in the classroom that day, so for the first time, we received a first hand account of what had happened. She was the principal's daughter. John really helped me out because of his past police experience and his two recent deployments in Iraq. John and Celeste, thank you for opening up your hearts and your home to us that day. The healing process has begun and I am glad you were there to help.

Epilogue

As I reflect on that day every May 16, the demons are getting scarce but the shadow still lingers. I recently reviewed the crime scene tape and listened to the dispatch tape. For the first time, I was able to view and listen to the entire tape.

In parting, I took the words of Celeste's father on April 29, 2005, "He healed his demons and so shall I."

Lyle Forrest
Cokeville Volunteer Fire Department
(Oral History - Telephone)

I was teaching school and Kevin Walker, another firefighter, came to school and told me that there was a problem at the grade school and that I needed to come report with the fire trucks. So I said, "OK," and we headed down to the fire station. I was an EMT at that time, too, but that day I was a firefighter.

We'd had a drill a few weeks before where this guy from the state came and called out fire departments and had them respond. He pushed his stop watch and said, "OK, we have your response time." This was just a few weeks before. So we were going down the street and here's the same guy on the street corner, looking up and down the street. I said, "OK, Kevin, this is a drill. Using school kids in a bombing or hostage drill situation is not a smart thing to do. If word gets out, people won't be happy."

Kevin said, " Lyle, I know it's real, I saw the people." I wasn't convinced. We got our gear on, pulled trucks out and staged on Main Street by the street into the school. I was thinking, OK this is really a big drill. I was the officer in charge that day because the chief and assistant chief were both at work out of town.

The police there told us that there were snipers on the roof of the school and if they saw us they would probably shoot us. I thought this was extreme for a drill. They told us to block the street off. About that time some sheriff's deputies came roaring into town. I'm still thinking, wow, this is a real big drill even to see how we respond and what goes on. I was listening to the chatter on the radio and one of the police officer's requested that the FBI be notified and to get them on their way here.

With that, I knew that it was real. I had a chill go up my back that didn't quit. I just knew that it was the real thing. About that same time Brad Anderson, who was our Wyoming Highway Patrol Officer, who lived in town at that time, requested that somebody go to his house and get his bulletproof vest. And within a short time police from all over started arriving. We had police from all nearby communities in Idaho, Wyoming, and Utah. A lot of them, when they heard of the situation, just told their dispatchers, "I'm going." We also had ambulances from as far away as Logan, Utah, and Rock Springs and Evanston, Wyoming and from Idaho.

There were police lined up, hidden in the bushes in all the backyards up and down the area on Main Street that faced the school. I have no idea how many police came to help. Kevin and I were standing in front of the fire truck just hidden by the house we were in front of. We heard a "whomp" kind of a sound. We looked and saw a black cloud of smoke rising up above the school.

We were standing in front of the truck and we got in the truck and drove about forty feet, turned the corner toward the school and drove about fifty feet more and there was a wall of kids running down the sidewalk. They reacted to the fire drill training they had had. They responded to what they knew they should do. Some went out the doors, some got tossed out the window by the teachers. They all got out faster than I could ever have imagined.

Just the week before at fire meeting we had practiced how we would attack the elementary school if it had caught fire. We had preplanned and practiced which hydrants we would hit. The pumper took the first hydrant. We took the second in the quick response truck and laid two and a half inch hose lines. We then met outside the window of the classroom.

The bottom window was open, top was still intact. I asked Allan Burton if he would go in with me. We were air packed up and I told the crew to break out the large top widow. And it was interesting, they had to hit it several times with a pick headed ax to get it to break. It was tempered glass. It wasn't easy. The firemen were amazed at how hard it was to break, we had never had to do that before.

Rifle and handgun ammunition was exploding and sounded like gunfire in the front of the room. I had the fire crew wet down the front right corner of the room and the popping sounds stopped. When we were ready to go in, I climbed up and just jumped in and landed on all fours on the floor. Allan did the same. He said he was sure they would shoot him as soon as he stood up and was silhouetted in the window. Smoke was so thick you couldn't see anything, even close to the floor.

Even before we went in, we were sure we would find the bodies and body parts of our grade school kids and teachers. We crawled around the room to make a right hand search. In the second corner, which was the front corner of the room, I was crawling over a pile of loose stuff. It felt weird. I put my face mask right down on the stuff and found I was crawling on a pile of guns, rifles and pistols. This was my first miracle; that the guns didn't go off. So I backed off of those and went around them. And then a few feet from that I encountered a pile of milk crates that were stacked up and had stuff in them. I started to crawl over those and I backed off. Later I discovered that was the second bomb that was armed and ready to go. I couldn't see what it was in the smoke. That was my second miracle.

We proceeded across the front of the room in our search and Allan found a body. We could tell it was a woman's body but we didn't know who it was. Smoke had risen six or eight inches off the floor. Just from what we could see, we both thought it was Allan's sister, Kim, who was one of the elementary teachers. Even though I knew better, I took my gloves off and I pulled off my mask and gave her mouth to mouth. Two no-no's in a fire. But when the air blew out a hole in the back of her head onto my hand, I knew there was no use. So we picked up the body and carried it to the window and passed it out the window to the fire crew.

A teacher who had been in the whole ordeal, said when he saw her, "She's the son of a bitch that did this to us!" They just placed the body on the grass outside the classroom window and left it laying there.

We then made a left hand search from the window back to the front of the classroom. Smoke had cleared now so that we had about three feet of clear air above the floor. There were no other victims in the classroom in the remainder of our search. We then started to check the hallway between the two classrooms where there was a small restroom. As I opened the door, I saw a deputy with gun drawn pointing right at me. There were several others following him through the hallway. We tried to talk to him but he just stood there. It seemed like a long time. Finally, he and the others turned and walked back down the hallway.

One of the officers told us not to look in the restroom because the "guy who held them all hostage had blown his brains out in there." We followed them outside. The lead officer with the gun said, "It was so smoky, I couldn't see who you were. I thought you were the bad guys. I almost shot you." The third of my miracles. We then went back in the school and searched for kids who might have run into another classroom to hide but we found no one.

We left the building when we knew everyone was out and there was no fire. We had to stand by so the bomb squad could get the bomb out. We had hoses charged. They said we would have a structure fire to work on if the bomb blew. They pulled the bomb out of the classroom, down the hall and clear outside with a wire. They dismantled it. We were on standby there for about an hour and a half after the event was over, waiting for them to get the bomb out. I let the guys who had kids in the bombing go and check on their kids. Up to that point no one knew about their kids.

After the bombing a small circus came to Cokeville to perform for the kids and everyone else. The afternoon before the performance, they had elephant races down Main Street. Becky, my wife who was an EMT also, and I were two of the lucky ones who got to ride the elephants.

During the show, they called for any EMTs to come over, so Becky and I went and a guy who worked for the circus was drunk and had been feeding the tiger. He had teased it with a big chunk of meat.

When he held the meat in the cage, the tiger caught his arm with sharp claws and opened his arm with a twelve inch laceration. So we had the distinction of being the only EMTs to treat an attack by a tiger in Cokeville. The patient refused to go to the hospital in the ambulance because he was broke and drunk. So one of the clowns in costume took him to the hospital in the clown truck that they used in the show.

Our kids had already graduated from high school so they were not involved. I picked Allan to go in with me because I knew I could depend on him. He had a sister and two or three kids in the bombing.

I had three chances for something to go wrong. Somebody was taking care of me.

What do I suggest? Training!. When you are well trained you just respond and do the things that need to be done without having to stop and figure it out and that improves your survival rate. I am still on the fire department. I retired from teaching. I think about the bombing occasionally when someone brings it up. I put it behind me and went on with life. It was one of those experiences you don't want to have to go through again. It affects everybody differently. Some of them still have problems to this day. They have problems being in a room where they don't feel like they can get out, get away easily. I was more in control of my situation, I knew I could get out any time. The kids and teachers couldn't.

Callan Fredrickson
Cokeville Town Marshal
(Handwritten Mailed Submission)

The day started with a burglary at the truck stop. I made a report on that. I had an appointment to get my patrol car worked on, the electronic carb was not working right. While at the appointment my wife called me and said there was a man in the school with a bomb. I told the people at the shop I had to go. They put all their people on it. They got the car going in short order and I headed for Cokeville.

Earl Carroll was on the phone talking to someone at the school when I got there. Somehow the phone line would get interrupted. I went over to the phone office and talked with the people there. I asked if they could keep the line clear. I had not been back at the office very long when Earl said, "Oh my God the bomb just went off."

I drove to the school and we started to get the children out. I went to the window of the room they were in and Frank Lazcanotegui and I started to pull kids out. I said that it sure would be nice if the opening were bigger. Frank pushed me to one side and took hold of the window and tore it out of the steel frame.

We finished getting all the kids out who were at the window.

I then went to the main entrance with Earl. He and I went in and started working our way to the area in the school where he (David) was. The smoke was so heavy you could not see much. At one point, working toward the classroom, a deputy and I almost shot each other. It didn't feel right to me and on the other end Brad Anderson was telling the deputy it was me. By then, I heard some more gunfire. That was when David shot himself. The rest of the day was spent working the scene and accounting for all the children and teachers.

I searched the school for any more bombs or anything he (David) might have put there. A teacher was shot by David but he was OK. The only people who died were David and Doris. There were a lot of mental scars for years on some of the children.

    This is in brief of the things I did that day. From the time I got up on the 16th it was forty-two hours before I got to sleep again. I can remember a lot of details and conversations that took place that day but I don't think it would add. We all had a lot of help that day that we could not see but it was there. I know it beyond a doubt. We all did things we could not normally do.

Lee Gardner
Afton, Wyoming Police Chief 1973-1996
(Oral History - Telephone)

When the media reports concerning the Cokeville bombing came across on public radio, I was actually on a Honda Goldwing motorcycle on a highway near San Bernadino, California, with my wife Linda on the back. We were on vacation on a motorcycle. We were going to visit relatives in southern California. We turned the motorcycle around and headed back to Wyoming, we drove back through the night and arrived the next morning at approximately 7:30 a.m. The bombing report was national news and I felt that I should be there to assist the Lincoln County Sheriff's Office. This incident altered our whole vacation.

When I arrived in Cokeville, the bomb had already gone off. The television media (in mass) were still there. I didn't really get involved in the investigation, but offered Sheriff Wolfley any assistance that was needed by the Afton Police Department. The Lincoln County Sheriff's Office did an excellent follow up investigation. Mutual Aid units from all over the area volunteered to assist in any way that was needed. This incident, while being a tragedy, also pulled all emergency services together and created a bond that had not been there previously.

I believe that the bombing incident in Cokeville was a wake-up call, that even in our rural communities anything can happen. It was a miracle that only the suspects died in this incident. I feel certain that the students, teachers and those who first responded have pondered the amazing outcome of the takeover and bombing of Cokeville Elementary School in 1986.

Greg Goodman
Corporal, Lincoln County Sheriff's Office
(Email Submission)

May 16, 1986 was my best friend, Ed Stephen's, birthday. Ed was a Sergeant with the Kemmerer Police Department and I was a Corporal with the Lincoln County Sheriff's office, working out of the Kemmerer office. That morning I had been at Ed's house to wish him a happy birthday before going home to take a nap. I woke up to the phone ringing and when I answered the voice on the other end was Maggie, a dispatcher from the sheriff's office, telling me there was a hostage situation at the elementary school in Cokeville and I was needed there. I could tell by the tone of her voice that this was about as serious as it gets.

I quickly put my uniform on, not bothering to shave or shower, jumped into my patrol car and floored it, going west on US 30 the forty odd miles to Cokeville. I went straight to the Cokeville Town Hall on Main Street. When I went inside the first thing I noticed was the crowd of people standing around, the place was packed and the closer I got to the resident deputy's office, the more crowded it got.

I pushed my way past the crowd and into the office where the sheriff, Deb Wolfley, and investigator Earl Carroll were attempting to identify and organize their assets. I got the sheriff's attention to let him know I was there and waited for direction. While I waited I learned that a couple and their daughter had entered the elementary school with a homemade bomb carried in a small, two wheeled grocery basket, the type you pull behind you. The couple had rounded up everyone they could in the school and herded them into one of the classrooms where they were threatening to blow them up. The daughter had second thoughts, left the building and was no longer in the school.

After waiting what seemed like forever, but was probably no more than a couple of minutes, I got the sheriff's attention and told him that it was apparent that I wasn't needed at town hall and was headed to the school see what I could do there.

Deputy Ron Douglas had arrived so I grabbed him and we headed down Main Street toward the school. It was my intention to set up a roadblock in front of the only access road leading to the school. I wanted to keep the small crowd of concerned parents and relatives that was forming away from the school. Someone in the crowd, I can't remember who, told me there was nothing we could do to keep him from attempting to rescue his child.

The Cokeville elementary school was new in 1986, it was a single story structure, a flat topped building plopped down in the middle of a very large and open field. There wasn't a tree or bush anywhere near the school. There was one access road leading to a large parking lot in the front of the building and, because it's an elementary school, the parking lot was virtually empty. The school is impossible to approach without being seen, in other words, the place was a fortress and a perfect place to hold hostages. In addition to the tactical problems with an approach to the building, no one at the sheriff's office had any kind of the specialized training needed to handle a situation like this. We had a hostage negotiator but he wasn't available. Even more disturbing was what I learned from the sheriff before I left Town Hall; that the man inside the school used to be a police officer in Cokeville.

As Deputy Douglas and I were trying to organize the roadblock and corral the relatives of those being held inside there was a loud explosion. I didn't have to look to know what had happened, I could see it in the eyes of those around me. I remember turning to run toward the school and the crowd of people who were running with me. I remember the thick black smoke pouring out of the school and the chaos.

The people running toward the school were my main concern. How could I protect them and myself at the same time? What if the bomb was a ploy and someone with a high powered rifle was waiting to take shots at us? I turned and yelled, "Stop! Go back!" It didn't do any good, they kept coming.

Douglas and I came to a skidding halt at the front doors to the school, with us was Brad Anderson, a Wyoming highway patrolman. We can see through the front doors that the hallway was filled with smoke, making it impossible to see clearly for more than a few yards. Brad and I entered the building and Douglas stayed behind to watch the front. We really didn't know which classroom to go to and, on top of that, the hallway was filled with smoke, limiting visibility to about twenty feet.

We moved down the hallway on the right side and pulled up next to a classroom door. As we were assessing our options I was startled to see a dark figure through the smoke cross the hallway in front of us. As far as I knew, we were the only good guys in the building so that must be one of the bad guys and he had a handgun. I pointed my gun at him and yelled, "Sheriff's office, stop!" I got no response so I yelled again, "Sheriff's office, stop where you are!" I got a response this time, the figure moved faster.

Brad was saying he thought it was Cal, Cal Fredrickson the Cokeville Town Marshal. I said I didn't think so, I hadn't seen Cal in town hall earlier and the guy was not in uniform so it couldn't be Cal. The mysterious figure moved away and vanished into the smoke. Brad's statement had kept me from squeezing the trigger. I found out later that, in fact, it had been Cal. I was so mad I could have spit. What the hell had he been thinking? He'd about gotten himself or perhaps one of us dead. As it turned out, Cal had come into the school from a side door and was there for the same reasons we were, to help the children.

The first classroom door we came to appeared to be the one we wanted. I slowly opened the door and could see that the room was absolutely filled with acrid black smoke, making it impossible to see or breathe. Brad and I moved inside to take a look; we lasted only as long as the air in our lungs before we beat a hasty retreat. When we were back in the hallway I told Brad that if there was anyone still in that room, they were surely dead. No one could breathe that smoke and live very long.

When Brad and I exited the school I noticed for the first time (since my earlier mad dash to the school) the children—they were outside. I didn't remember seeing them leave. How could I have missed that? To this day I don't remember the children leaving the school.

Deputy Sheriff Ron Hartley pieced together the events leading up to that day from the thousands of pages of hand written journals found in the bomber's vehicle. It would appear that they, that is the bomber, his wife and daughter, were planning to take the students hostage in order to extort money from the LDS church. Once they received the money they were going to load the money, themselves and the children onto a bus and blow it up in the hope that they would be transported to an afterlife. Their plans were only partially realized. The daughter's participation is a bit cloudy, she claims not to have known what was planned and in fact she fled the school after realizing what her parents were doing and went to the police.

The homemade explosive device they brought into the school that day had what's commonly referred to as a "dead man switch." The switch was a clothespin with two thumb tacks stuck into the jaws. Attached to the thumb tacks were two wires running to a detonator in the basket with the explosives. The switch, when closed, completes the circuit and fires the detonator, which in turn ignites the explosives. According to some of the hostages the "dead man" switch was on the woman's finger. It would appear that she accidentally closed the switch detonating the explosives. Her husband was in the bathroom at the time and when he heard the explosion, he ran into the classroom and started shooting at the fleeing children and teachers. One of the teachers was hit in the shoulder by a .22 as he fled the room. The man then went over to his mortally wounded wife and shot her and then himself.

God was surely watching out for those children on that day as the explosive device malfunctioned and only partially detonated. None of the children was killed.

I am still involved in law enforcement. My family and I moved to Kake, Alaska, in 1988 where I took the job of chief of police. We moved to Haines, Alaska, in 1991 and I was appointed chief of police of the Haines Police Department in 1999. My son, Evan, is in construction in Ketchikan, Alaska, and has a daughter, 10, and a son, 6 months. John is an aircraft mechanic in Anchorage and has a son, 18 months. My daughter Alixanne is a freshman at the University of Alaska, Anchorage. My wife, Carole Ann Thompson-Goodman, is a customer service representative with the local phone and power company.

Betty Allen Hansen
Cokeville EMT
Mother of Teacher Survivor
Grandmother of Four Student Survivors
(Oral History—Telephone)

It was just such a confusing day for everyone. When the little kids started running, they were all going in different ways. I was president of the EMTs at the time. I was on the sidewalk outside of Art Robinson's house. We had the ambulances all lined up and the bomb went off.

The little kids started running and Scott Miller lay down. He said, "I've been shot." Jamie came up to me and said, "Grandma." I said, "Just go find your mom, just go find your mom." We got Mr. Miller in the ambulance. Then we dealt with the kids. I couldn't find Gayle for a long time. We tried to keep track of where the kids were going. I wrote some down on my hands. It was really hard to keep straight which direction the kids were going, which ambulance.

When parents started asking where their kids were, it was hard to tell them. Some kids had run to their homes. Some had gone to Taylor's and other places. We were kind of watching as they came out but we couldn't see them all. Don Ferrin came over and told me Jennie was burned badly so we put her in the ambulance. Some people were good at telling us about the kids. After the ambulances were gone, I still tried to find Gayle. I didn't go on an ambulance at that time. I went later. I stayed to coordinate. We had drivers and EMTs.

I walked over to the school. The lady, Doris, was lying on the ground. I picked up the blanket and looked at her. I didn't know who it was under the blanket so I looked. Later I found Gayle. She said, "Mom, I could have been shot." I said, "Gayle, you are OK and I don't have time to talk about it." I've always felt bad I said that. But that's how it was just then. There was a lot going on.

It wasn't two weeks before, Earl Carroll, who used to be a policeman in Kemmerer, was a coordinator. He had been trying to get an emergency management training here. He had written all these letters and sent them out to us. He was trying to get a training going. He asked, "Betty, what did you do with all those letters?" I said they were at home. He told me to burn them. We weren't prepared. We were going to train but we weren't prepared.

I had Gayle and four grandkids, Melanie, and Justin, and Carol's two, Jamie and Jennie in that room. I didn't treat any of my own, except getting them on an ambulance. Parents mostly rode with the kids on the ambulances. Some were burned, and had to go to Salt Lake and get treatment. Some wouldn't sit down in the schoolroom, and kept wanting to wander around the room. Others stayed right by their teachers.

Right after, we had a few sessions talking about it. I went to Riverton to a fire seminar and they had a lot of EMTs from around the country there. We had a session on what had happened at that time. People who dealt with emergency management gave the seminar and they called us and asked us to go, just a few of us to help with questions. After that, we just kind of pushed it aside and moved on, we didn't really talk about it but tried to make the training better.

Rich "Big Rich" Haskell
Deputy/Bomb Technician Sweetwater County
(Oral History - Telephone)

I was (and still am) a certified bomb technician. At the time of the Cokeville incident I was the only one in the western half of the state of Wyoming. I was at White Mountain Junior High School in Rock Springs watching a basketball tournament when I was first notified; over the loudspeaker there was an announcement that said, "Deputy Haskell please come to the office for a phone call."

It was the dispatch center in Kemmerer. Sheriff Wolfley had left a message for me: "Rich, we have a hostage situation at the Cokeville school and they have a bomb." Well, I thought: holy mackerel! I didn't know the exact situation with hostages, how many there were, or what the background of the situation was. I contacted my sheriff, Jim Stark, and told him they were requesting my assistance. His response was, "And why are you are still here?"

I went home, changed clothes, grabbed extra clothing because I had no idea how long I'd be, jumped in my patrol car and drove to Cokeville. During the trip I was in constant radio contact with Kemmerer via the mutual aid channel and they kept me updated.

In the time frame of the Cokeville incident you were accustomed to thinking about bombs in terms of dynamite or pipe bombs, not incendiary devices or anything sophisticated. As I was driving up there it seemed like about Mach 3 but it actually took me about an hour and fifteen minutes to reach Cokeville. As I passed the off ramp/exit at Kemmerer, dispatch called me and told me the bomb had detonated. By then I had learned that they had taken the whole school hostage; there were 150 plus hostages involved.

It was snowing when I left Rock Springs and it was snowing when I went past Kemmerer. It probably was snowing in Cokeville, I don't remember. There was slush in the curves by Kemmerer or I would have made better time.

"Please respond," they said, and I continued on up there. When I arrived they had all the streets blocked, of course. They moved out of the way for me to get through. There were patrol cars at and around the scene from Utah and Idaho. There were law enforcement agencies from everywhere at the scene. I pulled into the parking lot and I could see the room where they were all being held because it was black on the outside of the room. I also noticed a body lying out on the lawn. I thought, oh, my Lord. I could just imagine bodies laying all over in the school.

I walked over to the body and I noticed it was a woman and part of her skull was missing. I did not know at the time that she was one of the suspects. I started talking to Deb Wolfley, and he explained to me what had taken place, that all the children had been transported to different hospitals, but it was feared there were still devices in the building. Another gentleman and I went inside and started clearing the building, looking for other devices.

We started going through all of the stuff outside that Young had lined up in the hallway. There was ammunition, guns, blasting caps and more components to build another bomb and from what we now know, he had planned to build another one. We took everything outside and stacked it up. We opened briefcases, remotely. We didn't have an X-ray machine. We used a shotgun and put it in sand bags and shot down through the end of it and opened it up through the seam.

Then we went inside the classroom. Oh, what a mess. So just looking around the classroom there was black smoke inside and on the ceiling, the ceiling tiles had been lifted up. They weren't where they belonged; they were in disarray. As soon as we made sure everything was secure, we started the investigation. Later that evening we were joined by ATF (Alcohol, Tobacco & Firearms) agents out of Cheyenne.

It took three days to do the investigation. We stayed at the Hideout Motel. ATF took all the recovered materials, equipment, and other evidence, and it all went to their crime lab. Any federal charges would have been more severe had these two people lived. It would have come from the federal government. I went inside to the bathroom and was told that he [the suspect] was in the bathroom, dead. They had handcuffs on him and he had shot himself through the bottom of the chin and up. He was dead and handcuffed. He was in that much trouble.

In the classroom, you could see little pieces of metal all over, stuck in the walls. Come to find out after many interviews, the device that went off inside the room had extra ammunition sitting on top of the bomb. When the thing went off, the heat ignited all of the cartridges, setting them off randomly all over the room. If I remember correctly, I walked into the room and the white board or chalkboard was off to my left hand side. As we tried to reconstruct everything, I noticed on that board, it looked a little strange. I said, "Hey that looks like the outline of an angel," and I said that not knowing that they were there.

So we put the thing all back together and tried to reconstruct what the device looked like from the description provided by the kids. We even went into the ceiling and found a .45-caliber slug there, up in the ceiling. It went in at an angle that made us ask, "How did that thing get up there?"

We tried to reconstruct and reconstruct and reconstruct. Then we found out that when it went off, Doris Young was on fire. The next time we asked, "how did it get up there," I said, "I'll tell you exactly how that bullet got there. He was in the bathroom and she was on fire. I can't even imagine the pain she was in. He came out and heard her screaming. He came out and saw thick black smoke. He saw his wife standing there burning, dropped down to one knee and shot, hit the bottom of her chin and it went out the top of her head. That's how she lost that piece of skull." Killed her instantly. I think he took her out of her misery. I can't even imagine that ungodly scream she must have made while on fire. Then he went back into the bathroom and he shot himself. We tried to reconstruct everything.

Looking at it from the bomb technician's point of view—and I've been around explosives a long, long time—I know how they are supposed to function. This bomb was designed to function just like these grain elevators that you see; they just explode. The tops blow off. Dust particles go in the air and then they ignite. These aluminum particles were in tuna fish cans, fine, like flour. Blasting caps went into each of those canisters. It was timed that when the blasting caps went off, particles went into air and then were ignited into a huge fireball.

The top of that building should have been gone. Had the bomb functioned the way it was designed, the top of that building would have been gone. But it didn't. There were just too many things that didn't function. He'd even tried the bomb out earlier in an old school bus and it functioned perfectly. It tore that bus apart. ATF found that out. They even found the bus. It was totally destroyed.

There were just too many things that came into play to not make that bomb go off all the way. And you can't explain why. He'd made it work before. As an example, the gas bottle was leaking. Why? I have no idea. If the gas deteriorated the plastic, I don't know. It leaked enough to fill the room with fumes and make everyone sick. Doris talked him into opening the windows. Now there's a vent. When the gas was dripping, it dripped into the powdered aluminum and made it a paste. I got to looking at the pile of rubber. One wire had been cut.

No reason that thing should have been like that. I still can't explain what happened to that. Why that wire got cut. The reason we know that is that it didn't go off, the blasting cap was still sitting there. What the bomb should have done, exploding like it did, it should have killed people that were in close proximity, within thirty feet. It was designed to go out in 360 degree circle. The top of the building is the weakest part and that should have been gone.

Why did this thing function like it did? Why didn't it go out to the sides? Why did it go up? Looking at what the bomb was capable of doing and then looking at the comparatively very little damage, it just didn't make any sense and I couldn't figure it out. I couldn't answer these questions for years. I knew there were angels in the room but I didn't know about the angels in the circle until later.

I'm really good friends with Ron Hartley. About two years ago, I was talking to Ron and I said, "Ron, I have never been able to understand why that blast didn't go out into the room." He said, "Let me have you talk to my son, Nathan."

I talked with Nathan. "Why didn't the blast go outward like it was supposed to do?" And when he told me what he did, you know, talk about hair standing up on the back of my neck. You could tell from the way the bomb funneled up in the air that his explanation is the only thing that could have happened. It is the only thing that stopped that bomb from going out in a 360 degree circle like it was supposed to. He told me what happened. He said that everybody in that room had an angel. He could see them. Even the bad guys had them. But right before the bomb went off, the bad guys' angels left. Nathan said, "We saw them, just before the thing went off. Angels just got in a circle, joined hands, and boom."

The kids didn't talk about these things because sometimes people didn't believe them. People laughed at them. Well, I believe. *Something was in there and that something changed everything.*

All of a sudden, it made sense to me. In other words, something had to direct that blast to go in the direction it went. It closed my report. No more wondering what on earth happened. And it closed the report for the other guy when I told him. A human body couldn't have made that go straight up. But a spiritual body, we don't know.

We had never interviewed kids before we finished our investigation. Different investigators were doing that. About three days later we all sat down and that's the first we heard about the angels. There should have been a lot of dead people in the room. None of us talked to any of the kids about this stuff. We had heard that kids were identifying their ancestors as the people that helped them out of the room.

Twenty years, I still think about it. When the Columbine incident and other things take place, we feel bad but also, you know folks, you forgot about what happened in Wyoming in a little Wyoming town called Cokeville that's just a small community. I've never seen so many helicopters in my life. Geez. I couldn't get a fast enough ride from Rock Springs to Cokeville but it didn't take the news media long.

I talk about the Cokeville incident constantly and the miracles and the things that took place there. I can't even imagine the things those kids have lived through and what they went through with those two people taking them hostage. Just the fact that they couldn't do anything. That two people controlled their entire destiny. Little kindergarten kids. No one understood what was going on. Those two people thought they had everything in control. No they didn't.

I find that parents don't talk about things and that kids do. I would love to sit down and talk to the kids just to hear from their own mouths what happened. Just to hear how that bomb functioned. I look forward to reading the book and finding out.

Nadine Hayes
Bear Lake Memorial Hospital News Spokesperson
(Interviewed by LaRee Baker)

Nadine Crane was named as the Bear Lake Memorial Hospital spokesperson by the news media that night on the 10:00 p.m. news. She recalled that it was because she was working in the admitting office and was the one that took the calls from the media. "We were even on CNN," she recalled. She remembers that the entire event had a calm organization about it and she felt the hospital handled the disaster very well.

Jean K. Hoopes
Star Valley EMT
(Typed Mailed Submission)

When the call came from dispatch on that horrible day we were told to go to the hospital for further instructions. I went in and Connie Jensen said the Cokeville elementary school children were being held hostage by a man with a bomb. My first thought was that we were having a disaster drill of some kind and I said, "You're kidding me." Then I looked at her white face and knew she was not joking. My heart sank and all I could think was, HURRY!!

I hurried to the ambulance and got a couple more EMTs loaded up and we headed for Cokeville. We were told not to use the siren and to park away from the school. When we got there I couldn't believe that a crisis was happening. The sky was clear and it was a beautiful day. There was no traffic on the street, no people around the school and the whole thing seemed surreal. We had only been there for a few minutes when we heard several POPS and then the children began streaming from the building. We moved the ambulance closer and began calming the children and reassuring them that they were safe now. They were hysterical and didn't know what to do. Someone got them lined up and we started treating them. At the same time parents came running from the surrounding homes frantically looking for their children.

After things calmed down a bit I walked over to the east side of the schoolhouse. Someone had put a quilt on the ground and Mrs. Young's body had been put on it. I thought it was a waste of a good quilt, but someone had shown a lot of compassion for the misguided woman.

We soon loaded up our ambulance with patients and headed for Afton. On the way the fan belt broke, this was on our new ambulance, of course. A truck driver stopped and helped Durk Lowe replace it and we were on our way again.

Fortunately the children we had were not seriously burned and were quickly treated at the hospital.

I think what stands out most in my mind was the mother of a young girl who rode on the jump seat with the little girl on her lap. She held onto that child like she would never let her go. I could see the love and relief on her face as we made the long trip to the hospital.

I think that the people in charge did a great job and the parents showed remarkable restraint during the ordeal and I feel privileged to write down my memories. It truly was a miracle.

Merlyn Jensen, LPN
Bear Lake Memorial Hospital
(Interviewed by LaRee Baker)

Merlyn worked at Bear Lake Memorial Hospital for many years prior to her retirement in 1997. She said, "That day stands out in my mind. We first got the call from Cokeville. We were told that school children were being held hostage and this man was threatening to set off a bomb if his demands were not met. We were told this was to be kept confidential.

"Then we got the next call that everything had broken loose and that many injured would be coming in. We started to call in as much help as we could. Every nook and corner of this hospital was used for the many who were needing assessment. I stuck close to Dr. Daines and we saw burn patient after burn patient. Those kids came in for a long time afterward having treatments and dressing changes. I also remember that we did one skin graft back in surgery at a later date.

"Dr. Daines contributed a lot. It wasn't just because of his training in plastic surgery. The connections he had to get that burn team here from Stanford was wonderful—just wonderful!"

Nina Jensen

Surgical Technician and Central Supply Manager
Bear Lake Memorial Hospital
(Interviewed by LaRee Baker)

Nina worked at Bear Lake Memorial for twenty-three years. She remembers that day well. She had already put in a full day's work and had just gone home when the call came, summoning her back to Bear Lake Memorial for the disaster. She states, "The timing was providential!" She was referring to the fact that as it was a Friday afternoon, everything was stocked to the hilt for the weekend. Every suture tray and all instruments were sterile and ready to go. Cupboards of sterile dressings were stocked to maximum capacity. We were ready for anything!"

She remembers well the system of numbering the patients as they came through the ER doors. "A number was put on the ER report which was on a clipboard and that same number written ON the patient's body—hand or other available part. It was a fast, simple, logical way to keep track of things. We had to have a system and this went like clockwork. She remembers helping other personnel at the ER doors giving out the numbers.

Nina, like many others, remembers that all were working as a team. She said, "The kitchen kept coffee and hot cocoa coming—everyone helped in their own way. Bear Lake Memorial Hospital got the most severely burned victims, of course, because we were the closest." She remembered Logan sending an ambulance and burn packs to us and them being very impressed to find us so well prepared to handle such a disaster. We did not have to open any of their packs.

She recalled, "Charlene Brown, a main news anchor, was right here at Bear Lake Memorial Hospital—interviewing people and asking questions. The story was on all the channels—Dan Rather and Tom Brokaw were talking about us, even CNN had coverage on the Cokeville disaster. I remember that Gail Dayton opened the basement supply room for any needed supplies and helped in any way needed. As soon as instruments were used, I got them packaged up and used both the small autoclave in the operating room (because it was fast) and the big autoclave to keep up with things."

On the Monday following this incident, Nina wrote in her journal that there were "71 ERs to process and that the majority of them were from the bomb disaster." She remembered many coming into the hospital during the following days and weeks, post injury, for the continued dressing changes. Nina remembers a skin graft surgery being performed on one of the burn patients at our hospital at a later date, by Dr. Daines and Dr. Wolff.

Nina said, "I guess my feeling at the time was disbelief that a small town could have something like this happen. It just did not compute. I just remember thanking God I had the ER and the central supply stocked for the weekend when those kids started rolling in. And, I was just so thankful for a great and well organized staff. Bear Lake Memorial was perfect!"

Tim Malik
Lincoln County Deputy Sheriff
(Email Submission)

I was on patrol for the Lincoln County Sheriff's Office at the time that the call came in to the North Lincoln Communications Center in Afton, Wyoming. I remember that I was serving some civil process at the time in the Lower Star Valley area. The radio call that I received asked me to contact Afton dispatch by telephone or come in to the Center to get a message. It sounded urgent and I thought it might be something in the Upper Valley area since the dispatcher knew where I was and gave me the option. I opted to go to the communications center for the information.

When I arrived I was told that there was a hostage situation at the Cokeville elementary school. That all the students were taken hostage by suspects with a bomb and they were threatening to blow everyone up if their demands were not met.

I remember picking up a sniper rifle and other gear to respond to the incident when I received word that I should not respond to the scene and that I should stay in Star Valley on patrol. Although a little perplexed about the order to not respond I thought that someone, with more knowledge about the situation than I had at the time, had made the call for a reason. That reason possibly being concern for other areas of the county in case the situation was a distraction for some other crime or crimes.

Since I was still concerned about the situation I had the communications center contact every off-duty deputy that they could find to send them in that direction. They did and sent some off duty Deputies to the scene from Star Valley.

I was detailed to do an in-depth background check on the subject believed to be holding the school hostage for negotiations and tactical purposes. I did perform this detail and relayed the information to the scene commanders.

I awaited more word on the situation. After hearing that the bomb had gone off and with no ability to contact anyone by radio at the scene of the incident, I started heading in that direction. While en route toward Cokeville, I was told that backup services were being requested by agencies at the scene of the crime.

When I arrived, the tactical and medical portion of the situation was starting to wind down. I was asked to secure the perimeters of the crime scene which I did that evening and the day afterward.

It wasn't until after this incident that the Lincoln County Sheriff's Office decided to put together a SWAT team so the training and equipment for any future events like this would be available from our own first responders. The team was put together and I trained and served as counter-sniper marksman on that team.

Leonard H. Matthews
Church of Jesus Christ of Latter-day Saints Stake President
(Email Submission)

A Stake President's Point of View

During the late afternoon of May 16, 1986, I was working at my mortuary in Montpelier. The phone rang and it was my counselor in the stake presidency, Dean Wiggington. He told me that he had just heard that the grade school in Cokeville had been bombed and they were bringing many of the children in to the hospital. We decided that we needed to go to the hospital and see if we could be of help.

As soon as I got off the phone I went to my knees and said a quick prayer for those that were involved. When we arrived at the hospital there were many children, most with parents, in the halls, in the rooms and anywhere they could find room for them. We obtained some consecrated oil from the hospital and proceeded to offer to give blessings to any that wanted them. I have no idea how many we gave blessings to, but I know we were there for a couple of hours trying to help those in need, in a spiritual way.

There were some that had already had blessings and there were a few that were not members of the Church of Jesus Christ of Latter-day Saints that refused our offer, but most of them wanted to be blessed.

I was totally amazed when I was told that none of the teachers or children had been killed. We were told of the circumstances surrounding this tragedy and to this day I am convinced that it was nothing but a miracle.

The next day I decided that I should go see the school. From the outside it was difficult to see any damage until someone pointed out the broken windows in that particular room where they were all held prisoner. I then went into the school and was told what took place at different points. As I entered the room where the explosion took place I felt much different that I thought I would. It was almost like walking into a temple. I knew I was in a room where a tragedy had taken place and yet I knew that angels from the other side of the veil had been in that room. I thought I would feel fear, but through my tears I had a quick little vision of angels helping children out of the windows and shielding them from flames. Looking at the room, I could not imagine why everyone who had been in there was not dead, and yet not one was except for the perpetrators of that heinous crime.

As I drove back to Montpelier, I had a very strong feeling that I had just witnessed how much power the Almighty has when we are faithful to Him. I knew that I was involved with some of the most special and faithful people on the face of the earth and that we had witnessed in a small but very important way what God can do when His saints are obedient to His laws and commandments. My life has been very blessed by my being connected with the great and good people of Cokeville. Thank God for good friends.

Scott Miller
Lincoln County Sheriff's Office
(Oral History)

If you don't believe there was Divine Intervention, then you weren't there that day. That's my story.

Steve Moore
Firefighter/EMT
Parent of Student Survivor
(Oral History—Telephone)

That day I came home late from work because I had to stop and rototill a garden for a guy. I went home and George, my brother, said, "Isn't Kristy in the third grade?

I said, "Yeah."

He said, "I heard a report that a guy is holding the third grade hostage and has a gun and some bombs."

We took a trip to city hall. Lyle Forrest was there. He said, "Yeah, that's true, the guy has a bomb and a gun." He said, "We have been having some mock accidents."

I said, "If this is a mock, it isn't very funny"

We found out David Young had the whole school in there. I went to the fire department. There were already enough EMT's. We were just sort of standing around waiting for something to happen when the bomb went off. I was in my gear. I was able to get over that big tall fence. A bunch of kids were coming out. I couldn't see Kristy. I just never saw her. We ran over to that window that everyone was at. I tried to play superman and punch it out. It just split my knuckle out was about it.

They got a fire ax and broke it out. Lyle Forrest and someone else went in. Rocky was the last one out and he got stuck. They hauled Doris out and said she was the lady who was doing all that. I went over and looked at her. I still didn't know what had happened to Kristy.

Someone said Wayne had gotten Kristy and Glenda Lorraine Nicholas ("Pixie") had picked her up and taken her home. When they told us and I went and I had to tell Luci, I told her the story George had told us. She acted like most people would when they heard that, she went to her mom's. Once they figured there was a bomb there, they wanted everyone there that could get there. They had Bear Lake, Rich County, Kemmerer and several other ambulances. We thought if that goes off with that many kids in there, we are going to have our hands full plus all the fire.

I guess I've decided I'm glad I'm not a God. I can't forgive him, the guy who did it. I don't know what caused him to do that or anything else. I'll let God decide what to do with him.

Donna Morfeld
Cokeville EMT
Mother of Two Student Survivors
(Oral History—Telephone)

Basically what I remember was I was a volunteer. At the time Cokeville didn't have paid EMTs. I was on my way home from work. I was working at the Red Dog café at the time. There were all these emergency vehicles on the street. Lyle Forrest and Craig Chadwick pulled me over saying, "We need you, now." Until I heard the bullets flying around in the classroom, I thought it was a national disaster drill. I was hesitant to believe that we were involved with a National Disaster Drill yet I had no impression that it was the real thing. I just didn't know.

I started hearing bullets going off, about that time I saw a cloud of smoke and kids coming from every direction. Someone said, "The bomb's gone off." I didn't know what to do. I saw kids that needed treatment. If I recollect properly, it's debatable at this point, I was standing in the middle of Main Street and I banged on the back of an ambulance door and said, "We've got kids who need treatment."

I felt two ways: I knew that to be able to function as an EMT, I had to shut down my parent mode. I was just an EMT. I had no idea what had happened to my kids. I think subconsciously I was looking for them. Consciously I wasn't looking for them because if I saw them and they had been hurt, I would lose it.

There were so many people who needed my help. I needed to be an EMT. I think that was as much for self-preservation as much as it was professional. We had no idea what we were facing. I've been bothered by the fact that I went into EMT mode instead of parent mode. We have to remember we are all individuals and we all do different things. That was a crisis. You have to be able to function in some capacity. Again, it's each individual's capacity and wherever their forté is, that's were you're going to go. You just have to go into a shut down mode in one so you can go into the other effectively. Guilt walks in. Did I make the right decision? Honestly speaking, that was a war zone, for me. You go in, you don't worry about yourself as an individual. You worry about the entire group that you are with. For me it was those fellow emergency responders and maintaining as many lives as we could.

We needed to set up a triage point. I think Betty Allen set that up. Someone suggested we go to the town hall. We tried to get people to move in that direction. It was so overwhelming that it was a major disaster. I remember somebody saying, "John's been shot," and I remember walking with him to an ambulance. I remember seeing Brad Anderson and he looked pretty crappy. I said, "You need to get some oxygen." He said that he wasn't going to use any oxygen until he made sure that the people that had detonated the bomb were dead. I told him I would walk over there with him, if he would use the oxygen. We walked over to the body, laying on a blanket and covered. I remember seeing the back of Doris' head, I don't remember if I voiced it or if Brad was thinking the same thing I was, but we both knew she had been shot. When he was convinced they were dead. I said, "You need to take care of yourself, now."

At that point, I don't remember much of anything until someone came up to me and told me that Tina had been burned and was in somebody's house. I went in to get her. She was the last child on the last ambulance out of town and I sank an IV into her. And the ambulance was just absolutely packed with people, medics as well as victims. They were all needing to be cooled off from their burns. Someone said that we were running out of sterile water. We had a whole damn box of IV fluid and we just cut the tops off and started pouring it on these people.

I remember asking Dr. Wolff to take a look at Tina. Someone handed me a phone and said it was a TV person for an interview. I said yes, I would speak with them. They wanted to know what had happened, but I didn't really know what had happened. I made the comment that there were going to be a lot of people who wouldn't sleep that night.

About that time, Dr. Wolff said Tina needed to go to Logan. I rode down in the Hutchinson car, if I remember correctly. I had to hold Tina down while they incubated her and catheterized her. I remember bouncing back and forth between Billy Jo and Tina. Then they decided they had to transport both girls to Salt Lake. Jack, my husband, and my sister and brother-in-law, connected with me in Logan and we drove to Salt Lake.

When we got to Salt Lake, we went to see the kids and they wouldn't let us in because they said one of the kids had pulled her tubes. We knew that was Tina. About that time Dr. Saffle came out and he met us at the door and explained that yes, Tina had indeed pulled her tubes. They didn't know if they would be able to re-intubate her or not. It could do more damage than just leaving it out.

My next memory is of being in a hotel room there in Salt Lake City. A guy from my hometown in Gillette, Wyoming, called to tell me that we could take our kids to Galveston, Texas. There I sat with one kid in critical care in Salt Lake City, one kid with Jack's niece, one kid— I wasn't sure where she was— and one kid, Leslie, she was a baby ,and was with Ron Hartley's wife. I wasn't sure what to do. Galveston is where the Shriner's had the closest burn unit.

What was really strange about this to me, that gentlemen from Gillette knew my folks. My folks had picked up all this information because my dad was a fireman at that time in Wyoming. Somehow in other parts of Wyoming they had pieced together what had happened even before the people in Cokeville knew what happened. I felt like we, in Cokeville, were totally isolated and that the people in the rest of the United States had more information than what we did.

From what I understood from what I had heard from Cal Fredrickson and Ron Hartley, they had totally shut down the town of Cokeville from all communication. What is frustrating for me now is that I have major gaps in the time frame that I will never ever fill in.

I had shut down as a parent, but I apparently functioned very well as an EMT. Everybody walked out of there except the Youngs. Do I give us EMTs credit? No, I credit it to a little higher power than that.

After the dust settled and the communication links were open again, my dad called from Salt Lake City and said that the ATF said that the bomb had only partially detonated and if it had gone off completely it would have completely leveled the school. Of course, I had this mental image in my head that we were damn lucky. I know that between the firemen, the law enforcement, and the EMTs it was a comedy of errors that worked out to be the best. The law enforcement was basically just not there that day. They all had things in other towns. Of course, I got there after it was all set up, got pulled into it blind. I am still amazed we pulled it off. I still sit here and wonder how did we pull it off, how did we save so many people? I know somebody else had to have hand in that.

Actually, it bothers me that I can't remember. I remember that Karen Stonecypher was there. She was pouring IVs into people. We'd taken the IV class together in Kemmerer.

Cokeville, the whole bombing thing, was broadcast over radio and TV news, it seemed like it was endless to me. I kept thinking, this is not good. Somebody is going to jump on this bandwagon and they are going to take it to the next level.

We moved to Sequim, Washington, within a year. Cokeville at that time had very little work. We had Monica and Tina, both kids in the same school here in Sequim. I was working in a nursing home and somebody said, "A bomb has gone off in the school."

I was so totally unbelieving until I found out it was nothing. Having gone through that with Cokeville, it was less than a year later that I re-experienced it here. A bunch of kids did something stupid like set off a cherry bomb. Obviously I totally lost it. It took me a while to get my ducks together again. Several months.

And then when Columbine High School had its...*episode*...I

walked into a room and this gentleman was sitting in his wheelchair sobbing his eyes out. He said, "Look at this TV. Tell me how anybody could do this." The image on the TV was kids flying out the windows at Columbine High School. I just about lost it. I came as close as I could to having a nervous breakdown. It was broadcast hours upon hours on the news. I don't believe then or now that that continuous broadcast of a disaster like that is healthy. I think there are so many weird people in the world right now that jump on that bandwagon and they take it to the next level. Unfortunately, innocent people get hurt and families are devastated.

I know that Jack and I were separated for a couple of years, we just moved back in to the same home this past August. He had told me that you gals were doing this book and he told me that he had a lot of stuff he wanted to share. He and I were never able to share our emotions with each other. It hurt too much. He never understood where I was coming from. I was never able to share effectively with him, "This is where I'm coming from." He suggested counseling, and I back that up 100%, counseling.

And then the other thing I think I want to clarify is, nobody should ever feel guilty because of the way they reacted.

Another thing is, Doris's daughter lived up the street from us— Bernie. I told Jack that we needed to go up there. We needed to speak to them. She not only lost her mother, she lost everything that her mother stood for. Doris's kids probably are going to take a lot of blame and guilt and they don't need to do that. Both Doris's kids and Bernie's.

We have some scars, yes we do. But the bottom line is, we didn't lose anybody. But Bernie did. For me, it was reaching out to somebody else. I have never lost my parents, thank God. But the pain she was going to feel, all directions. We went up. We cried together.

My girls now, we have a relationship. There was some bitterness because I went into EMT mode instead of Mom mode. They know that. They have mentioned that. But that's OK. My children are very close. I think that is because of the way the circumstances in our life happened. The three oldest girls are all married. Trish was in junior high school at the time. She now has three children. Monica lives by Seattle and has two children. Tina is married and has two children and also lives in Washington. All three of the girls have gone into the medical field. Leslie is in college pursuing an RN degree and I am in college hopefully going into social services. I am still a caregiver.

We went back into the classroom later. It was hard, but we thought the girls had to go in. There is no doubt that there were guardian angels. Even more miraculous than the fact that all the kids lived, is the fact that they WALKED out of there. All of them walked out, the possibility for massive bodily damage was huge. They are still walking as far as I know.

Bob and JaNene Nostaja
Cokeville Fireman, EMT/ Cokeville EMT
Parents of One Student Survivor
(Handwritten Submission by JaNene)

As our very first experience as new EMTs, I was leery about this being a real hostage situation thinking it might be a planned mock disaster. We had been told that we were going to have one and no one would know when or where. In the meantime, the mine workers had been notified and everyone, including Bob, headed home, making the trip in eighteen minutes.

When the bomb went off I could hear screaming. I jumped out of the ambulance parked in front of Glen and Mary Lue Birch's home. The first person I saw was John Miller, not knowing that he had been shot in the back. I'll never forget the terrified look on his face as he ran right past me, his body covered with smoke.

At that moment I was a mom with my little girl in there and I had just left her and all my friends and I walked away from working in the lunchroom to go over to the high school to finish up over there. I was supposed to go back to the elementary to clean for the afternoon.

Bob, being an EMT, fireman, and dad, was there at the window, pulling anyone through as fast as possible. He also helped remove Doris's body.

The emotions were so high that day and for the next weeks and months. Our innocence had been robbed. Yet in so many ways, our little community came together so closely. It was amazing to see what happened from all over the country. Still, to this day when we are in different places people will ask, "Cokeville, Wyoming, isn't that the place where those people took the grade school hostage?"

We believed that no matter what religion we were, we had been given divine intervention that day. We had seen a MIRACLE! Not one of our loved ones had died in there, and we had peace of mind that it would not happen again. The two people who had done this had died.

Time does have a way of healing and a lot of healing has happened over twenty year's time. But if we see a strange looking van our natural instinct is now to know who they are and what their business is here.

It doesn't seem possible that twenty years have passed and yet thinking and talking about it seems to bring a lot of feelings back. Not that they were all bad, because a lot of good was shown to one another and from strangers from all over the world.

We've always felt that Cokeville was a wonderful place to raise our family and if we had to do it all over again, knowing what happened twenty years ago, we would still raise our family here.

We're not just a little community, we're a community that cares about one another. We have a deep respect for life, because of what we have lived through.

Spencer Preece
Reserve Lincoln County Deputy Sheriff
(Oral History - Telephone)

Ok, this was quite some time ago. It was in May of '86, if I remember right. As I recall, I was working out at the power plant when this occurred. We got the word from people at work that there was a hostage situation at the Cokeville elementary school. We immediately excused the people from Cokeville to go home. There were several who had children in that school.

I remember I got off at 3:00 p.m. At the end of the shift I went home and I turned on my scanner radio and I was listening to the radio traffic and of course it was the emergency traffic and I thought, I bet no one has thought to take the morgue pickup truck down there. This is a covered truck with a camper on the back.

I called dispatch and told them I was available and I would drive it down for them if they needed me. As I recall, about an hour later they called me and asked me to do what I had volunteered to do. I jumped into my uniform and went to the Lincoln County retention facility. I got to Cokeville later in the day, sometime between four and five o'clock, in my mind, which may or may not be factual.

There were emergency vehicles everywhere and television cameras. I got permission to drive that pickup right into the elementary school. I could see one body on the front lawn and it was the lady. She was covered up and I assumed she was dead.

I found the nearest deputy in charge. We had one body that had to be put into a bag and another that was in the restroom and had to be brought out of the bathroom and bagged up. He had shot himself with a .44 special. It isn't a real powerful gun so it didn't go all the way through. There was no blood or mess or anything. He was laying on the floor of the bathroom. We grabbed him under the arms and pulled him out and rolled him into the body bag. He had shot himself in the mouth.

The bullet was later found under his skull.

We bagged him up and took him out on a gurney and put him in the back of the truck and then we loaded the lady. When the sheriff told me to, I took them back to Kemmerer and one of the jailers helped me put them in the morgue at the detention facility. That was the last I saw of them. That's just my story, it's just a little part.

I remember the school was all smoky and hazy with burned marks. I remember the story of how it went off. I think it was the hand of God that stopped the bomb from going off completely.

I retired from the power company. I retired in Aught of 1990 and I am now just a retired resident of the little town of Opal, Wyoming. In the first book by the Wixom's, there is a picture of bringing the body out. There are four men. I'm the one on the far left, in the back on the far side of the gurney. I have a uniform coat on. That particular incident is just one of many in my ten years as a reserve deputy and it brought me closer to my God. I realize how He can affect our everyday lives.

I want to commend you for doing this. It is a great civic thing, a great religious thing and I think it will help a lot of people.

Darlene Romrell
Nurse at Bear Lake Memorial Hospital
(Typed Submission)

We at Bear Lake Memorial Hospital were just completing our 7:00 a.m. to 2:00 p.m. shift when I received a phone call from the Cokeville, Wyoming, dispatch. She asked that I call our two ambulances to go to Cokeville where a hostage situation was in progress at the elementary school. She asked that the ambulances go in with their lights and sirens off, so as not to alert the hostage takers, and to also stay a block or so away, but to be ready to move at a moment's notice if they were needed.

We decided to go home and wait to be called, as we had no idea how long the hostage situation would last. It took me about fifteen minutes to get home and as I walked in the house the phone was ringing and it was the registered nurse, saying the bomb had just blown and I was needed fast. I hurried back to the hospital and arrived at the same time as the first ambulance arrived. Before the night was over we would attend to about fifty-four children and four to five adults.

As the children were brought in from the ambulances there wasn't any crying or anyone in a panic. They were all perfectly calm, because of their teachers and their calming effect on them. During the hostage situation the teachers had the children singing and praying with them. And because of their teachers' faith, they knew that their Savior, Jesus Christ, was watching over them.

I personally was assigned four children and two adult women teachers to take care of. One of those women was Verlene Bennion, who was one of the teachers. I put them all to bed and then I went to get supplies to clean them up and dress their burns. When I returned Sister Bennion was not in her bed, in fact she was not even in her room. I finally tracked her down in one of the other rooms with the children. I took her back to her room and to bed again, and asked her to please stay in bed, that I would keep her informed as to how the children were doing. I then went about taking care of my other little patients.

When I returned about fifteen minutes later to check on Sister Bennion, she was once again gone! I found her in yet another room with the children. When I told her she had to stay in her bed and let me take care of her, she said, "I don't care about me, I just have to know that my students are safe and being taken care of." At that point we felt she might have had a heart attack and that it was vital that she stay in bed, so I could attend to her. But every time my back was turned she would go to one of the other rooms. I kept putting her back to bed, and she kept leaving, until they transferred her to a larger hospital because of her heart condition.

She just loved those children so very much she just had to make sure they were all safe and being well cared for.

I found out later that Sister Bennion had pleaded with the hostage taker to keep her and let her children go free. She felt because of her age that it wouldn't matter what happened to her, but it sure mattered what happened to her young students. Many other children were taken to different hospitals around the area.

It should be noted that Verlene Bennion was one of the last people out of the room following the bomb blast. Because of the smoke density she crawled on her hands and knees in the room, searching for any children who might not have escaped. She suffered severe smoke inhalation.

RaDawn Ruud
Star Valley EMT
(Typed Mailed Submission)

It started out like most any other day at work for me at Star Valley Hospital. It was, however, a day that would linger in many memories for years to come. When our administrator, Carolyn Allen, came to get me out of the surgery department, she said, "I need you to gather all of the supplies you can and take them on the ambulance to Cokeville. They have a hostage situation at the Cokeville elementary school with bombs that are set to go off." It took a moment for the meaning of her words to sink in, then everyone shifted into high gear.

On the tense trip to our neighboring town, the ambulance crew discussed the best scenario hoped for and the worst possible outcome feared, and what we should do in either case.

As we drove in to north Cokeville, we could see the school west of us. All looked normal. Then it happened. Smoke burst from the windows of the school. There were immediate expressions of disbelief and horror from all of us on the ambulance as we realized the worst had just happened.

The next hour or so was a blur of frantic intervention of treating rescuers and children for smoke inhalation, finding the children who had been taken to homes for safety, cutting off bandages so we could cool burns, and loading ambulances with those who needed hospital treatment. I remember that oxygen became a precious commodity as all ambulances were quickly depleted of their oxygen supply.

I have two specific memories of this event that have stayed foremost in my thoughts. The first is the little boy that I took care of on our first ambulance trip to the hospital in Montpelier. He was handed up to me as I worked in the back of the ambulance. I don't even remember his name, only that I was told that he had the worst burns of all the children. I knew I needed to keep his burns cooled, find an IV site to start replacing fluids, and at the same time warm the boy to combat shock and hypothermia caused from all of the cooling.

It was a challenging trip. I remember thinking how brave the boy was being with the extent of his burns and the trauma he had suffered. I was so relieved to deliver him to the hospital along with the other children in our ambulance. We learned later that Montpelier Hospital was swamped with patients and the Star Valley Hospital was geared up for many more but had only six or seven children delivered to their facility. Radio and phone communications were totally tied up.

When we returned to the school, we began sorting equipment and trying to make organization out of chaos. The only humorous thing that happened for the day, was when a teacher asked me to check a student who was starting to have some breathing difficulties. While shining my pen light down her throat looking for signs of soot, redness, and swelling, I happened to glance up. There were fifty (well, it appeared like that many) cameras staring me in the face. It had taken that long for the news media to arrive. They had missed most of the action and I guess were desperate to film something patient-related. That picture of me looking down that girl's throat was sent nationwide over the news wires. It was the only thing I found to chuckle about in an otherwise tragic day.

My second memory is of the firemen who had all the ambulances around the school pull back to a safe distance because it was discovered that there were more bombs in the school that had not exploded. They had me and one other EMT take a jump kit (medical supply kit) and wait outside a window of the school. We were told they were handing an injured woman, possibly a teacher, out through the window for us to treat.

We spread a blanket on the ground and made ready what supplies we thought we might need. The woman was handed out through the window and placed on the blanket. Within only moments of checking her injuries, I was overcome with grief and frustration as I realized there was nothing that could be done to help her. Thoughts of the children she had taught, of a life snuffed out while still so young flashed through my mind. What a senseless waste! Then one of the firemen said that it was the woman who had held the children hostage and who had set off the bomb.

A flood of relief washed over me. I pumped my fist in the air and said to myself, *Yes! What justice!* Then I was filled with another emotion—that of guilt. I was trained to see only a patient, trained to treat, not judge. And oh how I had judged! Those moments of shame I felt have served to remind me throughout the last twenty years I have worked on the ambulance that all are God's children—that we should hate the act and not the person. That judgment is reserved for our Heavenly Father.

I have had numerous occasions since that day when those moments of shame have reminded me that people need compassion and love the most when they deserve it the least. From my personal point of view, it was perhaps the one positive outcome for me from that day of tragedy.

I have often wondered how the children, teachers, and parents involved in this life event have fared through the years. Maybe now we will all know.

Debbie Sparks
Cokeville EMT
(Oral History—Telephone)

I don't know exactly where to begin, I have struggled remembering details after all these years. It was such a traumatic thing that I think I have tried to bury it deep in my mind.

I had just finished my EMT course in April. That day I was not on call, but had a call radio and was kind of listening to the chatter. I was going about the daily duties of a mom with two young children when I heard a call about the school takeover on the radio. I was very concerned and knew I needed to respond. I quickly got the kids ready to go and called my mother-in-law to see if she could watch them. I dropped them off and went to the town hall. I was told what was going on, and was directed to the intersection of Spring Street and Main Street to stop traffic. About that time several ambulance crews from surrounding communities starting showing up to help out.

Soon after I got to my assigned place, my husband John, Alan Stahl, Kumeroa Chournos and Matthew Teichert drove up. They all worked in Kemmerer at the Naughton Power Plant. About an hour before, the plant supervision had heard enough about the situation to notify the Cokeville people and send them home. Alan Stahl had a child in the school. We had started to talk about what was going on when we heard the explosion and screaming of the children.

We were over a block away, but the sound was terrifying. They jumped out and took off running and I lost track of them in the confusion. I, too, started running to the school intersection.

As I looked toward the school I saw many children with black faces running down the road toward where I was waiting. I immediately started helping who I could. I was working with other EMTs and loading those who needed further medical attention into ambulances. I don't remember who went in which ambulance or to where. I tried to help group those remaining into families or classes. I was frantically searching for my two sisters and soon was relieved to locate them with their classes. They appeared to be physically fine and I continued helping those who had burns or needed attention.

I remember at one point I was with Mrs. Morfeld, a veteran Cokeville EMT. She and I were treating a young girl and somebody came up to her and told her that they had found her daughter. This was such a shocking thing to me, that she had been diligently treating children when her own daughter was one of the hostages. The thought went through my mind that she was extremely dedicated. I remember wondering what I would have done in that situation and whether or not I would be a terrible EMT since I had wanted to know about the safety of my sisters.

I went in one of the ambulances to Montpelier. We helped there with what we could until the doctors took over. I remember coming home and just being so scared. This fear continued over the next several days and I wouldn't let John go to work.

I think what bothered me the most was the reality that even in isolated Cokeville, our children were not immune to the evil of the world. The fact that someone did this in our school and to our children was hard to accept.

Things will happen every once in a while and I remember what we experienced on that day. We get so busy we tend to forget. We need to be reminded about the miracle that happened.

A couple of weeks ago I took my young daughter Emily to school. She hadn't felt well that morning but later felt well enough to go to school so she was about an hour or so late. She went to try the south doors and they were locked. I motioned her back to the car and we tried the back doors. They were locked. I drove her to the front of the school and told her to let Tina Cook know the doors were locked. I had a scary feeling and wondered if I should just take her home. When she came home later that day I asked her if she told Mrs. Cook. She said that Mrs. Cook knew they were locked. Just recently they started always locking the doors. It was a reminder to me about what happened in 1986. That's why we all have reminders. It is Heavenly Father's way of helping us remember the blessing and miracle that we all witnessed.

I agreed to tell my story as an opportunity to express my gratitude to Heavenly Father. This event could have had so many different endings, but with the way this situation ended, it is very clear to me that only through divine intervention, do I still have two of my sisters whom I love dearly. In our lives we seem to push traumatic things aside. I was an adult when it happened and twenty years later I'm still experiencing fear. I can only imagine the trauma those children went through and what they have lived with since. Maybe knowing that after twenty years I'm still scared will help them understand that even though sometimes awful things happen, we can still move forward and have productive and successful lives. We were so blessed on that terrible day. It gives me strength to know we are watched over and protected and I am grateful for occasional reminders of a modern day miracle.

DeeAnn Linford Stephens, LPN
Bear Lake Memorial Hospital
(Interviewed by LaRee Baker)

DeeAnn remembers that everyone dropped what they were doing and came in to help. Everyone came in asking what they could do to help. There was such a feeling of cooperation. She does remember the news media being here, everywhere, trying to get their stories.

John A. Teichert
Cokeville LDS Church Bishop
(Typed Submission)

May 16, 1986 is a date that will go down in history in Cokeville, Wyoming. I had been meeting with the Corps of Engineers out of Salt Lake City, Utah, and Sacramento, California, and also the State Civil Defense regarding a flood problem threatening the Town of Cokeville.

The Corp of Engineers had left to return to Salt Lake City. I was visiting with Kathy Davison, Lincoln County Civil Defense Coordinator, and Grant Sorenson from the Wyoming State Civil Defense Office in Cheyenne, when a young girl came running into the Town Hall in hysterics and reported the children at the Cokeville Elementary School were being held hostage by her father and stepmother, and that two men were handcuffed in the van in front of the town hall.

I didn't know what to make of the story, it was hard to follow her and the language would have put a well driller to shame. I did go out and check the van which had all the windows painted light gray to match the rest of the van. True, there were indeed two men who were handcuffed together. They were also hysterical, and with some apprehension they were released from the van. I was asked to stay with them until the sheriff's department arrived.

Kathy Davison took over the situation, having been a sheriff's dispatcher, she knew who to contact and what to do. I learned that the two fellows were friends of David Young, the man who with his wife, was holding the children hostage at the grade school. They reported Young had contacted them about a deal that would make them rich. He didn't tell them what it was until after they had been there a couple of days. They said they told him they didn't want any part of it. They were then handcuffed and driven around and threatened for several hours before they went to the school. The girl had gone into the school helping her father with the explosives, probably out of fear of her father, but then took off with the van and came to the town hall.

We spent three hours of waiting and wondering, while ambulances and law enforcement people came to the scene. I stayed at the town hall. All were asked to stay away from the school. My youngest son had moved out of the grade school the year before, but I had great concern, as about half the people in the school were members of the Cokeville LDS First Ward over which, at the time, I was serving as bishop. It was a frustrating period. About all I could do was pray. After being relieved by the sheriff's department I went back downstairs to my office in the basement of the town tall where I poured out my heart for the Lord's protection and safety of our children and teachers being held hostage. After some time I arose with a sweet, peaceful feeling that everything was going to be all right.

Immediately after the bomb went off, I went to the school and heard the kids yelling. It was like a herd of wild Comanches as they came running. I watched as concerned parents found and hugged black faced little children. I again received the assurance that everything was going to be all right.

It was hard to assess the damage as approximately seventy of the children and adults were loaded into ambulances and buses and transported to various hospitals. After looking at the damage to the classroom and the fact that the only ones that lost their lives were the Youngs, I have to agree with all involved—teachers, children, parents, law enforcement officers and others that there had to be Divine Intervention. One teacher was shot in the back and several students had severe burns, but it was a miracle that of the over 150 students and teachers that were crowded into one classroom, none lost their lives...

J. Russell Thornock
Lincoln County Commissioner, Chairman
Seven Grandchildren Student Survivors
(Oral History)

I was out on my ranch moving cattle. They came out and told me about it. Of course I went right in. The school was all blocked off. They wouldn't let people in. I told them I was the county commissioner so they let me in.

There just happened to be an emergency management coordinator from the county, Kathy Davison. We established a center in the town hall. I went over to be there and find out what was going on. I'm a little hazy with my memory. They were talking to this David Young. He asked for three million per child. If the city couldn't raise that money, he knew the Mormon church would.

About that time the bomb went off. I went back over to the school. I ran over. We live quite close to the school. Kids came to our house and were laying on the floor and all around. Ryan said the music teacher took him out with him so we are thankful to him.

Frank Lazcanotegui and several others went and helped get kids out the window. So many came to our house to be helped, it was pandemonium. My wife helped out and some other ladies came and helped get things settled down. Our grandkids didn't get hurt too badly but two got burned a little. My grandkids were in 2nd grade, Ryan Thornock, he is Ernie and Karen Thornock's son. Also Cameron Bird in the 2nd grade and he is John and Connie's. We had Karee Thornock in the 2nd grade and she is Linda and J.R.'s. Jason was in the 4th grade and he is Karen and Ernie's. Rusty Birch was in there in 4th and he is Glen and Mary Lue Birch's. Kimberly Thornock was 4th grade, she was J.R.'s and Kyle is J.R.'s, too and he was in 6th grade.

It was a wonderful thing that happened as far as the local people thinking it was a miracle. It certainly was a miracle as everybody survived. It was quite a hectic day.

It changed lives and we came closer to the church, our own churches, realizing the Lord protected the children. I think it brought the community together more than anything else that ever happened in there. This is a great community but we changed and became more united. I think it had a lasting effect. It still has.

Don and Gwen Toomer
On-Scene Helping Hands
(Handwritten Submission by Gwen)

Don and I had come home at spring break from the University of Wyoming. Both of us were substitute teaching in the Cokeville high school. When we heard about the bomb, we were out on the football field with P.E. classes. They called us inside and into the auditorium. We had a prayer together. We then went to a relative's home near the elementary school to wait. Don's sister had a daughter in the school and my sister had a son and a daughter. Don decided to go to the corner to wait.

Then the bomb went off. I remember going down the street and Don found one of our nieces and our nephew. Don's Levi jeans hurt our niece as he hugged her against him. He hadn't realized she was burned. We poured water over her burns while standing on the street corner. I don't remember where the water came from. It seems like someone had some pitchers. I wish we had taken her to Grandma's house to be able to cool her burns a lot faster. At the time, we thought we had better stay at the corner for them to get a count of the school children.

It was amazing when we went back to college how our lives and perspectives had changed. Our safe little home town had been invaded and so had our lives. Each day would mean more than ever before.

We are so very thankful, as we see these family members with beautiful families of their own now, that prayers were answered.

Cristy Transtrum, RN
Bear Lake Memorial Hospital
(Interviewed by LaRee Baker)

Cristy who is now DNS at Bear Lake Memorial, remembers this incident well. She put in many hours working with these patients. After almost twenty years, she says, "I think that we dealt with the initial physical care of those kids very well. I've worried about the lifelong emotional and psychological scars some of these kids may have. They had been through so much before they even came to us. Many of these patients had a long road to recovering—from both the emotional and physical aspects."

Kevin Walker
Firefighter/EMT
Father of Three Student Survivors
(Oral History)

Rachel wasn't able to talk about it for a long time, until last fall, 2004 at a fireside in Idaho. It was the first fireside Rachel had ever done with Katie and Glenna. I only say a few words at firesides. Not much. I have a whole different perspective than Katie and my wife Glenna's. Theirs is a spiritual side. Mine is a firefighter's side.

How it started was, I went to the town hall to tell NaDene, the town clerk, I was leaving for a few hours. I was taking some paperwork to Kemmerer, Wyoming. I was the public works director, had been working since '83 and director since '85.

At first, when Princess came into the town hall, she said, "My dad has your school held hostage. He's in the third grade."

I didn't believe her. I just wouldn't believe her!

She cussed and cursed.

I said, "I don't believe you, I just don't believe you."

She said, "Why not?"

"Because this is Cokeville, Wyoming."

She cussed and cursed some more. I told her she didn't have to talk that way.

"If I show you the two men handcuffed in the van will you believe me?"

"Yeah," I told her, "I will."

So we went out and I saw the men. They were handcuffed in the van just like she'd said. I went back in and told NaDene and Kathy Davison, "It's real."

The van was parked on the east side. They saw me walking in with the men to the conference room. I told the men to stay in the room. I don't know who stayed with them when I left. All the two men did for me was confirm what was going on. I didn't care what else they knew. That wasn't my job. I think if those two guys could have gotten free earlier, they would have told us the plan.

I took them to the conference room in the town hall. Then Kathy called dispatch. Other people were at the town hall, Kathy Davison and others. Emergency Management was in town, County and State, because they were looking at the flood plain. We were worried about the elementary school flooding. We were going to build a dike along Smith's Fork. Emergency Management called people.

I went home to tell my wife we weren't going to Kemmerer. Then I wanted to let Mr. Lamborn, the high school principal, know we needed to evacuate the high school. I talked to Mr. Lamborn face to face. I can remember talking to JaNene Nostaja, she was an EMT and she worked at the high school. I just told her what was going on and she had to get to the town hall. Everyone kept saying, "It can't be real. It can't be real." I kept saying, "It is."

Everyone kept saying, "It's a mock. It's a mock." I kept saying, "NO! I wouldn't let anyone do a mock like this." I was Emergency Management Coordinator for the town. I let the EMTs know. I didn't want to have dispatch send out a page because I knew Gayle Chadwick had a radio and was in the school and I didn't want them (Youngs) to hear the page.

I called or told all the EMTs personally what was going on. My wife and I were both EMTs at the time.

But can you imagine having to go home and tell your wife you have three kids that might get blown up? Can you imagine? Katie was in first grade. Rachel was in third grade. Travis was in fifth grade. The pain in my heart, telling the mother of those children that.

We had to get everyone away from the school or he would blow them up. I was to the point that if anyone had gone to that school I would have killed them.

Wayne Harmon with the town public works and DeMont Grandy blocked streets until we got the fire department going.

I knew it was David Young and his wife in the room and they told us they had enough explosive to blow that school apart.

We all got in fire trucks and ambulances and we blocked the elementary school off by the town hall at Pine Street and at Spring Street. We didn't let anyone in but emergency vehicles. I was in old CV10. Lyle and I, Doug Prows and Allan Burton were there. I can't remember who else was there.

Then it was just a waiting game. I can remember Delbert Rentfro coming to us and telling us where they were and what they were doing. He was custodian to the school but he got out. When they said they had a bomb, he just walked out of the school. He was able to give us very vital information about where they were located. We are glad Delbert did that.

I saw someone run around the school once. It was Doris, I found out later. We could tell by the clothes she was wearing. I don't know what that was all about.

One gentlemen said he was going in. I said, "Dave Young said if anyone tried to stop him he would kill a child. Don't go or I'll shoot you." I didn't even have a gun. Montpelier called us saying they had fire trucks ready. They wanted to know where they should go. I said to stay at Cook's Ranch because if this thing goes all bad we want you to pick up the pieces.

And then we noticed the helicopters coming in and circling the school. It was just before the school bells went off. I don't know what went on in the school. It came across on the news, that he (David Young) wanted so much money per child. We had our radios on, of course, but that information didn't get to us that way.

And I thought a million per child? I've got to come up with his amount times three! I can't remember the amount, I'd have to look it up. I said, "Lord, whatever I have to deal with, I'll deal with. But, I'm putting all my trust in You." I had to.

When the bomb went off, I expected to see the whole school totally disintegrate. We were there with the truck, CV10. We heard it.

Then we saw smoke running out the windows. I thought all my children were dead! Oh Lord be with them.

How do you deal with that? You just say, "I'm a fireman." When we were driving to the school, kids were flying from windows, from doors. Kids were coming out the windows and falling. They just kept coming. I didn't recognize anybody. All the faces were black. I should have known them all but didn't recognize them. They were in our kids' classes. Just thanked the Lord that some kids were alive because we saw them running.

Parents were running toward the school and the media running toward the school. I saw one parent literally tear the school window out of its window track.

I couldn't put an airpac on. I just couldn't do it. Lyle and Allan did. We pulled up by the 3rd grade classroom. I figured I'd deal with them outside, I was an EMT, too. I figured I'd help triage.

When I hooked the hose up to the hydrant I heard one gunshot. And when I was hooking the hose to the old truck (that's how we had to do it then), I heard the second shot. We had already preplanned who was going to do what and who was going to go in.

When we went up to the window to let Allan and Lyle go in, we heard popping. We didn't know what it was, it sounded like firecrackers. Later we found out it was the bullets. They went in the window. A few minutes later they came out with a body. The next time they came to the window they said, "Kevin, they're all out!" Thank You Lord for this blessing!

After the smoke was out and fire was out and the children were out, we turned it over to the policemen. We helped secure the scene because we knew there were still bombs.

Staying there was really, really hard. I knew my kids were out but I didn't know how badly they were hurt. Someone came up to me and said that Rachel was at Steve Taylor's house. She was the worst and Katie and Travis were OK. Then someone told me Rachel was going into shock. She was burned badly and they needed to take her in the ambulance. I went back to the town hall to change out of my fire stuff. Shane and Jana, they were in the other school, were down at Grandma and Grandpa Walker's house. Jana was our niece.

We just got cleaned up and went to Montpelier and saw Rachel. When we got to the hospital someone wanted to interview Katie and Travis. I said, "No." I remember beds lining the hallways. Stake President Matthews and counselors and executive secretary were there and as kids came in they anointed them and blessed them.

When I saw Katie, she came to me and said, "The angels saved us." Those were the first words she said to me. "The angels saved us." And I never doubted it. I said, "I bet you they did." I didn't know how literal it was. I didn't know the magnitude of her story.

I can't explain the terror I felt inside when I heard those kids were taken hostage. You wouldn't wish it on your worst enemy. Another thing that really bothered me, I didn't know what clothes my kids had worn to school. I had gotten up early to get things done. All those little black faces running by and I didn't know what to look for. I don't know how I got through it. The Lord carried me.

The anger I had in my heart. I couldn't describe...toward David Young...I couldn't describe it. I did not know him. I knew he had worked for the town but I did not know him personally. I hated him. The kids hadn't done anything and they didn't deserve that kind of trial in their lives. I lived in town and I was working for the railroad when he lived here. I just flat didn't know the man.

Rachel had some burns on the back of her neck and on both arms. It seemed like her left arm was worse than her right. I asked Dr. Wolff if we could go 'cause there was so many.

We stayed with Glenna's parents in Paris, Idaho, that night. Took the kids with us. Then went back the next day so they could scrub her burns. I can remember Rachel getting in that tank of water and having those burns scrubbed, tears running down those little cheeks and she never screamed. The strength she had was God-given. Now when Rachel fills her car with gas she smells the gas and remembers the fumes. Travis gets into a building and has to know where the exit is and nothing gets between him and the exit. None of my kids like total darkness.

Rachel didn't say a whole lot about it right then. It was the next week. Travis kept saying he was inspired about where to take his sisters. To take them to the window. Katie kept saying a dark haired lady came and talked to her. I kept thinking she meant Doris Young. Rachel said she had talked to people. She had seen people in the room. The dark haired lady said to Katie, "You don't know me, but you will some day." I didn't doubt them. I thought it was odd they didn't tell them who they were.

Travis had told the girls to stay by the windows. Then his friends called him over to the door. When the bomb went off, Travis was blown out the door.

I can't believe the outpouring of love from other communities. It was just beyond anything a person can imagine. And then I had to sort through my feelings. It took me a while. I didn't want to forgive David Young. I can remember Carol Petersen saying, "I have no animosity toward that man. I have no bad feelings." I thought, "How can she say that? Look at all the generations it would have taken out." But the Lord didn't let it happen. I knew if I wanted to keep progressing in this life, I had to forgive him. The Lord says you have to forgive all, no matter what.

Our family grew so much closer. There are no words to describe it. None whatsoever.

Twenty years made me realize that everything can change in a matter of minutes or seconds. What it all boils down to is you've got to rely on God's strength and on your testimony. I still thank the Lord every day in my prayers...for my kids.

As I stand back now and look at the whole picture, there must have been so many Angels helping kids out, answering prayers and protecting them. I have to ask myself, who did those kids see? Some said that I'd helped them out.

We had trained on fires at the elementary school the week before. The elementary school had a fire drill and after the bombing some of the children lined up on the grass outside of the building as they had been shown the week before.

I don't know how I'd have gone on without my kids. I would have but the Lord would have had to help me. You look at my family, twenty years after the bombing; Katie's married with two kids and one on the way. Travis is married with three kids. Rachel's married and has five kids.

For me, Princess was a key factor in not having kids killed at that school. She came and gave us time to get things set up. If she hadn't come, God only knows the impact it could have had on Cokeville. She had a "spark" of God's love in her because she was horrified that children were going to get hurt. I saw the horror on her face. I talked to Princess right when I got back to Town Hall. "I've got to know what my mom and dad did," she said. I said, "I can't tell you that but, it doesn't look good." That's all the compassion I could come up with for David and Doris. I knew they were dead.

Shane has two kids and one on the way. That's one thing I feel good about, the junior high and high school kids. Getting them out and home safe so David couldn't demand them, too.

All my children have a testimony of God and Christ. They all know of my love for them. The Lord blesses us each day.

To my children and grandchildren: I hope that as you live your life you will feel the love that I feel for you. There are no words that can be written that can describe the love I have for you. Always hold on to your families, they are an important part of life and they will be your eternal friends.

My testimony is I know God lives and that Christ died that we may live if we believe in Him. I know that without that knowledge we will not have eternal life. Prayers are answered every day. So pray to Heavenly Father and if it be the Lord's will, He will answer your prayers as He did that day, the 16th of May 1986. When I said in full firefighter outfit on the main street, "Lord, whatever I have to deal with, I'll deal with it. I'm putting all my trust in You," this prayer was answered. Throughout my life, prayers have been answered, some not in the way I would have chosen but in the way the Lord wanted because He knows what's best for us. May I be a Christ-like example to all.

Randall W. White
Deputy Sheriff, Lincoln County Sheriff's Office
(Email Submission)

My law enforcement career has been very diverse as I have worked for several agencies including federal, state and local. Law enforcement has been described by some as long periods of routine boredom interspersed with moments of pure terror. My career has been some of both. Let me start by giving a little background to show how I came to be in Cokeville, Wyoming, on May 16, 1986.

I was born in Twin Falls, Idaho, and grew up in the Magic Valley. I joined the U.S. Navy in March 1971 and started my career in law enforcement in 1977 when I attended the Army Military Police School in Aniston, Alabama, and was assigned law enforcement duties in the Seattle, Washington area.

I left active duty naval service to attend the College of Southern Idaho in 1980. I was hired by the Gooding County Sheriff's Office and worked nights and attended college classes during the day. After graduation I was hired by the Montpelier Police Department and was promoted to the rank of sergeant and assistant chief of police.

In November 1982 I married SunDee Crane, the youngest daughter of Jack R. Crane of Bennington, Idaho. The same month I was elected to the office of Bear Lake County Sheriff and served until January 1985, when I was hired as a patrol deputy by Minidoka County Sheriff's Office in Rupert, Idaho. In November 1985 I was hired by the Idaho State Police and left their academy in January 1986 when my shoulder was injured in a training event.

In March, 1986 I was hired by Sheriff Deb Wolfley to be the LaBarge resident deputy and because I had not found housing I was living with my wife, and sons Jared, 3, and Jordon, 1, in Bennington, Idaho, a small town with a population of about one hundred and fifty residents located about five miles north of Montpelier on State

Highway 30.

On the morning of May 16, 1986 I started my day early. I got up, dressed in my uniform, and kissed my wife goodbye, and as she usually did, she told me to have a good day, not knowing what the day would bring. I drove the thirty-eight miles from my house to Detective Earl Carroll's house in Cokeville, where I picked up my sheriff's office vehicle and checked in service on the police radio. There wasn't anything unusual about that morning. The sun was just rising and the streetlights and the lights of the truck stop parking lot were still on. The streets were quiet with only a few local farmers in their pickups on their way to meet at the local café. As was my routine, I patrolled the highway from Cokeville to Kemmerer where I stopped at the sheriff's office to check for messages, read any new bulletins and check in with dispatch.

I left the sheriff's office at about 10:00 a.m. and then worked my way north toward LaBarge, my assigned patrol area. The fifty miles of US 189 from Kemmerer to LaBarge was a long wide open stretch with very few homes or other buildings. The route passed by the Opal cut off, Fontenelle Reservoir and LaBarge Creek Road with only a few speeding cars to break up the trip. I usually only gave warnings for the speed as it was good to talk with someone on the trip.

I arrived in the town of LaBarge just after noon and was just pulling into the local hot spot, the Huskey gas station, when I got a radio call that changed the course of the day I had planned. The dispatcher told me to respond to the Cokeville elementary school. For a moment I wondered if she had made a mistake. I was in LaBarge about one hundred miles from Cokeville, surely there were other officers closer than I was. As the dispatcher continued I realized that all available officers were being dispatched to Cokeville. The dispatcher seemed to have a sense of urgency in her voice and then I heard her say that there was a man with a bomb at the school and he had taken the school hostage.

I turned around, turned on the emergency lights and siren and started the long return trip to Cokeville. As I raced toward Cokeville my mind was racing, as well. I started to think about strategies for dealing with the situation, the best route to take to get to the school and where to park my patrol vehicle among other things. As I drove I heard several calls on the radio as other officers were responding. Officers from Star Valley and Kemmerer were on the air. At one point I heard Sheriff Wolfley warn responding units about some sheep on the road near Salt Canyon area. I thought to myself that that was a long way from where I was. I heard several officers advise dispatch that they had arrived at the school and heard some of the actions they were taking and planning.

I was still about fifty miles away and the siren on my patrol vehicle seemed to be dulling and changing rhythm. It seemed that I was not covering the miles as fast as I needed to, even though I was probably averaging a hundred miles an hour. My mind was racing, my heart was beating fast, and I was wondering what was going on in the school as I drove. As I finally neared Cokeville, I noticed that the trip that had taken me most of the morning had now only taken me about an hour to cover the same distance.

As I entered Cokeville the scene was quite different from when I'd left only a few hours before. There were police cars, fire trucks, and ambulances all with the emergency lights flashing. Private vehicles parked haphazardly all over the streets in the area of the school and people on foot running everywhere, as if in a panic.

I radioed to dispatch that I was entering Cokeville and was told to go to Town Hall and meet with the detectives. At Town Hall I was assigned to interview Princess Young, the nineteen year old daughter of David Young.

I entered a small room where I saw a small table, a few chairs, and Princess with her head in her hands. I turned on my tape recorder and placed it on the table. I told Princess that I was a deputy sheriff and that I was assigned to interview her. Princess told me that she had already told officers that her father, David Young, and her stepmother,

Doris Young, were in the elementary school and they had guns and a bomb. I asked Princess to describe the bomb to me and she told me that it was made in a shopping cart and had gasoline and high explosives. I asked her how it was designed to be detonated and she told me that it was a switch, that if the person holding the switch were to let go of the switch, it would set off the bomb.

I asked about the events of the morning and Princess told me that they had stayed in a hotel in Montpelier the night before and had painted the windows of the van white so that people could not see in. Princess told me that they left Montpelier and drove to Cokeville early that morning. I thought to myself and wondered if they were on the road at the same time I'd passed through Montpelier on my way to Cokeville. I pressed Princess for a more specific time and she could only tell me that it was early in the morning.

As I interviewed Princess she kept asking what was going on in the school and if the kids were going to be OK. Princess told me about Doyle Mendenhall and Gerald Deppe who had been handcuffed and placed in the van by her dad because they did not want to hurt any kids. Princess told me that her dad talked about "the Biggie" and she did not know the details of what he was planning until this morning when he told the group that he was going to take over a school. I asked Princess what she thought "the biggie" was and she said she didn't know but thought it must be a plan to get money or rob a bank or something. While I was talking with Princess I heard a big boom and someone in Town Hall say that the bomb had just gone off in the school.

As I ran the two blocks to the east side of the school I saw several children running, several with their clothes on fire. As I got closer to the school I saw Sheriff Deb Wolfley standing by a fire department vehicle. The sheriff directed me and another deputy to put on the air pacs from the truck and find the suspect.

As I entered the hallway I saw several more children running out of the building with terrified looks on their faces and their clothes on fire. The hall was filled with smoke and the fire alarm was so loud that I could not hear what the deputy behind me was saying. I remember thinking to myself that this is one call that I might not be going home from. I heard several gunshots ahead of me. I then realized that each time I took a breath from the air pac that there was a noise from the regulator, and I would hear a gunshot ahead of me. Thinking that someone was shooting at me, I got down on my knees and crawled down the hall and opened a door to a classroom to my left.

As I entered the classroom I noticed several small shoes floating in the soot filled water. I also noticed that the deputy who was following me was no longer behind me. I didn't know if he continued down the hallway or if he had been shot. The fire alarm then went silent. I then heard a door close ahead of me. I moved in that direction and saw, through the clearing smoke, the door to a small restroom. I then heard another shot. Later several deputies and I placed David Young's body on an ambulance cot and removed it from the school.

Back in Bennington, my wife SunDee was not aware of the situation in Cokeville until her mother, who also lived in Bennington, called and told her that the radio reported that a bomber had taken over the school and was concerned that I might be in danger. SunDee knew that I was working in LaBarge and would not be in Cokeville and that her mother may not have gotten the news correctly. She thought that there must be something going on in Coalville, Utah. Then the dispatcher called her and told her that I was out of the school and I was not injured. My wife then realized that her mother was correct and that I was involved in a dangerous situation.

A short time after the Cokeville school bombing incident I purchased a new doublewide mobile home and moved to LaBarge. I also joined the Lincoln County Sheriff's SWAT team and continued to patrol in the LaBarge area.

In April 1987 Sheriff Ray Jarvis of the Minidoka County Sheriff's Office in Idaho hired me as a lieutenant and chief of detectives and later chief deputy. My family and I moved back to Rupert, Idaho, where I continued to serve until my retirement on April 24, 2005.

I have had several tense situations during my career. I have been shot at several times, knifed once, and injured a lung while attempting to arrest a person fighting in a bar. I also was shot once in the abdomen, and twice in the leg. The shooting took place on September 23, 2003, when two Wells County sheriff's deputies, a Utah highway patrolman, a Twin Falls Idaho police detective and I were attempting to arrest a bank robber who had fled to Cactus Pete's Casino in Jack Pot, Nevada. The robber came out of a hotel room, ran past the first few officers, and as I attempted to force him to the wall he fired four shots. I took one round in the abdomen, and two rounds in the upper right leg, shattering the femur and taking out about an inch and a half of bone. The fourth round struck the wall. I am now recovering from the shooting.

In July of 1992, my wife SunDee and I adopted two additional children, Michelle and Dalen. I now have three children in college and my youngest son is a senior in high school. I have a new job. A few days after retiring from the sheriff's office I was appointed as chief of police for the City of Rupert. I enjoy serving the citizens of Rupert in this, our centennial year, 2006.

I will always remember the events of May 16, 1986, and all the people whose lives have been forever changed by the events of that day. I shall also remember how the community and surrounding area came together in that seemingly hopeless situation. And I will never forget that our Heavenly Father answered the prayers of all that were there that day.

Dr. Noall E. Wolff

Bear Lake Memorial Hospital, Idaho

E.R. Physician/Family Doctor

(Oral History - Telephone)

We actually created a number of beds, space for kids that weren't really intended for patient beds. For example, the bed in the doctor's lounge had two kids in it. We had kids in the hall and we created a number of other spaces. We can only hold twenty-two in our little hospital. Some of the children were able to go home and some needed to check in the next day. I think we had forty-four in the hospital overnight. Every bed in the hospital plus a couple of others was full. I think eighty-four children we treated. We were able to handle most right here, a few of the more serious ones transferred out, the ones that needed intensive treatment at a major hospital. Every one of them that we saw was burned and had smoke inhalation. Plus we had one teacher that had a bullet wound.

Every one of these children did very well, the children we treated in our hospital. They had no permanent problems with lungs due to the smoke inhalation and truly minimal scarring with burns. All healed completely within sixteen to twenty-one days. I don't know otherwise. If that's not true I'd sure like to know. It was just absolutely astonishing to see them heal so well and do so well. It was just so rewarding to see that. And then over the years I've watched them to see what happened. I think about them all the time. I see them and I say, "There's a little miracle walking down the street."

T. Deb Wolfley
Lincoln County Sheriff
(Email Submission)

Where to begin?

My thoughts on this event can be viewed in law enforcement, community, personal and spiritual terms.

Being sheriff of Lincoln County for nine years, 1982 through 1990, was a very special time in my life. The job brought a lot of joy, headaches and many challenges. I believe that training and preparation pays off in any endeavor and helps a person to be prepared to handle what lies ahead. I attended a lot of law enforcement training over my law enforcement career and part of the training included hostage negotiations. Because Lincoln County is in a very rural area, I never really felt that I would be faced with some of the situations that big cities might encounter in law enforcement matters. Little did I know that one day things would change dramatically in law enforcement concerns for Lincoln County.

May 16, 1986 was a normal day for me in many ways, even though it was my birthday. I usually have very low-key activities on my birthdays, but this day would be much different. I worked in the morning at the sheriff's office and decided to play racquetball during the lunch hour time. I had just finished playing a game and was going to go home to shower and clean up. While at the rec center, I received a call from the dispatch center where Jerrie Burris told me that there was some kind of disturbance in Cokeville either at the town hall or at the school, but that it could be serious; something about some guns and a bomb. I decided to head over there and to get some deputies heading out that way. Earl Carroll and Randy White headed to Cokeville.

While headed to Cokeville, our dispatch center received more information from the town hall, thanks to Kathy Davison. Kathy had worked for Lincoln County for several years, many of those years as a dispatcher and at that time, she was working as the Emergency Management Coordinator. Kathy was in Cokeville with some state officials looking at the floodwater potential for the Smiths Fork River. Kathy was in the town hall when Princess Young came in and reported in a very excited way what her father was doing at the Cokeville elementary school. After Kathy had talked some to Princess and she called Jerrie at the sheriff's office, we knew something terrible might be taking place.

When I arrived at Cokeville, Earl had already talked briefly to Princess while Randy was talking to the two men who had been handcuffed in the back of a van. It appeared that David and Doris Young were holding all the kids, teachers and other adults hostage in the school. I met briefly with Princess and the two men who had been friends of David at one point in time. Their story of David's plan shocked me. I slowly began to realize that we had a very major problem on our hands from a law enforcement perspective.

At the school, David had allowed the principal, Max Excell, to leave the classroom to go to his office and communicate with law enforcement officials. I had set up our command post at the town hall, which is about two or three blocks away from the school.

I talked to Max on the phone to get a better idea of what was happening at the school and what David's demands were. Max relayed a horrifying story to me. David believed in reincarnation and he planned on killing the kids to start a "brave new world," but he needed $300 million dollars to help start this "new world." Max explained as best as he could on how the classroom was set up with the bomb in a cart and that there was an area taped off in the middle of the classroom and that no one could be in the "zoned" area. David made it very clear to Max that it would do no good for the sheriff's office to use a sniper to shoot him, or to rush the classroom and try to subdue him because David had the bomb set up to where if he fell (shot by someone) or if he was tackled, the bomb would be set off because of the way it was hooked to his body. He had a clothespin set up with screws in the ends that when the clothespin came together, contact would be made. There was a piece of wood between the ends of the clothespin, which prevented the bomb being detonated. The clothespin was tied to his wrist and body so that any sudden movement or if his arm was raised too high or away from his body, the piece of wood would come out, contact would be made and the bomb would explode.

As the afternoon wore on, we learned more about David's past and his background. I had forgotten that David used to work for the Town of Cokeville as their law enforcement officer a few years back. He did not last very long because of certain actions with guns and other matters, which caused him to be fired from the job. Apparently he'd lived there long enough to know that Cokeville produced some good kids. He knew of the strong families that lived there and of the religious beliefs of the people. According to David's diaries, that is why he picked the Cokeville kids to start his "new world." We learned that David had attended college and graduated in law enforcement. With his previous training he knew exactly what plans I would be making to try and resolve the situation. In so many ways, he had planned ahead to counteract our strategy to get the kids out safely.

From what Max reported to me, David had come prepared to fully execute his plans. David had brought into the school a large supply of guns, ammunition, blasting caps, chains, padlocks and many other items used to control people and destroy them. David also had brought with him many of his personal journals and writings. It was from these journals that we later learned more about his views and ramblings, though we never could figure them out. David almost bragged in his journals of the number of times that he put a bomb together exactly the same way each time, and that the bomb went off exactly as he planned. His writings all pointed to the day when he would start his "Brave New World."

The town hall, as our command post, turned out to be a very busy place. We soon had the task of keeping parents and other people away from the school. I certainly didn't blame them for wanting to get their kids out. We worked on getting medical personnel in place in case we needed them. We arranged for SWAT teams to come, along with bomb personnel to help us out. These teams came from neighboring counties. We had officials doing more background work on David. There were hundreds of other details to attend to.

Having kids being held hostage was very painful for me because I have six kids and I can imagine how I would have felt if my kids were in that school. Making it even harder was the fact that Ron and Claudia Hartley, who lived in Cokeville, were close friends of my wife and me, and they had most of their kids in that school. I remember very distinctly how I felt when Claudia came to me and asked what I was doing to get her kids out safely. I told her we were doing all we could and that things would work out. We both shed a tear and she walked away and I wondered what was going to happen. I recall feeling a very heavy weight on my shoulders; the responsibility of getting the kids out alive.

I was struggling in my mind as to what to do. At one point in time, somehow I was alone, walking down the hallway of the town hall. I remember saying a brief prayer in my heart and asking my Heavenly Father for help. I explained the situation to Him and told Him that I needed His help. I can testify to the reader of this article that my prayer was answered. A voice came to my mind and it was strong, clear, personal, and it told me that things would work out and everything would be OK. I did not question what would happen, how, or when, but I felt such a peace in my mind. I knew there was a higher power in control of the events happening in Cokeville that day. I am so thankful for that brief moment in my life when again my prayers were answered.

My solitude didn't last long. So many things to do, people to talk to and of course, working with the press /media. Officers reporting on how things were being taken care of with the perimeters set up, how many ambulances were in place, EMTs, fire trucks, how soon before the SWAT team would be here, bomb squad tech would be coming, when the FBI personnel would be coming and even getting food arranged for people. David would not talk to any of the local law enforcement officers; he wanted to talk to the president of the United States. David said he had all the time in the world to wait for the money, he knew the parents and local church leaders would put enough pressure on the government to get the money rounded up. The thing that worried me was the fact that it was getting close to time when school would normally end and the kids would want to leave. What was going on inside of the classroom, how were the kids doing and all the adults? Shortly after 3:30 p.m., my worst fears came true; the bomb went off in the school.

I remember that Earl and I were talking on the phone with Max when we heard the explosion over the phone lines. I recall wondering what carnage I would find as we all rushed over to the school. We could not drive, but had to run through all the people that were out in the streets. As I got closer to the school and the classroom windows on the east side of the building, I saw smoke billowing out of the windows and a boy was crawling out of the window. I ran over to the window and helped pull kids and adults out. There was one lady that I helped pull out the window and I later learned it was Doris Young.

There was black smoke in the classroom and I could hear the sound of gunfire or popping sounds, like .22 shells being exploded. The kids who came through the window had black on their faces, eyes wide as silver dollars and the look of fear was prevalent. The kids were running everywhere, looking for their parents or brothers and sisters. Officers were entering the building through other entrances, looking for David and Doris and getting the building secure.

As it turned out, the only people who died in that classroom were David and Doris. There were very few kids who were seriously burned; many had minor burns and smoke inhalation. One teacher was shot, but he survived and continued to teach. There are others who can tell their stories as to what happened inside the classroom, the miracles that occurred there and they have their own testimonies. My reflections consist of the many miracles that happened on May 26, 1986. My prayers were answered that day when I was by myself as I was in the town hall. The prayers were answered for all the parents of the kids. Later I found out about all the prayers that were being offered in the homes of people in Cokeville, out in the streets, in the classrooms of the high school building in Cokeville, in Casper, Wyoming, at the state track meet where Cokeville had some kids competing. There were prayers being offered all across the nation on behalf of the Cokeville kids.

The bomb did go off, but the power of the explosion and force were reduced greatly because of several factors, which in my mind was a result of Divine Intervention. Two main reasons stand out in my recollection of that day: David made one big mistake in preparing his bomb for that day; he got an empty plastic milk jug out of the Cokeville landfill and put gasoline in the jug. Later on in the day, the jug leaked and got much of the gunpowder, blasting caps and flour wet. The other factor was that two of the wires used in the bomb device had been cut so that only part of the blasting caps were activated. These wires had been cut by heavenly messengers or guardian angels; there is no doubt about this in my mind. Other things occurred to reduce the bomb capacity.

I am glad that things turned out the way they did. One hates to see anyone die, but David Young made the choice to shoot his wife Doris and then shoot himself after the bomb went off. This was a blessing because there was no criminal trial for the Youngs. The kids were spared the ordeal of going to court and reliving that horrible experience. I was able to relate to the news people what happened and to answer all the questions asked during the news conferences. I was amazed at the power of the press in broadcasting the story, bringing out the good things that happened, all the human-interest stories and the strong character of the people of Cokeville.

In closing, I am grateful that miracles still do occur. I am grateful that a Heavenly Father hears and answers prayers. I will always be grateful for all the people who worked together that day in Cokeville to save the kids. I'm grateful for all the volunteers who sacrificed their time and talents for others, grateful for the opportunities to meet with my staff at the sheriff's office and talk about what happened and the counseling we received from professionals to help us deal with our thoughts. I'm grateful for all the people, who sent letters, cards money, flowers and other things to help the kids recover. These actions reinforced my belief that there are many good people in the world who care and who want to help others in distress. I am also grateful for the people in law enforcement who put their lives on the line to protect others. I am especially grateful for my good wife; she always has supported and stood by me in all that I do.

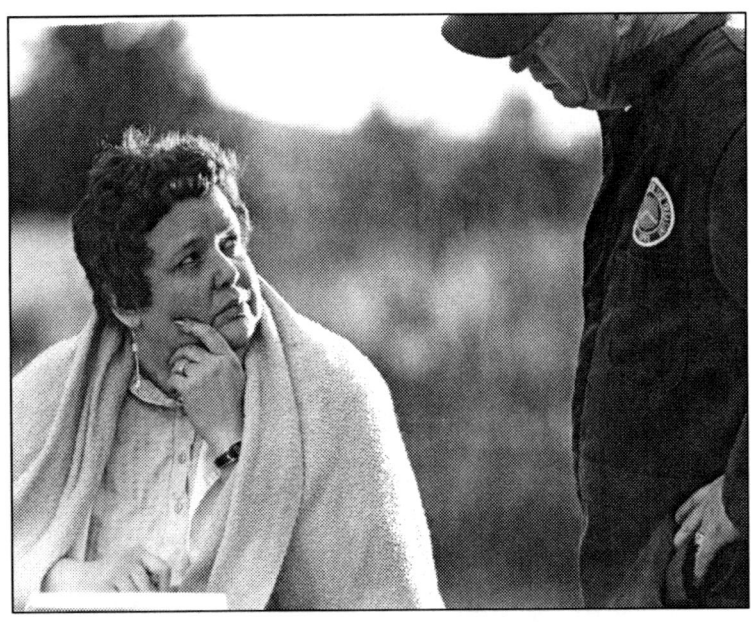

School Secretary Tina Cook and
Sweetwater County Bomb Technician Rich Haskell
Courtesy of the Casper Star Tribune Collection, Casper College Library

Parents and Spouses of Survivors

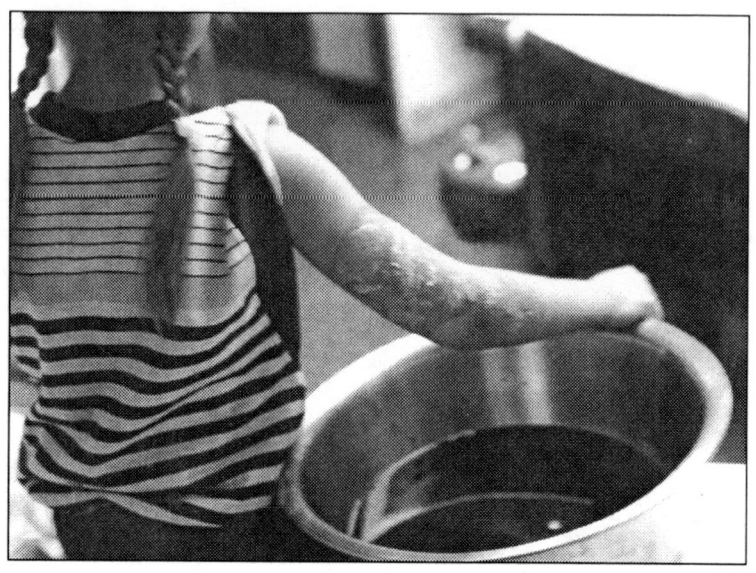

LuAnn Anderson
Mother of Absent Student
(Oral History—Telephone)

I know it wasn't meant to be for Julie to be there. I had driven the kindergarten bus that day. Dennis, my husband, was in Casper. He didn't know if I was in there or that Julie wasn't. Sometimes I stayed at the school after driving the morning kindergarten kids home and ate lunch with the kids at school. I didn't that day. I was going to Evanston to help my daughter and her husband move.

I got my car from where I left the bus. I had taken Julie out of school for the second half of the day. We went to get Wendy from the high school. At the high school, Julie said she had forgotten her homework at the elementary school. We went back to the elementary. The doors were locked and no one could get in.

Then we got to the railroad tracks and Wendy said, "I need to stay. We have a class party tonight." Julie added, "If she stays, I'm going back to class, too." Usually I would have said OK and taken them back. I didn't. I didn't even take my foot off the pedal, just kept going. The girls didn't say anything.

I basically passed the Youngs in the driveway at the elementary school. I don't remember seeing them. But, I had to have passed them. It was that close, within minutes.

Then we went to Evanston. I was writing out a check. Someone said, "You're from Cokeville? Have you heard what happened?" I ran out to my car and turned on the radio. Julie just started crying.

I really think it was meant to be that Julie was not there. That was the miracle. She was the kind of kid who was easily frightened. I know it would have traumatized her. It would have traumatized her. She was just not meant to be there.

Samuel O. Bennion, Jr.
Husband of Teacher Survivor
Father of Three Student Survivors
Son of Teacher Aid Survivor
(Oral History—Telephone)

My three oldest kids were in there. Jessie was not born yet. Janaan, Nancy, and Sam, were all in there. It was on the radio and I couldn't believe it. I didn't believe it. Denton Bartschi and I were together. I said I was going to leave, so I left. Denton went with me. His little girl was sick that day and she didn't go to school. I listened to it all the way home. I didn't realize the extent of it.

My mother's oldest grandchild, Jennifer Hart, was visiting for the week. I picked her up from here at the ranch. I told her to get her jacket and her coat. The car I was in didn't have much gas. I changed vehicles to my pickup so I could do whatever I needed to. As I pulled into town and parked, the bomb had just gone off and the kids were coming out in all directions. I did catch my wife. She told me the kids were out. She had seen Sam but didn't know where he was. She had the two girls. She had not seen my mother. It was just a few minutes more before I found my mother. We went to Marion Sparks'.

I took them to the hospital. I left my kids with my oldest niece at Marion's.

Cheryl Buckley
Mother of Three Student Survivors
(Typed Submission)

May 16, 1986. It was a beautiful spring day. The school year was drawing to a close and it seemed to be a fairly typical day. My husband Joe was on days off and out fixing a tire. I was busy doing housework when the phone rang. It was a good friend of mine, LaJean Pieper, calling. She told me a crazy man was holding our kids hostage at the school. At first I thought she was joking and told her so, but as she assured me it was true and told me a few details, I could tell by the terror in her voice, it was true. I was numb.

I went out to tell Joe and his reaction was much like mine—I mean really, we live in Cokeville, Wyoming, in peace and harmony where nothing too exciting ever happens! As soon as I convinced him it was true, he got his guns and went to his dad's house, Joe Buckley Sr., to pick him up and travel the twelve miles into town from where we lived out south of Cokeville. Later we found out we weren't the only ones who were ready to take this into our own hands. Many dads had the same idea and were ready to storm the school had it been necessary.

Now I was home with my three pre-schoolers, Joseph, Jessica, and Jared. Three of my children were in that school: Jamie, 3rd grade, Jennie, 2nd grade and Jolene was in the 1st grade. I made some phone calls trying to find out what was happening, all the while pleading in my heart for the Lord to protect all the kids.

I began to see police cars coming from Kemmerer, heading to Cokeville. I had to face the fact that my children were in grave danger. I decided I could wait no longer and jumped into my car with my three little ones and drove to town. I didn't even stop to put on decent clothes or shoes. I had on a pair of pink flowered polyester bell bottoms and bare feet, much to the embarrassment of my family, especially when I appeared on TV that night. As I was riding to town I remember wondering why the sky was still blue and everything seemed still and at peace when my children were in such perilous circumstances. I was afraid to ride into town, not knowing what I might encounter. As I came around the corner and looked down Main Street, I could see a lot of commotion coming from the school. I was frantic because there were people running everywhere and an ambulance in the middle of the street. Screaming. I grabbed Norene Thompson as she rushed by and asked her what had happened. She told me the bomb had gone off. I asked her if she'd seen my kids. She said a bunch of kids had run to her house and mine could be there. It's hard to explain the feelings I experienced as I found my kids and they were all alive!

Jamie had been burned up both her arms. We later found out the man had gone to the bathroom and while he was in there, the woman somehow turned wrong and set the bomb off that was tied to her wrist. She was on fire. The man came out of the bathroom and saw her on fire and shot her. He went into the bathroom and shot himself. The kids and teachers escaped out the windows and doors. Not one of the children or teachers lost their life. There were some bad burns and emotional injuries, but what a miracle!

We found out later that some of the children had had angels help them out of the school that day. A few days later one of the children was looking through a family album and saw her great-grandmother and excitedly told her mother, "There's my angel!" It makes a lot of sense to me that deceased family members would have been there that day to preserve their posterity for many wise purposes.

After gathering up all our family, we took Jamie to the hospital to treat her burns. That was another miracle, the way the kids healed up from their burns. That night we had a lot of phone calls from friends who had seen us on TV or heard the news over the radio. There was a lot of media coverage. For me, it was one of the most grateful days of my life. The school provided counseling for the parents and kids and I took advantage of that service.

It was so interesting to see how this incident affected different people. I loved hearing all the stories of how it had been for them and how they were handling life now. As for me, the week following the bomb was one of the happiest of my life because I was so grateful. I think my attitude helped my kids heal faster. I had no feelings of fear or hate or "why us"—only gratitude to have my little family still with me.

Every May 16th, all my kids can expect a call from their mother reminding them of the Miracle of that day and how thankful I am to have been a part of a modern-day miracle. I will never forget God's mercy to us that day. I remember the first Sunday after the bomb and hearing the children singing in the Primary room. What an angelic sound that was. I remember when the kids were all performing in the Christmas play and were all together for the last song. I thought, what would have happened to our community had the full bomb exploded? We would have had no children. I think our town would have died that day with the children.

Sometimes in quiet moments I like to think of all those children and the lives they are leading today. I like to think of my own children and their lives today. Jamie and Bill King have four children of their own. Their children will go to school in that same school their parents attended and where they had that experience. Jennie served a mission to Kentucky and now is married to Jeff Walker and has two boys she is raising. Jolene married Brad Bradshaw and together they just finished building a home of their own for them and their three children. Joe and I have since moved from Cokeville and have lived in different communities. I feel an obligation to share this experience whenever and wherever I meet new people to let the Lord know I WILL NEVER FORGET!!

Joe Buckley Jr.
Father of Three Student Survivors
(Handwritten Submission)

As I recall I was outside working on my truck. Cheryl came outside and said there was a crazy man holding the grade school hostage. I had three daughters in that school. I immediately got my gun and headed for town. I stopped and picked up my dad on the way. It seemed like a long way to town that day.

When we got there, the streets were all blocked off. We were told to stay back and not to attempt going close to the school. I found out that those in charge were trying to round up lots of money. I later found out they wanted two million per child. It seemed like the minutes were hours to me. I felt helpless. My mind was working on how to get something done.

It wasn't a long time after we arrived in town that things got crazy. I was standing just behind the blocked area when I heard an explosion and it came from the school. I was on my way toward the school. I didn't get too far before a cop stopped me and told me I could not go to the school. I told him I had three girls in there and I was going to get them, so he better move or get run over. As I got to the schoolyard I heard screams and there were little kids pouring out of the school and running away. I searched through the faces looking for my girls. I finally found Jamie. She was burned and crying. Jennie and Jolene somehow got by me and I later found them at Norene Thompson's house. They were just scared but not physically hurt. I took Jamie to the ambulance to get some help with her burned arms. After doing that I gathered all the family and we headed for the hospital in Montpelier. It took a while but we got everyone taken care of throughout the afternoon.

It turns out that the two who were committing this crime were killed during the explosion and chaos at the end. I think that was a blessing for everyone.   No one was lost but the ones who were doing wrong.

The most important thing to me was I got my girls back that day.

Sherrie Cornia
Mother of Three Student Survivor
(Email Submission)

I wrote this May 18, 1986. A slightly altered version was printed in one of the newspapers. Every time I read it I feel like I am there, standing in that classroom, humbled and grateful for miracles.

Reflection

I stood silently, staring at the smoke blackened classroom. The horror of what my children had survived seeped deep and heavy. My eyes walked up the gray walls covered with school papers and dulled displays, over scattered building blocks and crayons, into tipped over chairs and empty shoes, around the masking-taped line that had framed the lethally loaded shopping cart, up to the broken ceiling panels where the bomb's explosion had found partial escape, out the windows and doors where heroes had lifted, carried, pushed and pulled our precious heritage to safety.

I stepped over to the corner and studied the graceful folds of red, white and blue hanging in quiet dignity, altered only by a thin film of black dust. A symbol of the freedom that had been held hostage. The standard had been tested, and terror had failed. Our freedom was intact. Our children were alive. Pain would pass. Burns would heal. God does hear and answer prayers.

As reality settled into reverent gratitude, the words of a small son gently echoed through my calming thoughts, "and Heavenly Father, please bless that it won't ever happen again."

Susan Cory
Mother of Two Student Survivors
(Typed Submission)

May 16, 1986 started out like any other school day. Wake up the kids, have them get dressed, feed them breakfast, brush through Jennifer and Heather's waist length hair and drive Jennifer to school. Come home, clean things up a bit, have lunch and take Heather to the school for afternoon kindergarten. Drive back home and put my four year old son and ten month old daughter down for an afternoon nap so I can possibly get something accomplished for the day.

Then the phone rings and my husband is on the line telling me that terrorists are holding the children hostage at the school. I can't believe this is happening. What if I never see them again? Did I tell them I loved them before I dropped them off at school? I immediately get down on my knees and plead with my Father in Heaven to spare the lives of my daughters and the others held hostage.

I call my mother-in-law, she comes down and we have the television on and the radio on listening and waiting for any news. I am frustrated. I want to go to the school but my little ones are napping and we would just be in the way, so I sit and listen to the radio. At 3:30 my mother-in-law says she will drive down to the school to see what is happening. Shortly after she leaves, the radio announces the bomb has gone off. I can do nothing but sit and wait.

Several minutes pass by and then my mother-in-law comes in with Jennifer and Heather both crying and showing signs of burns. Jenn's fingertips are burned on one hand and her eye is very red and starting to swell. Heather has spots on her face and hand that have the top layer of skin burned off and is complaining of her knee hurting. When I remove her intact leotards, I find the skin burned off her knee as well. I run cool water over Heather's burns and get a dish of cool water for Jenn to soak her fingers in and a cool washcloth for her eye.

I then go and find my husband's EMT book and look up how to treat burns and shock.

On a normal Friday afternoon, after I picked up the kids from school we would head to Montpelier to give my husband a ride home from work. He is a track inspector for the railroad and travels by motorcar on the track. We go pick him up and stop and visit my parents. As I read more on burns and shock I decide my daughters probably should be seen and treated at the hospital for the burns and Heather seems to be in the shock stage.

My mother-in-law and I drive them to the hospital in Montpelier where they are admitted. I try to contact my husband. He had gotten a car from the Ford dealership in Montpelier and headed for home. The lines are all busy. I have an aunt who works in the office at the hospital. She continues to try and get hold of him. Finally around 10:30 that night by husband arrives at the hospital. He has been on a bus with the injured kids from the bomb who went to the Kemmerer hospital. My family is all together now and I feel great relief.

I felt then as I still do now, deep gratitude to my Father in Heaven for sparing the lives of my children and all the others who were held hostage that day. It was truly a miracle that the only lives that were lost were that of the perpetrators.

In writing this letter for the book I have very mixed feelings about continually bringing it to life through the media every five, ten and now twenty years later. Part of me just wants to put it in the past and leave it, even though I will forever carry the miracle in my heart. And then there are the emotional scars that my daughters carry.

The summer after the bombing they did not enjoy the fireworks on the 4th of July. And on our family campouts the next few summers they could not roast hot dogs or marshmallows over the campfire. Two years after the incident we had the big fire in Yellowstone Park that was continuously on television and the smoke penetrated the skies of Cokeville and one of my daughters began to have fears of our home burning down and would get up in the night and shut off the heat, even though it was the end of September and starting to get cold enough to require extra heat in our home.

The psychologist explained to me that things like the fire could trigger her memories of the bombing. We saw that again five years after the bombing when we had a small chimney fire in our home one morning and she was hysterical and I had to hang up from 911 and drive her to her grandma's house so I could deal with the fire. The physical scars that they carry are minimal but the emotional scars run deep and will forever remain, only to manifest themselves more at certain times of their lives than at others.

Has this changed our lives? Yes! We witnessed a modern day miracle and know that our Heavenly Father does hear and answer our prayers today and for that I am truly grateful. I became an EMT a few years later and then went on to pursue my childhood dream of becoming a nurse and to work at the Montpelier hospital with those who gave such good care to my daughters.

Sharon Dayton
Husband of Teacher Survivor
(Typed Submission)

Chores done, when I drove up to the ranch house six miles north of Cokeville JoAnne Metcalfe was standing outside the door by the cellar. As I got out of the pickup she said, "I think there's something wrong over at the school. Somebody's holding the school hostage." Outwardly JoAnne is one of the calmest people I know and she was worried! Her youngest three children were in the elementary school.

It didn't take long to reach town in the old blue International pickup truck. My first stop was my house on Main Street where I took my 30.06 rifle from its scabbard, grabbing also my belt of cartridges and an extra box of shells. Wanting to know more of what was happening I stopped at the town hall where several cars were gathered. I had qualified as rifleman "expert" in military training and we had ranch property close to the west side of the school so I figured I could cover any attempted escape to the west or north.

Entering the city hall I found a clustered group discussing the hostage situation. "They have a bomb," I heard. "There's a pin attached to a string and tied to their arm and if anyone tries a rescue, they'll pull the pin and set off the bomb. They say they'll be there as long as ten days waiting for the ransom." My wife Janel was in there with the rest of the teachers and children.

Abandoning any rifle plan, I left the truck parked where it was and began the two block jog toward the elementary school. Halfway there I heard the explosion and then saw billows of black smoke pouring up from the area of the school. Peering over a tall whitewashed fence I saw the Cokeville Fire Department truck next to the school, its volunteers preparing for their work, and I heard the school fire alarm and the screams of the children for the next five minutes.

Repositioning myself on the roadway that led to the school

I watched as the children poured past. Some had blackened faces and some faces were burned white. After the bomb exploded, parents gathered as close as law would allow, and searched for their children among those who came past. Ambulances, buses and law enforcement vehicles waited for the injured. Lawmen and a SWAT team entered the smoking building for possible rescues and to recover any dead.

The blanket-covered body of Doris Young was soon brought out on the lawn and following several shots we were informed that David Young had shot himself in the children's bathroom.

All teachers survived and were frantically trying to account for all their students, some of whom had run to the homes of relatives. My wife, Janel, was among those doing their counts. All the children made it out alive, several critically burned. Seventy-eight of the hostages were temporarily hospitalized. Many suffered severe trauma.

Subsequent to the event an older son read to us an entry in his diary recorded two weeks before the bombing. "Last night I had a terrible dream. I saw smoke pouring out of the elementary school and heard the children screaming."

That is what I remember best.

Gilbert and Trixie Eastman
Parents of Two Student Survivors
(Oral History—Telephone)

It's made us stronger for what our lives have been through. We are very thankful everything turned out the way it did with the bomb. We know that our kids were protected by a higher power.

Carl O. Eggleston
Father of Two Student Survivors
(Oral History—Telephone)

I was on a railroad working. When I found out we were up the track. I didn't have a radio. Gilbert Eastman came up the road and told us. He was working in Kemmerer and when he saw us he told us. I think Art Hess and Craig Taylor were working there that day, too, but I can't remember.

We had to wait to get track time so we could put a motorcar on the track and get back to the main house, down at Sage.

When we had done that, why, they had just heard on the radio that the bomb had just gone off. And, I think Carla just got home a little while before. The bus had just brought her home. She said that was the hardest thing she ever had to do, to come home and tell her mom the kids were held hostage.

Lamar Thornock and Rose, they went and got their car and we jumped in and went to town. YoLonda and Carla and I went. When we got in there, everyone was gone and out. It was just a matter of locating the kids, finding out where they were. Neither one of ours was hurt seriously. I think Carl John had a little burn on the back of his neck.

I know it was a miracle or there would have been people killed. Jodie went with this one lady she knew. Carl John was one of the last ones out because he went back in hunting Jodie. He wasn't that old and yet he kinda knew about getting everyone out. Where they had the desks piled up by the bathroom, well that's where he went out. He took other kids out that way, too. We took him to Kemmerer on the bus to check him for smoke inhalation. He had some hair on his forehead singed and some on the back of his neck. He was OK.

They were kind of like heaven was living with them for a while after that happened. They liked everybody real good. They knew they might not have had each other for a long time.

YoLonda Ann Eggleston
Mother of Two Student Survivors
(Oral History—Telephone)

Well, Carla came home. She just barely got off the bus. The bus had turned around and they said the bomb went off right about that time. It had just gone off when she got out. And so when she came in the house and told me, I was petrified. I couldn't even talk. Our neighbors had been to town, Kemmerer, and they had heard so they stopped. They asked us if we wanted a ride into Cokeville. They'd heard it on the radio. We rode into town. I don't remember who told me where to find Jodi but she was over at the neighbor's. She was scared we wouldn't know where to find her.

She remembers they were singing Primary songs and they thought that was getting to the bad people. She was playing with clay and you're not supposed to remove things from the school and she had this clay in her hands. That always bothered her.

I think it was a miracle. I know the Lord stepped in. He was the One that stopped it. He was the One.

Carol Ferrin
Mother of Two Student Survivors
(Oral History—Telephone)

I am very grateful to have all of them, my two kids, Jamy and Jenny, my sister, Gayle and her two kids, Justin and Mel.

The rest is just something I haven't dealt with yet. I haven't written yet in my journal or my personal history. I really should do something with that.

Pam Grandy
Mother of One Student Survivor
(Handwritten Submission)

The miracle of Cokeville remains a very special and sacred memory for me, knowing that my Heavenly Father loves each of His children and answers prayers!

Thinking of the Cokeville bombing conjures up many mixed feelings and memories. Books which have been written and the movie which was made, only partly touched on or scratched the tip of the truth. Each person's perception was and is different. Regardless of each person's perception, all involved recognized there was no "man-made" reason the school stands today and the children of the bombing are going on to bear witness of the Lord providing a miracle.

For our family, I guess the "bombing story" started many years ago. It was not too long after our marriage in 1977 when DeMont had a dream where he was frantically looking for something valuable at the scene of a red brick building with billowing smoke. We couldn't place the building or identify what he was seeking. I dismissed the "nightmare" and told him not to worry. However, he frequently had the same dream and he would often say, "I had it again." It was if the Lord was preparing us for what was in our future.

I will never forget that Friday in May. Mont had brought in people from the county to assess the spring flooding damage in the Cokeville area and the workings were in place for a miracle. When David Young's daughter came to the town hall, Mont's office became the hub of activity as authorities were contacted and initial cordoning off of the area became critical. I was oblivious to the situation until I happened to call his office at about 2:30 p.m. He said, "Haven't you heard? I'll be home in a minute." I was puzzled and waited a few minutes.

As Mont came in the house he fell in front of me on his knees crying, "He's going to die." I didn't understand. He proceeded to tell me our son, Carl, the teachers, and students at CES had been taken hostage by a madman and that they wouldn't be released until he received a huge sum of money. I fumbled with what to say, not really believing what he had just told me. Knowing Carl and another student had serious medical conditions which required daily medication, I stupidly commented, "We'll just take in medicine and food and wait it out!" I immediately gave him a hug as he asked that I stay home with our other children since he was needed at his office.

I remember calling my mother at her business in Salt Lake City and relating the events. She, like many others, didn't believe the event transpiring in Cokeville. Phone lines in town, shortly after that, were tied up and regular communication had stopped when she later tried to call back.

In shock and feeling my life had been shaken, knowing the situation was critical, I to fell to my knees. I poured my heart out to my Heavenly Father in prayer and as I was quiet, I felt a calm. I know He listened. A peaceful feeling came over me and I knew Carl and the others would be safe. I didn't know how the situation would be resolved, but that all would be OK. It gave me strength.

I went outside and stood on the corner to wait. Just that morning I had stood on that corner and watched as Carl had ridden his bike the half mile to school. It is a straight shot and I could always watch Carl to make sure he made it to the school parking lot, until he had to turn. Wait. All I could do was wait. JoEllen and Brad were napping and I periodically checked on them and returned to the corner. It was SO quiet. The birds were not even singing. I heard some "pops," like gunshots heard from the firing range in the summer, and immediately following, the sounds of noisy children. It was a good sound to me, yet I didn't know what it held.

A short time later, Mont brought Carl home in Joanna Petersen's car. He was as black as the ace of spades! All you could see were the whites of his eyes. Carl was so unrecognizable, wrapped in a blanket, that Mont had passed several times before John Toomer stopped him. Our son was fortunate. Under all that soot his burns were not extensive. But because of his seizure disorder and extreme smoke inhalation in addition to the burns, he spent a short time in the hospital.

Carl remembers the taped square, Mrs. Young in flames and reading Mr. Young's notes. It was an awful scene and he has had a hard time understanding why someone wanted to kill with a bomb. Even today he is very wary of the room in CES and when he is upset, he will ask why I hated him so much that I sent him to school. We have to remind him that he is alive because of a miracle. Also, that there are consequences for our actions and the Youngs made bad choices resulting in a very high price.

It was a blessing to live in a small community where people look out for each other and to go to a hospital where you knew the staff personally. Fear was alleviated because you were with friends and family. The love of God was everywhere. Going back to the school a couple days later and time have brought healing. For some it has taken years. In a way the intrusion of the outside world was not good. Most have been kind in their help but others have continued to concentrate on the negative aspects for personal gain. I recognize people have had questions and were fascinated by the bombing but I wanted to be left alone and I wanted to shelter my family. Left as a community, we pulled together and relied on each other for answers and closure.

Looking back, Cokeville's children and families are stronger because of this experience. There were so many preparatory things like; fire drills out of one room, ceiling tiles which absorbed most of the shock, the open windows, emergency personnel in the area and caring citizens that day which enabled our Heavenly Father to perform a miracle. There will always be memories too numerous to count and little reminders.

As for the dream, DeMont did spend time looking for our son, Carl, as the Cokeville Elementary School billowed smoke. A month or so later, he realized that the dreams had stopped. Every day I am grateful for the knowledge that my Heavenly Father heard the prayers of children and their parents.

A miracle occurred in Cokeville that day when the birds were so quiet and we gratefully heard the children's voices. There are still days which are challenging, one being when they put the big propane tank in at the school. I saw it as a potential explosion. The unlocked doors at the south end and Carl's occasional comments and fear for his siblings as they have gone to school continue to remind me that each of us needs to feel secure and that self worth is very fragile. Life is not always easy but God has a plan and we are instruments in His hands. In faith we have to go on.

Claudia Hartley
Parent of Four Student Survivors
(Typed Submission)

How does one describe a nightmare turned miracle?

It was a Friday. The house was clean and organized so I was working on Ron's mother's life history. A telephone ring disturbed my concentration so I reluctantly answered it. "Claudia, this is LaJean. Have you been listening to the radio? There's a bomb at the elementary. Some guy's holding the school hostage." Disbelief and dismay took my breath. "I'm going down there," I said.

I called the sheriff's office. Jerrie, the dispatcher, sounded agitated and I could hear a lot of radio traffic in the background. I asked, "Is there something going on at Cokeville Elementary?" Jerry answered, "Yes, there is Claudia." "Is it serious?" I asked. "Yes, Claudia. It is. I can't talk now."

I felt like someone had hit me in the chest with a fist of fear. I had to go down there. After hanging up, I realized that I was babysitting James Dayton, age one, and Leslie Morfeld, age two. I also had my little Sabrina. There was no way I could expose them to danger. I was so agitated that I picked something up and put it down in the same place repeatedly. It seemed to take hours to get the kids ready and in the car. I drove them to LaJean's and asked her to keep them. How thankful I was that she was willing. This once, when Sabrina cried I just told her she had to stay and I left.

I remembered Ron's two-way police radio in his car and went home to take it with me. It would provide information on what was happening. Ron was in Utah. He and Rob Erickson had gone to Price to talk with his brother, Jim, about a business deal. He was due home that day. I decided to call Jim so he could tell Ron to rush home but there was no answer. I next called his brother, Larry. His wife, Karol, answered and said she hadn't heard from Ron at all. I told her about the situation and she asked how she could help. I just said, "Please send Ron home!"

I next reluctantly called Ron's parents. I didn't want to lay this on them before I had to but I'm glad I did now because in a short while it was on the national news. I wouldn't have wanted them to hear it that way and not be able to get in touch with me. Dad said he would check the last place he knew Ron was going. Later, I found out that they also called the highway patrol to look for him.

How I yearned for Ron to drive into town! As I drove into town I felt like screaming. *Four children! That's half of my family! Why don't we have a SWAT team? Please Lord, save my children!*

The thought came to me that I could go into town behaving like a crazy woman and be shoved away or I could keep my senses and try to help, thus also being able to be close enough to the action to know what was happening. Not knowing would be far worse than having all the terrible details.

I saw Doris Moore and stopped to ask her what was going on. She told me that a man and a woman were holding the third grade hostage. I may never forgive myself for thinking, *at least it's only one of my children.* It was as though somehow I could survive the loss of one child but certainly not four of them.

Ron's radio was full of talk of fire trucks, ambulances and SWAT teams. It confirmed my fears that this was more than a nightmare. The investigator, Earl Carroll, was at the city hall. He said some crazy man and a woman had the whole elementary school as hostages in the third grade room. My chest tightened at the realization that Nathan, 6, Jason, 7, Cindy, 9; and Brenda, 11, were at the mercy of those people. What were they feeling? Were they afraid? Were they being hurt?

"Please Lord, help my children!"

The town was very quiet. People were standing on the streets talking. They looked very concerned but I saw no crying. It was as though there were heavy weights laying on all of our hearts.

I had learned from Ron's training and by watching the news that this could go on for days. I also knew that we could not pay them a ransom. If we did pay them and they were successful in our school there would be crazies all over the world doing this to other children. As much as I loved my children, I could not condone this action. I have learned since that many people were offering money, land, ranches and homes to pay the ransom. They were willing to give everything for our children.

My greatest fear was that the hostage-takers would take our children one by one and shoot them to prove they were serious. All of these thoughts rushed through my mind. The brain must have a safety valve because when I felt like falling apart those terrible thoughts left me and I just concentrated on the tasks at hand.

The city hall was a maze of people. I was glad that my status as Ron's wife allowed me to go straight through to the sheriff without being told to wait outside. The sheriff, Deb Wolfley, gave me a hug and asked how many I had in there and when Ron was going to be home. Earl asked me questions about the layout of the school. At first, I gave him the wrong information but later corrected it. I then ran errands for them for about an hour. Earl then asked me to find him some cassette tapes. I couldn't buy any so I returned home to pick some up. I knew I was probably in for a long day so I changed my blouse and refreshed my makeup.

When I returned, I asked Earl and Deb if they'd like me to find Bernie Petersen for them. I had just learned that the woman in the school was her mother. Earl didn't seem to think it was important but I pressed it. She was a link to getting those kids out and we needed all the breaks we could get. He finally said, "I guess it couldn't hurt." I don't think he felt the anguish I could see on the sheriff's and deputy's faces. I hope I'm wrong but it seemed to be very exciting to him.

I couldn't get a phone line out. I knew Bernie wasn't home because I noticed her car was gone when I came down. I drove past her mother-in-law's home and all around town looking for her to no avail.

I stopped at the Lazy T and used their phone to call her husband Brent's workplace. Maybe he would know where she was. After three calls to locate him someone told me that he had the next two days off.

Two days! They could be on a trip!

I returned to the city hall to tell Deb. He seemed frustrated by it.

I asked Kathy, the county disaster coordinator, to please put me to work so I didn't go insane. She was so concerned about me but I felt very much in control and wanted to help.

She asked me to please go downstairs and comfort people. The ladies downstairs were very calm but Jeff Petersen, Bernie's brother-in-law, was almost hysterical. He was trying to find Brent and Bernie for us. I have since learned that most of the teenagers were very upset and scared. They had gathered together in a prayer circle to pray for their little brothers and sisters. Jeff was trying to call his father so I went to see what was happening. I noticed that it was very quiet so I looked and saw that everyone was gone but a crying teenage boy being comforted by an older woman.

"What has happened?" I asked.

"The bomb went off!" she said.

"Oh, no!" I cried.

The worst possible thing had happened. Four little faces popped into my mind at that moment. Were my sweet little Cindy, Jason, Brenda and Nathan dead? Were they terribly hurt? I was visualizing little bodies strung out across the schoolyard. Again the safety valve turned and I pushed the terror from my head. All these thoughts flashed in an instant as I was running up the stairs before the boy finished his words.

Kathy met me at the top. She told me to wait and she'd get her coat and told me to get mine. I didn't want my coat, I wanted my babies!

I started running and she caught up. I saw two Cornia children, Wade and Allyson, alive and well, coming down the street. Some of them must be all right! Maybe my children were all right!

I saw Sherrie Cornia and told her I had seen two of her children. She knew they were OK and said she had seen Jason.

I rejoiced and mentally counted, *that's one.*

There was a crowd of people across the main street from the school road. As I came closer I saw Jason. He was a filthy, black figure whose big, scared eyes looked out from a pale face. I rushed to him grabbed his face and said, "I love you. I'm so glad you're all right." Before I could finish asking him if he'd seen the others, Brenda ran to me. *That was two.* She was crying and very frightened. I told her I loved her and asked about Cindy and Nathan.

I think she took me to them. Numbers three and four were lying on the grass crying.

"Oh, thank you, Lord!"

Nathan had a blistered burn across his back where his shirt and pants met. Brenda had a silver dollar shaped burn on her back in about the same place. Cindy was black from smoke and very frightened but OK.

I couldn't believe it. These kids had just come out of a classroom in which a bomb went off and all they had were small burns. I looked around and there were kids all over crying. Many had burns but they seemed minor. Later these burns got much worse but at the time they really didn't seem bad. These were not the terrible injuries I'd thought of when I heard the news. We put cold water on the burns mainly by soaking gauze and spreading it over the burned area. I learned that a few children were badly burnt and in an ambulance on their way to the Montpelier hospital. Everyone was talking about Mr. Miller, the band teacher, being shot. They said he was very "bad off." We were afraid he'd die.

Nathan and Cindy were very upset so I tried to comfort them. We kept them lying on the grass to avoid shock. Jamie Buckley had a badly burnt arm and was hysterical. I was trying to hold all three at once. Jamie's father soon came and took her.

I asked Brenda to stay with Nathan and Cindy while I checked on others. Clark Bedell was very scared so I asked Jason to stay with him. Some women were standing there crying so I told them to grab a child whose mother wasn't there and hug him or her. Our babies were so frightened. The teachers and everyone were desperately trying to account for all the children. It was wonderful when someone would ask, "Have you seen Jenny or Billy or Greg?" and the answer was always affirmative. I only had to answer, "No," once to Austin Henderson's mother but later I learned that he had run all the way to his father's store.

I clasped every little face that I saw between my two hands and said, "I'm so glad you're all right!" We all did the same. One child later exclaimed that he didn't know so many people loved him. I was so thankful my children were safe but I can truthfully say that every child there was like my own. I loved them dearly.

Dana Thornock asked me if she could take my children to her home to wait until I was through helping the others. I gratefully answered, "Yes," but I kept Cindy and Nathan lying on the grass because they seemed too close to going into shock. They were both frightened but I think Nathan was more frightened of having cold water put onto his back than anything else.

I guess some of the children went to Russ Thornock's house and some to the corner where I was. Many more had run out of the school and all the way home. It was terrible for those poor teachers. I could hear the cries of, "Sixth grade, gather here!" "First grade, meet by the tree!" "Has anyone seen Jimmy?" One teacher was frantic. "I can't find my kids. Where are all my kids?" Soon we learned that the room had been cleared and no one was in it so we didn't have to account for children anymore.

The rest of the evening was spent in hospitals having the burns and lungs checked followed by a long bus ride home. The hospital we went to was in Kemmerer which was forty-five miles away. It was 9:00 p.m. when we pulled back into town. I saw my sister-in-law, Sandy Baker, out my window. She had driven sixty miles because she couldn't get through on the phone. She told me that Ron was there and wanted me to come to him as soon as we got back. I piled the kids in the car and drove to where he was. He picked me clear up off the ground and hugged me with big tears running down his face. "Are they all right?" "Are you all right?"

All I could say was, "They're alive! They're alive!" I remembered when I found all the children right after the bomb had gone off. I smiled through tears and exclaimed over and over again, "They're alive!"

Ron then picked up each of his children and cried with them. I had been through a hard experience but Ron must have experienced what hell is during the time he waited for us. The next hours and days were very busy with many calls and visits from concerned relatives and friends. How grateful I was to have Ron's parents and my mom and sister come. I guess they were like Ron. We could tell them the kids were all right but they had to see those little souls for themselves to know for sure.

I felt totally numb for the first three days. I really couldn't even cry for a long time. Then, as Ron learned more of just what these people had planned, it dawned upon me just how much the Lord loved us. He literally had performed a miracle. All of us in Cokeville went through our daily tasks whispering, "Thank You, Lord. Thank You. How can we ever repay You for this blessing?"

I've found that I cry very easily now. I cried when John Miller came to school and took off his shirt to show the children the small scab where the bullet had entered. That bullet had passed under the skin and right over his spine lodging under his shoulder blade. A different angle and he would be paralyzed now.

I cried when I saw the beautiful Cory girls with terrible burns on their pretty faces. I cried again when I saw them the next week and could barely tell they'd been burned. I cried when the nurses asked, "Why aren't these burns hurting these children more?" The children seemed to feel very little pain from them. I cried when we had a testimony meeting and my friend told of her daughter having a great feeling of peace just before the bomb went off. I wept as a young mother thanked me because my Brenda had played with her daughter so she wouldn't be afraid while being held hostage in the school.

The miracles were so many. Just two weeks before the bombing, the school had fire drills in which they made the kids crawl out on their knees. When the bomb went off, the kids crawled out. There was very little smoke inhalation. One boy felt his shirt on fire so he dropped and rolled to put it out. He was eight years old. How did he remember to do that?

A few parents have told of their children having had nightmares about bombs since the Christmas before. They were afraid the Russians would bomb us because they kept having these dreams. One mother asked her daughter if she was afraid and she said, "No, I'm finally rid of that terrible fear of bombs I've had for so long."

One little girl had absolutely refused to go to school that morning. Her mother demanded, cajoled, and pleaded but to no avail. That child would not go to school that day.

My good friend, Pat Bennion, was substituting for third grade (Cindy's class) that day and she and her mother-in-law stayed until last in that smoke-filled, fiery-hot room because, as Pat said, "I couldn't leave knowing there were children still in there." Her mother-in-law, Verlene Bennion, searched the floor before leaving and found a little crumpled body that was probably Tina Morfeld.

These ladies helped my children out of that room. I shall never be able to thank them enough for what they did.

Little Tina almost died in the University Burn Center. How we all prayed for her. She came home and was sent to school for a few days. Someday I know her little face will be normal and pretty again because you see I not only believe in miracles, I *know* they exist because I have seen one. I have seen how the miracle goes on and on. I have heard self-proclaimed atheists say, "Someone must have a had hand in this. This was not just luck." I have felt the love and the spirit of the Lord in our town and not only with Mormons.

Someday, I want to forget the horror of these past few weeks, but I never want to forget that, for some reason, the Lord decided to save the children of Cokeville, Wyoming. I never want to forget that they must be very special spirits and that I have a great responsibility to the Lord to teach them correct principles. I never want to say, "Yes, weren't we lucky."

The days following were passed in an out-of-this-world stupor. We could not believe this had happened to our little town. My children seemed to be doing well. Their grandparents had come and given them much love and comfort at a time when my husband, who is an investigator for the sheriff's department and I could only just try to function and comprehend what might have happened.

As time passed, I began to notice that the children were suffering trauma from their experience. Jason became argumentative and would strike out, hurting his brother and sisters for no reason. Brenda was having nightmares but they seemed to be few and far between. Cynthia talked and talked and talked. This was great because when we all told our story so many times we became bored with it and pushed it from our minds.

We began to be very concerned about our six year old Nathan though. I had taken all the kids to the library, which is a real treat for them. Nathan wouldn't get out of the car no matter how much I coaxed. I had to go to the store and he wouldn't even come with me. When I came out, he was hiding between the seats. He said that he had seen some strangers and didn't want them to pull him out of the car.

He began to run fevers of 103/104 degrees. He had gotten a third degree burn across his back but it was healing well so it couldn't be blamed for the fevers.

I took him to Dr. Wolff in Montpelier. He prescribed antibiotics and dressing for the burn. Still, the fevers didn't go away. I took him again and more antibiotics were given. They didn't help. Nathan was beginning to look like a sad little old man. He said he was having bad dreams at night and when he'd wake up they were still there.

He said, "Mom, all I can see is the bomb. It won't go away." The sparkle was gone from his usually snappy brown eyes. I knew then what hopelessness looked like.

When Doug Ford, a psychologist, called I made an appointment for Nathan. During his session Doug discovered that Nathan had tripped over a "man" who wouldn't wake up no matter how much he told him to get out. That "man" would have had to have been Doris Young, who had been badly burned before being shot by her husband. I don't know if that was what was making him so unhappy but after that session Nathan did well for a week or so. We spent much of that time in Utah visiting relatives. He did best when not at home.

However, when we returned home, so did his fevers. Again we went to Dr. Ford. Nathan spent a long time talking with him and then I was called in. Dr. Ford began by asking me if I knew what angels looked like. I answered in the negative and he asked, "Would you like me to describe them to you?"

"Sure," I said.

Then he told me that Nathan said he had seen angels. He said that Nathan's great-great-great grandmother had told him the bomb was going to go off and he'd better get out. Dr. Ford said that, as a Mormon, he'd like to believe Nathan had seen angels but, as a psychologist he had to believe it was made up.

Afterward, on the way home, I asked Nathan if he had seen an angel. He said, "Yes," and that it was his great-great-grandmother. I named his Grandma Baker? Grandma Hartley?

"No. Neither of them."

"Was it Grandma Meister."

"Yeah. It was Grandma Meister."

Grandma Meister is living in a resthome in Pinedale, Wyoming. I thought then that he must have dreamed it up.

At home, I told Ron what Nathan had said and he became very angry with the psychologist for "filling his head with that stuff." He asked Nathan what had happened and this is the story he told:

"Just before the bomb went off, angels came down through the ceiling. There were about ten of them holding hands, protecting the children. (Note: Later he said that there were many angels, one for everybody in the room.)

"One was very close to me and she was my great-great grandma. She told me the bomb was going to go off and David and Doris would have to die because what they were doing was bad. She told me to sneak very quietly toward the window. All the angels told us to run to the window again and again but before I recognized what they were telling me, the bomb went off.

"When it went off, the angels went up through the ceiling and then came down again. My grandmother touched me where I got burnt. The angels looked nice and smiled. They made me feel good. Some of them were big and some were little. They had gray hair. They looked like light bulbs." (Note: Nathan said later that when he was going for the window in all the black smoke, he looked back and saw the angels still in the room. He also said the angels had rags on their feet. At first, he insisted that they had wings but later said, "Angels don't have wings or rings around their heads.)

When Ron and I had heard his story we wanted to believe it but things like this happened to other people, not us. Besides, how could it have been Grandma Meister if she wasn't even dead?

Ron asked me to get a picture of Grandma Meister so we could settle the matter. I could only think of one picture we had of her so I got our Book of Remembrance out. In it, we had a snapshot of Ron's grandma and my grandma sitting together in our wedding reception line.

I pointed to the picture and said, "Nathan, do you know either one of these people?"

He pointed to the picture of Ron's Grandma Elliott and said, "Yeah, that's my angel!"

The world stopped and it seemed as though even my breathing stilled. I looked at Ron and read emotions of awe and shock on his face.

Grandma Flossie Elliott had died three years before. Nathan had seen her only once before in his life. We have a picture of him seated on her lap in the midst of his sisters and brother. He was one year old at the time.

We knew then that he really had seen angels. Though everyone in town had felt sure that it was a miracle that the hostages lives were spared, we now knew just how that miracle had been accomplished.

For some reason, I felt no surge of joy. I felt instead a heavy weight of responsibility. Why did Nathan see them? Why was he saved from serious harm and not the others who were sitting next to the line as he was? How could I ever be worthy of such a gift? What if after having been given the opportunity to raise my children, I failed and they turned away from God? Do I tell? Is this too sacred to reveal?

Well, as time passed we did tell. And with the telling it became easier and easier. I do now feel a great responsibility to tell the world that we are not alone. God lives and cares and will protect us. And He had angels to help Him do it!

Nathan has forgotten many of the details now. Every once in a while he'll mention the angels and he always insists he really did see them but the details are getting fuzzy.

I believe he saw them. It all fits in. His burn is two inches below his pant line. He would have been crouching down, ready to crawl toward the window when the bomb went off shooting those flames toward his little body.

Some children and adults say they felt the most calm just before the bomb went off. Of course, they did. That was when the angels came down. They also said David Young became very nervous and perspired a lot before the bomb went off. I believe that when the hosts of heaven entered the hosts of hell had to leave and David Young was left alone to carry out his evil plan.

I wish I could draw. I have a wonderful picture that comes to my mind every once in a while. If it could be drawn it would teach marvelous things and give the gift of hope to the world.

It would be a pencil sketch. It's of an elementary school

classroom, but the only way to know this are the bookshelves under two tall narrow windows. At the bottom of these windows are two foot by one foot smaller windows that a ten year old child is pulling open. He is opening the window because it's congested in the room.

The room is crammed with 154 people. By far most of them are children but there are adults there too. The adults are good, kind people who are holding children in their arms and on their laps. Some of the children are crying and all the adults are looking concerned if not frightened. There is also a man and a woman with a bomb, sitting in a taped off square in the center of the room.

Above all this, there are figures suspended in the air. They are dressed in white and their personages radiate love and warmth. Some are old and some are young. They are whispering to the people below them. They are guiding and warning them. Some of the children are looking toward them. Some see them—most do not.

In the center of the room, very close to the taped-off square, a six year old boy is on his knees. He is looking into the face of one of the angels. She is old with white hair and has a kind loving face. She is touching the dark haired lad upon the shoulder.

The horror of the day will always be with me. But I would like to hang a picture of the miracle in a quiet place. It would be a place where I could go when the horrors of life overwhelm me. I could look at the sweet face of my son looking into the loving eyes of his grandmother and remember how close heaven is.

A shaded outline would surround the picture. It would be a silhouette of a man. No, much more than a man. It would be Christ, our Lord, and He would look as He does in the picture on our Relief Society Manual. The personification of love.

Yes, I wish I could draw.

Marlene Hess
Mother of One Student Survivor
(Oral History—Telephone)

I knew there was something going on, because of all the cops. I do remember David Young was a cop because he came to my house. He lived in Rocky Moore's house. We were just out visiting once. All the kids called him Wyatt Earp, because he had that big long gun. Just like Wyatt. I can remember that plain as day.

It was one of those days, you know, you have a thousand things to do and you can't do any of them—riding up and down the street trying to find out what was going on.

When they all came out of there, you couldn't tell whose kids they were. All you could see were the whites of their eyes and their teeth. They were so covered with smoke. Their faces were black. We didn't recognize them.

BranDee was on the lawn with some of them. I know she lost one of her new tennis shoes in there. I was going to keep it, cement it and make a planter of it. She said, nope, she didn't want it. I kept it a long time and then I got rid of it. I told her that she needs to get the scrapbook out and show her kids. She says she will, someday.

It was miracle. God was with us. Each and every one of us. That's the only reason we survived.

Don Himmerich
Father of Four Student Survivors
(Typed Submission)

I would like to express my feelings and a few thoughts about the very stressful and scary day at Cokeville Elementary School on May 16, 1986. I am so grateful for the blessing the Lord handed out that day. Having all those children come out of the doomed situation was truly a miracle. I know the Lord had a hand in this miracle and for this I am truly grateful.

Four of my children were in school that day: Brandi, Rick, Jamie, and Trini. Micah was only four at the time. I was working on a powerline project in Wyoming from Alcova to Thermopolis. We had a field office in Powder River, Wyoming. At about 3:30 p.m. that day one of our employees came into the office and said he had heard on the radio that the school in Cokeville had a bomb threat and all the children were being held as hostages until the bomber's demands were met.

I immediately tried to call home but all the circuits were busy. I tried several times to call other people including the Perkin's service station but the circuits were always busy. I also tried to charter a flight out of Casper but they had all been taken by the news media. When I found out that the media were the main reason the circuits were busy and the charter flights were not available I was frustrated.

After not getting a flight or making phone contacts I started driving home. I was hoping a cop would stop me so I could possibly find out some more information, but I had no such luck. I was able to listen to the radio and get pieces of information. I was surprised that later on all the radio stations were carrying the story and I was finally able to hear that the bomb had gone off and that all the children and faculty got out without any loss of life. I made it home faster than usual and I was surprised that my big red Ford had that kind of get up and go in it.

All my children got out without any injuries, although some had stressful times later. Ricky was one of the first out of the school after the bomb went off. Judy said he ran so fast she could not stop him or catch him. He jumped over the fence south of the school about four feet high without touching it. When Judy found him, he was home hiding. Brandi was one of the last ones out because she was helping other children out through the window.

I got home at about 10:00 p.m. to see a lot of media vans and helicopters in town. I was happy to see my kids and to share some of the experience with them. How grateful I was to have them still with us after hearing the entire story and how it unfolded.

I am so grateful that I have all my children in my life, and now my grandchildren. They are my life. I have been truly blessed. I love them with all my heart. They are all married now and have families of their own.

Brandi and Ken Bill live in Colorado Springs and have a daughter named Savannah. Rick and Kristi Himmerich live in Pocatello and have a daughter named Morgan. Jamie and Ryan Teichert live in Cokeville and have a son named Lochlyn and two daughters named Rylee and Reagan. Trini and Camren Bowen live in Pocatello and have two sons named Hunter and Camden. Micah and Camille Himmerich live in Logan and have a daughter named Gracie.

Colleen King
Mother of Two Student Survivors
(Fax Submission)

My story starts in Montpelier at the hospital. I had taken my son Christopher King out of school about forty-five minutes before they took the school hostage. He had to go get stitches out and I also had to pick up my dad from the hospital. None of my other boys knew that I had taken Chris.

We were wheeling my dad out the door of the hospital and saw Dr. Wolff and a lot of activity going on. I said to Dr. Wolff that they must have a big one coming in and he said that they did. He didn't tell me anything about it.

We stopped at the Maverick and I asked the clerk what was happening. She said that a bomb had gone off at the Cokeville elementary. I freaked. I went to the truck and Larry and I went back to the hospital to wait for our kids. We saw lots of Cokeville kids, but not ours. That is a most terrifying thing to not know where and how your kids are. Sometime later my mother got through to us, (The phone lines were very tied up and she said our kids went to Kemmerer and Judy was with them.)

We had a trailer full of wood and we just dropped it in some farmer's yard and took off. About six miles out of Cokeville, we were stopped by a highway patrolman. Larry jumped out and told him if he wanted to give us a ticket he could mail it because we were going to Kemmerer to find our boys. He said that nobody was hurt so we didn't need to speed. Anyone who knew Larry can probably understand what he told that idiot.

When we got to Kemmerer it was packed but we found our boys. We were some of the lucky ones because our boys had some flash burns but were OK. Johnny didn't have any shoes, they were lost in the shuffle.

David was in seventh grade and waiting outside the elementary. He caught Johnny and told him to go home fast. Bona Taylor found him on the road and just picked him up and kept him. David found Billy, but he couldn't find Chris. He was running all around trying to find him. Finally Kim Casper found him and told him we had taken him out of school.

I believe that the reason the kids that weren't in school that day, that they were absent or gone, was because they were the ones who might not have been able to handle it. They weren't supposed to be there. There is a reason for everything and that day was one of those reasons. There was no reason that those other bombs didn't go off. There are many children that were burned and scarred, those that had nightmares and things to fear, but that day was really one of the most lucky days of our life. We could have ended up with a town with few children. There really is a God and we should thank Him every day of our lives. That is the miracle.

Margaret McKinnon
Mother of One Student Survivor
(Oral History—Telephone)

Travis was in 1st grade and Julie was in kindergarten. Monte and I had to go to Kemmerer to the bank. We took Julie with us, we didn't have anyone to pick her up after kindergarten. We had gone and done our business and just out of Kemmerer, here came all these cop cars. We knew something had happened somewhere, but we didn't know where it was.

We had just come home and changed our clothes and here comes Justin, Georgeanna, and Lisa off the bus. I asked them what they were doing home. They said, "Mom, they've taken the school hostage." I said, "You guys are funny" They said, "Mom it's real."

I grabbed my clothes. Got dressed on the way. Monte and I drove in with the kids.

Several children had been playing cowboys and Indians back in the corner, before the bomb went off. When it did, it was totally black in there. Mr. Moore went over to the window, he was going out, and he got his belt buckle stuck on the window. Those kids had to wait for him to get unstuck.

Travis didn't want to go to school that day and I told him no, you need to go to school and learn.

He was under that big pine tree by Steve and Jane Taylor's. He was so black I couldn't tell it was him. They had laid him under that tree. He wasn't doing too good. He was in shock. I started cleaning him up. He said, "Mom, if you had just let me stay home today like I wanted to, and if I had gone with you, I wouldn't have been in there."

They took him over to Montpelier. It was a chaotic mess. I wasn't sure where he had gone when they took him. I guessed Montpelier. We spent the night there. There were two kids to a bed in some places. Travis had that smoke in his lungs, he kept coughing up this black stuff. They said the smoke that went in his lungs, just like he'd smoked for twenty years. I consoled a whole bunch of kids. Ryan Taylor was in his room and some others.

One thing that was amazing to me was when they let us into the school that Sunday was that outline on the wall. It was amazing. It would have knocked your socks off. It was like the outline of Jesus.

One thing that happened at the time, the community really pulled together. They were just kind and sweet. A lot of the nitpicky went away. Stake President Matthews came over, he just felt like he needed to be here. He got up and spoke during the Sacrament Meeting on Sunday.

For a long time after that happened, it took its toll on Travis. I think it took a toll on all of us. I think it was a miracle how all of the bomb didn't go off. I think it was a miracle that more people didn't get shot.

President Herman Teichert said something to the effect that, "The Lord held a court and convicted the guilty and the innocent went free."

The one good thing, the kids didn't have to worry about that guy coming back. They didn't have to worry about a trial. It didn't have to drag on. It was taken care of and over. The Lord took care of it. They just had to heal.

Jack Metcalfe
Parent of Three Student Survivors
(Handwritten Submission)

I had the seniors on their annual trip to the Utah State Prison the day of the bombing. They were returning home that afternoon when we stopped in Evanston, Wyoming, for ice cream. The store attendant asked if we were from Cokeville and I replied, "Yes we are." They then asked what was going on with the hostages. I had everyone immediately reload the bus with no ice cream. I told the bus driver to go as fast as he could home and I would pay the ticket if he got one. I'm the drivers education teacher and I don't advocate speeding!

Everyone on the bus had someone in the school, so there was a great deal of prayer going on in the bus. Just out of Woodruff, Utah, we heard on the radio that the bomb had gone off and Mr. Miller was shot. Worry was the concern of everyone because the radio announcer had no further information on the people in the school.

When we finally arrived in Cokeville everyone was surprised to see the elementary school in one piece, so we scrambled off the bus to see where our family members were located.

I found my wife Joanne and she told me that Joanna, Jaime, and Jay were in three different hospitals, but Jay was hurt the worst with burns on his face, back and arms.

Some years later I realized how fortunate we were that none of the children were killed in the bombing as I sat in a church sacrament meeting. At the time, the teenagers were attending a youth conference. It came to me that those absent young people were the same group that had been saved in the bombing and the half empty chapel where I sat was the way it would have been had they not survived. Our community would not have survived had Providence not showed its merciful hand and allowed all those children, teachers and townsfolk to be with us.

Joanne Metcalfe
Mother of Three Student Survivors
(Typed Submission)

One of the worst things a person can say when you answer the phone is, "Just try not to get upset, but something has happened at the school." Now completely "upset" and with rising apprehension, I was told that the elementary school had been taken hostage by a gunman, words too improbable to be believed! My kindergarten child, Sandra, just off the bus from her morning class, was beside me, but my other six were in school, and three of them at the elementary. I stood there trying to absorb this incredible news, but could not make sense of it at all. This kind of thing couldn't happen in a quiet, little, off the beaten path town like Cokeville, Wyoming. I thought, *this is nuts, it can't be right! What should I do?*

I decided to call the school and find out at the source. Surprisingly, my call was picked up immediately, "Mmm...Max?" I stammered, hoping it was him.

The principal, Max Excell, was incredulous as he recognized my voice, and he said, "How did you get through? I've got calls out all over the state: the police, the Governor, everybody I can think of. I've barely been off the phone!"

I replied, "IT IS true then. Is there anything I should do?"

"Don't come into town...people are already starting to gather; it'll be best for you to stay out there." "All right," I said. "Things will be fine; we'll keep the kids safe. I've got to go now," he said kindly and hung up.

Slightly dazed, I wandered outside and found my neighbor, Judene, standing on the driveway talking to Cindy, a friend from town. They had heard the news and were not quite sure what to do next, but were hoping their husbands would show up soon. I knew that my husband would not be home quickly because he, a teacher, was on a school field trip to Salt Lake City. We seemed to talk in circles for awhile because we really didn't know much, not even that a reporter from Kemmerer was broadcasting the story over the radio at that very moment from the scene in town. Then we were surprised when a school bus brought some of our older children home and let them off at the top of the lane.

Judene invited us into her trailer as she expected her husband to come home any minute, and sure enough he soon came in, grinning hugely and packing an enormous armload of papers and mail. She tried in vain to get his attention to tell him about the crisis at the school, but he was totally preoccupied turning the pages of a magazine trying to find his latest published article. He seemed completely oblivious to the fact that his living room was cluttered with nervous, harried-looking, hand-wringing women. Suddenly the trailer door crashed open, slamming against the wall; we all jumped a foot as papers flew every which way!

"The bomb went off!" was the shout we heard. We all rushed outside and scattered in different directions. The shouter of the horrific news was my seventeen year old son, Aaron.

"Let me drive Mom, you're too upset," he exclaimed.

Actually, I had enough adrenaline pumping to run along beside the car, but I warily agreed and then lived to regret it. Aaron drove those seven miles to town in less than five minutes, and I had my eyes closed most of the way, praying we would make it in one piece.

As we careened around the corner onto Main Street an unbelievable sight greeted us. There was no visible fire coming from the still standing elementary school, but the street was massed with cars, ambulances, fire trucks, and grown-ups trying their best to help. Children were wandering about, running, being carried, being hosed off, lying on lawns or just looking lost.

A child came running toward us with arms outstretched in gladness. She was one of my own, Joanna, a 5th grader who had been in the school. She and her two siblings, Jaime and Jay, had been together when the sudden bomb blast sent her flying through the air and crashing into the wall of the classroom, becoming wedged between two pieces of furniture. As her senses returned, all she could see was dark smoke, but above the noise and confusion came the voice of Mr. Mitchell, "Get down, get out!" he shouted over and over.

Joanna began to crawl, keeping close to the wall until she reached the door, then she got to her feet and ran out of the building. The air was so good to breathe as she ran, but she suddenly pulled up short and turned back toward the building knowing she couldn't leave the others behind.

Jaime, our 4th grader, had been pushed out the small window by Mr. Moore, a teacher. Totally panicked, she ran screaming and crying across the lawn toward her sister, her face blackened with soot from the gasoline explosion. As they stood comforting one another they saw their 1st grader brother, Jay, walking to them, and they rushed forward to hug him. When he cried out in pain at their touch, they realized he had been badly burned and immediately began to look for help. Someone took one look at Jaime's dark face and snatched her from that little group and took her straight to a waiting ambulance. Jay, who didn't look too bad yet, was directed to Emma Lue Birch's house to be evaluated.

Inside that small classroom, Jay had been kneeling on the floor with his back to the taped "magic square" where the man had placed himself with his bomb. Jay was just beginning to color a picture when the woman accomplice, who had been left in charge, turned to answer a question and accidentally detonated the bomb. The enormous blast sent burning gasoline onto the woman and flaming fireballs streaking out randomly through the room. A brother standing right next to his sister could be hit with fire and she could be totally spared. Jay was hit square on his back, and also the whole right side of his face and arm was hit by the fire spewing from the blast.

Standing nearby, Kliss Sparks saw that Jay's hair was smoldering, so she placed her hands on his head and smothered the smoke. He then followed the voices and made his way outside.

Parents were searching and calling for their children. Mr. Miller had collapsed to the ground and was being treated, having been shot in the back by the bomber when his plans went awry. Joanna grabbed onto my hand to take me to Jay.

The inside of Emma Lue's house seemed dimly lit and filled to bursting with people, and children were sitting in every corner. We found Jay perched on a tall stool in front of the kitchen sink. Volunteers were wetting down and wringing out large white towels to place on his back where the skin was already beginning to slough off in big sheets. He sat shivering and mute as I took over the task, the pain evident on his tear stained face. The blue polyester pullover shirt he'd been wearing lay in a heap on the floor. It still looked to be in good shape, except for the cut straight up the back they had made to get it off of him. I was so very thankful when only a short time later he was in an ambulance on his way to Bear Lake Hospital in Montpelier.

I knew that Joanna was fine, and that Jay was in good hands on his way to be treated, but where was Jaime and how badly was she hurt? After being told she'd been sent to Star Valley Hospital, I hopped in the car and drove the fifty miles to Afton to see her for myself. Could she have been terribly burned underneath all that soot? What would they find when they cleaned her face?

That hospital didn't get many of the bombing victims, so they knew exactly who I wanted and pointed me straight to her room. There she was in clean bedclothes, sitting up in bed, being attended to by nurses. Her face was glowing, hair washed and shining, and she was eating a big plate full of fried chicken and mashed potatoes with gravy.

"Hi Mom!" she said with a happy grin.

The doctors had found two tiny burns on her face, one on the side of each nostril. I kissed her quick, and said we'd be back soon to spring her from the hospital and then dashed back down the mountain to go to Jay.

The hospital in Montpelier was like a madhouse; parents and

relatives crowded the halls as doctors struggled to be heard over the din of voices. The children were being sorted by the severity of their burns, some being treated and released, and others being sent to rooms for overnight stays.

A doctor told me that Jay had been burned over seventeen percent of his body. Jay was almost unrecognizable when I found him because the right side of his face had ballooned to three times its normal size. Thick, white, creamy medicine was being smeared gently onto the affected areas and then covered loosely with yards of gauze. He was assigned a room down the hall and around a corner, nicely out of the way of the reporters who were beginning to prowl around for their stories. The first good smile we got out of Jay was when he found out that his older brother Aaron, the speed demon high school junior, would stay with him in his room, even if he had to sleep on the floor.

Two days later, a Sunday, he was released because we were told nothing more could be done for him there, so we brought him home.

The interior of our turn of the century old farmhouse seemed too dark and unhealthy for a burned boy swathed in bandages. He sat himself carefully on the very edge of the couch so that nothing would touch his body. In silence we all stood there, helplessly eyeing this poor, miserable little guy and wondering where to begin to relieve his pain.

Then his dad remembered hearing that a team of burn specialists from Logan Regional Hospital was coming to the school to evaluate victims that very afternoon, so we quickly took Jay into town.

There were quite a few children at the school with deep red colored splash burns on their arms and faces. The doctors turned their attention to Jay when we entered, and zeroed in on the ugly wound on the backside of his arm. After examining it closely, they said it was a third degree burn that would not heal by itself, and we should take him at once to the burn unit in Logan.

It wasn't a tough decision to take him there because we knew he needed special help. But, I still wince at the memory of what burn victims must endure on their road to recovery. Not many adults could take what those eight or nine hospitalized youngsters did without crying buckets of tears. The treatment was the debriding pool, where after soaking Jay's skin, a nurse then had to scrape off the scabs that had formed in order for correct healing to take place. It was almost unbearable to watch, much less be the person doing the scraping, but excruciatingly painful for the one enduring it all.

We now also discovered other wounds that had gone undetected. There were splash burns on the back of his lower leg where the pants had ridden up, exposing flesh while he knelt on the floor. The doctors came to us and said that Jay would need a skin graft on his arm and surgery was set for the next day. A large square of skin was removed from the front of his right thigh and grafted onto his right arm. The thinking seemed to be that because he was a boy, it didn't matter how it looked later. The graft was successful, but Jay was overly conscious for years of its mean, puckered appearance.

There are outward scars and there are inward scars that we deal with on life's journey. Our three children never seemed to think of themselves as victims, but they learned that day that their world was not as safe a place as they had once thought it to be. They learned that a smiling face can hide deceit and that people can be deranged, sick or just plain evil; a sad, difficult lesson to have to learn at so young an age.

On the other hand, they also found great joy from the gift of life that God had given them and the other innocent participants of that potentially deadly incident that day. Each one of our children had seen true caring and love from family, friends, townspeople, and even from complete strangers; a fact that we all marked well in our minds. The whole experience became a part of us, mostly for our good, and cemented our feelings of love for one another as a family in the years that have passed.

Larry and Cathy Miller
Parents of Two Student Survivors
(Oral History—Telephone with Cathy)

Well that morning I probably shouldn't have put my kids in school. My kids, at different times, came to me and told me they had stomachaches and didn't want to go to school. I gave them pepto bismol and sent them anyway. I never sent them again with stomachaches.

We were moving that day. Didn't have the phones in yet. We were at the Feuz Ranch, moving from the house to a trailer. I didn't know anything was even going on until the school bus came at 2:00 or 2:30 and this foreign exchange student got off. It was a weird time. I went down and talked to the foreign exchange student. He told me that some people had a bomb and was holding the grade school hostage.

So, then I went and got my husband and told him we had to go to town because they were being held hostage at the elementary school. He wanted to get a gun but I told him we had to go. We had to find out what was going on.

Then we went into town and the police wouldn't let us go in. We told them we had kids there, so they let us go in. And I guess the bomb had already gone off by the time we got there. Kids were out and on lawns. We found our kids on a lawn. I don't know whose lawn. It was pretty chaotic. There were people all over the place. There were kids on lawns all over town.

Kellie (2nd grade) she got a few burns and went on a bus to the hospital in Kemmerer. Bobbie (6th grade) got pushed down and walked over the top of when they were all trying to get out of the school. Kellie's burns all went away. The back of her hands had big blisters when we were going over to the hospital. Her hair was burned off to a quarter inch and her nose was burned but she had covered her eyes. You can't even tell it happened now. Kellie healed really pretty quick. I don't even think it scarred.

     I was really thankful that I still had my two girls. It's made me closer to the kids. That's what's important to me, my kids, my grandkids and my family. I love my little kids. I have three children. Jamie had been with us about a month and a half but she went home. Jamie just barely missed it. I have six grandchildren. Bobbie's three are Gavin Lee, Mia Lauryn, and Bree Cathrene. Kellie has little Josh and Jamie has Kaden and Nicholis. We still live in Cokeville.

Jack Morfeld
Father of Two Student Survivors
(Email Submission)

There's a Bomb in the School

I was forty miles east of Cokeville, Wyoming, working in a ditch, doing my job, when I heard the darndest commotion. I looked out over the ditch I was in, and I saw my buddy driving recklessly up the hill in his old Ford pickup, bouncing and fishtailing all over the rough gravel road. As he slid to a stop, throwing gravel and dirt all over me, he shouted, "Get in. There's a bomb in the Cokeville elementary school!" My heart stopped. I had two daughters in that school. The first thing I saw in my mind was the elementary school in Cokeville, Wyoming, lying in a big pile of rubble, little bodies buried under all of it, and screams of terror coming from beneath the rubble.

Suddenly, this tragedy made me realize how important my family was to me.

I jumped out of the ditch and into that Ford pickup, and before I got the door closed we were heading back down that rough gravel road for Cokeville. As we sped down the highway we listened to the radio broadcast, and no one seemed to know anything for sure, except that the bomb had gone off and there were injuries and one teacher had been shot in the arm.

When we drove into Cokeville, the main highway, all roads and side streets leading into or out of town were blocked with Wyoming state patrol, sheriffs, and city police vehicles; there were emergency vehicles with flashing lights and emergency personnel from three states everywhere in this little community of five hundred people. Also, all phone lines had been blocked, so no calls could come in or out of town. Since it was a small community and everyone knew each other, we got right through to the school where the children were. I saw mass confusion; people and children were everywhere with parents trying to find children, children looking for parents, and brothers and sisters involved in the bombing trying to find each other.

Smoke was still rolling out of the school windows, and teachers were trying to get their classes together to make sure all the students had made it out of the school. EMTs were working on children.

Before we had stopped, I was out of that pickup looking for my two daughters and my wife, who was also a volunteer EMT. After about ten minutes that seemed like an hour, I found one of my daughters standing in a yard looking frightened and all alone. When I first saw her, I had to smile to myself because her whole face was covered in black smoke from the bomb, except for those big blue eyes that shone brightly, and I think maybe with a little anger and frustration over what had just happened. I grabbed her and gave her a big hug and asked if she knew where her sister or mother was, and she said no. I finally talked to an EMT who knew my wife, and he thought that she and my other daughter had taken an ambulance to the hospital, but he didn't know which one.

I took Monica, ten years old at the time, to the hospital in Montpelier, Idaho, to get checked out for burns and injuries. The doctor examined her and said her burns were superficial and he didn't think they were serious. He gave us medication for the burns and told me to keep a close watch on her for twenty-four hours. I asked around to see if anyone had seen my wife and daughter. No one had, so I took Monica back to Cokeville to find my other two kids; one was in middle school, and the other one was at the babysitter's house, but my niece had already picked them up. When I found my niece, she said that my wife Donna and my daughter Tina were in an ambulance getting ready to leave for the Montpelier, Idaho, hospital. I left Monica with her sisters and my niece, and headed back to Montpelier.

The hospital was so busy no one could tell me where my wife and daughter were, so I just started walking through the hallways looking in each room as I went past. I walked past one room and looked in; there was someone small lying on the bed with her whole face wrapped in medical bandages. A doctor and nurse were standing over her. I saw my wife sitting in that room so I stepped in and very quietly asked her if that was Tina under all of those bandages. She said, yes, it was the daughter I'd been looking for for the last four hours. When I first realized who was under those bandages, I asked myself how much damage had been done to that pretty little face. I remember seeing those big blue eyes looking out of those bandages, looking at me, and I smiled and asked her if she was getting ready for Halloween.

Donna told me that Tina had found her at the school while she was working on the other children and Donna had put Tina, eight years old at the time, in the ambulance with her and another student to transport to the Montpelier hospital. They were trying to get a tube down Tina's throat, so if her throat closed off she could still get air into her lungs. Tina had been standing next to the bomb when it went off. When she inhaled, it had burned her throat, lungs, and face. They were getting her ready to transport to Logan, Utah, by ambulance because it was a bigger and newer hospital, better set up to care for burn patients.

By the time I went back to Cokeville and told my niece and two daughters (Trist, twelve years old and Leslie, two years old) what was going on and gathered up a suitcase for a stay in the motel, my sister and her husband had arrived. I rode with them to Logan, which was about one hundred thirty miles from Cokeville. By the time we got to Logan Hospital, the doctors there had examined Tina and called the Salt Lake City Burn Center to talk to the head doctor in the burn center. He suggested that they put Tina in a helicopter and airlift her to Salt Lake City Burn Center because of her throat being burned and the extent of the burns on her face. Salt Lake City at that time had one of the three biggest burn centers in the United States.

So after talking to the doctor, Donna, my sister, her husband and I were back in the car headed for Salt Lake, which was another one hundred forty miles from Logan and two hundred sixty miles from Cokeville. It was the beginning of a long day, which wasn't over yet.

After four days in the burn center, Tina was finally taken off the critical list, and we could begin to relax a little. We started hearing parts of the story of who had done the bombing and why from different sources around us. To this day I don't think law enforcement knows exactly what the so called "terrorists" had in mind when they planned this. We found out the only two people involved were an ex-city police officer who had been fired from the Cokeville police department, David Young, and his wife, Doris. People who knew David said he could read an encyclopedia and memorize it. With the information the law enforcement officers were able to gather, they believe David and Doris were going to ask for three hundred fifty million dollars for the hostages. Then they were going to take all the blond-haired blue-eyed, children and blow them up with themselves and the money and go to another world and start a perfect civilization.

I am not a religious man, but on that day I believe the Lord was on our side. If everything had worked according to plan, the bomb should have flattened the whole school and killed everybody in it. The bomb was made of gasoline, gunpowder, and Styrofoam cups. When melted, Styrofoam acts like napalm and burns right through you. The bomb was hooked up to a car battery, with two wires and a clothespin for the triggering device. There was a string hooked up to the clothespin for the Youngs to hold on to. The gas container had a leak in it, the gasoline leaked down on the gunpowder, and wet gunpowder will not explode.

With the smell of gasoline in the small room, the teachers convinced David to let a couple of teachers open the windows to let some of the fumes out of the room because some of the kids were beginning to get sick. David had given Doris the string to hold while he went to the bathroom. When she turned to answer a question—Monica and Tina both said she liked talking with her hands—she accidentally pulled the firing mechanism to the bomb, setting the bomb off. But when the gunpowder did not explode, the gasoline exploded a little bit and the gunpowder turned everything black in the room.

David stepped out of the bathroom, saw what had happened, shot the teacher in the arm, shot his wife in the head, then shot himself in the head. Luckily, the kids and teachers were too busy getting out of the classroom to notice what was going on inside. The teachers were scared to let the students use the main doors because they had been told that all the outside doors had been booby trapped with explosives. Even then, it only took about five minutes to get one hundred fifty students and teachers out through the windows.

Tina spent ten days in the burn center in Salt Lake City. After showing Donna and me how to get the correct water temperature and how to wash her burns gently but firmly to get the dead skin off, we were able to take Tina home. She was doing a real good job of healing up and exercising her muscles so they wouldn't stiffen up. When we got her home, all my girls wanted to go see the classroom where it had all happened. To everyone's surprise, as we walked into the classroom door, we saw on the far side of the room a big spot in the wall that was completely white, while the rest of the room was black from gunpowder smoke. The white wall looked like the outline of an angel standing guard to everyone in that room.

To my knowledge, everyone is doing fine who was involved in the bombing on May 16, 1986. All my girls are doing fine. The thing that amazed me was that when Donna and I talked to them openly about what happened and why, my girls never did seem to be too scared. They would walk into a dark house or go outside at night without fear that something would happen to them. Monica and Tina still carry outside scars from the blast; Tina is now twenty-eight, married, with a family. We all carry scars inside of us from that day: I guess this is to remind us just how lucky we really are.

Dennis Nate
Father of Two Student Survivors
(Oral History—Telephone)

We had been in Salt Lake on a school trip and we stopped on the way back in Evanston. I was the bus driver and I was with Metcalfe's class. We were in a Star Valley bus. We stopped to get something to eat and when we pulled up and got out someone said, "That was a terrible thing that happened to your neighbors in Cokeville." We said, "What happened?" They told us, "Someone just blew the elementary school up." We couldn't get back to town fast enough. We passed the ambulances going to Kemmerer on our way to Cokeville. Of course, by the time we got there all the kids were out. There were cops and news helicopters all over. It was a mess. I had two boys in it. They went to my mother's home. They both ended up being all right. I was concerned because my wife was in Montpelier that day and no one was at our house. The kids all ended up Grandma's.

Lynette Nate
Mother of Three Student Survivors
(Typed Submission)

I felt no premonitions of evil; I had no uneasy feelings; I heard no whisperings of the Spirit as Katie, my five year old, and I kissed each of the four school-age children and told them how much we loved them before they left for school that Friday, May 16, 1986. I didn't, but Lori did.

Keith and I were the parents of five children. Traci, 14, was a student at CJHS; Brian, 12, was a sixth grader at Cokeville Elementary School, along with fifth-grader Lori, 11, and Kevin, 7, a first grader. Katie was five and still my best helper at home, too young for kindergarten that year. Truly, we were in the best years of our lives. Keith and I loved each other and we were exactly where we wanted to be, doing what we wanted to do; raising a family and worshiping our Heavenly Father. Living in Cokeville and being active members of the Church of Jesus Christ of Latter-day Saints were helping us accomplish our dream.

Family prayer and scripture study had gone well, and as the children left the house, I had no inkling that my time for teaching them faith in prayer, our family, the temple, and especially their Heavenly Father, was over. Today was going to be an eternal test day for all of us, and I didn't even realize it. I didn't, but Lori did. Three times that day our Heavenly Father would try to move Lori out of harm's way for her protection and three times Lori would resist the Spirit because of her personal integrity.

Lori and I have always been close, reading-each-other's-minds close, so when the first prompting came after school first began that day, Lori thought something was wrong at home, with me. The feeling told her to go home, but she wasn't sick and couldn't think of an honest reason to leave. So she stayed. Morning recess brought another strong impression to go home and by lunchtime she was literally beginning to feel sick with worry about me, as again she was told, "Go home!" In retrospect, I know Heavenly Father knew Lori's personality, and the potential for psychological injury to her as EVIL was at that very moment preparing to push its way into her young life.

Lori decided to obey the fourth prompting that came after lunch during music when Mr. Miller didn't return to the classroom after leaving to get a video of the previous night's concert. Lori was beginning to tell her classmates that they needed to go outside. She knew they could all get in trouble and this was very unlike Lori. Still, she knew something was very wrong somewhere in her world. Just as she began mentioning it to her friends, a strange woman came in the room, telling them to follow her to an adventure. The dread was so heavy inside Lori that moving was difficult and when she saw the guns lined up across the blackboard in the room she knew it was no ordinary assembly. Lori KNEW immediately that she and all of the children in Cokeville Elementary School were facing death. David and Doris Young's opening statements confirmed it in her mind. She looked at her brothers and thought of her mother, then she began to pray with all her might.

Brian Nate was never afraid of anything! Not any horse or cow or bull or motorcycle, four-wheeler, haying-equipment, or anything else on Nate Ranches. There wasn't another football player, basketball player or wrestler that he had ever competed against that he was afraid of. But, he was afraid now. Brian was scared for Kevin, his little brother, who had never held still a day in his life. He was afraid for the younger children and the special education students who might not understand just how serious David Young was about shooting anyone who tried to leave the classroom that afternoon. He was scared of the string tied on David Young's arm, connected to the shopping cart full of explosives. He couldn't think of anything to do about that, but he could stand by the door and keep the children from absentmindedly wandering out in the hall. Brian could hold and comfort some of the crying smaller children—like Meaghan Thompson, and keep an eye on Lori and Kevin. And he could pray.

Kevin had never seen so many guns in his life. His dad hunted and owned a few guns, and he had heard Grandpa Perkins talk about World War II, but he had never imagined so many guns in one spot, belonging to one person. Kevin's photographic memory began to memorize every detail about the guns. Brian told him to hold still and not cry. So Kevin thought about Ammon in the Book of Mormon, and how much he wanted to be like him. He didn't like David Young and he didn't like his wife either. She talked like a grandma, but Kevin didn't believe her. His grandparents loved him, and would never put him in this kind of danger. He was glad there were police cars outside, and he was glad for the prayers that had been said. That's what Ammon did when he was imprisoned—he prayed, and the whole building fell down, but Ammon was saved.

I don't know what time I found out about our children in the elementary school. I do know it took a short time for it to really sink in. Cokeville didn't have money or oil like some of the communities in Wyoming, so I could not come up with a reason anyone would take our children. Standing outside the perimeter the police had established, it soon became very real. Mingling with the other parents, information was scarce. Stories containing fact and fiction were being shared. I didn't know what to believe, no one did. We just wanted our children to be safe.

Needing to be alone, I took Katie and got in my car. I don't remember her making a peep, whining, or crying. Sitting there, I began to feel the warmth of the Comforter, easing my troubled mind, as I poured out my heart to Heavenly Father, asking for the protection of the teachers and children in that school—and for Traci at the high school from which there had been no information. I loved them so much. As I began to think of each one individually, the spiritual pain was so severe it was almost physical. Then the comforting thoughts began to enter my mind as I realized that I had done everything possible to protect my children. We had read the scriptures and prayed together that morning, and I began to look at the long term—the eternal perspective. Not only had I done every possible thing that morning to insure those children, I had every eternal ordinance in place to insure they would be mine eternally.

What a blessing my temple marriage was at that moment. I might not see them alive again after today, but I would have them eternally, if I lived worthy of them. I made a solemn promise to myself and my hostage children that I would live so that we could be together again. They loved me and their father and we loved them. Everything we had done up to May 16, 1986, we had done because of love—for God, for each other, and for our children. Our being with them may be delayed for a time because of some crazy person with a bomb, but we could be together in the future, the much more important future.

As my head remained bowed, another truth was made known to me through the Spirit. The day was not in the hostage-taker's hands, it was in the Lord's hands. IF my children died that day it would be in answer to a call from a loving Father in Heaven, not because evil people had sent them to their deaths. THE LORD WOULD DECIDE. Hope and comfort filled my breast. I did not have complete knowledge, but I had complete faith in the Lord. Everything would be OK, one way or the other, and I gave Lori and Kevin to the Lord, just as I had Brian years earlier.

Keith and I had lived on a ranch in Idaho for seven years. We had our first three children very quickly. Traci was barely three when Lori was born and Brian was right in the middle at eighteen months. Brian never seemed like a little boy, though. He loved his dad more than anything and would do anything to be with him. I had run more than one race against his tiny legs, as he would sneak out of the house to be with his father. We had some close calls, because Keith didn't always know that Brian had gotten away from me. We had already had Brian stitched up several times because of bad falls and accidents. I was truly afraid for his life. I believed in the scriptures, literally. I remembered how Samuel's mother had given him to the Lord, so one night I did the same with Brian. I told Heavenly Father if he had a mission for Brian to fulfill on this earth, He would have to keep him safe until he had fulfilled it. Keith and I had been obedient by marrying in the temple and having children. I loved my little son, but could not keep him safe. Would Heavenly Father please help me? Remarkable things began to happen. Bri fell from a horse running full speed—no injury. Six bales of hay fell from thirteen tiers up. The first three formed a triangle over Brian before the others lit on him. A twelve hundred pound dead heifer was dragged over the top of Brian; it peeled his snowsuit right off of him, but not a scratch. In my car, I thanked Heavenly Father for the miracles that had happened in Brian's life and prayed for one more.

Some time later, the high school students were sent home. Traci found me on Main Street and I took her and Katie home, along with older Neil Cornia children. They lived out of town and had students in the elementary as well. I don't know how long I was at the house; time had no relevance to me that day. There was only *before* the bomb and *after* the bomb. While driving back toward the school, Sherrie Cornia and I heard the bomb explode. I parked my car and began running toward the school, passing children who were blackened and some with skin hanging down. My brain and heart had stopped, only my legs were working.

Suddenly, there they were, three black children running together toward me and jumping into my outstretched arms. Surely no celestial reunion will be any sweeter. The boys were talking as fast as they could. Lori was hugging me so tightly I could hardly breathe. I knew it was a miracle, and more so as the next few days passed and more information became available. Brian had been blown out the classroom door, literally flying through the air. Many thought he had been killed, but he had not been hurt. He ran past David Young, fully expecting to be shot in the back. Lori had stayed in the classroom to look for Kevin, and saw Doris Young burning as she crawled over debris looking for her little brother. Kevin had been sitting next to Billy Jo Hutchinson, the most badly burned child, six feet from the bomb when it exploded. He had no burns, only a scrape from exiting through a window. Physically we had survived in great shape.

Obviously the children we sent to school were not the same as the ones we got back. They were in shock. Brian was so angry. Kevin couldn't be quiet about the guns, and Lori wouldn't say or do anything. She just sat by herself and stared. Our hearts were full of gratitude for the miracle, and prayer for those more injured than we were. I was very naïve, not realizing that at least one of my children was very injured. We toured the school, attended the town meeting, and were assigned a counselor for help if we needed it. No one needed help more than I did. We all slept in one bedroom, with the light on. Brian apparently thought that since no one could blow him up, he must be invincible. His risk-taking reached a whole new level. Kevin was taking the neighborhood children hostage and Lori couldn't do the simplest task, and even more upsetting, she was refusing priesthood blessings and never slept. Within twenty-four hours every family was sick with the flu or colds. It was all normal—except for Lori.

My prayers were prayers of exhaustion as I tried to stay awake with Lori. Not only had she read David Young's intentions correctly, but she had come up with a plan. She knew as the afternoon wore on and the children became sick and restless. David Young would try to drug them. She told herself over and over that she would not take the medication. Somehow Lori would stay awake and prevent David Young from falling asleep, pulling the string and exploding the bomb. It was so ingrained in her brain that even in safety she could not sleep. She refused priesthood blessings because she had ignored the warnings of the Holy Ghost therefore she was unworthy. The only relief Lori had gotten from her plans was when David Young left the schoolroom momentarily. Lori had a good feeling enter and the evil feeling left. She received a voice in her mind which told her where to stand and to get ready.

I knew Heavenly Father had not saved Lori to suffer so profoundly. She was a beautiful, pure daughter of God, but all of my pleadings and explanations could not break through. I had never been so humbled by anything in my life, and yet I knew our prayers were being answered baby step by baby step.

Counselors came to the parents' meeting and I was led with others to the room where Dr. Vern Cox, a psychologist from Star Valley, was waiting to advise and assist us. The children were so afraid of strangers that a plan was devised where the parents, usually the mothers, would meet with the counselor, then go home to help their children. My first group meeting with Dr. Cox was reading scriptures on forgiveness. We had to move on if we expected our children to move on. The key to that was forgiving David Young. We had neither time nor energy to waste on him. I am still so thankful for that lesson. Getting David Young out of the way allowed me more closeness to my Heavenly Father. There was no anger or hatred in me, just love for my children and a sincere desire to do what was right for them.

Gradually, Lori began to respond, although she never slept a full night until August of that year. Her self-esteem slowly returned as did her capability to do things that she had always done before the bombing such as answer the phone or tend her little sister. I sobbed through her first priesthood blessing. She finally began to feel worthy to pray again. The exhaustion was leaving and we were truly healing.

I do not know why we got the miracle that day when it seems so many are denied the miracles they need. We never considered ourselves more worthy of a miracle than anyone else. Living worthy of such an enormous blessing provides a challenge of its own. I know our God is a God of miracles, and since the bombing I find miracles more often. To say God is aware of each of His children and knows each of His children is an understatement. Every blessing He grants while given to many at the same time is personalized as well, meant just for you or for me. God is the most powerful force in the world and goodness will reign in the end. Evil can never outdistance good. How can I ever show my gratitude for the miracle of the restoration of my children. The Lord saved them physically and has provided a way for them to be saved spiritually. My ten grandchildren are a living reminder to me of that restoration. I love my Heavenly Father. I know He loves me. What greater happiness can there be?

Terry Nate
Mother of Two Student Survivors
(Oral History—Telephone)

I was actually in Montpelier doing some errands and I was at the bank going through the drive thru. My mother heard something on the radio. I was busy with the teller so I didn't hear it. She turned it up and we got bits and pieces. I panicked and went to my mother's house. I called home to Alva. All the radio had said was it was a hostage situation. It didn't say what. I didn't know it was the school.

I thought it might be Knouse's service station because it was on the corner of the main highway. That's not what the name was but that's what we called it. That's where everyone went. I remember thinking maybe I shouldn't go. Maybe my kids are on the ambulance coming over here. I was just torn. I started to head home. I saw car after car going to Montpelier. I thought I was a failure as a mom. All those parents there helping their kids. I wasn't there to be with mine. Of course, no cell phones then so you couldn't call anyone to see what was going on.

I saw the ambulance go by. Speeding. All those cars going past. I didn't know what to do. I just kept going. I got to town and went to Alva's. As I went in, Greg and Brad both came running to me and just broke down crying. There were tears of joy from me and also tears of sadness that I wasn't there for my two little boys.

Grandpa was there outside waiting for them. Grandpa and a few other guys were going to go to the school and storm it. That's what they were saying. And people told them they couldn't do that. Of course, no one would have let them.

At that point, they told me Greg was one of the first ones out. He was by the window. As the older brother, he felt it was his responsibility to find Brad. Greg and Grandpa Orson were looking for Brad. They couldn't find him. They were scared to death. Most people had left, it seemed and they couldn't find Brad. Then they found out he was the first ones out and went running straight to Grandma's.

Greg didn't shed a tear. He felt like he had to be the big brother and take care of his little brother. He felt a lot of responsibility. Brad cried and got it all out and seemed to be fine. Greg was very strong and seemed to be fine but later in the summer a motor home pulled in here at our place and wanted to stay by our hay shed. They were from Europe and they felt unsafe in the park. They wanted to stay somewhere where people were.

Dennis said yes and he showed them where to park. Pretty soon Greg and his cousin Kyle Thornock, who were playing together, came and talked to me. They were just scared to death that his dad hadn't come down yet. They were really worried about him.

Greg didn't like white vans. He didn't like vehicles of any kind stopping on the highway in front of our house. They slept on the floor by our bed on makeshift beds for a good month or so. A year later to the month we had gone to Pocatello to see some relatives and on the way home, everyone had fallen asleep. Brad started yelling out NO! NO! I got up and made my way to the back of the van and woke him up. I found out he was dreaming about the bombing. I had thought we were over the hump.

Since then I don't remember anything about it coming up. However, Greg has never been one to stay at this house alone, to this day. Doesn't like being alone. He won't admit it. But if he comes here and we're not here, he'll go in and visit with Grandma until someone comes home.

We ran the boys over to Kemmerer. Linda's boys were in Kemmerer. They had hair singed. We thought for safety measures we'd better run to Kemmerer and have them checked out for smoke inhalation. We wanted them looked over and checked out. They got counseling through the school. It didn't seem like my kids needed as much as some of them. They suggested we go back and walk through the school with the kids. The boys told us where they were standing and where they were sitting so we did that and talked about it. We spent time with them and talked about it as a family.

There was a group about that age and they went to the window to have a prayer and be alone. They were trying to look out the window and see the people, too. Greg and Brad both went out the windows I think. My understanding is nothing was open. No windows. There wasn't a lot of circulation. Everyone was getting irritable because it was hot and stuffy. David Young was getting irritable because everyone was getting irritable.

As people have said here, and I don't think anyone understands it like we do, Cokeville is special. We are a very different community. We are mostly Latter-day Saints and we are not free from mistakes by any means but everyone is striving. Like little kids having a prayer. That's from upbringing in your home. No matter what religion you are. You know that there is a Supreme Being who was listening to those children's prayers.

I know for sure it was a modern day miracle.

It makes you realize how much more it was a miracle when you get stats from people who saw the bomb and what was in it. They say they could see no flaws here and they didn't know why it didn't go off. You hear the things the kids tell you and there was no way to deny the fact there was some Divine Intervention there. The kids were truly blessed. For me and I'm sure for many, many others it was a way of saying and reinforcing what it was. That it was a miracle. That's only what it could have been. A miracle.

I can't even begin to say how horrible the fear was. We were living out here in a nowhere land. You feel so totally helpless. Some had children that were more involved and more injured than my children. Everyone was in a different situation doing and seeing different things. Dennis was driving a bus, visiting the prison on a high school field trip. They stopped to have dinner in Evanston, I think, and someone came up and asked them about it. They were back on the bus as quick as they could, trying to get here. Rick Payson was in the high school and he went up to the band teacher's wife, Mrs. Miller—I can't think of her first name right now—and put his arm around her trying to comfort her. Everyone was coming up to me later saying your son was so sweet, trying to help her out while he had two brothers in it. She had a husband who had been shot but it was not fatal.

And still, I think that must have been the Spirit telling me to keep going to Cokeville when all those cars and ambulances were passing me going the other way. I didn't know if my little boys were in one of those vehicles but I kept going to Cokeville.

I've tried to teach all of my children to always remember a miracle that happened in their lifetime—and always show thanks to their Savior for answering their prayers and being with them during a very frightening time.

DottyJo Pope
Mother of Two Student Survivors
(Through the Eyes of Her Daughter, LaFond)

This was written shortly after the bombing by LaFond Pope Hall

The Day the Bomb Went Off

On the afternoon of May 16, 1986, David Young and his wife Doris Young, filled with an obsession to obtain three hundred million dollars either from the people of Cokeville, the Congress of the United States, or the Mormon Church, entered the elementary school in Cokeville, Wyoming, with guns and bombs and took 150 children, teachers, and personnel hostage. The following is the true story of only one of the many families involved in the drama.

It was a couple of minutes after 1:00 p.m. on that afternoon. Dotty Jo Pope was running a little behind schedule—not too unusual for this busy rancher's wife, mother of ten, and church and community worker.

She pulled the old sedan up in front of the Cokeville elementary school and opened the door. Six year old Jody, a blonde, pixie-faced kindergartner, kissed her mother goodbye and skipped up the walk to the door. In spite of being late, she turned to blow kisses to her mother and younger brother and sister in the car. Dotty's heart welled up with gratitude for the beautiful, loving little girl, for the sunshine of the spring afternoon, for the peacefulness of the small town, and for life in general. She pulled away from the school and headed back to her ranch home only three miles away.

Once there, Dotty unloaded Lacy Jo and Jade, her two youngest, and went inside to resume her work. She put the youngsters down for naps and busied herself with household chores.

Time sped along, but even so it startled her to glance out the window and see the yellow school bus stop on the highway and fourteen year old Justin run up the lane. Where were Shiloh and Jody? She looked at the clock and realized that the bus was at least a half hour early. Puzzled, she met Justin at the door. "What in the world are you doing home early, Son?" she asked.

"Mom, haven't you heard? Two crazy people have all the kids in the grade school locked in the building. They have bombs and stuff, and they have been there for a couple of hours. Our principal didn't know how many bombs might be planted around and he decided to send us home early. He called us into the auditorium and told us what had happened. Then we all had a prayer and got on the buses. I didn't want to come. Shiloh and Jody need help but the law officers won't let anybody close to the school at all. They're keeping everybody way back."

Dotty's heart sank. Had she unknowingly sent Jody into that kind of danger? Indeed she had. As Jody had bounced through the door of the school, a woman's voice had commanded her, "In here, quick." But that wasn't her room. It was Shiloh's room, and he was in the first grade. What was going on? The bewildered child obeyed and found herself in the first grade room, a classroom measuring 30' by 30', crowded with all the kids in the school. "Find your teacher," ordered the woman, who was holding a gun and standing close to a cart with bottles and wires and stuff in it.

"Stay on the other side of that line," the woman told her, and Jody saw that the woman and man were standing inside a square marked off with masking tape. They had promised to shoot anyone who stepped across the tape line. Jody looked around, searching for Shiloh or her teacher in the mass of kids who were standing around whispering apprehensively. She was frightened, and a sob rose in her throat, but she swallowed it and watched with big eyes.

There was a funny smell in the crowded room and it was very hot. Several children became nauseated and soon the odor from the waste basket into which they vomited was as bad as the gasoline-like odor from the cart. The teachers tried to keep young minds occupied by singing songs, but, as Jody recounted afterward, "I didn't feel like singing. I just kept watching that man and lady. They had guns and they said that the bomb would blow up if they wanted it to." Slowly the minutes turned to an hour and then two.

As soon as Dotty Jo got the word from Justin, she said, "Watch the kids, Justin. I'm going."

"No, Mom, it won't do any good. They asked us to tell everybody to listen to the Kemmerer radio station and they'll tell us the best thing to do. They're doing everything they can. They said to please keep the phone lines clear, too."

At that instant the phone rang. "Hello," Dotty managed, in spite of her growing panic.

"Hi, Mom. This is Linda." Linda, sixteen, was in Casper, Wyoming, participating in the state track meet. "We won't be getting home very early tomorrow. We had a snowstorm here and some of the events have been postponed until tomorrow morning. We...Mom, are you crying? What's wrong?"

Dotty had no choice but to explain that all the elementary kids in town were being held hostage by a pair of kooks.

"Mom, that's awful. What can we do?"

"Get the kids on the track team together, honey, and pray. OK?"

"OK. We will. I love you. I'll call back soon."

As the receiver clicked down, Dotty realized that somehow she must get in touch with Evan, who had left early that morning for a stock auction in Blackfoot, Idaho. Where could she find him? Who could she call? It then occurred to her that she must not tie up the phone line with a series of calls, and so she dialed her married daughter Lorie in Swan Lake, Idaho, roughly a hundred miles away. Explaining to her what was happening, she asked her to try to make contact with her dad; then she hung up the phone.

In the meantime, Linda, in Casper, had passed the word to her teammates, many of whom had younger brothers and sisters in elementary school and all of whom felt very close to someone in the school. They gathered in the motel room of Linda and her roommates and knelt around the bed. Each of the eleven young people prayed silently and fervently, joined by their common fear and concern. One by one, they rose and stood around helplessly. It didn't take long to discover that the radio and TV coverage had no new information to offer.

Repeatedly for the next hour Linda tried to get in touch with her mother, but all circuits were now busy. She then called her older sister, Lisa, a co-ed at Brigham Young University in Provo, Utah.

"Lisa, do you know what's going on?"

"Not really. All the kids here have been calling me to let me know what they have been hearing on the television, but I can't get a line through to Cokeville. Lorie called me. She hasn't been able to get hold of Dad and she's on her way to Cokeville now. She promised to call me as soon as she knows anything."

"OK, I guess we'll just have to keep trying to find out. And pray. Pray hard for Jody and Shiloh and everybody."

"You know I will. 'Bye, Linda."

In Logan, Utah, 120 miles from Cokeville, Shane Pope, 24, and his bride of a few months, Laura, went into a jewelry store. Ordinarily Laura worked at the Cokeville high school as an aid, but she had taken a leave day to accompany Shane to a dentist in Logan. Now they were ready to head home but decided first to have Laura's diamond checked to make sure it was secure in its setting. A radio was playing soft music, but suddenly that was interrupted by a commentator bringing "the latest details in that hostage situation in Cokeville, Wyoming."

As they listened, Laura squeezed Shane's hand tightly and looked up at him, her face pale. "Shane, 150 hostages. That's all the kids in the school. That's awful." Attempts to call home brought them the all-circuits-are-busy response, so they hurried to their car and headed home.

In Blackfoot, Idaho, a young woman was leaving the auction

arena where she worked. She was troubled. A few moments before, her colleague had taken a call from a very distressed girl who was trying to find her father. The information she had received from the girl who took the call was garbled, but it dealt with some kids in a Wyoming school that were being held hostage and a Mr. Pope who had come from there was urgently needed at home. Since he had not responded to the paging, it was assumed that he had gone.

Impulsively, she turned her car into the downtown area of Blackfoot, a fairly small town, and drove slowly down the street scrutinizing license plates carefully. In a few minutes she spotted an old truck with a stock rack, a loaded stock trailer behind and Wyoming license plates. She stopped and approached the red-headed man with cowboy boots and a Stetson hat. He was conversing with a truck salesman on a used car lot.

"Mr. Pope?"

"Yes, young lady. What can I do for you?"

She poured out what little she knew. Evan thanked her quickly and then headed for a phone booth. All circuits were busy. He called the Blackfoot City Police Department but either they did not have information or could not give it to a stranger over the phone. One last call. The Wyoming lines were tied up, but he did get a call through to the Bear Lake County Police Department in Paris, Idaho. He identified himself and the dispatcher told him what she knew—that a bomb had gone off a few minutes before and that many children were on their way in ambulances to area hospitals. None had yet arrived in Montpelier. Evan hopped in his truck and headed south. It was more than a hundred mile drive, and he could pick up only bits and pieces of information on the radio as he drove.

"Heavenly Father," Evan prayed. "Bless my kids. Bless all those kids. Help Dotty to be brave." Somehow he knew that Dotty would do what she had to do. She might fall apart tomorrow, but as long as she was needed, she'd be OK. Why did this have to happen when he was away? If he had been at home...and then an unusual calm came over him. He thought of his many friends in Cokeville, the members of his ward (the divisions of the LDS Church) and as he thought of them one by one, he could count more than a dozen who he knew would do as much for his kids as they would for their own.

Dotty was holding together. News of the explosion came over the radio station at about 3:40 p.m.. Justin grabbed his sleeping brother and sister, one under each arm, and ran to the station wagon, Dotty three steps ahead of him. Less than five minutes later they arrived at the school and could see smoke pouring from the windows of the first grade room. Children were being loaded into several ambulances that were on hand, having been summoned by the police department as soon as the seriousness of the situation became apparent. (The nearest hospital was thirty miles away in Montpelier, Idaho, but ambulances had also come from the Star Valley Hospital in Afton and from Kemmerer.) Dozens of children were lying on the ground covered with blankets. The community's core of medical technicians had also been summoned and were on hand administering first aid in all directions.

"Find Jody, Mom," Lacy Jo, nearly four, told her mother through her tears. "She's my bestest friend."

Dotty moved quickly through the confusion of the school yard. Many children were crying and parents were helping the injured while looking for their own children.

Justin found Shiloh within a minute or two, teary and frightened, under a tree. "I'm all right, Justin. When everything went yellow, I just jumped out the window."

Everything "had gone yellow" when David Young had left his wife to go to the restroom. He took the string attached to the bomb release from his wrist and wrapped it around hers. Then he left the masking tape fortress and went to the restroom. Shortly thereafter a comment from one of the hostages caused Doris Young to turn quickly. Inadvertently she jerked the string and the bomb exploded.

Initially it was thought that she was killed instantly, but later investigation led to the belief that when Young stepped from the rest room a few seconds later and shot the music teacher in the shoulder, he also shot her before turning the gun on himself. In any event, pandemonium ensued, and children ran out the doors and jumped out the windows. Teachers like Verlene Bennion, 66, and Kliss Sparks stayed in spite of injuries until every child was out of the room.

It took a few minutes more to locate Jody, huddled under a blanket in the ambulance. Medics had poured cold water over her badly burned arm and her face and eyes hurt.

A couple of ambulances pulled away and Jody and two other little girls were in the ambulance from Afton, Wyoming. (Afton is located in Star Valley, more than fifty miles from Cokeville.) Justin said he could take care of Shiloh and the two little ones, so Dotty climbed into the ambulance as it headed for the hospital. Once seated, Dotty felt both relief and gratitude well up within her. "Thank You, Heavenly Father. Thank You. Please continue to bless Shiloh at home, and Jody here, and Evan on the road, and all the injured children, and everyone who helped, and..." Quiet tears ran down her cheeks.

A few miles out of town, however, more frustration! By Todd Dayton's house, the engine of the ambulance began smoking and it was necessary to stop. Within minutes several truck drivers had assembled to help the driver. A broken fan belt was determined to be the culprit and someone miraculously produced one. Soon they were on their way again, taking with them the best wishes and Godspeed of the truck drivers. Dotty was later to explain, "I guess I always thought that truck drivers were kind of a hard, crude lot; but I'll always have a soft spot for them in my heart. They were kind and concerned. A couple of them stuck their heads inside the ambulance to speak to the little girls and offer encouragement to me."

Upon their arrival in Afton, they discovered that three doctors had flown by helicopter from Jackson, Wyoming, to join the local doctors at the hospital to treat the burn victims. (They had had no idea how many might be brought to Afton. As it turned out, there were only a few, and so they got immediate and expert attention.)

A short time later, Evan arrived in Montpelier, Idaho. He had heard on his truck radio that a number of children had now arrived there. As he ran into the hospital corridor, he saw many of his friends and neighbors.

Robert Cory greeted him first. "Evan? What are you doing here? They took Jody to Star Valley."

"Is she bad? What about Shiloh? What about your kids?"

Monte McKinnon joined them. "One arm, I think, Evan. I'm not sure about Shiloh, but I don't think he was injured. Are you in your truck?"

"I have a load of stock."

"Take my car and go. I'll take care of your truck and unload the cattle."

"Thanks, but you'll need your car. I have a friend out here a mile or so. I'll be able to unload the cows there."

Evan stepped into a room to speak to Travis McKinnon and checked quickly with several other families. Then he hurried to his truck and drove to his friend's corral to unload.

It was fifty miles to the Star Valley Hospital in Afton, but he could breathe a little easier now, knowing that no one had been killed except the two perpetrators, that most of the children had not been critically injured, and that his own youngsters were in relatively good shape. He offered prayers of thanksgiving as he drove and also prayed for all those who had been injured and frightened. He wondered as he drove how the bomb could have exploded without much greater devastation. A devout Mormon, whose two oldest sons had each served two-year missions for the Church, he thought how fortunate it was that Shiloh had been spared and that he would one day perform such service. Justin, too, of course. It occurred to him that in that school room there had been dozens of boys who were being trained up to serve as missionaries. Again gratitude brought tears to his eyes as he thought of how blessed the community had been in the face of such an ordeal.

Leon, 25, had been trucking cattle to a summer

pasture in Fish Haven, Idaho. About mid-afternoon he was driving through Paris, en route to pick up another load, when he decided to drop in and say hi to his wife, Lynne, who worked in the courthouse as secretary to the county agent.

"I'm so glad you stopped," she greeted him. "I didn't know how to find you, and something terrible is going on at home. Several people have called to tell me that the radio is broadcasting that all the Cokeville kids are being held captive in the schoolhouse."

Lynn had been unable to locate her boss to explain, so she simply locked up the office and let neighboring office workers know the situation. Then they started for home. The route led them through Montpelier, then south to Cokeville. By the time they were about mid-way between Montpelier and Cokeville, they began passing ambulances and many cars going the other way. They recognized many of the hometown folks in the cars and debated whether to turn back to Montpelier or go on. It occurred to Leon that those who were on the road would have adequate professional help and that possibly they could be of more help in Cokeville and so they sped onward, realizing as they passed carload after carload of their friends and neighbors that many youngsters, indeed, had been injured.

Arriving at the schoolyard, they found some people still milling around and a number of children still confused and weeping. Most of the injured, however, had by now been transported to area hospitals—including one school bus load of children who had been taken to Kemmerer for treatment of minor burns. Soon a family friend, Kumeroa Chournos, one of the EMTs who had been helping, approached them. "Oh, Leon, this has been awful."

"Kumeroa, have you seen my folks? What do you know about Jody and Shiloh?"

"Shiloh is OK. He is frightened but he is still all right. He went home with Justin. Jody's arm looked awful bad to me, and her eyes were burned some. Your mother went with her in an ambulance, but I don't know which hospital."

"We'll drive home right now. It looks like you have done everything you can, too. You had better go home and get some rest."

Leon and Lynne, after talking with several friends and realizing that there was nothing further to be done at the school, drove out to the ranch to be with Justin and the three smaller children. There they found that Lorie had come with her baby daughter and soon Shane and Laura also arrived. They called the Montpelier hospital and learned that Jody was not there. A call to Star Valley revealed that she had been admitted, but somehow no one could find Dotty Jo and the nurses had nothing to report on her condition. Within an hour, however, they were able to talk to Dotty and found out that their little sister was going to be fine. Her eyes were not seriously burned and the arm would heal. Besides that, her dad had arrived and was with her.

Good news at last to report when Lisa called from Provo and Linda called from Casper. Realizing how much nationwide coverage the incident had had, Leon got the first open circuit to call Grandpa and Grandma Pope in Gooding, Idaho, and learned that they had tried dozens of times, to no avail, to get a circuit through.

Gradually the excitement subsided and exhaustion—physical and emotional—set in. Before Leon and Shane left for their own homes, the family gathered in the living room to kneel together and give thanks for their blessings and to pray once more for those who had been seriously burned. They felt very close—close to their parents and Jody, miles away in the hospital, close to Linda in Casper, close to Lisa in Provo, and close to their Heavenly Father.

In Casper, Linda knelt once more at her bedside, this time with her two roommates, and poured out her thanksgiving that she had finally been able to make contact and find out that things would be OK. In Provo, Lisa, having made arrangements to drive home the next morning, offered a similar prayer. Brad Gamble, Lorie's husband in Swan Lake, knelt and offered thanks that things had turned out as well as they had for the family he had married into and so much loved. In the hospital in Afton, Jody had fallen into a fitful sleep and at her bedside, Evan, holding tightly to Dotty's hand—she still hadn't had a chance to fall apart—bowed his head to express gratitude. In a few moments he smiled at Dotty.

"Hey, Sweetheart. We're richer than we knew. We always knew the kids were worth a lot, but some guy who didn't even like 'em thought they were worth two million apiece."

Janet Prows
Mother of Two Student Survivors
(Typewritten Submission)

When I was approached to put something in this book I was told it wasn't going to be about the horror of May 16, 1986, it was to be about the impact that day had on my life. I have two children who could have been taken from me that day through evil. But because my Heavenly Father loves me so much, he spared my children as He did every child and teacher in that room. What a gift. The power of that love is renewed in my heart every day as I have been able to see those children grow. I feel that love when I hold my grandchildren in my arms who never would have been born without the miracle He gave me that day. I feel it takes away from the gift of life he gave me that day to hold onto the evil and horror of what happened. I have left that day where it belongs, in the past, and I enjoy every day I have with my children.

Brent Roberts
Father of Two Student Survivors
(Oral History as told to his wife Tamra)

Brent was in Kemmerer, Wyoming working at the time. His sister, Joy Cassels, was working in the van and heard the news and excitement over the radio. She alerted Brent and he was sure she heard wrong. They continued to listen and of course realized the seriousness of the situation. Brent recalls driving faster than his truck could really go and knew the motor was going to fly out. He was just entering Cokeville when the news came over the radio that the bomb had gone off. He tells of the emotions going through him at that time and said it was one of the most terrifying times in his life. They had the roads barricaded off so he just ran and soon located Heidi and Aaron.

Miracles happen in our days, we have the proof of all the Cokeville children and their providers.

Tamra Roberts
Mother of Two Student Survivors
(Typed Submission)

I was in Logan, Utah, the day of the bombing. My mom, Una Dayton, had a doctor appointment and we had left early that morning. As we were coming back we passed a lot of fire trucks and police cars in the canyon and we both mentioned that there must have been a fire or a bad wreck. I took the Westside road and again we were amazed at all the fire trucks and were sure the McKinnon Ranch was on fire. We soon found that was not the case.

I was stopped at the railroad crossing in Cokeville and was told about the situation and informed that all the children were accounted for. I could not comprehend what had really happened. Our safe little Cokeville, how could this possibly happen? Not being in the middle of all the confusion and the waiting and coming into it at the end, it was almost like it was untrue. By word of mouth I was getting more information, but still it seemed to be so unreal.

I did finally locate our family. Kari, our oldest daughter, who was a senior and Shellie, our second daughter who was a freshman had our two hostage children safe. Heidi was in sixth grade and Aaron was in third grade and all were found at their grandmother, Jenny Roberts's, home.

I can remember holding them and trying to comfort them. They did not get burned or hurt, only frightened to death. Heidi's hair was burned and had turned green. Aaron was like he was speechless, he didn't want to talk about it then or now.

We had some very special spiritual moments with both of them. We did a lot of praying and teaching and with the help of our Heavenly Father and Jesus Christ they were able to carry on with their lives. This is not to say that we did not have a lot of sleepless nights and a lot of tender moments to help them but feel grateful they were blessed with peace through the gospel of the Church of Jesus Christ of Latter-day Saints.

Barbara Sorensen
Mother of One Student Survivor
(Oral History)

There is a lot about that day that I don't want to recall, but I do remember someone calling and telling me that the elementary school had been taken hostage. I don't even remember who called. I just recall feeling scared. I jumped in the car and sped into town to find roadblocks going into the school, so I went over to my mom's house. I tried frantically to get in touch with Andy who was working in Kemmerer for the railroad at the time. I never was able to contact him, but he had heard it broadcast over the local radio station, KMER. He was then on his way home to save his daughter. He passed numerous ambulances and police cars on his way home.

I spent the afternoon wondering if I would ever see Jennie again. I battled with myself internally wondering if I told my baby that I loved her that morning. I couldn't even recall if I had kissed and hugged her before she made her journey to school. I am sure I did, but I wanted to hold her right then. I felt so out of control. You never want your children to be in harm's way.

My dad and mom came home from work early to console me. The dread of not knowing what was taking place in the school was frightful. I remembered Dad saying, "Everything will be all right. We will take care of things." He then headed out the door and down the street to wait on the corner with several other concerned people. The whole town shut down, wondering what was going to happen to all our loved ones.

We sat in the big front room window of the Toomers's home and watched as helicopters landed on the football field. Philip, my son who was only four at the time, remembers all the great big helicopters. He also remembers a few years down the road when there was a propane truck leak and threatened to explode at the school. The whole elementary school was again evacuated in fear of their lives. It turned out to be properly taken care of, but a lot of the kids and teachers remembered their fears from the bombing situation of 1986.

I received a call from my good friend, Ann Clayton from Green River, who had also heard on the radio that the school was taken hostage. She was concerned and tried to comfort me. I told her that Andy had not made it home, but I knew he was on his way. In a way, I think it was good Andy did not make it because he would have gone in after his baby girl.

After pacing back and forth for several hours, we heard the loudest explosion we had ever experienced in our whole lives. One earth shattering noise that I will never forget as long as I live. I got the sickest feeling that we had just lost our kids and all the adults that were at the school with the children. I took off down the street. People were running and swarming toward the school. The police and others stopped us at the corner of Sage Street. My dad and brother Don, were some of the few who were able to go closer to the school before they closed the road off. They figured those men who were already headed to the school would help get the children out. Then we saw children escaping from the school and my heart was grateful. I just prayed I would soon see my daughter. It seemed so weird that the bomb really went off in our safe little school.

The miracle was that I did see my daughter again! I will never forget the chills of pure joy I had to see my dad and little girl coming safely home. I can still picture her black, tear stained face. I can't imagine the fear she had to endure that day, but was glad she and the other hostages were brave and safe.

Andy was so glad and thankful that Jennie was safe. When he did finally make it home, there were tears of joy to see his family safe. We were so glad that Jennie only had a few minor burns on her knee and shoulder, but I do remember the pain on her face when we peeled the plaid pants from her burned knee leaving a plaid impression on her skin. Luckily, we treated her at home and thanked Heavenly Father every day that she was still with us.

Her legacy lives on. I have two beautiful granddaughters and more grandchildren to come who constantly remind me of the miracle that my daughter is still with us. I am not going to say the last twenty years have been easy, but I will say that through many sleepless nights from nightmares and lots of good counseling our miracles are still continuing.

Craig D. Taylor
Father of One Student Survivor
Cokeville EMT
(Oral History)

I was at work on the railroad with Carl Eggleston and Art Hess and I think Boyd Sparks, when Gilbert Eastman came down the road in his car, and if I remember right, he said, "Some crazy fool is holding the kids hostage at the school with a bomb and I just heard, the bomb went off."

We were in the middle of Nugget Canyon. I jumped in the car with Gilbert and we headed to town. We hurried and got to town and they had all the traffic stopped about where the Valley Hi Motel is. We had to park the car there and run all the way down the street to the elementary school from there. I was an EMT and I had a boy in there. They still wouldn't let me in. By the time I got to the school, several ambulances had taken off. I couldn't find my boy and I was starting to panic. By then, I couldn't have done a thing as an EMT.

When I arrived at the scene, I asked where my son, Ryan, was. They said he was already taken by ambulance to Montpelier. I asked how badly he was burned and they didn't know but they knew Kliss Sparks had rubbed out the fire on his hair. There were a couple of ambulances going to Montpelier and I jumped in the back with some kids. I was there as an EMT but my father instincts had kicked in. I stood back there and rode. I was in a daze and I can't remember to this day what kids were in there. By the time I got to Montpelier and got to Ryan, I couldn't tell how bad he was burned. He was all wrapped up.

My wife Rachael and daughter Mandy had gone to Logan that day to a dentist appointment for Mandy. That morning Ryan begged and begged to go with them. His mother told him no. So he stayed. It was through Ryan's grandparents, Jean and Solomon Romero, that they were able to get hold of Rachael in Logan. Rachael and Mandy both arrived at the hospital later that evening.

     When I got to the hospital and looked at Ryan, the first thing that popped into my mind was, he needs a blessing. I know that President Leonard Matthews and I administered to him. They shipped some of the seriously burned kids out. They kept Ryan. I had enough trust in Dr. Wolff that he could do the job. You can only see a little scar on his hand and by his eye now. The doctor said that the glasses saved his sight and eyes from severe burns. You could see the flash burn. His ears swelled up to three times their size and his fingers swelled up, too. They took some skin off the side of his legs and put it by his eye. Skin graft. The railroad was good enough to me that they gave me a week off.

     Ryan remembers in the classroom that the shopping cart was taped off. The little kids were in the front and the bigger kids were in the back. When the bomb went off, Ryan went out a door. He remembers somebody helping him out the door.

     What I remember the most is that it was a miracle that the kids got out without anyone getting hurt except the two people that were holding the kids hostage.

     As a dad, I remember seeing Ryan lying in the hospital and how bad he was hurt and how much pain he was in. It was the next day, I recall, he had to start getting benodine treatments in a whirlpool tub. They had to take the bandages off, set him in a whirlpool tub, scrub off the dead skin from the blisters that had popped so the new skin could be exposed, and when his hands came out of the water and was exposed to the air, he would just scream because of the pain. That was the only time he would cry. The rest of the time you could just see him in bed with his little glasses on. To this day, he still has a whole box of mementos of that day and he still won't talk about it. There will be some times that he will take that box out and he will look at them and go through the day again and realize how lucky he was.

     I'm a firm believer that if it weren't for the Priesthood blessing that Ryan received, he would have been scarred worse than he was. To this day, I'm a firm believer that Ryan and all the children had help from above getting through the bombing and out and as well as they did.

We don't have a means to all things or to understand all things. It's not our place to question why things happen. We don't need to know everything. One day we will meet our Maker and we'll know and have the answers to the questions that we certainly all have.

Danalee and Gordon Thornock
Parents of Two Student Survivors
(Email Submission)

They were standing midstream up to their knees in the cool Pine Creek water. Laughing, yelling to each other, throwing water and love of life. Five girls, four ours and one belonging to the neighbors, were enjoying the summertime. Viewing this scene no one would guess the torments nighttime brought to nine year old Kara's life.

On May 16, 1986 I was stunned by a phone call informing me that our entire grade school was being held hostage by a couple who had a bomb in a shopping cart. We lived in a tiny town in Wyoming, safe, or so we thought, from the violence of the world.

I immediately grabbed our two-year old daughter, Jaclyn, and drove twenty miles to get my husband, Gordon, who was trailing a herd of cows out onto the summer range. He was the bishop in the second ward and I knew there were many people who would need him in addition to his family. As Gordon moved the cattle along he had noticed many police and rescue vehicles on the highway going toward Cokeville but had never entertained the thought that it might be our grade school and his two daughters in danger.

On returning home we found the high school students, including our sons, Scott, 16, and Shawn, 13, had been sent home. We got our five year old daughter Krista, who had attended morning kindergarten and was playing with a neighborhood friend, and told our sons to stay at home and tend their two sisters. As I handed the girls to Scott he said to her, "Mom I don't like to be helpless." We had always taught him to find a better way, to take charge and solve his own problems. We weren't helpless and we didn't have to accept things as they were. Our previous instructions to him didn't apply in this situation. We ALL felt helpless!

We then went to join the other parents and relatives and friends who were standing outside the police perimeter, fear numbing us as we thought about having a town and families without these children. Gordon began phoning nearby banks to see if the ransom for these priceless children could be somehow met.

We stood there hugging, comforting, fighting tears and fears for about a half hour. Although we didn't hear it, someone said that the bomb had gone off. And then we heard a sound that will forever haunt us. The cries of the escaping children were not loud but unlike any we had ever heard. The pitiful cries proclaiming their loss of innocence were heart wrenching.

Our eleven year old daughter, Leigh, was one of the first to come running down the street from the school and we hugged her with relief and then started hunting Kara. It seemed we searched for a long time but in reality it was only a few minutes until we found Kara, black with smoke and wandering around disoriented. We all embraced and then started helping others find their family members. Praying in our hearts with gratitude for our daughters' safety and hope that all families would be complete.

As we observed Leigh through the heavy soot we could see that she was badly burned so she was taken by ambulance fifty miles away to the hospital in Kemmerer. Dana followed. Because Leigh's burns were serious and Kara hadn't been burned, Dana spent the next days primarily with Leigh. Even in the emergency room Leigh began talking about her frightening experience. She told us how scared she had felt and we cried together. One teacher later told us that Leigh had come to her during the time they were hostages and said that she needed to go home because she knew her mother wouldn't want her to be in a room where there was a bomb. Another one of our teachings, to get up and leave a threatening situation, proved to be useless at this time.

When Leigh and Dana returned from the hospital Dana discovered that Kara had been sleeping by her dad and that she didn't want to talk about the afternoon she had spent crowded with 150 others in a schoolroom with a bomb.

Leigh had deep physical scars on her arm and Kara had deep scars on her heart. During the daytime everything seemed normal but as night and darkness approached Kara would stay very close to us. She slept with us and we held her close and told her we realized how awful her experience had been. And each night before she went to sleep we would talk about everything she liked to do; riding her bike, reading, singing, playing the piano, collecting rocks, etc.

After a few weeks Kara decided she wanted to try sleeping in her own room. And for the first few nights had no problems falling asleep. Then one night she came sobbing and shaking into our room. And we decided we needed to take a new approach with her. Our telling her we knew how horrible the experience had been or avoiding the issue by talking of her favorite things was not getting the nightmares to cease. We told her that we needed to talk about her hostage experience. As she talked we all made a surprising discovery. Everything that happened that May day was not something we needed to avoid or forget.

First Kara told of being taken to the classroom and how her third grade class sat close together along a wall. And that one of the teachers had passed her some magnets to play with her friends. Then they handed out some books to read. Leigh said she couldn't concentrate on the book but she was able to read to a first grader. Kara remembered how she always tried to keep her eye on her fifth grade sister across the room. Some of the time the teachers told them stories and sang with them. Kara was concerned that she couldn't remember how she got out of the school. They realized how much they loved their family and friends. And Kara, along with her sister Leigh, had prayed out loud and silently and continually.

We remembered that we heard from people we hadn't seen since childhood or college. The Cokeville phone lines were so busy that many tried for hours before getting through. All our family members from Hong Kong to Texas and those close by cared about us. We found our teachers were great under stress and our children had the self discipline to do as they were asked. Our ambulance crews and police departments were extremely competent. The neighboring communities were very unselfish, caring and helpful. The bomb had not completely detonated and all the children and adults involved lived. And the most important thing was that prayers were heard and answered. Prayer works anytime, anyplace and in any circumstance. As we focused on the positive aspects of the experience, the healing process began.

Glenna Walker
Mother of Three Student Survivors
EMT
(Oral History)

The day started in a normal way. The children got ready for school. Kevin and I had planned on going to Kemmerer with our niece. I was waiting for Kevin to pick up our niece, Jana, at the high school. He was late and I kept wondering where they were. This was approximately 12:30 and we were supposed to have left around noon.

I heard a car in front of the house. Kevin pulled up and told me we had an emergency at the elementary. He had just talked to Princess at the city hall. Her father had the children hostage and wanted two million for each child there. It was unbelievable. I kept asking him questions. I can't imagine this happening. He was very, very upset. I knew he was not trying to trick me. He told me to get our other son from the junior high and if they released them, to have him stay with me.

He also told me to report to the EMT barn as quickly as I could. He told me to get blankets ready and whatever else we could use in case of an emergency. I tried to call the junior high and the line was busy. So I went to the EMT barn and Becki Forrest and I pulled the ambulance out of the bay and proceeded up Main Street. Kathy Davison and I wondered if it was a mock accident. I felt very disturbed at that time and felt that if they tried to test us in this way, I didn't want to be a part of the EMT group.

We stayed on Main Street, outside of the school road and talked to several townspeople. People started coming and asking if they could get to their children of if they could help in any way. We started seeing other people and fire departments and ambulances from other communities coming. We were told that they released the junior high students. I wondered where Jana and our son Shane were. They had gone to their grandparents and were safe at their home.

We waited for about two and a half hours and the time was approaching that the elementary would be dismissed for the day and we wondered what would happen if the bells rang and if the children would know what to do. I remember the bomb going off and it was such a different sound than anything that you would ever imagine a bomb sounding like. It sounded more like a dull thud maybe inside of a can and we wondered even what had happened or if it was a gunshot.

Total chaos happened at this time. I can remember looking up and seeing vehicles proceeding forward toward the front of the line and several local people were running toward the school building. I opened the side of the ambulance and jumped inside and then decided I needed to be outside to help the children.

The next thing I remember seeing is the children coming, running to us. They came through Russells' yard from the school to Main Street where we were parked, about a block straight through from the school. Coming through private property. The children were so terrified and would run to us and would throw their arms around us and ask us to help them. Some were scared for their families and grandparents at home and wanted to go get them and leave before David could get to them also. He had told them he would come after them if they left.

One little girl came to me and told me that she was on fire and I showed her that she was not on fire and she kept crying that she was burning. We put her in the back of the ambulance. She started taking her pants off and her skin was red from the heat of the fire. We started trying to triage the children and keep them in groups so that their parents or teachers could locate them. Many of the grandparents were there to take care of their children.

I remember some of the children who were burned severely. Someone had turned on the hose at the house on the corner so we could cool their burns. At that time I saw my youngest daughter, Katie, sitting on the ground with her arms folded and rocking back and forth. And when I went to her and caressed her, she told me that "they" had saved her. And she was so glad to see us. I asked where her sister and brother were and she didn't know at that time.

Someone came and got me and told me that Rachel was in the Taylor home and that she was going shocky and wanted permission to start an IV. I asked if anyone knew where Travis was and right then he came running to me. At that moment, they wanted to load Rachel in the ambulance and start toward Montpelier and so I told someone from the EMTs that I was leaving with my children to go to the Montpelier hospital.

The ambulance was full in the back and I held Travis and Katie on my lap in the front. We had three that were severely burned when we left here in the ambulance and the children were crying. We were trying to keep them from going into shock. When we arrived in Montpelier at Bear Lake Memorial Hospital many news reporters were there from all over the area and asked if they could interview us. Our main concern was getting the children the medical help they needed.

Rachel was hospitalized with burns on her arms and back. And she had small pieces of metal from the bomb in her back. The next few months were a time of many trials and also blessings. Our children kept telling us about people who helped them out of the room, and wanted to know if we knew who it was that had helped them.

There were many obstacles for the children to overcome. Their fear of darkness, smells, and people they were not sure of or trusted. We were involved in a counseling group for the adults and one night one of the mothers had asked the counselor if we needed to be concerned because our children kept talking about the people who had helped them out of the building and wanted to know if we knew who they were.

This jarred my memory. My children had kept asking about "the woman." The counselor told us to go home and talk to our children, and see what they had to tell, and see if they had any concerns. He felt that maybe there was something that they needed to talk about, because he had also talked to the children and many of them keep telling him stories about people who had helped them.

I went home and visited with my husband Kevin and we decided to talk to our children and let them tell us what they remembered and what they wanted to talk about.

What an incredible experience that was. Yes indeed they did have something to share that was most precious. And to this day, it is one of our greatest blessings.

We asked them if they could describe the people who had helped them, and they told us about the teachers who were sitting by them, and how they had comforted them the whole time. But then they started telling us about a wonderful beautiful lady who had come and told them to go by the window and to stay there. And if they would listen to her and do what she said, they would be saved and protected. Our son, Travis, had been over by the door that exited the room and was prompted to get his sisters and put them by the window. He had walked to the opposite side of the room and told his sisters to stay by the window. Then he went back to one of his friends that had called him back to the door. So he had returned to the door and this was at the very moment that the bomb detonated.

Travis was forced into the hall from the impact. And he went back four times to try to get his sisters. The teachers kept telling him to leave but he kept trying to get to his sisters. Rachel and Katie had been put out the window so it took Travis a little time to find them outside. That is why I didn't find him for a few minutes also.

When we visited with our children, Travis kept taking so much blame. We couldn't understand his guilt but after we heard the whole story we understood better. As soon as we asked the girls to describe the women they saw, they said, "She had hair like yours, and big brown eyes like yours, she had a beautiful long white dress and white slippers." We had tried to trick them and ask if she was in pants, or tennis shoes or pajamas, but they both described the woman the very same way. She had said that she loved them. She told them that she would always be with them to help them and she loved them very much.

We decided to get family photos out to see if she looked like anyone in our family. I had a very small locket that had my mother's picture in it. The very moment I opened the locket, they became very excited and said, "There she is, there is the lady that helped us out of the building. She kept us safe."

They were so excited that I knew who she was and that they knew who had helped them out of the building. They told us they had prayed together in groups and asked the Lord to help them. We know that this was a miracle from the Lord as that they were protected and saved and directed what to do so they would be protected and saved so their lives could continue on. Their grandmother (my mother) had died in 1971 and they, of course, had never known her in this mortal life, but they certainly know her now and know of her love for them.

It gave them so much comfort that we finally knew who they were talking about that so much of their fears and anxieties began to leave. So much made sense to us and them that their healing seemed to be accelerated.

The summer after was such a time of love and concern for all of the children. And all of the people involved were concerned and prayed for the children that the healing would continue and things would get back to normal in our little community.

We've learned so much from this experience. We've learned that the Lord hears and answers our prayers and that love and concern can transcend even the veil and that we are protected and watched over.

This is such an incredible story for our family, it is so precious to us and them that sometimes it's hard to share. But it has had such a powerful effect on us and others that it's hard to keep it hidden.

It's now twenty years later and we have so much gratitude to all the people and the heroes who were in that room and who helped and comforted our children during that time of trial. So thankful to all the EMTs and firemen that helped those children who came out of the building. There were so many communities available to us to help our children. I remember letters from all over the world, people expressing their love and concern. It was incredible to feel that love and concern for our children.

Our family has continued to grow and all our children are now married and have children of their own. Our lives could have been very different that day but we are so thankful that our children were spared and were able to carry on and we testify of this wonderful miracle.

I testify to my posterity of the truthfulness of this wonderful miracle and wish to express my love to all of you. I love you with every fiber of my being. And just like this incredible love that was given at the bombing, I pray we may always remember and that you will also know of my love for each of you. I testify that God lives and answers prayers and that Jesus is the Christ. We give all glory to God for this wonderful miracle in our lives.

LaVonne "Bonnie" M. Wathen
Mother of One Student Survivor
(Oral History—Telephone)

I wanted to keep Willie out of school. Some kind of sixth sense. Bill said no because there was nothing wrong with him. We watched it all from the shop and I thought, I could just go through the field that is behind the shop to the school. And then I thought, no, that is dumb. When that bomb went off, Willie came running over to the shop and said, "When that bomb went off I ran like hell!" Then he added, "Am I going to get in trouble for swearing?" He didn't.

I'm just thankful it wasn't as serious as it could have been.

JoAnna Wiscombe
Mother of Three Student Survivors
(Fax Submission)

May 16, 1986 was a day of shock, fear and terror. It was also a day of confidence, peace and prayer. As I reflect on the experience of twenty years ago I am most thankful for the wise, calm responses of teachers and administration, for the prayers of friends, neighbors, and fellow countrymen. I am absolutely sure that the prayers of all the people across the country saved our children that day. It was perhaps all of these factors plus unknowns that saved our children's lives that day. Some say they saw ancestors. I know my children did.

I refer to my journal on the experience: *The principal Mr. Excel spoke in church. He said, "I did not see any angels but I know they were there." Brother Dayton, our neighbor, said, "Miracles do take place and one has taken place in our little town." The Deseret News was in town Sunday taking pictures and interviewing. This little town's been bursting with activity for the past few days. Byron was on the news.*

I just want to conclude that I am most appreciative and thankful for the miracles that took place. As I visited with each of my children regarding the experiences of that day, I realized how much trauma they each felt. Putting this together has been truly a healing experience for each of us. We thank each of those who have brought this about.

Steven A. Wiscombe, Sr.
Father of Three Student Survivors
(Fax Submission)

Cokeville Flashbacks

I was working at the Exxon jobsite seventy miles away. The situation was over by the time I learned about it. I was not able to reach my wife, JoAnna (who was six months pregnant) so I called a neighbor who told me that all the children had survived although some had serious injuries. I was able to leave the jobsite soon afterward.

My children we all safe with their mother on my arrival. Our children had minor injuries—splatter burns, singed eyelashes and eyebrows, scrapes and bruises, etc. Three of our four children were in the explosion. Our preschooler, Steve, had attended the school earlier in the day for the morning session and was back home.

Joshua, kindergartner, was one of the first kids out the main door but he tripped and was trampled over by dozens of other kids before he could stand up and start running again. He immediately ran toward the bicycle rack to get his new bike. Officers were yelling at him to get away from the building and come to them Josh still ran to get his bike.

Stephanie, in 4th grade, told of seeing a large blue hand in front of her face at the time of the explosion. Her toes were on the line of the taped area surrounding the basket that held the bomb.

At the end of the day, the only dead were the instigators, David and Doris. Conclusion: Tragic circumstances can occur in small town rural America as well as in larger cities.

We "got over" the situation almost immediately and the children did also. We moved on with our lives. I'm convinced that the children and teachers in the classroom that day were protected by guardian angels and/or relatives who had passed on. The gods can intervene when they choose to do so. The prayers of many across the nation that day were answered.

Hartt and Judene Wixom
Parents of One Student Survivor
(Email Submission)

Where are we now? After twenty years, how does the Cokeville miracle affect our lives? Probably in more ways than we are conscious of.

There are those we meet who never heard of what happened in Cokeville, Wyoming, on May 16, 1986. There are many who vaguely remember hearing about "something," and a few who recall it in some detail. Still, as the story is recounted, all are amazed that things didn't turn out differently. And in the telling, I am always struck with the same sensation: I am telling this in first person, but I can't believe it really happened to me–my family, my friends and neighbors! It's a strangely detached sensation of something so very real and personal. Still, the tears always come.

Now as I watch our son who was one of those gathered in by David Young, going about living a productive and meaningful life as a husband and father, a Scout leader, a commercial artist, I see somewhat the same thing...unless we get into a conversation about the details of that event. Then he looks off into space, connecting to the realities of that extraordinary experience with his peers, yet resisting connecting too much with the emotion of it. Some tears come in spite of his effort, but always he mentions the prayer circle in the corner of the classroom, and the remarkable sense of well-being he had, simply waiting out the conclusion.

As a family we have discussed how we never want to forget the lessons of that day:

—don't take too much for granted, whether it be the freedom to go about daily tasks or that the intentions of a stranger will always be honorable;

—friends and family are more important and vital than

supposed, and relationships should be nourished;
    —life is good and worth giving our best effort to;
    —God is aware of us, and prayer connects us!

A professional writer always wants to "be there" for the big stories. This is one that could not have been foreseen. Yet something drew us to the little town of Cokeville, Wyoming in 1981, and kept us there four years longer than planned. Part of it was the adventure of experiencing the difference from life in a big city. Much of it was the opportunities for participation in a small but vibrant/spirited school and community. Most of it was the heart of the people we associated with daily that made it more of our life than we could walk away from. But the "big story" happened just before we moved back to take a job in the city.

It was an event so bizarre and personally impactful, the story of it almost escaped me—the real story. At first it was just being interviewed by a student reporter for a college daily. Then it became a magazine article, which grew into a book and later a made for TV movie. The latter was a learning experience of its own.

The book afforded us the opportunity, along with several others in the community, to speak to interested groups around the country. An interest in angels spurred a film producer to seek us out for further development of the story for a movie. He was sensitive to the remarkable situation; some of the writers involved were not. "What is the dark side of all this?" one writer kept asking, the "dark side" of the community, the people, the event. Our take: in the end there was a bright side, and that was the important story.

His original story depicted the faculty as lacking the courage to overwhelm the intruder and take away his bomb. When we read the script, we contacted the producer; we could not allow our names to be attached to this production unless the school faculty was given proper credit for handling the situation with extraordinary courage and sensitivity. Eventually, the first writer was dismissed and another turned more light on the subject. Still, no one knew how to deal with the angels. "Hollywood doesn't know about angels," we were told.

Since then, of course, multiple shows and successful series have evolved in response to the evidence of that unseen world.

The pressure to tell the story with appropriate balance was immense. This was our community, our friends and neighbors. It had to be told in a way that would help the world understand what truly was taking place in Cokeville lives without causing more pain. We felt a great weight on our shoulders to tell the story as it happened, and to do it justice, to interview others and include their perspective. This was Cokeville's story, not just ours.

Statements in the book may be used freely by anyone in the community to help explain what happened. In the contract, we asked that the community receive some remuneration for their cooperation in helping share the story with the world.

In summary, we are grateful, along with many others, that lessons were learned from this ordeal rather than lamenting it for twenty years. We have gained something positive from it and are stronger for it. Looking back, we are more grateful than ever that none of the hostages was killed and we received what in retrospect seems to be, more than ever, Divine Intervention.

All the Rest

Ron Bird
Parent of Morning Kindergartner
(Oral History)

The way I found out about it, I was working for the county at the time, I was just in town. My boy, Zach, was in the morning kindergarten class so he was home when this happened. He had just gotten home. I was really grateful. I couldn't do anything because the police were around and the state patrolman and they wouldn't let anyone do anything. That's OK. They were doing their job. I was grateful for them. My son being home, it just made me so thankful. I went home and I hugged those two kids like I never had before, I tell you. You wouldn't believe it. I stayed around town because I was on standby with the county for radio communication. I didn't really do anything but I was there if they needed something.

I wasn't there when the bomb went off. I was in town somewhere. I heard when they first took them hostage. It was unreal. That's all I remember.

Miracles? I'm sure of it. I'm positive of miracles. A message? "There's always hope."

It didn't affect Zach badly. He was OK. I don't like to read, so I didn't read the book. I thought the TV show was far-fetched. Out there a little bit.

Clara Dayton
Cokeville High School Teacher
(Typed Submission)

On that fateful day, May 16, 1986, I was a Cokeville High School teacher. I remember all teachers and students were held at the high school until a more clear assessment of the terrifying situation could be made. After some time we were dismissed with clear, strict orders to go directly home and not to go near the elementary school.

I was distressed but did take Dan Mitchell home with me. He was concerned as both his parents, Jack and Jean Mitchell, were elementary teachers. He also had a younger brother at the school. I did manage to keep him with me.

I was not directly involved in this horrible situation as I had no immediate family members threatened.

This situation made national and international news. The morning after the incident a cousin in New York City was contacted by relatives from Trentino, Italy, who had seen TV news which said a teacher had been shot and a policeman killed. Since they could not reach me by phone they feared for me (as the teacher) and my husband (city policeman at the time). The next day I did get calls from the grateful New York City and Trentino relatives.

Dan Dockstader

Publisher, *Star Valley Independent* Newspaper
(Email Submission)

Star Valley Independent memories of 1986 Cokeville Bombing

In the spring of 1986 I still considered myself to be new on the job as editor of the *Star Valley Independent*. Only seven months into the job I was faced with the task of covering a major national story in Cokeville, a community that was included in the *Independent's* regular weekly coverage. This was largely due to the fact that the Cokeville schools were an important part of Lincoln County School District No. 2.

In fact, the evening before the bombing, May 15, 1986, I was in the Cokeville elementary school covering a LCSD No. 2 school board meeting. Little did I know that the next day and for several days following I would be in Cokeville covering the aftermath of an elementary school hostage crisis.

Star Valley Independent staff member, Irene Jeppson, arrived first on the scene that Friday afternoon, taking photographs and gathering statements from those who had rushed from the school as the bomb exploded in the form of a fireball. She compiled detailed reports of the event. Jeppson, a former resident of Cokeville, was honored by the Wyoming Press Association along with all of the newspaper staff for coverage of the event. The association presented the *Independent* with a Special Recognition Award for the May 22, 1986 edition, which devoted numerous pages to the event.

Headlines, reports, charts, and photos told the story. *Interruptions lead to terror, when will the nightmare end? Cokeville chosen because of location and people. Cokeville is bombed with news media, Cokeville injury update, Cokeville students return to school, Victims are recovering from hostage crisis, Bomb aftermath, Counselors help cope with crisis*, were just some of the headlines in the

Independent that week.

For me personally, there are two photos from that event that created feelings on each end of the emotional spectrum. One photo showed former Lincoln County Sheriff T. Deb Wolfley speaking to the press and explaining the lined up rifles and pistols on the floor below him that were taken from the school. Deep feelings of concern overwhelmed me as I thought of what could have happened had the event progressed any further. However, feelings of joy came from our front-page photo showing Cokeville first grade teacher Jean Mitchell sitting in a circle of resilient students after they had just returned to school on Wednesday, May 21st, for the first time following the crisis.

Now twenty years later, I find myself still associated with the *Star Valley Independent* and to this date the Cokeville story is the most emotionally moving story that I have covered.

Robin Douglas
Wife of Lincoln County Sheriff's Deputy
(Typed Submission)

May 16, 1986 dawned like any other spring morning in Wyoming. There was the usual rush to get everyone ready and out the door. I had to get the boys to daycare, my husband off to work as a Lincoln County Sheriff Deputy, and myself to work as assistant manager of Coast to Coast/Ben Franklin in Kemmerer, Wyoming. That day was a day just like every other day of the week for the Douglas family.

I was kept busy in the morning with incoming freight orders, stocking shelves and placing orders for new inventory. I took my lunch early to run a few personal errands and was back at work by noon. At this point I was working on the floor assisting customers. It was around 1:00 p.m. when a co-worker, Ann, asked me if I had heard about the hostage situation in Cokeville. I was stunned and shocked at the word "hostage." This was a quiet, little town in Wyoming, where nothing exciting happens. As the wife of a deputy sheriff I took comfort in the quiet part of Wyoming. All this changed that day.

When Ann asked me about the hostage situation I ran to the other side of the store to listen to the radio newscast to hear what was going on. This is what I remember about the newscast: A husband and wife team had taken the elementary school in Cokeville hostage and was demanding a ransom from the federal government. When I heard that I knew the guy was crazy and I started to worry about my husband being on patrol that day. Then I received a telephone call from another deputy's wife. She said I should go to the hospital because they were taking my husband there. She did not know what had actually happened but just told me to go to the hospital. She would pick up our boys from daycare. I remember telling the store owner I had to go to the hospital and ran out of the store.

When I arrived at the hospital there was confusion due to the different county and state agencies involved. Nobody was sure which hospital he was being taken to or the nature of his injury. I was a bit frantic when an ambulance pulled up to the hospital entrance.

I ran to the doors and sure enough there was my husband looking pale and dazed but not bleeding or looking harmed in any way. He was on oxygen and struggling to breathe. The smoke from the bomb was toxic and the oxygen was dry, causing his lungs to burn. After a short period of time he was released from the hospital. He wanted to go back to Cokeville to assist with processing the crime scene. All the deputies were still in Cokeville so I drove him back to the school. During the drive to Cokeville he was very quiet, he was trying to find places within himself for all the events of the day. When we arrived at the school it was emotionally difficult for me to watch him walk back into the damaged school.

I never really heard the complete story of the Cokeville hostage situation until recently. We made a special trip to Cokeville to visit the school and to calm some of the emotion that surfaces every May. It was a step in the healing process for us. John and Celeste Jackman were instrumental in assisting us with entry into the school, reuniting us with adults who were children held hostage that day. Just talking and writing about the events of that day has helped heal many wounds I thought we'd left behind. Thank you.

Mike Duran
Cokeville Resident
(Oral History)

I was working for Lynn Dimond at the time. Kevin Dimond and I were headed up to do some fencing. I heard it on the a.m. radio. We turned around and headed back to town. We went to the corner station, Knouse's. I just stayed there. We watched and listened. I was brand new on the fire department. I didn't go. I should have gone but I was new. Looking back now of course, I should have gone.

Corrine Fredrickson
Wife of Town Marshal
(Handwritten Submission)

I remember sitting in the front of our home which is about 1 block from the school. One mother was concerned about her son, who is diabetic.

I said we might need to see if we could fix some food for the kids and see if they would get it in to them. About that time the bomb went off we all ran as fast as we could, expecting to find the worst.

The kids coming out were covered with black smoke. And it was hard to know how bad the burns might be so we had wet blankets someone had brought. And it had started to snow and we took as many as we could to homes in the neighborhood and the EMTs got the worst in the ambulance or school bus to transport.

Jackie Holmes
United States Postal Worker
Cokeville Town Committee Member for Donated Funds
(Oral History)

Joyce Dayton was the postmaster and I was working for her that day. She probably came in and told me or called me on the phone and told me what was going on. As I looked out the window of the post office, there was a van with Arizona plates. That was what people were talking about. I thought, "Oh my gosh! They are here at the post office!" I was pretty scared for a minute. But that was just a coincidence. It wasn't them.

Everyone who came in wanted to know what was going on. I didn't know what was going on. It was scary. I couldn't leave the post office to find out what was going on. I probably had the radio on. I didn't have any family in the bombing.

I think we will always think how fortunate and blessed we were not to have that as bad as it could have been. I still work at the post office, I am the postmaster now, and people still come in and ask about it. People who do come in want to know if this is the place, how did it happen, where the school was. Not as much now but it still happens.

A committee was formed after the bombing and then we met often and ministers and bishops and someone from the council or school district from Star Valley came. We talked about different things, what to do to help. Just different things like that. As it went on and on and on, we didn't meet anymore as that committee. It got to the point where there were just a couple of families that had ongoing medical bills, luckily. It could have been much worse. They got the money. I was on that committee, I was happy to be involved in some way with that. I was honored that they asked me to be on that committee. We met often at first and then through the years we just, you know, pretty much just authorized the checks for people who needed gas money and money to go to the doctor. NaDene Dana and I ended up being the ones who signed the checks. Then it was ten years or was it six, and then they gave the money to the graduating seniors who were in that situation. Then when they were all gone, that was the end.

Jana Hansen Hottel
High School Student, Cousin of Three Student Survivors
(Hand-written Photocopy Submission)

My name is Jana Hottel. At the time of the Cokeville Bombing my name was Jana Hansen and I was living with my aunt, uncle, and cousins, the Walkers. I was in high school at the time.

That particular day I had left school at lunchtime to go home so I could travel to Kemmerer to get my driver's license. Uncle Kevin had to go to town hall, where he was working, to pick up his paycheck. I decided to ride with him. When we got there, he parked out front and told me to stay in the car. Shortly after Uncle Kevin went in an old white full size van pulled up. A girl with long dark hair jumped out of the van and ran into the building. There were two men left sitting in the second seat of the van.

It seemed like it was taking Uncle Kevin a long time. So, I went in to find him. I went in and could hear a lady's voice yelling hysterically, "He will kill them all, you don't understand."

I saw Uncle Kevin standing in front of her trying to talk to her and calm her down. She looked over his shoulder and saw me and tried to walk toward me saying, "You have to listen to me, tell them to listen to me."

At that point Uncle Kevin turned to me, he hadn't known I was there, and told me to go back out into the car and wait and not to come back in.

I knew something wasn't right but I didn't know what or how bad. After what seemed, again, a long time, Uncle Kevin came out to the car. He opened my door and told me to drive home to Aunt Glenna.

"Do not say anything, just go home and stay there. I will be home when I can."

So I did. When I got home I was a little upset but tried not to say anything. After a few minutes I remember telling Aunt Glenna, "Something isn't right. I think something is wrong."

And she questioned me, "Like what? What are you talking about?"

I said I didn't know it just felt like something wasn't right.

At about that time or a short time later we heard Uncle Kevin come home in the green city truck. It came screaming in the driveway and he came running into the house. We could tell right away something major was going on and he wasn't going to tell us.

Aunt Glenna and Uncle Kevin got into an argument and Aunt Glenna told him, "You have to tell us what is going on, you just can't leave."

So he told us what he knew which was that someone named David had the whole elementary school held hostage, had bombs and a huge gun arsenal. It wasn't much but enough to stop us dead in our tracks—it was like shock—almost, now looking back, like an out of body experience—watching yourself go through it but not really going through it.

Aunt Glenna told him it couldn't be true, it was some kind of drill for the firemen and EMTs. Uncle Kevin had to go back to town hall to notify proper personnel. Aunt Glenna and I ran next door to the neighbors, they had just gotten home from buying groceries and were taking them in the house. We informed them of what we knew.

Some time passed and I am not sure how long or what went on. The next thing I remember is that Aunt Glenna and Uncle Kevin were both gone and I was in the backyard standing—I think waiting for my cousin Shane—the oldest of my four cousins and the only other one not in the elementary school—to get home. I think we were instructed to go to Grandma and Grandpa Walker's when Shane arrived home.

Again not knowing how much time passed and we were at Grandma and Grandpa Walker's and Shane suggested we mow Grandpa's yard for him to keep our minds occupied. We were doing that when we heard something. We knew it must have been a bomb going off. I remember running and running and running—closer to downtown toward the elementary school and seeing people everywhere running, kids black with smoke and saying that they were burning and crying and we were looking for my cousins and aunt and uncle and we didn't know where anyone was or if they were alive or dead or OK or anything.

We finally saw Travis, the next oldest, and I remember running to him and hugging him and asking him if he was OK and where Rachel and Katie were. He didn't know, but he seemed OK, just dazed. I took him to a house on Main Street, the Thornocks's, I think. We were still looking for the others.

I went farther down the street to the corner of Main and the street where the school was—it was chaos!! Ambulance and police and people were everywhere and I found Aunt Glenna. She was an EMT and was helping burned children. She asked if I had seen Travis or Katie and I told her I had Travis and he was OK. But not Katie. Rachel was burned and in that house or in an ambulance, she wasn't sure.

We had the water hose and were just hosing kids off as they came up and were crying and stuff. Putting the worst ones in the ambulances and putting others in lines for immediate and less immediate care. Katie was located and OK, also. I don't remember much after that except just staying with Aunt Glenna helping kids. But as for later that evening or night, I am not sure what we did.

For awhile after—a few weeks, maybe months—I remember times of waking up and being damp with tears and sweat from nightmares. Remembering the facts I can do, but to try and remember the feelings and thoughts is hard, it drags everything back and always brings tears and some fear. I am married now with two kids of my own, who are almost as old as I was then. I am very happy and love my family.

Marty Linford
Star Valley High School Student
(Handwritten Submission)

I remember sitting in high school in Star Valley when they announced it over the intercom and I thought, "Oh, crap! My cousins are in there." Then I remember watching it on TV that night.

Jan Petersen Moody
High School Student
(Typed Submission)

When the idea of a book was first presented, I was concerned about the affect it might have on those who were in the Cokeville elementary school and the memories it might ignite. I have family members who were there that day and know that the horror of the event has had a great impact on their lives. But as I visited with one, I came to believe that telling her story might finally begin a healing process that was twenty years past due.

I was a junior in high school when the Cokeville elementary was taken hostage and can still remember the events of that day. I would like to share with you a little of what I wrote in my journal about that day:

Friday was the worst day of my life.

It was going along being a pretty normal day. In the middle of sixth hour, Kevin Walker came and got Mr. Pieper. No one would tell us what was going on. Then Bob Dayton came into the classroom and said that the elementary was being held hostage and there were bombs involved. All of us thought it was a joke. We just couldn't believe this was happening to us.

Mr. Lamborn said over the intercom that we were not to leave school at 3:30. We went on to our seventh hour class. Nobody could do anything. Mr. Lamborn got on the intercom again and said that the people holding the kids hostage wanted two million dollars for each kid and if he didn't get it he'd start shooting. They decided it was better if we went home. They let school out early and we had a prayer all together before we left.

The buses had to take a detour because Main Street was blocked off. While I was sitting at home, Jerry and I got anxious. We went up to the top of the lane and looked across the way with binoculars. We couldn't see a thing. After a while ambulances were going by and we didn't know what had happened. Mom came flying by and we stopped her. She was rushing Jamie to the hospital because she was burned. The bomb had gone off. They had to throw the kids out the window. When we got to the hospital there were all these poor little kids burned. Mr. Miller had been shot in the shoulder.

As I read my journal other memories came to me: I remember trying to comfort a classmate, whose parents and brother were in the building, as we all prayed together. I remember the feeling of panic but then a calming that everything would be all right. I remember Sunday going to church and it was Rick Excell's Mission Farewell. The primary children sang as members of the congregation wept. I remember going back into the building Sunday afternoon and feeling claustrophobic as we entered the small blackened room knowing that it had been filled just a couple days before with terrified children and wondering if any of them would ever be the same. I remember the circus coming to town the week following the bombing and watching children who were bandaged and burned enjoying such a grand event.

Now almost twenty years later, and a mom with five children of my own, I think of the prayer of a mother as she waited, praying desperately for the safety of her child or children. As a reporter for the *Cokeville News*, I wonder what my column would have said that week. I believe I would have included; "I believe an innocence in all of us was taken that day but in its place came a deep faith and hope knowing that a Father in Heaven was watching over the little town of Cokeville that day and spared the lives of so many."

I pray that as this twenty year reunion approaches that we find that lives were mended and faith was restored and that we are all stronger for the trial of the Cokeville elementary school bombing.

Rosa Moseman
Preston, Idaho Newspaper Reporter
(Oral History - Telephone)

I remember the incident from the time I was working at the newspaper in Preston. I talked with Teddy Stamm, who was the editor of the *News-Examiner* at the time. We talked about how much coverage dailies and TV stations had given it, rightfully so. Teddy wanted to talk to law enforcement before doing anything at the *News-Examiner*. I kept expecting to hear of the death of some of the children. There were none.

When they had the hostages in Russia and the bombing at the school in Colorado, we remembered the Cokeville incident. Dozens and hundreds of children were killed and none in Cokeville.

My own personal beliefs? It was a miracle. I believe that there are angels that help us. I am LDS; I believe angels intervene on occasion.

Kathy Mower

Cokeville EMT—Out of Town on May 16,1986
(Oral History)

OK, I don't know really where to start because I had all the girls in my car, OK? My mother was even with us. We were at Connie's state track meet in Casper. I'm sure it was Casper. Anyway, there was the Pope girl, Linda, I can't remember who all was in the car, me, mother, Linda, Connie. I had four of the girls in the backseat. The radio was on. All of a sudden I heard there was a hostage situation in Cokeville. All those girls sat up. I said, "Shhh for a minute." They were yakking and then they sat straight up.

We were going to KMart. Everyone wanted to go shopping. We didn't go shopping. We headed back to the motel. We heard Max Excell was dead and that Miller the teacher was dead. We heard the school was being held hostage. Two people at least held it and they were asking a ransom.

All those girls started bawling in my car on the way to the motel. It was awful. It was a sick, sick feeling. There were a bunch of people in the lobby watching when we got there.

We got there and went to my room. I started calling, trying to find out what was going on. We couldn't get a line into Cokeville. All those kids with brothers and sisters, they were just sick.

I called Bear Lake Hospital and told them who I was and where I was calling from. They told me they had kids and what was going on. Everybody wanted to know about their own. You want to know about your own. We found out exactly what was going on.

The whole state track team did not do well. We did stay until the track team finished and then we headed home. We went home on Saturday. The whole team, everybody, was sad. We didn't find out that the teachers weren't dead until later. Everyone was just devastated. Being in the motel room, it was really a challenge.

I didn't know David Young well but, he looked just like Wyatt Earp. I was in the bar once, and he walked in and acted like he was King Kong. His composure was just so arrogant. Just like, "Don't talk to me. OK?"

You could see on the wall afterward, angels, in the classroom. There were .22 shells all over. There were a zillion in the walls.

People that say there aren't any angels—yes there are. Yes there were. The smoke, you could just see it. Cokeville is blessed. We had angels guarding our children. Guarding people. We went after to check out the room. A lot of people will tell you the same thing. There were white spots and then dark spot, white spots and then dark spots.

I did Bernie's hair all the time. She is Doris Young's daughter. David Young kept calling it the Big Day. There's going to be a big special day. Bernie did not know. I had no idea. I don't blame her. She didn't know.

I wish people weren't still angry. The Youngs died. Why should we have to feed those people the rest of our lives with our anger? We shouldn't do that.

Randy Nate

8th Grader, Two Brothers and Cousins Student Survivors
(Oral History—Telephone)

I think it's a good thing what you're doing.

I was in 8th grade English class. Mr. Birch said, "I just can't believe it." They took us all in the auditorium. Amy Dimond said a prayer. Then we all went home. They weren't going to let us go home and then they let us go early. They said not to stop and add to the chaos. So my younger brother, Rick, and I, that was before Rick got killed, started to go home, and were just pulling into the yard and the radio said the bomb went off.

We turned around and went back. We picked up my brothers and they were all black and covered with soot. We went to Grandma's and just stayed there. Dad was driving a bus. Mom was shopping in Montpelier. She didn't know if she should come home or stay because ambulances would be going that direction.

I think it was a day of miracles for sure. That, and going through his diaries and the things he wrote. He tried the exact bomb he'd built before, which had gone off flawlessly. Then the bomb didn't work. It was a gasoline bomb. I went in and walked through the classroom a few days later when they let the public in.

I had a lot of cousins in it. My brothers, Greg and Brad, had smoke inhalation. The got checked and went home.

The thing that amazed me the most is how strongly the community pulled together on the whole thing. Some parents wanted to go in and storm the school, of course. But the people were all helping each other. Families whose kids weren't as bad as others would help those who had kids that were worse. The whole thing of the community helping each other is the miraculous thing.

We would have lost a generation, K-6, gone. Young planned on killing them all. There was chaos, there was people everywhere. There were parents going out and getting kids as they ran across the lawn and out the door. Frank Lazcanotegui was one up there by the door trying to get them out. Paramedics were helping those who were burned.

When the Columbine High School event happened and some other things, we relive it to some degree. But we don't talk about it all the time. I've never really talked to anyone about it besides my family and my wife.

Once, when I was guiding elk hunters from Michigan, they said, "Were you in that bombing, did you know anyone in it?"

I told them, "Yes, I had two brothers."

"Are they OK?"

"Yeah." And that was the end of it.

I don't know how those other towns are doing it without the church. For weeks, that's what people talked about and bore testimony about.

Gladys Nelson
Cokeville Resident
(Interview)

I wasn't living in Cokeville. My husband had died and I was living with my sister in Santa Maria, California. I was at her house and a niece called telling us to turn on the TV to such and such a channel. We didn't get that channel so we had to turn on a different one. We saw reports on the news.

When I called people in Cokeville, they didn't even know it was going on. What I don't understand—what no one has ever said that I've heard is, what did they do with those two bodies? I knew the man. I didn't *know* him, you know what I mean, but this shows how little I know. I thought he was a good police officer. He used to sit up on the second balcony of the hotel and look around Cokeville. I'd walk home from work and see him sitting up there and I thought, well good, someone finally cares about Cokeville. Someone cares enough to look around and see what was going on in town. That shows how little I know.

Brent Petersen
Family in Bombing
Son-in-law to Doris Young
(Email Submission)

I don't know how to begin, so I'll just start from about a week before the Cokeville grade school incident happened in May 1986.

I was living in Cokeville and had all my life, except for two years serving a mission for The Church of Jesus Christ of Latter-Day Saints in Texas, at the Dallas Mission. I was exposed to a whole different world on my mission but this experience was a lot different and I hope I've been able to deal with it in a positive way.

As I said, I grew up in Cokeville and my wife, Bernie, moved to Cokeville in 1976. In the spring of 1986 we had two boys, Ryan, age 5, and Jon, age 4. I worked for Utah Power and Light as plant mechanic. I drove to Kemmerer, Wyoming, almost every day for work. I also helped on the family ranch when possible.

The Sunday afternoon before the bombings, my mother-in-law, Doris Young, had come up from Tuscon, Arizona. She pulled into the yard and said, "If my daughter isn't going to call me for Mother's Day then I'm going to Cokeville and see her." It was a great surprise to see her, especially since she didn't have David with her. Needless to say, a few says later he came around doing other things, as I later found out.

The week went about like any other week. I went to work and then, on Friday, I had plans to go haul hay with my dad. We—my dad , two uncles and a cousin and I—were going over to the Bridger Valley area to haul hay that the ranch had bought back to Cokeville.

Friday morning I got up early and went out to the ranch to get the trucks ready. We came into town to get some things and I was going to see my wife and kids before I left. Bernie had come up to the corner to see me and when I talked to her, I could tell that she was a little down. I asked her if she wanted to go to the movie later that night when I got home. She said all right but that still didn't cheer her up. I talked to her for a while but she still wasn't happy, so I asked if she and the boys would like to go with me to get a load of hay.

She surprised me by saying yes, because she never went with me when I was working on the ranch, especially when it came to hauling hay.

I told her to go to the store and get something for her and the kids to eat because it would be well after noon before we would be finished loading the trucks. She got the food and she and the boys met me at the ranch south of town about forty-five minutes later.

We got to Mountain View around 10:30-11:00 and we started to load all three trucks, which took a few hours. Sometime in the afternoon, as we were loading one of the trucks, my cousin was listening to the radio and I heard something about a bomb in Cokeville. I asked him what was going on and he said some guy tried to blow up the grade school. I thought to myself, David wouldn't do something like that. I knew David had come around a few days before, but I hadn't seen or talked to him. I didn't hear any more about the bomb because I went back to work.

That was all I knew until I turned on the radio about half way between Mountain View and Kemmerer. The local radio station had announced that David Young and his wife had taken the Cokeville grade school hostage and that a bomb had gone off. Several people had been injured and that David and his wife had been killed. Life for us changed that instant. My wife was hysterical and I was trying to stop the truck as fast as I could without wrecking. I got the truck stopped and got her calmed down and she got the kids calmed down. All we could do is drive on home and find out what had happened.

As we came passed Kemmerer and headed to Cokeville, we passed several ambulances with lights on and many people coming from Cokeville. When we got to the ranch south of Cokeville, I pulled the truck into the yard. My mom had left a note in our vehicle that said we needed to come to their home as soon as we got town. When we got there, we found out that we couldn't go to our home because the ATF (Alcohol, Tobacco, Firearms) Department and police were going through our home to see if David had left a bomb or something there.

The next day my wife and I had found out that David had planned this "big thing" and that he had taken everybody in the grade school hostage, saying that he had a bomb and would kill everyone if he didn't get what he demanded. We also found that David and Doris had gone out to our house to get Bernie or to see her. They didn't know that she and the boys had gone with me that day. I don't know what would have happened if Bernie and the boys had been home.

As the days passed we were hounded by reporters trying to get interviews. We would turn on the TV and there would be something about the bombing and we still didn't know what David and Doris had been trying to do and why.

One thing I was grateful for was my family being there for us and for their support. We also had some great friends who supported us because we found out that there were some people that thought that Bernie had something to do with it. Bernie never did know what was planned, she just thought that her mother had come to visit her.

A couple of weeks after the bombing I was able to go into the schoolroom where everyone had been held hostage. The classroom had been left like was when the bomb went off. On the wall about three feet above the ground was a silhouette of a person with arms extended outward. The room was blackened from the smoke except for that spot on the wall.

We had talked with some friends of ours, the Hartley family, sometime afterward and they were telling us of the experience that their son had in the school before the bomb went off, and later of many other stories that the children told. There were angels that were there that day and someone was there to save many from getting hurt. I know that someone was watching over me and my family that day because they could have been there, also.

I was able to talk to investigators on the case and they told me that the bomb was designed to blow the entire building up and everyone in it would have been killed but it was like someone had pulled the plug or muffled the blast.

It's been almost twenty years since that happened and I still have people ask me if I knew anything about the bombing in Cokeville. For a long time I didn't want to say anything but then, the more I realized the miracles that happened that day, the more I would talk and let people know that miracles do happen and we don't understand why this happens or why this doesn't. Things have changed some in these last twenty years and some changes were very challenging and hopefully everyone realizes that God is watching over us at all times.

I don't live in Cokeville anymore but it is a place I love and I'm grateful I grew up there. I work at different power plant but I still find people asking about the bombing in Cokeville. I have four boys now that are all grown up, two of whom were born a few years after the bombing. My youngest son will graduate in May 2006.

Life keeps on going and there are changes and challenges that come into our lives every day, it's just a matter of how we accept these challenges—as stumbling blocks or stepping stones. I'm grateful for what I have been given and what I can give back because life is a test as to how we deal with it. I know miracles happen each and every day and our Heavenly Father is watching over us and trying to help us. Jesus Christ is alive and He and the angels were there to protect those children and adults in Cokeville that day in 1986. He's been there ever since in my life and I'm grateful for that.

Gwen Petersen
Grandmother of Three Student Survivors
(Email Submission)

Being the seminary teacher in Cokeville, I had just taken invitations to the elementary teachers for seminary graduation, and was driving away when I saw a strange looking van with painted windows drive up to the school. I wondered who it belonged to. I drove on down to the post office where I met and exchanged greetings with elementary principal, Max Excell. Neither of us was aware of what was going on at the school.

After running a few errands, I returned home. Shortly after, I received a very disturbing phone call from my daughter Cheryl, frantically telling me that the children at the elementary were being held hostage. Three of her children were in the school. Being the news reporter for the town of Cokeville and the grandmother to these three children, I rushed to the school, only to find that I couldn't get close or I might endanger the lives of the children. I ran to a neighboring house, Barbara Bartschi's, to call the *Kemmerer Gazette* and inform them as to what was going on. She was on the phone and the crises had already been reported to the *Gazette*.

I waited around anxiously for some time before deciding to take our exchange student, Edward Delgado, to a dental appointment in Montpelier. I kept the radio on for any news and when we got about fifteen miles out of town, an announcer shouted out that the elementary school had been bombed. I whirled the car around and headed back to Cokeville. By the time I got there, most of the children were gone, either to neighboring hospitals or home. The bodies of David and Doris Young were in bags on the front lawn of the school.

We drove back to Montpelier to the hospital to check on the children there. I was surprised when my daughter Cheryl came running out of the hospital to report, with no shoes on. My granddaughters were

OK, I was so thankful. But my nephew's daughter, Billie Jo Hutchinson, was badly burned.

I was shocked in the aftermath of this event, the effect it had on the hostages. I was walking partners with Janel Dayton and Carol Petersen, both teachers at the elementary. One morning after the bombing, we were walking up to the dump when a strange car went by. Carol immediately said, "Who was that?" I could hear the fear in her voice. She said it always bothered her to see a stranger. Then Janel told us of an experience she had had when she was carrying groceries into her home. Her arms were full so she hadn't shut the screen door. The wind blew it shut with a bang and it terrified her. I tried to understand what my friends were going through but there was no way I really could. My granddaughters seemed to do OK at first but the nightmare has never completely gone away.

Robert "Robbie" Scott Petersen
Serving LDS Mission
(Oral History)

I was serving a mission for the Church of Jesus Christ of Latter-day Saints in the Japan, Osaka mission. I was in Kuzaha. I happened to be in a library and there was a newspaper that I saw. On the front cover, I didn't see the headlines but there was a picture. At first I was thinking, that person looks familiar. Then I realized I knew that person. I can't remember who I recognized, I think a teacher. I read the caption. The only thing I remember was COKEVILLE. Oh my gosh!

I was sick. I read the story and I was sick. I knew the people involved, that was my hometown. Stuff like that shouldn't happen in a small town like that. I knew him, David, he was the cop. I had dated his daughter, Princess. Also Brent, my brother, was married to Bernie, Doris's daughter.

After a bit, everyone knew I was from Cokeville. It was big news and Church headlines and all that. The guy thought if the parents didn't pay the Mormon Church would. I had some cousins in the bombing. After receiving so much mail from people at home about the bombing, I got tired of reading it so I wouldn't open any thicker letters. I wanted to concentrate on the work at hand.

LaJean Pieper
Cokeville Resident
(Typed Submission)

It is difficult to express in words, how a person feels when an emergency pager goes off. Anxiety, sadness, fear, apprehension, and an adrenaline rush are just a few. That day, when the pager sounded its alarm, it seemed like any other normal spring day. My oldest child, Benjamin, hadn't been home for very long from the morning session of kindergarten. My husband, Richard, was a volunteer fireman for the Cokeville Fire Department and also an emergency medical technician for the Cokeville ambulance service. Since he wasn't "on call," he had left his EMT radio home that day while he was away at work.

The words of the dispatch are still clear in my mind, "We need all firemen and EMTs to report to the city hall immediately." Richard reported later that he had arrived at the city hall and found someone from the State Emergency Management Office (who just happened to be there by coincidence). Richard thought they were calling him to a big mock emergency drill that they had been planning. But, it was certainly not a mock emergency! This became apparent when one of the community members who was there at the city hall had learned of the emergency situation and became hysterical. It was very obvious that a true emergency was taking place because the person from the state office did not step forward and tell them that it was "just a drill."

My cousin's wife, Gayle Chadwick, was also an EMT and had her ambulance pager with her at the school. She was the librarian there at that time and when the pager went off, therefore the perpetrator was alerted that she had it. He took the pager into his possession and listened to everything that was going on with the police department and any communication that was taking place over the radio.

The information being relayed on the radio was horrible! "We have a man and his wife who have taken the Cokeville elementary school hostage. They have gathered everyone into one single room. They have rifles lined up along the walls of the room. There is a bomb roped off in the center of the room with a detonator attached to it. The perpetrator is holding the detonator, and all he has to do is pull it. If they see anyone come close to the school, or even see anyone through the windows, they will start shooting the children."

It seemed like an eternity, listening to all of the heart wrenching information that was being given. An eternity, because many dear friends, loved ones, and innocent children were in the school being held by someone who was serious about hurting them. My first thought was to turn the radio off so I wouldn't have to listen to the threats, but I couldn't do so, as I felt like I needed to know what was going on.

About an hour or so had passed, and then another emergency tone sounded on the pagers. This time it was, "We need all EMTs and firefighters to move to the scene. The bomb has apparently been detonated!" Richard reported that, as he was with his fellow firefighters a little distance away when they heard the bomb go off. His heart sank as he thought to himself, we are going to have all kinds of dead teachers and children.

The fear that many people had been harmed and killed was indescribable. As the firefighters, EMTs, and police officers approached and assessed the scene, they found only two dead bodies—those of the perpetrators. Our family thanked our Father in Heaven for having this miracle take place. Yes, many people were burned and many had emotional scars, but not one single soul from Cokeville had lost their life. All of the innocent people had been spared and we will never forget the Lord's guardian angels watching over the wonderful people who were in the elementary school that day.

Bette Rentfro
Cokeville High School Secretary
(Handwritten Submission)

When I returned to school after lunch, about 1:00 p.m., I walked into the north entrance and could see no one in any of the rooms or halls. I entered my office. I had a really strange feeling, everything was much too quiet. I left my office. Still, no one was around. In the hall, Steve Taylor walked toward me. Looking at him I knew something had happened. He told me what was going on at the elementary school. I didn't believe him. I told him he wasn't being very funny. He then took me to Principal Lamborn's office, where several teachers were. Then I knew Steve was telling the truth. Everyone was in tears or close to it. For a time no one could speak. The high school students were all together in one room, you could have heard a pin drop. There was crying. Some were sitting as if in a trance. Not a word was spoken.

Later, as I talked with some of the students, they asked if I knew what was happening. Many of them had family in the elementary school. The Jack Mitchell children were really upset as their parents and brother were in the elementary school. Delbert, my husband, was in the building, also. I was very concerned. I was concerned about everyone—students and faculty.

Principal Lamborn asked me if I would stay at the high school and answer the phone, as that was the only phone anyone could get at the school. I received calls from all over the United States, even one call from England. Newspapers all wanted to know what was happening.

Mr. Lamborn came over often to let me know what was happening. It was such a traumatic experience for everyone. Mr. Lamborn ran into the office at one point and asked me to call Teresa Miller and tell her John had been shot. He couldn't tell me how badly he was hurt at that time. This was one of the hardest calls I had ever made. I couldn't believe how calm I felt as I talked to Teresa. I was so relieved when I found out John would be OK. I was relieved when Mrs. Dana called and told me Delbert was out of the building and safe.

The hostage situation was something no one in Cokeville will ever forget. Everyone has been deeply touched by this experience. Each of us knows how blessed we have been as a community. We are so grateful that everyone was all right.

Pat Swenson
Mother of Absent Afternoon Kindergartner
(Oral History)

I recall the day of the bombing well. Britney, my kindergarten age daughter, was ready to go to school that afternoon. She was in the afternoon class and was always ready to go to school. My younger daughter, Shantell, had a doctor appointment that day and I had left Britney on many previous occasions as Shantell and I attended appointments. There was almost a feeling of guilt every time I left Britney.

This particular May day, I decided to excuse Brit from school to spend time with me and Shantell. I had no feeling of anything out of the ordinary that day except that I knew that I needed Britney to go to Salt Lake with us for the day.

As the day went on and I found out what had happened at the Cokeville elementary school where Britney would have been, I was very grateful that I had taken Brit with me that day.

I returned to my Cokeville home to find helicopters scattered across the football field in front of our house, police cars and ambulances galore, and a lot of people running in different directions.

There was something telling me I needed to take Britney that day. It was a feeling I had. She was ready to go school and I took her with me. I think it was a blessing that I took her.

Wendi Wixom Taylor
Sister of Student Survivor
(Typed Submission)

A whole twenty years after the Cokeville bombing tragedy, I still find it difficult to write about it. Not because it is so difficult emotionally, but because I connect with it on so many different levels. I guess I don't know what part to share, and what to leave out.

On the afternoon of May 16, 1986, my husband was returning home from a road trip. We had moved hundreds of miles away from where my family lived in Cokeville, yet I sensed something was terribly wrong. This was very unlike me. I'm known for being steady and calm. But I began crying, sobbing and sensed that a loved one was in danger. Was my husband in a serious accident? I thought how awful it was that I had never asked him where he wanted to be buried....

As it turned out, he was alive and well and listening to the news broadcast about the hostages at my brother's elementary school. He feared I had heard it, too, and had pulled over to find a phone to call me. Assured that he was OK, I now knew my brother was in trouble. The bomb had exploded. I called my parents' home—no answer.

The next morning a neighbor came over with a newspaper, the *Tucson Daily Star*. "Isn't this your mom?" he asked. On the front page was a large photo of my mother, her eyes closed, embracing my twelve year old brother. His eyes were wide open. Haunted eyes, I thought, and then I noted the jacket my mom was wearing. It was the one she always wore on our camping trips. I thought it would smell like campfire, and I hoped my brother would find comfort in that.

In addition to the wife/sister/daughter perspective, I am also a schoolteacher. How well I know those tender, protective feelings a teacher has for the students entrusted to her care. I know how closeknit Cokeville is. Teachers watch entire families grow up from kindergarten on. When the book *Trial by Terror* (now published as *To Save the*

Children) first came out, I relived the incident through each teacher's eyes. The appalling invasion of a classroom, the compelling need to do something to shield the children from trauma, the helplessness and the fear that must be disguised because they are teachers. I felt all that, right along with them.

So how do I write about being a sister to a hostage, knowing that my other siblings were victimized as well, standing in the parking lot of a school, hoping nobody died?

How do I write about my father's writing, the most objective, fact-finding man I've ever met, reporting that some students had seen angels which protected them from death?

And, twenty years later, how do I look at a society that no longer considers "school shootings" as front page news?

I always hoped the teachers wouldn't blame themselves for walking their kids into a death trap. Hindsight is great, but in 1986 people just did not consider elementary schools to be a center stage for violence. The fact that those children were so well behaved under such catastrophic stress speaks well of every educator in that classroom.

Norene Thompson
Cokeville Resident
Grandmother of Two Student Survivors
(Oral History)

I was living in my house, on Sage Street, just down from the elementary school. I gave shelter to children of school teachers and parents who had left town on ambulances to be with other children. I had one of Jack and Jean Mitchell's boys and noticed after high school let out, that his older brother was riding up and down the street on his bicycle. I motioned for him to come over. He had gone home and found no one there and was riding around looking for someone.

Since my home was directly across the street from the football field, the children watched three helicopters land and park there. They wanted to go look at the helicopters. It had started to snow and was getting cold. They had left their coats in the school, but I found some old sweatshirts to put on them and took them across the street for a closer look.

The children wanted to watch themselves on TV and would comment on what the different reporters said, such as, "That isn't what happened" or "Yes, that's right." They also wanted to keep switching from channel to channel to get the different views.

I had two grandchildren in the school, too.

Witness To Miracles

Elvina Thornock
Cokeville Resident
(Oral History)

The bombing of the grade school, 1986, a Salt Lake radio station called me to see what I saw. I told them that I did not see anything because it was the grade school several blocks from where I lived. I don't know why they called me. They probably called someone and asked who lived by the school and they got my name.

The elementary school was brand new at the time so out of town people would not have known that the children were not all in the same building. Up to that time, the elementary school children were all in the north end of the old high school. And then another party called me from out of town. They'd heard it on the radio and asked how come the helicopters had landed on my yard? I said, "They didn't, they landed on the football field."

Then my son called me from Alaska. He, too, had heard it on the radio. He'd run in and called the radio station there in Alaska and asked them what they knew about it. They told him what he had heard on the radio was fact. And then, he told me, "Mom, when I heard it on the radio that the school had been bombed, I saw you out working in the garden and when the bomb went off, the bricks falling down on you." (I am right across the street from the high school). He didn't know that there was a new grade school. My daughter in California didn't know that it was the grade school, either. She tried and tried to call me but all the lines were tied up. She didn't get through until two in the morning.

There were several miracles that there weren't as many people hurt as there could have been. If it had been meant to be, the thing would have gone off. There would have been no saving anybody. Yeah, it was a miracle. The thing that I think about, is those kids who were burned, how good they look and how good they are doing. Things are going well for them. It could have been just the opposite.

Emma Lue Thornock
Grandmother of Seven Student Survivors
(Quote from Journal, with permission from her husband, Russell)

About 1:00 Lydia Harmon and I were in the front room quilting and the phone rang. It was from the sheriff's office in Kemmerer wanting to let Russell know of the situation at the school, and that was all she would tell me. I said to Lydia that's a funny call. The next thing, cops were flying by and fire trucks across the road...

Children were brought here in our house and we treated them for first and second degree burns. Jay Metcalfe being the worst and little Morfeld girl and the Jamison boy. (Emma Lue's husband, Russell, inserts here that the Hutchinson girl was the worst hurt.)...

The man...used to be a cop here in town. Boy Cokeville knows to pick the winners for cops. Boy we can be thankful that the bomb wasn't a more blasting one and the children weren't hurt any worse.

Jenny Wixom Thurber
Sister of Student Survivor
(Typed Submission)

I can't explain how or why. I just knew everything would be all right. Somebody was threatening to hurt my brother (Kamron) and then I reminded myself of reality and how it WASN'T going to be all right. When I heard what was happening, I wanted to get inside his school and be part of it. I had to know. But my thoughts were furious and sometimes they become your first priority.

I wasn't scared. I knew everything would be fine. Something or someone told me and I listened. But also I was mad. Too mad to be calmed, too mad to believe. But my heart won and my thoughts subsided. And I understood and believed. I believed until I heard everyone listening to their thoughts and their thoughts smothered mine.

I saw their faces and doubted myself and thought I must be wrong. The adults were worried and they must have known more than I did. And then the news gave exaggerated stories about the bomb going off and children screaming with blood running down their skin. Everyone panicked. Everyone panicked me. My heart lost and my thoughts won. I didn't want them to win but I let them. I lost my comfort and my belief. I saw my brother on the news come out of the building and he was OK. But I already knew that before; I just forgot. Something or someone told me, before the camera ever did. And I got my brother back and everything was right again.

On May 16, 1986, I learned to trust myself, my spirituality, and not follow anyone else's thoughts or beliefs. I could have been more comfort to others; instead, I let others take mine away from me. Sometimes thoughts are dangerous. I learned at that time, spirituality isn't in a church building; it's in our hearts, and it is so easy to let someone make you doubt your belief. Those children in the school building were so much stronger. They listened to the angels they saw, and to their hearts, and they survived.

Brian Toomer
Uncle of Student Survivor
Serving LDS Mission
(Oral History)

I was serving on a mission for the Church of Jesus Christ of Latter-day Saints in Dearborn, Michigan.

I had a member call me, "Aren't you from Cokeville, Wyoming?"

"Yeah."

"I just saw your town on the news, a school was taken hostage and a bomb went off."

I said, "No." I knew it wasn't my town. "No, you have the wrong town. Not Cokeville."

They said, "You need to come over and see the news."

They finally convinced me to go. I saw the news. That night the mission president called and asked if I had family in the school. The next day I got the *Detroit Press* and it was all over the paper. Sounds like it was a miracle.

Shirley Toomer
Grandmother of Student Survivor
(Oral History)

I was home tending my grandson, Bradley, while Don and Gwen substituted at the high school. I was out on the front lawn and Orson Nate was driving by and stopped and told me they had taken the Elementary School hostage. I asked what grade and he said, "the whole school!" It just got worse from there. It was the most horrible time of my life. I don't even know how many hours it was. I probably walked up and down that road (Sage Street) a hundred times packing the baby. They wouldn't let us go across the street.

We heard the bomb and people started screaming, "The bomb went off!" I'm not sure how we knew there was a bomb. I think my husband, John, heard at the corner and came back and told us. There were some fathers who said they were going to go home and get their guns and kill the Youngs, but they wouldn't let them near the school.

Then we heard the kids come out screaming. Kids were coming out all directions screaming. John saw Jennie running and he went and picked her up. She was screaming, "Put me down!" and "Let me go!" She did that until she realized it was her grandpa. He was by Art Robinson's house when the bomb went off and they all went running to the school.

When the bomb went off, I went back down to the corner. I saw John with Jennie. After the bomb went off, she was crawled on her hands and knees past the bathroom door. David Young was shooting. That's when John Miller got shot.

There were ambulances from Kemmerer, Star Valley, and Montpelier. Jennie had some burns on her back and knee but that was about it. We checked her out. Her mom took her to a doctor later, but she was all right.

The school psychologist worked with all of them. Two or three days afterward they went back to the school. Doc Sandall said it was the best therapy for Jennie—going back. I'll never forget going in the room and seeing, in the corner, an image of a person with his arms out. It's hard to describe what it looked like. Heavenly Father was watching His kids. It was something.

It was something seeing those helicopters on the football field.

Later, looking at some family pictures Jennie said, "I know these people." They were pictures of my mother and my Aunt Ruth. I said, "Jennie, no you don't. They were dead before you were born." She told me, "I've seen them before. They helped me out."

It brings you closer to the church. You say lots and lots of prayers. I very definitely believe it was a miracle. Those two (the Youngs) were killed and no one else. There were some burned, yes, but it was a miracle. After twenty years I say we should believe in miracles because miracles do happen. Just stay close to the Lord.

Shane Walker

Seventh Grade Student Brother of Three Student Survivors
(Typed Submission)

My name is Shane Walker. I was in 7th Grade when the elementary school was taken hostage. Our Junior High/High School met in the auditorium where they told us about the situation. They told us that people were doing all they could to get the students out of the elementary school safely. They told us we were going to be dismissed, but we needed to stay far away from the elementary school.

It was a shock to say the least. My mind began racing and I felt panic. I thought about my brother Travis and my sister Rachel and my sister Katie in that school. I wondered if someone was coming to take our school hostage. I remember thinking, "I want out of this school now!" A group prayer was given and we were dismissed. I ended up at my grandpa's house with my cousin Jana. We told my grandpa what was happening, but we didn't tell my grandma because we didn't want her to worry.

I decided we should mow the lawn to keep our minds somewhat occupied. During that time I was trying to hope for the best. I wanted to know the motive for the hostage situation. I wanted them to give the criminals whatever they wanted so that my family could be safe. I also wondered why someone didn't just shoot the evil people responsible.

The criminals, David Young and his wife, were more deranged than I could have imagined. They were crazy enough to carry out their plan to blow up the school. There was no simple solution. There was nothing we could do but wait and pray. Many prayers were offered throughout the town and inside the school that day. I didn't realize it then, but those prayers were being answered in miraculous ways.

After awhile, I began to see elementary school kids being brought home by their parents. I ran to tell my grandpa that we needed to get over to the school to see what happened.

At the school it was chaos because the bomb had gone off. Kids were running around everywhere. Adults were trying to account for all of the children. Paramedics from all over were giving medical attention.

Eventually I was reunited with my family and we took my sister over to Bear Lake so she could get help for her burns. We had maternal grandparents and cousins over there that we stayed with. The magnitude of what had just happened began to sink in.

My mom was a paramedic and my dad was a firefighter so they had both been in close proximity to the building. I started to think about the fact that in one split second I could have lost my entire family. I wanted us to all stay together in Bear Lake where it seemed safer to me. I wanted to tell them that I loved them over and over. That tendency never left me, neither did the feeling that I could lose them. I am so grateful that I was spared the loss of my family. The time I have had with them is priceless.

There were many miracles that occurred during that tragedy to prevent any innocent lives from being lost. The only deaths were those of David Young and his wife. Details of those miracles aren't mine to tell, but I will share the lessons that I have carried with me from that experience: People like to be in control, yet there are some events in life that are beyond control.

I write this in the wake of Hurricane Katrina. As I watch the devastation and the losses of those people, I'm aware that not everything happens the way our situation did. Even people who believe in God may still wonder how God could let such tragedies happen. I don't have all the answers, but I know that He doesn't leave us alone during those times. If we will turn to Him, He will strengthen us and comfort us. It may take time, but He will give us the power to heal. If we trust Him we can overcome anything, move on and enjoy life.

Pam Weston
Cokeville High School Teacher
(Typed Submission)

May 16, 1986, is a day that will live forever in my memory. As much as I'd like to forget it, it remains too vivid. That was the day David Young and his wife entered Cokeville Elementary and held the school hostage. This deplorable act was unknown to the rest of the town for a while. Mr. Excell, elementary principal, was able to call out and alert the authorities.

I was teaching several 8th grade boys in a literature class. We were involved in a "good" story when over the intercom Mr. Lamborn, high school principal, announced that the elementary school was being held hostage, further instructing us that we should remain calm, avoid the area near the elementary, and that the buses would soon arrive to take the students home. After this announcement my students and I looked at each other in horror and amazement. We then thought that perhaps it was another of Mr. Metcalfe's ways to make a point to his American History class about some aspect of history.

Hearing a lot of commotion in the hallway I went to check things out. The look on Mr. Lamborn's face assured me that this was no American History gag. I returned to my classroom and informed the boys that it was the real thing. Justin Pope, one of my students, began pacing back and forth. He walked over to me and said, "Mrs. Weston do you think they'll exchange me for my little sister?" I assured him that "they" wouldn't because he was too strong and people who do such terrible things usually pick on young and innocent children.

I walked back out into the hall and many students were sobbing about the possibility that their little brothers and sisters might be hurt. Several students were extremely worried about their mother, father, or both who were teachers there. I asked Mr. Lamborn if we could have a word of prayer to help the students and for the safety of the elementary. He announced over the intercom for all students and staff to meet in the auditorium. After we were assembled, he said the most heart-rending, wonderful prayer. I still get goose bumps remembering how it seemed to calm and assure us that things would be OK. The buses arrived and students boarded them for home. Students who lived nearby walked to their homes.

An eerie gloom rested in my heart...I felt absolutely useless. I should do something! But what? As I headed home I stopped at the crosswalk and asked those who seemed to be in charge if there was anything I could do to help. I can't remember whom it was who said, "Just go home. There's nothing you can do." Oh, that dreadful gloom! I tuned in to KMER radio station and listened to the broadcaster giving updates to the hostage situation. As I turned down the lane to my home, he hollered, "The bomb went off, the bomb went off!" Panic filled my heart, tears streaked down my cheeks; there I was safe and sound as those elementary students, teachers and staff were in harm's way. I had no immediate family involved in the bombing, but oh, so many dear friends and fellow teachers were there.

Soon the announcer said that ambulances from Montpelier, Star Valley, and Kemmerer were pulling into the parking lot to give assistance and transport injured to area hospitals. Several youngsters were also taken to the Logan Regional Hospital. That evening I just had to go check on the condition of the children. I just couldn't remain at home. We drove to the hospital in Logan and visited with Verlene Bennion, an aid at the school, and several children who had been near the "taped area." Their fathers were at the bedside of their little ones. Those youngsters were children of some of the high school teachers.

The next day my daughter, June Marie, and I went to check on our neighbors, the Joe and Cheryl Buckley children and the Cornia children. They all seemed shaken, but fine physically. We went on to Montpelier and visited with the children there. We stopped in at Cokeville and visited with those folks who were standing near the school. I needed to know what had happened. Tina Cook gave a stirring and thorough account. While visiting with Herman Teichert he stated something to the effect, "The Lord held a trial and the guilty were punished."

Steve Wiscombe Jr.
Brother of Student Survivors
(Email Submission)

Short memories of May 16, 1986, Cokeville Wyoming

I was just two months shy of my fifth birthday at the time and so my memories of the event are somewhat short, yet they are some of my first memories and even now they are very vivid. I suppose it is the feeling that I remember most—a grateful and whole feeling that filled our home for weeks afterward.

Mom made me take naps every day. Some days I would elude her and sneak next door to the Jameson's after she had drifted off to sleep. But often enough, with her loveable sleepy-time rhymes and songs, Mom would lull me into blissful sleep. May 16th happened to be one of those days. I slept through the terror of it all. I keenly remember the image of my three siblings—Josh, Byron, and Steph—all together in the bathtub. I laughed at first, thinking how silly that was, and wanted to join them. Quickly enough, though, I realized that something frightening had happened. I could feel it in Mom's presence—the way she was leaning over the tub cleaning black soot off Byron's face and by the trembling of her pretty hands. And the bathroom smelled strange, like burning hair, though I wouldn't have known that then. No one spoke.

We still joke today about how Josh, who was in kindergarden then, tripped on the way out and was trampled by most of the kids in the room before he could get out. They told the kids to run home and find their parents. Josh refused to leave his stylish banana seat bike. He still gets really tense about loud noises like popping balloons. Byron was, at least in our own family lore, one of the small group of "older boys" that was planning some kind of tactical coup against David's wife. I can't remember if it was Chinese stars or a switch-blade knife—true to form Byron has always been courageous and innovative. Steph was our great storyteller. I'm not sure how much of that habit may have been prompted by the events of that day, but for years to come Steph always told fascinating tales about the four of us losing our way home and brushing with death—though never fatally—we were always willfully braving the storm. And always we triumphed and found our way home.

Photo courtesy of The Kemmerer Gazette

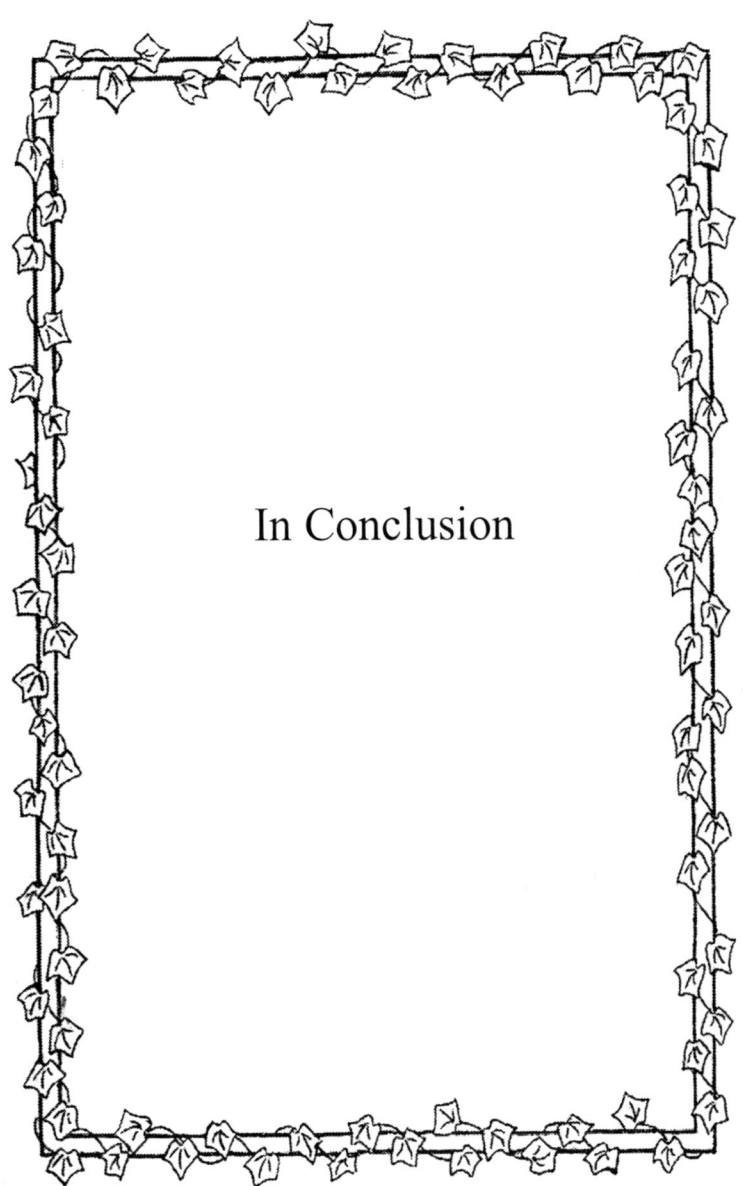

In Conclusion

Photo courtesy of Lincoln County Sheriff's Office

Vern A Cox

High Country Counseling and Resource Centers
Marriage and Family Therapist
(Oral History—Telephone)

I really enjoyed working with them. I had an opportunity to learn a lot of things. Both because we had a lot of training and because of the kids we worked with. I hope that the "leaders" of the community of Cokeville learned something because they were not very encouraging at first. They wanted the kids to pull their bootstraps up and say, "We will get on with life, right now."

It was a wonderful opportunity for me, to be able to help then. Those kids had quite an ordeal and I thought they went through it very courageously.

When you have an experience like this you do need to talk about it. It doesn't mean you are weak to talk about it. But the feelings don't go away without talking about them. It's time to let it go. But by simply saying it, they won't go away. You have to have resolved your beliefs and feelings and thoughts about the experience in a way that allows you to move on.

The event does not make you who you are. We have to say, "It's not who I am, it doesn't define me, it was horrible, frightening, unfair, unjust. But I can move on."

I like the idea of forgiveness. "I can no longer blame my behavior on something that happened." That's moving on. Even if you don't feel like Heaven's Hand was in it for you, you can still feel like like you lived through fear, you got past it. "I am now the creator of my own destiny."

Nohl "Doc" Sandall
Psychologist
Typed Submission

It is useful, from a perspective of twenty years later, to examine some effects and outcomes of what happened on May 16, 1986. Accounts of what specifically happened have been numerous. This will be more of note about the recovery process that began at the time, and realistically, probably still continues.

There was need, at the time, to recognize that such events cannot just "be forgotten about," or "put out of your mind." There was a need to deal with those memories more directly and in a manner that insured the least interference possible with future and long term success for all involved. This had some potential to be problematic. While all had shared the same experience, each person experienced it in their own way.

Two major assets emerged that helped accomplish this. One was the great strength and capacity for support within the community. The other was the outpouring of help from across the country from well intentioned sources who wanted to help in any way possible. The many facets from both resources needed to be coordinated to maximize effectiveness in response to individual needs. From the vantage point of one closely involved with many aspects of the recovery it is difficult to think of ways this could have been improved.

This is not to say that all is now totally well. As indicated, events such as the one noted here are not, "just forgotten." They will always be remembered. In that sense, many personal and other efforts continue to insure that memories interfere as little as possible with achieving goals, maintaining quality relationships, achieving peace within oneself, and living successful lives.

A number of valuable principles have emerged that serve well. One is that individual resilience, along with families, loved ones, and communities coming together are of immeasurable value in strengthening, helping and mending lives.

An other is that there are many many good people, 'out there,' who deeply and sincerely care, and when shown the way, make an important difference.

Still another is that individuals, with God's and each other's help, can triumph over potentially harmful experiences.

It is also meaningful to know that opportunities for growth, learning more about ourselves and how to improve our lives are always around us, even in the most trying conditions.

Taking advantage of them means a lot.

Twenty years ago many good people did many good things really well. That needs to be recognized. It continues now and it is important.

Transformation

HOSTAGE was my NAME,
for just a single day.
But manage tormenting thoughts within—
it's more than I can say.

That day should be left behind, ignored
as just ONE page in my book,
It's in the past. It's done.
There's MORE to me – Just look!

Talk about it? I won't, or simply can't.
Now, I only try to let it go.
I'd like to tuck that day away,
to keep the thoughts remote. But... NO!

For history has recorded it,
and people sometimes bring it up.
With narrowed eyes I grumble to myself,
"That day is MINE! My personal cup."

How can anyone have gratitude
for a day that haunts and sears?
It's hard to speak a single part
of the hurt, the pain, the fears.

When will the past, stay PAST?
"Let it be gone," I often say.
I'd like to leave it all behind.
I'm not grateful for that day.

Enough! Let it rest! Be done!
I've LIVED another day.
I'll just breathe and grow and age
for I've chores to do today.

As years go by, I've known good times,
yet buried memories remain.
There seems so little left to me
but some thanks I must contain.

Am I fully thankful? And for what?
Parents and family gave me much.
But on that day, I could have…DIED!
Yes, I *am* grateful for such.

Thankful to whom, I ask myself.
Heaven helped us some.
My life, it's true, was spared.
To be thankful must surely come.

While thoughts of thanks may comfort me,
and time some pains restrain,
when the past IS gone, one truth rings on…
Heaven's hand will still remain.

A life I have! I AM ALIVE!
despite those somber memories.
But to withhold my thanks from God Divine's
no longer an option for me.

I ask: could others learn from me?
What should that day within me mold?
Because of my eternal gratitude,
is it time my story's told?

Despite that unchanged past,
and deepest cries of pain,
my THANKS come, too. Now I see
that SURVIVOR, is my name.

Collective reflections from stories for the book,
Witness To Miracles.
The Cokeville Miracle Foundation Book Committee.

Photo courtesy of Lincoln County Sheriff's Office

The 154 Survivors

"The Promise of Cokeville is passed from generation to generation and from neighbor to neighbor, through love and concern, acts of kindness, and a belief in the Almighty. It cannot be described as a singular act or in a collaboration of words but rather felt in the tingling of skin and in the warmth of the soul"
—From *Cokeville's Promise Through History* as published on the website at www.cokevillewy.com

Kindergarten
Teacher: Kim Kasper
Students:
Sam Bennion
Paul Clark
Heather Cory
Linzie Jo Conner
Jodie Eggleston
Jamy Ferrin
Trini Jo Himmerich
Julia Jamison
Joshua Jones
John King
Jody Pope
Bret Taylor
Gina Taylor
Joshua Wiscombe

First Grade
Teachers: Janel Dayton, Jean Mitchell
Students:
Jolene Buckley
Shelley Burton
Burton Clark
Jennifer Cory
Fawna Eastman
Chad Etcheverry
Carl Grandy
Nathan Hartley
Billie Jo Hutchinson
Jeromy Lamb
Hilary Larson
Joni Larson
Travis McKinnon
Brenna McNamara
Jeremiah Moore
Jay Metcalfe
Emily Murdock
Kevin Nate
Shiloh Pope
Heather Prows
Collin Roberts

Shawn Stahl
Jennie Sorensen
Ryan Taylor
Meaghan Thompson
Katie Walker

Second Grade
Teacher Carol Petersen
Students:
Clark Bedell
Nancy Bennion
Cameron Bird
Brandon Brooks
Jennie Buckley
David Burton
Melanie Chadwick
Michelle Coates
Wade Cornia
Tareesa Covert
Jodi Dayton
Carl John Eggleston
Jason Hartley
Austin Henderson
Jamie Himmerich
Nanette Holden
Chad Madsen
Kellie Miller
Tina Morfeld
Levi Murdock
Karee Thornock
Ryan Thornock
Willie Wathen
Byron Wiscombe

Third Grade
Substitute Teacher Pat Bennion
Students:
Andy Bagaso
Jamie Buckley
Matthew Buckley
Justin Chadwick
David Clark
Joelle Dana

Ranelle Dana
Hyrum Esterholdt (H.J.)
Jenny Ferrin
Cindy Hartley
Bill King
Heather Larson
Joe McNamara
Chad Mitchell
Kristi Moore
Scott Mower
Aaron Roberts
Joey Sweat
Michael Thompson
Karalyn Thornock
Rachel Walker

Fourth Grade

Teacher Kliss Sparks
Students:
Rusty Birch
Jerry Dayton
Dustin Etcheverry
Sandy Hymas
Ricky Himmerich
Lana Holden
Adam Hymas
Jeana Jamison
Joe Mackey
Jaime Metcalfe
Monica Morfeld
Jamie Taylor
Jason Thornock
Kimberly Thornock
Stephanie Wiscombe

Fifth Grade

Teacher Rocky Moore
Student Teacher Kris Kasper
Students:
Amy Bagaso
Janaan Bennion
Elisabeth Clark
Shaneil Cornia
BranDee Hess

Jeromy Jamison
Amber Larson
Colton McDermott
Joanna Metcalfe
Brad Shane Nate
Lori Nate
Angie Nostaja
Adam Prows
Justin Sweat
Michael Taylor
Leigh Ann Thornock
Travis Walker

Sixth Grade

Teacher Jack Mitchell
Students:
Kent Cassels
Christy Clark
Tammy Coates
Allyson Cornia
Drew Cornia
Celeste Excell
Brenda Hartley
Brandi Himmerich
Paul Lazcanotegui
Kimberly Madsen
Bobbie Jo Miller
Brian Nate
Greg Nate
Cameron Roberts
Heidi Roberts
Anna Stewart
Kyle Thornock
Kamron Wixom

Faculty:

Max Excell, Principal
Tina Cook, Secretary
Gloria Mower, Special Ed.
Verlene Bennion, Teacher's Aid
Gayle Chadwick, Librarian
John Miller, Band Teacher

Others;

Eva Clark, parent
Kathy Clark, preschooler
Cynthia Cowden, job applicant
Sandy Gonzales, UPS driver

Absent:

3rd Grade Teacher Briant Teichert
Britney Swenson, K
Chris King, 1
Wendy Bartschi, 2
Vern Setser, 3
Mandi Taylor, 3
Julie Anderson, 4
Lea Kae Roberts, 4

Deaths since May 16, 1986

Verlene Bennion, Elementary Aid
Died June 4, 2001
in Cokeville, Wyoming
(Reported by Samuel O. Bennion Jr.)

Earl Carroll

Richard Leonard
Lincoln County Attorney
Died September 23, 2005
in Colorado Springs, Colorado
(Reported by Joseph B. Bluemel)

Cokeville landmark Rocky Peak, historically known as Rocky Point, faces the elementary school and will remain as a silent witness to the events of May 16, 1986.

About the Cokeville Miracle Foundation

In August of 2003 the original thirty-five director/members banded together, approved by-laws, and incorporated. Early in 2004 they elected officers and began to fulfill their stated mission: "The purposes for which the Cokeville Miracle Foundation is formed are in general to promote, sponsor and carry out projects which will enhance the community quality of life, encourage personal and community growth, encourage and recognize worthy achievement, acknowledge the blessings of heaven, assist fellow citizens and create extraordinary memorials to great lives and events that have effected our community and the larger world."

Director members include state and county dignitaries, city leaders, educators and a cross section of the community's citizens.

The vision of director/members and officers has prompted them to take the initiative in a number of projects including:

    Organ donor education and registration
    Meetings with guest artist and authors
    An annual service scholarship
    Citizen assistance (financial and medical)
    Community Yearbook Sponsorship
    The Minerva Teichert Memorial Art Show sponsorship
    Missing and Exploited children poster enhancement
    and placement
    Assistance in publishing a community newspaper edition
    Compilation and arrangement for publishing this book,
    Witness To Miracles

In November of 2004 the Foundation received 501 (c) (3) IRS status as a public charity, making citizen contributions tax deductible.

More information about the Cokeville Miracle Foundation or this book can be obtained by writing to:

P.O.Box 37, Cokeville, Wyo. 83114
Email: cmf@cokevillewy.com
www.cokevillewy.com/cokevillemiraclefoundation

Cokeville Miracle Foundation Board Members:

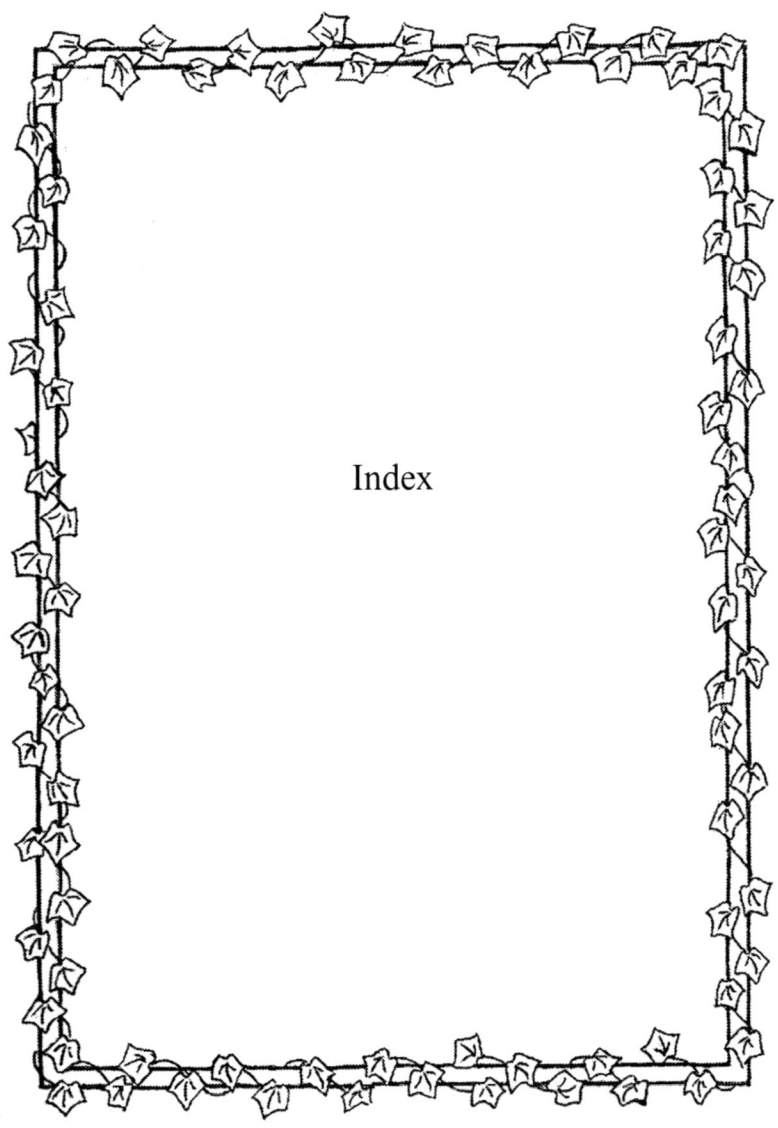

Index

Photo courtesy of The Kemmerer Gazette

My Story

My Story

Printed in the United States
205408BV00002B/2/A

9 781932 636215